D1224098

F. B. COSTELLO S. J.

THE POLITICAL PHILOSOPHY OF
LUIS DE MOLINA, S. J. (1535-1600)

BIBLIOTHECA
INSTITUTI HISTORICI S. I.
VOLUMEN XXXVIII

FRANK BARTHOLOMEW COSTELLO S.J.

THE POLITICAL PHILOSOPHY
OF LUIS DE MOLINA, S.J.

(1535-1600)

INSTITUTUM HISTORICUM S.I.   GONZAGA UNIVERSITY PRESS
Via dei Penitenzieri 20   SPOKANE
ROMA
1974

FRANK BARTHOLOMEW COSTELLO S.J.

THE POLITICAL PHILOSOPHY
OF LUIS DE MOLINA, S. J.
(1535-1600)

INSTITUTUM HISTORICUM S.I.   GONZAGA UNIVERSITY PRESS
Via dei Penitenzieri 20   SPOKANE
ROMA
1974

IMPRIMI POTEST: Romae, die 3 Dec. 1974. ANDREAS SNOECK, S.I., Del. Praep. Gen. S.I.
Con approvazione del Vicariato di Roma, in data 18 Decembris 1974.

TYPIS PONTIFICIAE UNIVERSITATIS GREGORIANAE — ROMAE

For my Parents:

Bartley and Catherine

IN PIAM MEMORIAM

Bartholomew was father to us all
And lover to his wife,
On whom he carefully begot us.
His wife, strong, visionfull and small,
Let grow the life
He planted. How they sought us!

WILLIAM T. COSTELLO, S. J.
(1914-1963)

PREFACE

J. W. Allen observes that the student who aspires to write of the political thought of any period requires a thorough knowledge of the conditions—social, political, and economic—under which that thought was developed. Such knowledge can hardly be too thorough; it is perhaps impossible that it should be thorough enough. Knowledge of texts, however, exhaustive, or patience, even indomitable, is not enough. He must possess power of accurate analysis, he must miss no subtlety of argument or distinction or connection. To be an historian is not enough; he must be something of a philosopher, too. He must sympathize with all points of view. He must love ideas for their own sake. His questioning must be ceaseless; his scepticism untiring. He needs above all that pure desire to understand which is his only defense against bewildering bias. "Thinking of these things," Professor Allen concludes, "he may be aghast at his own temerity." [1]

Every student who has rashly undertaken a dissertation topic soon realizes that the only thing which is saving his project from disaster is the wise guidance of those who have cultivated that field of study. I was singularly fortunate to have had in the graduate program at Georgetown University the expert counsel of the late Professor Heinrich A. Rommen, world's foremost authority on Jesuit political thought in the sixteenth and seventeenth centuries. It was he who first suggested the present topic to me; it is he to whom the study is indebted for whatever worth it may have. I am also deeply grateful to Professor Ulrich S. Allers and Father Gerard F. Yates, S.J., for their careful reading of the manuscript, their insight and ever-helpful suggestions.

More recently I have had the invaluable assistance in Rome of Father Ernest J. Burrus, S.J., one of the foremost Jesuit historians in the world. His kindness and encouragement were of immense help to me. In addition, I am affectionately grate-

---

[1] J. W. Allen, *A History of Political Thought in the Sixteenth Century* (London: Methuen & Co., Ltd., 1957), pp. xviii-xix.

ful to a here unnamed but never forgotten, host of my fellow Jesuits on whose generosity I have outrageously imposed in hundreds of ways, from borrowing their insights and ideas to imposing on them the tedious task of checking Latin footnotes with the original edition. To my sister, Helen Costello Petrich, I am grateful for her gentle prodding of me to finish the work. Finally, I acknowledge my indebtedness to two typists, Mrs. Edgar Hummel of Washington, D.C. and Mrs. Beverly Mahrt of Spokane, without whose unfailing good humor and skill the production of the manuscript would have been impossible.

Anne Morrow Lindbergh said that one can never pay in gratitude; one can only pay in kind somewhere else in life. I sense that each of the above would exact no more payment from me than that I return in kind to someone else. I pledge myself to try to carry out this challenging responsibility.

February 2, 1974

FRANK B. COSTELLO, S.J.
Gonzaga University
Spokane, Washington

CONTENTS

BIBLIOGRAPHY

ABBOTT, Walter M., S.J., General Editor. *The Documents of Vatican II*, with Notes and Comments by Catholic, Protestant and Orthodox Authorities. New York: The American Press, 1966.

ACTON, Lord. "Sir Erskine Mays' Democracy in Europe" in *The History of Freedom and Other Essays*. London: Macmillan and Co., 1909.

ALDAMA, J. A., S. J. "Luis de Molina S. J. *De Spe*: comentario a la 2ª2ᵃᵉ. 17-22," *Archivo teológico Granadino*, I (1938), 111-112.

ALEXANDER, Edgar. "Church and Society in Germany: Social and Political Movements and Ideas in German and Austrian Catholics (1789-1950)" in *Church and Society:* Catholic Social and Political Movements 1789-1950. Edited by Joseph N. Moody. New York: Arts, Inc., 1953.

ALEXSON, E. *Portuguese in South-East Africa, 1600-1700*. Johannesburg: Witwatersrand University Press, 1960.

ALLEN, J. W. *A History of Political Thought in the Sixteenth Century*. 3d ed. London: Methuen & Co., Ltd., 1957.

AMADO, G. "La question de la définition de l'agression," *Revue de droit international de sciences diplomatiques politiques et sociales*, XXX (1952), 147-155.

ANDRADE, Alonso de. *Varones ilustres de la Compañía de Jesús*, 9 vols., 2d ed. Bilbao: El mensajero del Corazón de Jesús, 1891.

ANSELMO, B., S. J. "Gli elementi di una giusta pace nella dottrina di Ludovico Molina, S. J.," *Civiltà Cattolica*, IV (1943), 307-316.

——. "La guerra difensiva nella dottrina di Ludovico Molina, S. J.," *Civiltà Cattolica*, II (1953), 354-363.

——. "La guerra offensiva e l'autorità necessaria nella dottrina di Ludovico Molina, S. J.," *Civilà Cattolica*, IV (1943), 25-38.

——. "La guerra offensiva nella dottrina di Ludovico Molina, S. J.," *Civilà Cattolica*, III (1943), 270-281.

AQUINAS, St. Thomas. *Scriptum super Libros Sententiarum Magistri Petri Lombardi Episcopi Parisiensis*. 4 vols. Parisiis: Lethielleux, 1929-1947.

——. *Summa Theologica*. 5 vols, Parisiis: Lethielleux, 1939.

ARNOLD, Franx X. *Die Staatslehre des Kardinals Bellarmin*. München: M. Hueber, 1934.

——. *Zur Frage des Naturrechts bei Martin Luther:* Ein Beitrag zum Problem der naturlichen Theologie auf reformatorischer Grundlage. München: Hueber, 1937.

ASTRAIN, Antonio, S. J. *Historia de la Compañía de Jesús en la Asistencia de España*. 7 vols. Madrid: Sucesores de Rivadeneyra, 1902-1925.

BAINTON, Roland H. *Christian Attitudes Toward War and Peace*, A Historical Survey and Critical Re-evaluation. New York: Abingdon Press, 1960, p. 230.

BALLIS, William. *The Legal Position of War:* Changes in Its Practice and Theory from Plato to Vattel. The Hague: Martinus Nijhoff, 1937.

BAÑEZ, Domingo, O.P. *De Fide, Spe et Charitate.* Salamanca, 1584.
——. *Scholastica Commentaria in Primam Partem Necnon in Secundam Secundae Summae Angelici Doctoris Sancti Thomae.* Lyons: S. Michael, 1638.
BARCÍA TRELLES, Camilo. "Las 'Relecciones' de Vitoria—El problema de la conquista de América," *Anuario de la Asociación Francisco de Vitoria,* I (1927-1928), 187-197.
——. "La autoridad universal del emperador," *Anuario de la Asociación Francisco de Vitoria,* I (1927-1928), 197-213.
——. "La ocupación como medio adquisitivo de la soberanía," *Anuario de la Asociación Francisco de Vitoria,* I (1927-1928), 229-629.
BARKER, Sir Ernest. "The Study of Political Science" in *Church, State and Education.* Ann Arbor: The University of Michigan Press, 1957.
BELLARMINO, Roberto, S.J. *Opera Omnia.* 12 vols. Parisiis: Apud Ludovicum Vivès, 1870-1874.
BELLOC, Hilaire. *Milton.* Philadelphia: J.B. Lippincott Co., 1935.
BELTRÁN DE HEREDIA, Vicente, O.P. "Doctrina de Francisco de Vitoria sobre las relaciones de la Iglesia y el Estado y fuentes de la misma," *Ciencia Tomista,* LVI (1937), 27-39.
——. "La enseñanza de Sto. Tomás en la Compañía de Jesús durante el primer siglo de su existencia," *Ciencia Tomista,* XI (1915), 388-408; XII (1916), 34-48.
——. "El maestro Domingo de Soto, Catedrático de Vísperas en la Universidad de Salamanca (1532-1549)," *Ciencia Tomista,* LVII (1938), 38-67 and 281-302.
——. "El maestro Domino (Francisco) de Soto en la Universidad de Alcalá," *Ciencia Tomista,* XLIII (1931), 357-373.
BENKERT, Gerald Francis, O.S.B. *The Thomistic Conception of International Society.* Washington: The Catholic University of America Press, 1942.
BIEL, Gabriel, *Collectorium seu Epithome in Magistri Sententiarum Libros Quatuor.* Lugduni, 1514.
BIGGS, Herbert W. (ed.). *The Laws of Nations:* Cases, Documents and Notes (2nd edition). New York: Appleton-Century-Crofts, Inc., 1952.
BITTREMIEUX, [n.n.]. *Lessius et le droit de guerre.* Bruxelles: Dewit, 1920.
BLAKE, J.W. "The Slave Trade (ii)" from *Africa from Early Times to 1800* (edited by P.J.M. McEwan). London: Oxford University Press, 1969.
——. "European Beginnings on the West Coast" in *Africa from Early Times to 1800* (edited by P.J.M. McEwan). London: Oxford University Press, 1969.
BLIC, J. de. "A propos des origines du probabilisme," *Revue des sciences religieuses,* 1930, pp. 460-464.
——, "Barthélemy de Médine et les origines du probabilisme," *Ephemerides Theologiae Lovaniensis* (1930), 46-63, 264-291.
BODIN, Jean. *Six Books of the Commonwealth.* Abridged and translated by M.J. Tooley. Oxford: Basil Blackwell [n.d.].
BOUVIER, Pierre, S.J. "Jésuites: La théologie morale dans la Compagnie de Jésus," in *Dictionnaire de théologie catholique.* 15 vols. Edited by A. Vacant and E. Mangenot. Paris: Librairie Letouzey et Ané, 1929. Vol. VIII, cols. 1085ff.
BOWE, Gabriel, O.P. *The Origin of Political Authority:* An Essay in Catholic Political Philosophy. Dublin: Clonmore & Reynolds, Ltd., 1955.

BOXER, C. R. *Race Relations in the Portuguese Colonial Empire 1415-1825.* Oxford: Clarendon Press, 1963.

——. "The Slave Trade (iii)" from *Africa from Early Times to 1800* (edited by P. J. M. McEwan). London: Oxford University Press, 1969.

BOYE, T. "Quelques aspects du développement des règles de la neutralité," *Recueil des cours de l'académie de droit international,* LXIV (1938), 161-165.

BRECHT, Arnold. "Sovereignty" in *War in Our Time.* Edited by Hans Spier and Alfred Kähler. New York: W. W. Norton, 1939.

BRIÈRE, Yves de la, S. J. *La communauté des puissances:* D'une communauté inorganique à une communauté organique. Paris: Beauchesne, 1932.

——. *Le droit de juste guerre:* tradition théologique adaptations contemporaines. Paris: A. Pedone, 1938.

BRITO, A. H. Dantas de. *La philosophie du droit des gens:* Une étude de critériologie juridique. Washington: The Catholic University Press, 1944.

BRODRICK, James, S. J. *The Economic Morals of the Jesuits:* An Answer to Dr. H. M. Robertson. London: Oxford University Press, 1934.

——. *The Progress of the Jesuits, 1556-79.* New York: Longmans, Green & Co., 1947.

——. *Robert Bellarmine 1542-1621.* 2 vols., 2 ed. London: Longmans, Green & Co., 1950.

BUCHAN, Alastair. *War in Modern Society:* An Introduction. New York: Harper and Row, Publishers, 1968.

BULLÓN, Eloy y Fernández. *El concepto de la soberanía en la escuela jurídica española del siglo XVI,* Madrid: Liberia general de Victoriano Suárez, 1936.

BURRUS, ERNEST J., S. J. "The Impact of the New World Discovery upon the European Thought of Man" from J. Robert Nelson (editor) *No Man Is Alien:* Essays on the Unity of Mankind. Lieden: E. J. Brill, 1971, pp. 85-108.

——. (ed.) *The Writings of Alonso de la Vera Cruz.* 4 vols. Rome: Jesuit Historical Institute, 1968-1972.

BUTLER, Sir Geoffrey and Simon Maccoby. *The Development of International Law.* London: Longmans, Green and Co., Ltd., 1928.

BÜTTNER, H. "Aus den Anfängen des abendländischen Staatsgedankens," *Historisches Jahrbuch der Görresgesellschaft,* LXXI (1952), 77-90.

CAMPBELL, Lewis. *Sophocles:* The Seven Plays in English Verse. Oxford: Oxford University Press, 1936.

CANAVAN, Francis P., S. J. "Subordination of the State to the Church According to Suarez," *Theological Studies,* XII (1951), 354-364.

CARLYLE, A. J. and R. W. *A History of Medieval Political Theory in the West.* 6 vols. London: W. Blackwood and Sons, 1903-1906.

CARRO, Venancio, O. P. *Domingo de Soto y el derecho de gentes.* Madrid: Revista de las Españas, 1930.

——. *Domingo de Soto y su doctrina jurídica.* Madrid: Imp. Hijos E. Minuesa, 1943.

CASTRO, Alfonso de, O. F. M. *Adversus haereses libri XIV,* Parisiis, 1578.

——. *De justa Haereticorum punitione.* Parisiis, 1578.

CATTON, BRUCE, "The Civil War—First Modern War," Gaston Lecture at Georgetown University, December 9, 1957. Copy in Georgetown Archives.

CHENU, M.-D., O.P. "L'évolution de la théologie de la guerre," *Lumière et vie*, XXXVIII (1958), 76-97.

CHILCOTE, Ronald H. *Portuguese Africa*. Englewood Cliffs: Prentice Hall, Inc., 1967.

Chronicon Polanci. Monumenta Historica Societatis Jesu. 6 vols. Matriti: Augustinus Avrial, 1894-1898.

CHROUST, Anton-Hermann. "Hugo Grotius and the Scholastic Natural Law Tradition," *The New Scholasticism*, XVI (1943), 101-133.

Church and State Through the Centuries: A Collection of Historic Documents with Commentaries. Edited by Sidney Z. Ehler and John B. Morrall. Westminster, Maryland: The Newman Press, 1954.

CLIFFORD, Sir Hugh Charles. "The Maylay Peninsula," *The Encyclopaedia Britannica*, 11th ed. 32 vols. New York: Encyclopaedia Britannica, Inc., 1911.

The Constitution of the United States of America: Analysis and Interpretation: Annotations of Cases Decided by the Supreme Court of the United States to June 30, 1952. Edited by Edward S. Corwin. Washington: Government Printing Office, 1953.

CORREA, Gaspar. *Lendas da India*, 4 vols. Lisboa: 1860-1922.

CORWIN, Edward S. *The President*: Office and Powers 1787-1948: History and Analysis of Practice and Opinion. 3d ed. New York: New York University Press, 1948.

COVARRUBIAS, Diego de. *Opera Omnia*. Lugduni, 1586.

CREHAN, J.H., S.J. "The Inspiration and Inerrancy of Holy Scripture," in *A Catholic Commentary on Holy Scripture*. Edited by Dom Bernard Orchard *et al*. London: Thomas Nelson and Sons, 1953.

CURTIN, Philip D. *The Atlantic Slave Trade*: A Census. Madison: The University of Wisconsin Press, 1969.

DAVIS, David Brion. *The Problem of Slavery in Western Culture*. Ithaca: Cornell University Press, 1966.

DAVIS, Henry, S.J. *Moral and Pastoral Theology in Four Volumes*. 6th ed. London: Sheed and Ward, 1949.

DAVIDSON, Basil. *The African Slave Trade: Precolonial History 1450-1850*. Boston: Little Brown and Co., 1961.

DEAGUILAR, J.M., O.P. "The Law of Nations and the Salamanca School of Theology," *The Thomist*, IX (1946), 186-221.

"Debates of the Federal Convention of 1787 as Reported by James Madison" in *Documents Illustrative of the Formation of the Union of The American States*. Edited by Charles C. Tansill. Washington: Government Printing Office, 1927.

DEEN, M.H. *The Laws of War in the Late Middle Ages*. London: Routledge & Kegan Paul, 1965.

A Defence of Liberty Against Tyrants: A Translation of the *Vindiciae Contra Tyrannos* by Junius Brutus. Historical Introduction by Harold Laski. London: G. Bell and Sons, Ltd., 1924.

DEMAN, Th., O.P. "Probabilisme," in *Dictionnaire de théologie catholique*. 15vols. Edited by A. Vacant and E. Mangenot. Paris: Librairie Letouzey et Ané, 1929. Vol. XII, cols. 417-619.

DEMPF, A. *Christliche Staatsphilosophie in Spanien*, Salzburg: A. Pustet, 1937.

DEMPSEY, Bernard, S.J. *Interest and Usury*. Washington: American Council on Public Affairs, 1943.

DENZINGER, Henricus, S.J., Clementus BANNWART, S.J., and Johannes Bapt. UMBERG, S.J. *Enchiridion Symbolorum*: Definitionum et Declarationum de Rebus Fidei et Morum. 23d ed. Friburgi Brisgoviae: Herder & Co., 1937.

DÍEZ-ALEGRÍA, José Mª., S.J. "El Conimbricense Ignacio Martins S.J. y el concepto de ley de las lecturas de 1570 en la Universidad de Evora," *Revista Portuguesa de filosofia*, XI (1955), Part II, 546-553.

——. *El desarrollo de la doctrina de la ley natural en Luis de Molina y en los maestros de la Universidad de Evora de 1565 a 1591*: Estudio histórico y textos inéditos. Barcelona: Consejo superior de investigaciones científicas, 1951.

——. *Etica, derecho e historia*. Madrid: Sapientia, S.A. de ediciones, 1953.

DOBIE, J. Frank. *A Texan in England*. Boston: Little, Brown and Co., 1945.

Documenta Indica, edited by Joseph Wicki, S.J. 12 vols. Roma: Monumenta Historica Societatis Jesu, 1948-1972.

DONNAN, Elizabeth. *Documents Illustrative of the History of the Slave Trade to America*. 3 vols. New York: Octagon Books, Inc., 1965.

DOWNEY, W.G., Jr. "Captured Enemy Property: Booty of War and Seized Enemy Property," *American Journal of International Law*, XLIV. (1950), 488-504.

——. "The Law of War and Military Necessity," *American Journal of International Law*, XLVII (1953), 251-262.

DRIADO, Juan. *De libertate christiana*. Lovanii, 1540.

EAGLETON, Clyde. *The Attempt to Define Aggression*. "International Conciliation," No. 264. New York: Carnegie Endowment for International Peace, 1950.

Epistolae Mixtae ex Variis Europae Locis ab Anno 1537 ad 1556 Scriptae. "Monumenta Historica Societatis Jesu." 5 vols. Matriti: Augustinus Avrial, 1898-1901.

Epistolae P. Hieronymi Nadal S.J. "Monumenta Historica Societatis Jesu." 4 vols. Matriti: Augustinus Avrial, 1898-1905.

EPPSTEIN, John. *The Catholic Tradition of the Law of Nations*. Washington: Catholic Association for International Peace, 1935.

ESPANCA, Trilio. *Évora*. Évora: Livraria Nazareth, 1971.

FAGE, J.D. "The Slave Trade (i)" from *Africa from Early Times to 1800*, (edited by P.J.M. McEwan). London: Oxford University Press, 1969.

FARRERA, Celestino. *El derecho internacional en la antigüedad y en la edad media*. Caracas: Lit. y tip. Varbas, 1927.

FIGGIS, J. Neville. *From Gerson to Grotius, 1414-1625*. Cambridge: Cambridge University Press, 1916.

——. "On Some Political Theories of the Early Jesuits," in *Transactions of the Royal Historical Society*. Vol. XI (New Series). London: Longmans, Green and Co., 1897.

——. "Political Thought in the Sixteenth Century" in *The Cambridge Modern History*. Vol. III: 1756-1759. Edited by A.W. Ward, G.W. Prothero, and Stanley Leathes. New York: The Macmillan Co., 1905.

FIGUEIREDO FALCÃO, Luiz de. *Livro en que se contém toda a fazenda e Real Patrimonio dos Reinos de Portugal, India e Ilhas adjacentes e outras particularidades copiado fielmente du manuscripto original.* Lisboa, 1859.

FITZPATRICK, J. "Some More Theology about Tyranny," *Irish Theological Quarterly*, XVI (1921), 1-15.

FRAGA IRIBARNE, Manuel. *Luis de Molina y el derecho de la guerra*. Madrid, 1947.

FRIEDE, Juan and Benjamin Keen (eds.). *Bartolome de las Casas in History*: Toward an Understanding of the Man and His Work. De Kalb: Northern Illinois University Press, 1971.

GARCÍA, Rubio Leandro, "La población civil y la guerra aérea moderna," *Revista española de derecho internacional*, 1953.

GEMMEL, Jakob, S. J. "Die Lehre des Kardinals Bellarmin über Kirche und Staat," *Scholastik*, V (1930), 357-379.

GIERKE, Otto. *The Development of Political Theory*. Translated by B. Freyd. New York: W. W. Norton and Co., 1939.

——. *Natural Law and the Theory of Society 1500-1800*. 3d ed. Translated with an introduction by Ernest Barker. Boston: Beacon Press, 1957.

——. *Political Theories of the Middle Age*. Translated with an introduction by Frederic William Maitland. Cambridge: At the University Press, 1951.

GILBY, Thomas. *Between Community and Society*: A Philosophy and Theology of the State. London: Longmans, Green and Co., 1953.

GILSON, Etienne. *The Unity of Philosophical Experience*. New York: G. Scribner's Sons, 1937.

GOUGH, J. W. *The Social Contract*: A Critical Study of Its Development. 2d ed. Oxford: At the Clarendon Press, 1957.

GOYAU, Georges,. "L'Église catholique et le droit des gens," *Recueil des cours de l'académie de droit international*, VI (1925), 125-239.

GRABMANN, M. *Geschichte der katholischen Theologie seit dem Ausgang der Väterzeit*. Freiburg im Breisgau: Herder & Co., 1933.

GRICE-HUTCHINSON, Marjorie. *The School of Salamanca*: Readings in Spanish Monetary Theory, 1544-1605. Oxford: At the Clarendon Press, 1952.

GROTIUS, Hugo. *De Jure Belli ac Pacis Libri Tres*, translated by Francis W. Kelsey *et al.*, for *The Classics of International Law*, ed. James Brown Scott. Oxford: At the Clarendon Press, 1925.

——. *The Law of War and Peace: De Jure Belli et Pacis Libri Tres*. Books I-III, translated by Francis W. Kelsey. Indianapolis: The Bobbs-Merrill Company, Inc., 1962.

GUNDLACH, Gustav, S. J. *Zur Soziologie der katholischen Ideenwelt und des Jesuitenordens*. Freiburg im Breisgau: Herder & Co., 1927.

GUTIÉRREZ, Marcelino, O. S. A. *Fray Luis de León y la filosofía española del siglo XVI*. El Escorial: Real monasterio de el Escorial, 1929.

HALÉVY, Élie. *L'ère des tyrannies*: Études sur le socialisme et la guerre. Paris: Gallimard, 1938.

HALKIN, Leon E. "The Moral Physiognomy of Philip II," in John C. Rule and John J. Tepaske (editors). *The Character of Philip II: The Problem of Moral Judgments in History*. Boston: D. C. Heath and Company, 1963.

HAMILTON, Bernice. *Political Thought in Sixteenth Century Spain*: A Study of the Political Ideas of Vitoria, De Soto, Suárez, and Molina. Oxford: At the Clarendon Press, 1963.

HANKE, Lewis. *Aristotle and the American Indians* (London: Hallis and Carter), 1959.

HEARNSHAW, F. J. C. *Some Great Political Idealists of the Christian Era*. London: George G. Harrap & Co., Ltd., 1937.

HELLÍN, J., S. J. "Derecho internacional en Suárez y en Molina," *Estudios eclesiásticos*, XVIII (1944), 37-62.

HESSELBERG, Arthur K. "A Comparative Study of the Political Theories of Ludovicus Molina, S. J., and John Milton." Unpublished Ph. D. dissertation. The Catholic University of America, 1952.

HEYDTE, F. "Francisco de Victoria und sein Völkerrecht," *Zeitschrift für öffentliches Recht*, XIII (1933), 239-268.

HOBBES, Thomas. *Leviathan*. Introduction by A. D. Lindsay. Everyman's Library. New York: E. P. Dutton and Co., 1950.

HÖFFNER, Joseph. *Christentum und Menschenwurde*: Das Anliegen der spanischen Kolonialethik in goldenen Zeitalter. Trier: Paulinus-Verlag, 1947.

—. *Wirtschaftsethik und Monopole im fünfzehnten und sechzehnten Jahrhundert*, Jena: Verlag Gustav Fischer, 1941.

HOLZHAUER, Jean. In a review of *The Angry Scar*: The Story of Reconstruction by Hodding Carter, in *The Catholic Messenger*, Davenport, Iowa: February 12, 1959, p. 11.

HOW, W. W., and J. WELLS. A Commentary on Herodotus. 2 vols. Oxford: Oxford University Press, 1949-1951.

HUBER, Max. "Die kriegsrechtlichen Verträge und die Kriegraison," *Zeitschrift für Völkerrecht*, VII (1913), 351 ff.

HURTER, Hugo. *Nomenclator Literarius Theologiae Catholicae*: Theologos Exhibens Aetate, Natione, Disciplinis Distinctos. Innsbruck: Wagner, 1906.

Initiation Biblique: Introduction à l'étude des Saintes Écritures. Edited by A. Robert and A. Tricot. Paris: Desclée & Cie., 1954.

IZAGA AGUIRRE, Luis, S. J. *El P. Luis de Molina, internacionalista*. Madrid: Razón y Fe, 1939.

——. "El P. Luis de Molina, internacionalista," *Razón y Fe*, CX (1936), 43-55, 192-206, and 491-513.

JAMESON, Russell Parsons. *Montesquieu et l'Esclavage*: Étude sur les Origines de l'Opinion Antiesclavagiste en France au XVIIIᵉ Siècle. Paris: Librairie Hachette et Cⁱᵉ, 1944.

JÁSZI, Oscar and John D. LEWIS. *Against the Tyrant*: The Tradition and Theory of Tyrannicide. Glencoe, Illinois: The Free Press and The Falcon's Wing Press, 1957.

JEFFERSON, Thomas . *The Papers of Thomas Jefferson*. Edited by Julian P. Boyd. Princeton: Princeton University Press, 1955.

JESSUP, Philip. "The Birth, Death and Reincarnation of Neutrality," *American Journal of International Law*, XXVI (1932), 789ff.

——. "The Crime of Aggression," *Political Science Quarterly*, LXII (1947), 1-10.

JESSUP, Philip and Francis DEÁK. *Neutrality*: Its History, Economics and Law. 4 vols. New York: Columbia University Press, 1935-1936.

JONES, W. T. *Machiavelli to Bentham*. Vol. II: *Masters of Political Thought*. Edited by Edward McChesney Sait. 2 vols. Boston: Houghton Mifflin Co., 1950.

KANTOR, McKinley. *Andersonville*. Cleveland: World Publishing Co., 1955.

KILGER, LAURENZ, O. S. B. "Die ersten Jesuiten am Kongo und in Angola (1547-1575)" *Zeitschrift für Missionswissenschaft*, XI, (1921), 16-33.

KINGSFORD, Charles Lethbridge. "Thomas Netter," *The Dictionary of National Biography*. 22 vols. Edited by Sir Leslie Stephen and Sir Sidney Lee. London: Oxford University Press, 1937-1938.

KLEINHAPPL, Johann, S. J. *Der Staat bei Ludwig Molina*. Innsbruck: F. Rauch, 1935.

KOMARNICKI, W. "La définition de l'agresseur," *Recueil des cours de l'académie de droit international,* LXXV (1949), 5-110.

KOPELMANAS, L. "The Problem of Aggression and the Prevention of War," *American Jornal of International War,* XXXI (1937), 244-257.

KOTZSCH, Lothan. *The Concept of War in Contemporary History and International Law.* Genève: Librairie E. Droz, 1956.

KUNNETH, Walter. "Die evangelisch-lutherische und das Wiederstandsrecht" in *Die Vollmacht des Gewissens, hrsg. von den Europäischen Publikationen.* Band I. Munich: H. Rinn, 1956.

KUNZ, Joseph L. "Chaotic Status of the Laws of War and the Urgent Necessity of Their Revision," *American Journal of International Law,* XLV (1951), 37-61.

——. "Individual and Collective Security in Art. 51 of the Charter of the United Nations," *American Journal of International Law,* XLI (1947), 872ff.

KURZ, E., O. F. M. *Individuum und Gemeischaft beim Hl. Thomas von Aquin.* Munich: J. Kösel & F. Pustet, 1932.

LAMADRID, R. S. de, S. J., "Luis de Molina S.I.—De Bello: Comentario a la 2.2, Q. 40," *Archivo teológico Granadino,* II (1939), 155-231.

LANSEROS, M. *La autoridad civil en Francisco Suárez.* Madrid: Instituto de estudios políticos, 1949.

LASKI, Harold J. *A Grammar of Politics.* London: George Allen and Unwin, Ltd., 1925.

LATOURETTE, Kenneth Scott. *A Short History of the Far East.* 3rd ed. New York: The Macmillan Co., 1957.

LAURES, John, S. J. *The Political Economy of Juan de Mariana.* New York: Fordham University Press, 1928.

LAVERSIN, M. J., O. P. "Droit naturel et droit positif d'après S. Thomas," *Revue Thomiste,* XXVIII (1933), 1-50 and 177-217.

LEA, Henry. *The Moriscos in Spain: Their Conversion and Expulsion,* Philadelphia: Lea Brothers & Co., 1901.

LECLER, Joseph, S. J. *The Two Sovereignties:* A Study of the Relationship Between Church and State. London: Burns Oates & Washbourne, 1952.

——. "L'argument des Deux Glaives dans les controverses politiques du Moyen Age: Ses origines et son développement," *Recherches de science religieuse,* XXI (1931), 299-339; XII (1932), 151-177 and 280-303.

LECLERQ, Jean, O. S. B. *Jean de Paris et l'ecclésiologie du XIIIᵉ siècle,* Paris: Librairie philosophique J. Vrin, 1942.

LE FUR, Louis. "La convention de Londres et la définition de l'agression," *Revue de droit international de sciences diplomatiques politiques et sociales,* XI (1933), 176 ff.

LEITÃO FERREIRA, Francisco. *Noticias chronologicas da universidade de Coimbra.* Coimbra: Universidade de Coimbra, 1944.

LEW, D. H. "Manchurian Booty and International Law," *American Journal of International Law,* XL (1946), 584 ff.

LEWIS, Ewart. *Medieval Political Ideas.* 2 vols. London: Routledge and Kegan Paul, 1954.

LIDDELL HART, Basil Henry. *The Revolution in Warfare.* New Haven: Yale University Press, 1946.

LIGUORI, Alfonso Maria de. *Theologia Moralis.* 2 vols. Taurini: Marietti, 1892.

LILLEY, A. L. "Francisco Suarez" in *The Social and Political Ideas of Some Great Thinkers of the Sixteenth and Seventeenth Centuries*. Edited by F. J. C. Hearnshaw. London: George G. Harrap & Co., Ltd., 1926.

LIPPERT, Peter, S. J. *Zur Psychologie des Jesuitenordens*. Freiburg im Breisgau: Herder & Co., 1923.

Litterae Quadrimestres. "Monumenta Historica Societatis Jesu." 7 vols. Matriti: Augustinus Aurial, 1894-1932.

LLANAS, Manuel Lasala y. "Conceptos y principios fundamentales del derecho de gentes, según la doctrina del P. Vitoria," *Anuario de la Asociación Francisco de Vitoria*, I (1927-1928), 269-305.

Lo GRASSO, J. B. *Ecclesia et Status*: Fontes Selecti Historiae Juris Publici Ecclesiastici. Roma: Apud Aedes Pontif. Universitatis Gregorianae, 1952.

LOSADA, Angel (ed.). "Juan Ginés de Sepúlveda," *Demócrates Segundo o De las justas causas de la guerra contra indios*. Madrid: Instituto Francisco de Vitoria, 1951.

LOTTIN, Odon. *Le droit naturel chez Saint Thomas d'Aquin et ses prédécesseurs*. Bruges: C. Beyaert, 1931.

LOYOLA, Ignatius, St. *The Spiritual Exercises of St. Ignatius*: A New Translation Based on Studies in the Language of the Autograph by Louis J. Puhl, S.J. Westminster, Md.: The Newman Press, 1953.

LUGO, Juan de, S.J. *Tractatus de Justitia et Jure*. 5 vols. Parisiis: Apud Ludovicum Vivès, 1863.

LUMBREAS, P., O.P. "De peccato originali quaedam Molinae placita," *Angelicum*, XVII (1940), 257-262.

MACCOBY, Simon. "Reprisals as a Measure of Redress Short of War," *Cambridge Law Review* (1924), 60 ff.

McCoY, Charles N. R. "Note on the Problem of the Origin of Political Authority," *The Thomist*, XVI (1953), 71-81.

McHUGH, John A., O.P. and Charles J. Callan, O.P. *Moral Theology*: A Complete Course Based on St. Thomas Aquinas and the Best Modern Authorities, 2 vols. New York: Joseph F. Wagner, Inc., 1958.

McILWAIN, Charles H. *The Growth of Political Thought in the West*. New York: The Macmillan Company, 1932.

McKENZIE, John L., S.J. *The Two-Edged Sword*: An Interpretation of the Old Testament. Milwaukee: The Bruce Publishing Co., 1956.

MADDEN, Marie R. *Political Theory and Law in Medieval Spain*. New York: Fordham University Press, 1930.

MAIR, John. *Commentarium in Libros Sententiarum Petri Lombardi*. Parisiis, 1510.

MAKTOS, J. "La question de la définition de l'agression," *Revue de droit international de sciences diplomatiques politiques et sociales*, XXX (1952), 5-9.

MALAGÓN-BARCELÓ, J. "Covarrubias y Leyva, Diego de." *New Catholic Encyclopedia*. 15 vols., Vol. IV. New York: McGraw Hill Book Co., 1967.

MANN, F. A. "Enemy Property and the Paris Peace Treaties," *Law Quarterly Review*, LXIV (1948), 492-518.

MARIANA, Juan de, S.J. *The King and the Education of the King*. Translated by George Albert Moore. Washington: The Country Dollar Press, 1948.

MARITAIN, Jacques. *Man and the State.* 7th ed. Chicago: Phoenix Books, The University of Chicago Press, 1958.

MARTIN, A. "The Treatment of Enemy Property under the Peace Treaties of 1947," *Transactions of the Grotius Society,* XXXIV (1949), 77-97.

MATEOS, Francisco, S.J. "El Padre Luis de Molina y la Trata de Negros," Miscellanea Antonio Pérez Goyena, *Estudios Eclesiásticos,* XXXV (1960), 209.

MEERSMAN, G. "Le droit naturel chez S. Thomas d'Aquin, et ses prédécesseurs," *Angelicum,* IX (1932), 63-76.

MENENDEZ, I. - REIGADA, O.P. "El sistema eticojurídico de Vitoria sobre el derecho de gentes," *Ciencia Tomista,* XXXIX (1929), 307-330.

MESNARD, P. *L'essor de la philosophie politique au XVI⁰ siècle,* Paris: Boivin & Cie, 1936.

MESSINEO, A., S.J. "Le rappresaglie nella dottrina degli antichi," *Civiltà Cattolica,* I (1941), 101-109.

MIRKINE-GUETZÉVITCH, Boris. *Les constitutiones européenes.* Paris: Presses Universitaires de France, 1951.

MOLINA, Luis de, S.J. *Concordia liberi arbitrii cum gratiae donis, divina praescientia, providentia, praedestinatione, et reprobatione, ad non-nullos primae partis D. Thomae articulos*: Doctore Ludovico Molina primario quondam in Eborensi Academia Theologiae professore e societate Jesu autore. Adjecti sunt duo indices, rerum alter, alter eorum scripturae locorum, qui vel ex professo, vel obiter explicantur eodem autore. Olyssipone: Apud Riberium typographum regium, 1588.

——. *De Justitia et Jure.* Vols. I-II. Moguntiae: Sumptibus Arnold Mylii, 1602.
      Vol. III. Antuerpiae: Apud Joannem Keerbergium, 1615.
      Vol. IV. Coloniae Agrippinae: Sumptibus Hermanni Mylii, 1614.
      Vol. V. Antuerpiae: Sumptibus Martini Nutii, 1609.

——. *Los seis libros de la justicia y el derecho.* Edited by Manuel Fraga Iribarne. Madrid: J. L. Cosano, 1941-1943.

MOORE, John Bassett. *A Digest of International Law.* 7 vols. Washington: Government Printing Office, 1906.

MORENO, Isidoro Ruiz. *El derecho internacional público antes de la era cristiana.* Buenos Aires: Facultad de derecho y ciencias sociales, 1946.

MULLANEY, Thomas U., O.P. *Suarez on Human Freedom.* Baltimore: The Carroll Press, 1950.

MURRAY, John Courtney, S.J. "Contemporary Orientations of Catholic Thought on Church and State in the Light of History," *Theological Studies,* X (1949), 177-234.

——. "The Natural Law," in *Great Expressions of Human Rights.* "Religion and Civilization Series." Edited by R. M. MacIver for the Institute of Religious and Social Studies of the Jewish Theological Seminary of America. New York: Harper and Bros., 1950.

——. "The Problem of State Religion," *Theological Studies,* XII (1951), 158-159.

——. "Reversing the Secularist Drift," *Thought,* XXIV (1949), 45-46.

——. "St. Robert Bellarmine on the Indirect Power," *Theological Studies,* IX (1948), 491-535.

——. "Theology of Modern Warfare," An address to the 31st Annual Conference of the Catholic Association for International Peace, Washington, D.C., October 24, 1958. Reprinted in the Catholic Messenger (Davenport, Iowa), November 6, 1958.

MURRAY, R. H. *The Political Consequences of the Reformation.* London: Ernest Benn Ltd., 1926.

MURROW, Edward R. "A Broadcaster Talks to His Colleagues," *The Reporter*, XIX (Nov. 13, 1958), 34-35.

NAVARRUS, M. Azpilcueta. *Manuale sive Enchiridion Confessariorum et Poenitentium.* Lugduni, 1575.

New York Times, September 8 and December 31, 1942.

NOONAN, John T., Jr. *The Scholastic Analysis of Usury.* Cambridge: Harvard University Press, 1957.

NUSSBAUM, A. "The Significance of Roman Law in the History of International Law," *University of Pennsylvania Law Review*, X (1952), 678-687.

NYS, Ernest. *Le droit de la guerre et les précurseurs de Grotius.* Bruxelles: Librairie européenne C. Muquardt, Merzbach et Falk, éditeurs, 1882.

——. *Études de droit international et de droit politique.* Bruxelles: A. Castaigne, 1896.

——. "Les juresconsultes espagnols et la science de droit des gens," *Revue de droit international et de législation comparée*, 2d serie, XIV (1912), 360-387; 494-524; 614-642.

——. "La publicistes espagnols et les droit Indiens," *Revue de droit international et de législation comparée*, XXI, 539ff.

O'BRIEN, William Vincent. "Military Necessity: The Development of the Concept of Military Necessity and Its Interpretation in the Modern Law of War." Unpublished Ph. D. dissertation, Georgetown University, 1953.

OLIVEIRA DIAS, José de. "En torno do duelo Fonseca-Molina: Uma argumentação suicida," *Verbum*, XI (1954), 37-63.

——. "Fonseca e Molina: Os últimos ecos dum litigio plurissecular," *Revista Portuguesa de filosofia*, XI (1955), 54-67.

OPPENHEIM, Lassa F. *International Law*: A Treatise. 2 vols. 7th ed. Edited by H. Lauterpacht. London: Longmans, Green and Co., 1948-1952.

O'RAHILLY, Alfred. "Some Theology about Tyranny," *Irish Theological Quarterly*, XV (1920), 301-320.

Patrologiae Cursus Completus: Series Latina. 218 vols. Edited by J. P. Migne. Paris, 1844-1855.

PEGIS, Anton C. "Molina and Human Liberty" in *Jesuit Thinkers of the Renaissance*: Essays presented to John F. McCormick, S.J., by his students on the occasion of the sixty-fifth anniversary of his birth. Edited by Gerard Smith, S.J. Milwaukee: Marquette University Press, 1939.

PERENA, L. Vicente. *Teoría de la guerra en Francisco Suárez.* 2 vols. Madrid: Consejo superior de investigaciones científicas, Instituto 'Francisco de Vitoria,' 1954.

PHILLIPSON, Colman. *The International Law and Custom of Ancient Greece and Rome.* 2 vols. London: Macmillan and Co., Ltd., 1911.

POHLE, Joseph. "Molinism," *The Catholic Encyclopedia*, X (1913), 439-440.

POLANYI, Karl. "Sortings and Ounce Trade in the West African Slave Trade," *Journal of African History*, V (1964), 381-393.

POLITIS, Nicolas Socrate. *La neutralité et la paix.* Paris: Hachette, 1935.

POLLEN, J. H., S.J. "Dr. Nicholas Sander," *The English Historical Review*, VI (1891), 36-47.

——. "Nicholas Sander," *The Catholic Encyclopedia*, X, 1913.

POMPE, C. A. *Aggressive War*: An International Crime. The Hague: Martinus Nijohff, 1953.

POPE-HENNESSEY, James. *Sins of the Fathers*: A Study of the Atlantic Slave Trade 1441-1807. New York: Alfred A. Knopf, 1968.

PRIBILLA, Max, S.J. "An den Grenzen der Staatsgewalt," *Stimmen der Zeit, Monatsschrift für das Geistesleben der Gegenwart*, CXLII, (1948), 410-427.

——. "Der Eid nach der Lehre der katholischen Moraltheologie" in *Die Vollmacht des Gewissens, hrsg. von den Europäischen Publikationen*, Band I. Munich: H. Rinn, 1956.

PRIDA, Joaquin Fernández. "Ultimos títulos justificantes de la soberanía," *Anuario de la Asociación Francisco de Vitoria*, I (1927-1928), 329-345.

PRIETO, Lucas García, O.S.O. *La paz y la guerra*: Luis de Molina y la escuela Española del siglo XVI en relación con la ciencia y el derecho internacional moderno. Romae: Pontificium Institutum Utriusque Juris, 1944.

Pressed Copies of the Opinions of the Attorney General. Vol. XXXV. Justice and Executive Section. National Archives, Washington, D.C.

PUFENDORF, Samuel. *De Jure Naturae et Gentium*. "The Classics of International Law." 2 vols. Edited by James Brown Scott. Oxford: At the Clarendon Press, 1934.

PUTNEY, Alfred H. *Executive Assumption of the War Making Power*. Sen. Doc. 39. Washington: Government Printing Office, 1928.

QUEIRÓS VELOSO, José Maria de. *A Universidade de Évora*: Elementos para a sua história. Lisboa: no publisher, 1949.

RABENECK, Joannes, S.J. "Antiqua Legenda de Molina Narrata Examinantur," *Archivum Historicum Societatis Jesu*, XXIV (1955), 295-326.

——. "De Ludovici de Molina Studiorum Philosophiae Curriculo," *Archivum Historicum Societatis Jesu*, VI (1937), 291-302.

——. "De vita et scriptis Ludovici Molina," *Archivum Historicum Societatis Jesu*, XIX (1950), 75-145.

——. "Quis prior Proposuerit Doctrinam de Scientia Media, Fonseca an Molina," *Archivum Historicum Societatis Jesu*, XIX (1950), 141-145.

RALSTON, J. H. *International Arbitration from Athens to Locarno*. Stanford: Stanford University Press, 1929.

RAMSEY, Paul. *The Just War*: Force and Political Responsibility. New York: Charles Scribner's Sons, 1968.

RANKE, Leopold. "Die Idee der Volkssouveränität in den Schriften der Jesuiten," in Vol. XXIV: *Abhandlungen und Versuche*. "Sämmtliche Werke." Leipzig: Verlag von Duncker und Humbolt, 1877.

REGOUT, Robert, S.J. *La doctrine de la guerre juste de Saint Augustin à nos jours*. Paris: A Pedone, 1935.

"Reports of the Committee on Effect of War on Enemy Property," *Reports of Conferences of the International Law Association*, XXXV (1932), 245-247.

RODICK, Burleigh Cushing. *The Doctrine of Necessity in International Law*. New York: Columbia University Press, 1938.

RODNEY, Walter. "Portuguese Attempts at Monopoly on the Upper Guinea Coast, 1580-1650," *Journal of African History*, VI (1965), 307-322.

RODRIGUES, Francisco, S.J. *História da Companhia de Jesus na Assistência de Portugal*, 4 vols. Porto: 1931-1950.

ROMMEN, Heinrich A. "The Natural Law in the Renaissance," in *University of Notre Dame Natural Law Proceedings*. Vol. II. Notre Dame, Indiana: College of Law, University of Notre Dame Press, 1949.
——. *The Natural Law*: A Study in Legal and Social History and Philosophy. St. Louis: B. Herder Book Co., 1947.
——. *Die Staatslehre des Franz Suarez, S.J.* M. Gladbach: Volksvereins Verlag, 1926.
——. *The State in Catholic Thought*: A Treatise in Political Philosophy. St. Louis: B. Herder Book Co., 1945.
SABINE, George H. *A History of Political Theory*. Rev. ed. New York: Henry Holt and Co., 1953.
SALA, Isidoro Beato. "Examen de los títulos 2.° y 4.° de la 'Relectio prior de Indis,'" *Anuario de la Asociación Francisco de Vitoria*, I (1927-1928), 305-329.
SÁNCHEZ GALLEGO, Luis. "Luis de Molina, internacionalista," *Anuario de la Asociación F. de Vitoria*, V (1932-1933), 41-69.
SCELLE, Georges. *La Traite Négrière aux Indes de Castille*, 2 vols., Paris: Librairie de la Société du Recueil J. B. Sherry & Du Journal du Palais, 1906.
SCHILLING, Otto. *Naturrecht und Staat nach der Lehre der alten Kirche*. Paderborn: Druck and Verlag von Ferdinand Schoningh, 1914.
——. *Die Staats und Soziallehre des heiligen Augustinus*. Freiburg im Breisgau: Herdersche Verlagshandlung, 1910.
SCHMITT, Albert, S.J. *Zur Geschichte des Probabilismus*. Innsbruck: F. Rauch, 1904.
SCHNEEMANN, Gerardus, S.J. *Controversiarum de Divinae Gratiae Liberique Arbitrii Concordia Initia et Progressus*. Friburgi Brisgoviae: Herder, 1881.
SCHUMPETER, Joseph A. *History of Economic Analysis*. Edited by Elizabeth Boody Schumpeter. New York: Oxford University Press, 1954.
SCHUSTER, J. B., S.J. "Was versteht Fr. Suarez unter Jus gentium," *Zeitschrift für öffenliches Recht*, XVI (1936), 487-495.
SCOTT, James Brown. *The Spanish Origin of International Law*: Francisco de Vitoria and His Law of Nations. Oxford: Oxford University Press, 1932.
SEMPIL, Aniceto Sela y. "Vitoria y los medios de adquirir la soberanía territorial," *Anuario de la Asociación Francisco de Vitoria*, I (1927-1928), 213-229.
SHERRARD, O.A. *Freedom From Fear*: The Slave and His Emancipation. New York: St. Martin's Press, 1959.
SIDJANSKI, D., and S. CASTONOS. "L"agresseur' et l"agression' au point de vue idéologique et réel," *Revue de droit international de sciences diplomatiques politiques et sociales*, XXX (1952), 44-45.
DA SILVA REGO, A. "Portuguese Contributors Towards the Geographical Knowledge of Africa During the XVIth and XVIIth Centuries," *Estudos de Ciéncias Politicas e Sociais*, N.° 58. Lisboa: (1962), 192-198.
SIMON, Yves. *Philosophy of Democratic Government*. Chicago: The University of Chicago Press, 1951.
SMITH, Abbot Emerson. *Colonists in Bondage*: White Servitude and Convict Labor in America 1607-1776. Chapel Hill: University of North Carolina Press, 1947.
SMITH, Gerald, S.J. *Freedom in Molina*. Chicago: Loyola University Press, 1966.

SMITH, H. A. "Booty of War," *British Yearbook of International Law*, (1956), 227-237.

SODER, J. *Die Idee der Völkergemeinschaft*: Francisco de Vitoria und die philosophischen Grundlagen des Völkerrechts. Frankfurt am. Main: A Metzer, 1955.

SOTO, Domingo de, O.P. *De Justitia et Jure Libri Decem*. Salamanca, 1550.

STEGMÜLLER, Friedrich. *Geschichte des Molinismus*. "Beiträge zur Geschichte der Philosophie und Theologie des Mittelalters." Münster in Westfalen: Verlag der Aschendorffschen Verlagsbuchhandlung, 1935.

——. "Zur Literaturgeschichte der Philosophie und Theologie an den Universitäten Evora und Coimbra in XVI Jahrhundert" in *Gesammelte Aufsätze zur Kulturgeschichte Spaniens*. Edited by K. Beyerle, H. Finke, and G. Schreiber. Münster in Westfalen: Aschendorff, 1931.

STONE, Julius. *Legal Controls of International Conflict*. New York: Rinehart and Co., Inc., Publishers, 1954.

STRATMANN, Franziskus M., O.P. *Weltkirche und Weltfriede*: katholische Gedanken zum Kriegs-und-Friedensproblem. Augsburg: Haas und Grabherr, 1942.

STRAUSS, Leo. *On Tyranny*: An Interpretation of Xenophon's Hiero. Glencoe, Illinois: The Free Press, 1948.

STRUPP, Karl. "Le droit du juge international de stateur selon l'équité," *Recueil des cours de l'académie de droit international*, XXX (1930), 337-348.

STUBBS, William. *Seventeen Lectures on the Study of Medieval and Modern History*. Oxford: Oxford University Press, 1886.

STURZO, Luigi. *Church and State*. New York: Longmans, Green and Co., 1939.

SUÁREZ, Francisco, S.J. *Opera Omnia*. 28 vols. Parisiis: Apud Ludovicum Vivès, 1856-1878.

——. *Selections from Three Works of Francisco Suárez, S.J.* 2 vols. Edited by James Brown Scott, Oxford: At the Clarendon Press, 1944.

TAUBE, Baron M. de. "Les origens de l'arbitrage international," *Recueil des cours de l'académie de droit international*, XLII (1942), 5-114.

TAVARES, Severiano. "A questão Fonseca-Molina: Reposta a uma crítica," *Revista Portuguesa de filosofia*, XI (1955), 78-88.

TEIXEIRA, Antonio José. *Documentos para a historia dos Jesuitas em Portugal*. Coimbra: Imprensa da Universidade, 1899.

TERNUS, J. *Zur Vorgeschichte des Moralsysteme von Vitoria bis Medina*. Paderborn: F. Schoningh, 1930.

THIRRING, H. "Was ist Aggression?" *Oesterreichische Zeitschrift für öffentliches Recht*, V (1952-1953), 226-242.

THOMPSON, Elizabeth H. *A.L.A. Glossary of Library Terms with a Selection of Terms in Related Fields*. Prepared under the Direction of the Committee on Library Terminology of the American Library Association. 4th Printing. Chicago: American Library Association, 1956.

TISCHLEDER, Peter. *Ursprung und Träger der Staatsgewalt nach Thomas und seine Schule*. M. Gladbach: Volksverein-Verlag, 1923.

TROMP, S., S.J. "De evolutione doctrinae potestatis indirectae R. Pontificis in res temporales," *Actus Congressus Juridici Internationalis*. III (1936), 55-107.

TUCKER, Robert. *Just War and the Vatican Council*: with Commentary by George C. Higgins, Ralph Potter, Richard H. Cox and Paul Ramsey. New York: The Council on Religious and International Affairs, 1966.

ULLMANN, Walter. *The Growth of Papal Government in the Middle Ages*: A Study of the Ideological Relation of Clerical to Lay Power. London: Methuen & Col, Ltd., 1955.

——. *The Medieval Idea of Law as Represented by Lucas de Penna*: A Study of Fourteenth Century Legal Scholarship. London: Methuen & Co., Ltd., 1946.

VALENTIA, Gregory de, S.J. *Commentariorum Theologorum 2ª 2ᵃᵉ D. Thomae*. Lugduni, 1609.

VANDERPOL, Alfred. *La doctrine scolastique du droit de guerre*. Paris: A. Pedone, 1919.

VANSTEENBERGE, E. "Molina," *Dictionnaire de théologie catholique*. 15 vols. Edited by A. Vacant and E. Mangenot. Paris: Librairie Letouzey et Ané, 1929.

VASUEZ, Gabriel, S.J. *Commentaria in 1ᵃᵐ 2ᵃᵉ S. Thomae*. Venetiis, 1600.

VAWTER, Bruce, C.M. *A Path Through Genesis*. New York: Sheed and Ward, 1956.

VEALE, F. J. P. *Advance to Barbarism*: The Development of Total Warfare from Serajevo to Hiroshima. New York: The Devin-Adair Company, 1968.

VITORIA, Francisco, de, O.P. *Comentarios a la Secunda Secundae de Santo Tomás*. Edited by Vincente Beltrán de Heredia, O.P. Salamanca: Biblioteca de teólogos españoles, 1932-1935.

——. *De Indis et de Jure Belli Selectiones*. Translated by John Pawley Bate and edited by Ernest Nys. Washington: The Carnegie Institution of Washington, 1917.

VLISSINGEN, Clementinus, O.F.M. Cap. *De evolutione definitionis juris gentium*: Studium historico-juridicum de doctrina juris gentium apud Auctores Classicos Saec. XVI-XVIII. Roma: Apud Aedes Universitatis Gregorianae, 1940.

WALKER, W. L. "Recognition of Belligerency and the Grant of Belligerent Rights," *Transactions of the Grotius Society*, XXIII (1930), 177-210.

WEIDEN, Paul. "Necessity of International Law," *Transactions of the Grotius Society*, XXIV (1939), 105-132.

WEIGERT, Hans, *et al*. *Principles of Political Geography*. New York: Appleton-Century-Crofts, Inc., 1957.

WEINKAUFF, Herman. "Die Militäropposition gegen Hitler und das Wiederstandrecht" in *Die Vollmacht des Gewissens, hrsg. von den Europäischen Publikationen*. Band. I. Munich: H. Rinn, 1956.

WARNER, G. "Les prisonniers de guerre," *Recueil des cours de l'académie de droit international*, XXI (1928), 6-24.

Wiederstandsrecht und Grenzen der Staatsgewalt: Bericht über die Tagung der Hochschule für Politische Wissenschaften, München, und der Evangelische Akademie, Tütsing, 18-20 Juni 1955. Edited by Bernhard Pfister and Gerhard Hildmann. Berlin, 1956.

WILKIN, Robert N. "Status of Natural Law in American Jurisprudence" in *University of Notre Dame Natural Law Institute Proceedings*. Vol. II, Notre Dame, Inc.: College of Law, University of Notre Dame, 1949.

WITTMAN, Michael. *Die Ethik des Hl. Thomas von Aquin in ihrem systematischen Aufbau dargestellt und in ihren Geschichtlichen, besonders in den antiken Quellen erforscht*. München, M. Hueber, 1933.

WRIGHT, Quincy. "The Concept of Aggression in International Law," *American Journal of International Law*, XXIX (1935), 373-395.
——. *A Study of War*. 2 vols. Chicago: The University of Chicago Press, 1942.
ZALBA, Marcelino, S.J. "Molina y la ciencias jurídico morales—un aspecto poco conocido de su actividad literaria," *Razón y fe*, CXXVII (1943), 530-543.
ZAVALA, Silvio. *La filosofía política en la conquista de América*. Mexico City: Fondo de Cultura Económica, 1947.

THE POLITICAL PHILOSOPHY OF
LUIS DE MOLINA, S. J. (1535-1600)

CHAPTER I

INTRODUCTION

It has often been said that biography is the best gateway to history; biography is likewise often the best approach to political theory, but in this case it is a narrower gate. To narrate accurately what a man has done is hard enough; to chronicle and understand his thoughts, even when he has left a written record of them, is much more difficult.

But a man's thoughts will never be understood if nothing is known of him or his background. The Gettysburg Address has a certain universality that transcends time and place, yet the reader who knows nothing of the American Civil War would miss most of its important nuances.

The purpose of this chapter is to place Luis de Molina in his setting. Mostly factual, the chapter aims to narrate those details which will assist in an understanding of his political theory. It makes no claim to be a biography, much less a definitive biography.[1] There never has been and never will be a definitive biography of anyone: every crystal changes color with every shift of time. By placing Molina in his setting, however, it should be easier to interpret the light reflected from the cut and polished surface of his mind.

Luis de Molina was born in September, 1535,[2] in Cuenca,[3]

---

[1] This chapter relies heavily on the carefully documented biographical sketch of Molina prepared by Joannes Rabeneck, S.J., "De vita et scriptis Ludovici Molina," *Archivum Historicum Societatis Jesu*, XIX (1950), 75-145. Hereafter cited: Rabeneck, "De Vita et Scriptis."

[2] Until recently Molina's birth year was considered to be 1536. Stegmüller published a letter from Molina to Fr. Claudio Aquaviva in which, on August 29, 1582, Molina gave his age: "Mi edad es de quarenta y siete años, los quales cumpliré este setiembre que viene" (Friederich Stegmüller, *Geschichte des Molinismus* ["Beiträge zur Philosophie und Theologie des Mittelalters"; Münster in Westfalen: Verlag der Aschendorffschen Verlagsbuchhandlung, 1935], Part I: *Neue Molinaschriften*, p. 556).

[3] "Nació el P. Doctor Luis de Molina en la nobilísima cuidad de Cuenca, honra del reino de Toledo, por el lustre de sus moradores, por su santa y esclaracida Iglesia Catedral, de las primeras de España, y el Obispado, de los

Spain. His father was Diego de Orejón y Muela, his mother
Anna García de Molina.[4] In the fall of 1547 he began the
study of Latin in Cuenca. This four-year course was finished
in 1551 and that year he entered the University of Salamanca
as a law student.[5] One year in law was all the training the
future author of *De Justitia et Jure* received. We know nothing
of Molina's stay in Salamanca. There is even no record of his
enrollment at the University.[6] It would be satisfying to be able
to conclude that he studied under the distinguished Don Diego
de Covarrubias who was lecturing at Salamanca at that time.
As will be pointed out later, Molina quoted Covarrubias when
he treated the question of slavery. But there is no evidence
that he attended his lectures at Salamanca. For an unexplained
reason he transferred the next year to Alcalá.[7] It was there

---

mayores del orbe, la fortaleza de sitio y la amenidad de sus riberas y fertili-
dad de sus campos, y no menos ilustre por haber dado al mundo un hijo
tan insigne en letras y religión como fué el P. Luis de Molina" (Alonso de
Andrade, "P. Luis de Molina" in *Varones ilustres de la Compañia de Jesús*
[9 vols., 2d ed.; Bilbao: El Mansajero del Corazón de Jesús, 1891], VIII, 315).

[4] As was frequently the custom, Luis took his mother's name. Fr. Jerome
Nadal, who was sent to Portugal by Ignatius of Loyola as Visitor, had set
down some norms in this matter. Baptismal names would remain unchanged
but the family name could be changed, especially if it had a strange ring
(*Epistolae P. Hieronymi Nadal S.J.* ["Monumenta Historica Societatis Jesu,"
4 vols.; Matriti: Augustinus Avrial, 1898-1905], IV, 201. Hereafter cited: MHSI
Epp. Nadal). The literal translation of Luis' father's name would be "James
of the Long Ears and Tooth," which is strange sounding, indeed.

Very little is known of his family, but Andrade (*op. cit.*, V, 785) carefully
notes that Luis' parents were thoroughbreds—*limpieza de sangre*. Concern
with racial purity became an obsession with some of the Jesuits at that time.
James Brodrick (*The Progress of the Jesuits, 1556-79* [New York: Longmans,
Green & Co., 1947]) discusses the matter and indirectly throws some light on.
Molina's ancestry. Writing of Antonio Araoz, Provincial of Castile who admitted Molina to the Society, Brodrick states: "*Limpieza de sangre* had become
a kind of religion in Spain in those days and Antonio Araoz was one of its
high priests" (p. 119. Hereafter cited: Brodrick, *Progress*).

[5] In July, 1561, Molina wrote Nadal: "Habré estudiado doze años, quatro
de grammática en Cuenca, uno de leyes en Salamanca, y obra de seis meses
de súmulas en Alcalá: todo esto antes de entrar en la Compañía" (MHSI:
Epp. Nadal, I, 666, n. 5).

[6] "Im Register der Matrikeln der Universität Salamanca kommt in Jahr
1551/52 ein Luis de Molina (Orejón, Muela, Garcia) weder unter den Legisten
noch Kanonisten noch Artisten noch Theologen vor. Ebensowenig unter den
dann folgen die von 1551/52. Es besteht daher die Möglichkeit, dass das juri-
stiche Studium Molinas schon in das Jahr 1550/51 fällt" Stegmüller, *Molinismus*.

[7] "Alcalá, the Spanish form of the Moorish words, *al kala*, the castle, is
unfortunately the name of no less than thirteen Spanish towns, all founded
by the Moors. But the only one that concerned the Jesuits was the great
Alcalá situated on the river Henares, seventeen miles north-east of Madrid.

he met Jesuits for the first time. In August, 1553,[8] he was admitted [9] to the Society of Jesus by Antonio de Araoz, Provincial of Castile. [10] Molina was sent by Araoz to Coimbra in Portugal to begin his novitiate. [11]

There has been considerable controversy in recent years about Molina's Coimbra sojourn. Two questions have been discussed at some length. The first is when did Molina's philosophical studies begin. Stegmüller maintains he had a two-year novitiate: "Molinas Philosophiestudium dauerte vom Herbst 1555 bis Herbst 1559." [12] Another German scholar, this time a Jesuit, insists that Molina began his philosophy in 1554: "Certum omnino est Molinam Conimbricae annis 1554-1558 integrum philosophiae cursum audivisse." [13] Rabeneck's conclusion, in the light of the evidence he produces, seems to be preferable.

The second question is of more importance: Under whom did he study at Coimbra? Again Rabeneck's careful research has produced evidence that Sebastian de Morales was his teacher during the last two years of the four-year course. The importance of this conclusion is that it removes both Ignatius Martins and Pedro de Fonseca from the list of Molina's philosophy professors. [14] Of Martins more will be heard during Molina's stay

---

... Both St. Ignatius [Loyola] and Nadal had studied at Alcalá, and a flourishing college had grown up there" (Brodrick, *Progress*, p. 117, n.).

[8] The conflicting testimony on the exact year Molina joined the Jesuits is discussed by Stegmüller, *Molinismus*, p. 3*, n. 4.

[9] Molina recorded that he was admitted to the Society by Fr. Francis de Villanueva, then Rector of the Jesuit college in Alcalá: "Fuí recebido por el P. Villanueva, que nuestro Señor tiene. ..." (MHSI: *Epp. Nadal*, I, 667, n. 5). Strictly speaking, only a provincial in the name of the General may admit candidates to the Society. What Molina obviously intended to convey was that Fr. Villanueva made all the arrangements with the Provincial for admission—a matter which even to this day is often handled by the local rectors.

[10] For an interesting vignette of Araoz, nephew of St. Ignatius, see *MHSI. Epp. Nadal*, II, 42-43. He appears to have been a cantakerous individual, hard on himself and hard on everyone else. Molina must have been lucky to be sent off to Portugal to make his novitiate.

[11] A possible reason for sending Molina off to Portugal was the poverty of the Castilian province. In June of that year Emmanuel Lopez wrote from Alcalá to St. Ignatius: "Muchos desean ser admitidos en la Compañía, pero el poco apareio que para ello tenemos, no lo sufre por agora" (Epistolae Mixtae ex Variis Europae Locis ab Anno 1537 ad 1556 Scriptae ["Monumenta Historica Societatis Jesu," 5 vols.; Matriti: Augustinus Avrial, 1898-1901], III, 354). Hereinafter cited as *Epp. Mixtae*.

[12] Stegmüller, *Molinismus*, p. 4*.

[13] Joannes Rabeneck, S. J., "De Ludovici de Molina Studiorum Philosophiae Curriculo," *Archivum Historicum Societatis Jesu*, VI (1937), 302.

[14] *Ibid*.

Cf. Friedrich Stegmüller, "Zur Literaturgeschichte der Philosophie und Theo-

at Évora [15] and Fonseca will be considered in connection with
the doctrine of *scientia media*. But neither Jesuit taught Molina
at Coimbra between 1554 and 1558.

During the time of his philosophical studies his intellectual
ability began to manifest itself. The rector of the Jesuit college,
Leo Henriques, writing to Rome in 1555, included Molina "son
los que meior entienden." [16] The following year Molina participated in a public disputation that began at the ungodly hour
of 7:00 A.M. and lasted until 10:00 A.M., resuming in the after-
noon at three and ending at six-thirty. Molina merited special
praise for his defense of theses taken from logic and philosophy. [17] By April, 1558, Molina, with two others, had successfully passed the oral examinations at the Royal College in Coimbra and devoted the remaining part of the year to studying
theology. [18]

In Coimbra the Jesuit scholastics studied theology at the
public university. They attended certain repetitions at the
Jesuit college and in 1560 were ordered to be present there at
the daily *casus conscientiae* in moral theology. [19] It is likely
that one of Molina's professors at the University was the Dominican Martin Ledesma. [20] Molina was praised during his
studies for his unusual intellectual ability and was deemed an
apt prospect for the position of teaching theology. [21] He filled
in for ailing professors at Coimbra and spent a month substitut-
ing for a professor of theology at Évora. He later admitted

---

logie an den Universitäten Evora und Coimbra im XVI. Jahrhundert" in *Gesammelte Aufsätze zur Kulturgeschichte Spaniens*, ed. K. Beyerle, H. Finke,
and G. Cchreiber, III (Münster in Westfalen: Aschendorffschen, 1931), 385-430,
for a detailed listing of the professors and courses at Coimbra and Évora
during Molina's day.

[15] José M. Díez-Alegría, S.J., "El conimbricense Ignacio Martins S.J. y el
concepto de ley de las lecturas de 1570 en la Universidad de Evora," *Revista
Portuguesa de Filosofia*, XI (1955), Part II, 546-553.

[16] *Litterae Quadrimestres* ("Monumenta Historica Societatis Jesu," 7 vols.;
Matriti: Augustinus Aurial, 1894), III, 453.

[17] *Chronicon Polanci* ("Monumenta Historica Societatis Jesu," 6 vols.; Matriti: Augustinus Aurial, 1894-1898), VI, 715, nos. 3092-3094: "Eminuit inter alios
Ludovicus Molina, quamvis omnes strenue admodum in respondendo se ges-
serunt. Disputarunt autem qui majoris erant auctoritatis, cum omnibus locus
nec tempus dari non posset, qui se bene armatos accesisse fatebantur; sed
partim tres praedicti discipuli, partim qui eis assistebant, tanta cum facilitate
et claritate argumenta disolvebant, ut multum omnino auctoritatis apud Univer-
sitatem nostris scholis conciliaverit."

[18] Rabeneck, "De Vita et Scriptis," p. 86.

[19] *Ibid.*

[20] *Ibid.*

[21] Stegmüller, *Molinismus*, pp. 577ff.

that these jobs were harder on him than two years of regular teaching. In his third year of theology Molina was ordained a priest. [22] By May of the next year Molina was in Évora to do graduate work in theology at the University. But before Christmas, 1563, he had been recalled to Coimbra to teach philosophy in the Jesuit college, where he remained until 1567. During this time his health, which was never much to boast of, caused some concern in Rome. Father General Lainez ordered the Provincial of Portugal to have a special care for Molina's health and to see to it that he was not overworked. [23] The first year at Coimbra he had seventy students, including fifteen Jesuit scholastics, and a report was made that he gave great satisfaction [24]—no mean accomplishment for any teacher of young Jesuits. The content of his lectures will be noted later in this chapter.

During this period in Coimbra pressure was exerted on Molina's superiors to have him returned to his native Spain. The shadowy figure of the Marchioness de Cañete, wife of the Viceroy of Peru, had petitioned Father General Borgia to have Molina returned to Toledo. The Provincial of Portugal protested the move as unfair, alleging (with considerable exaggeration) that Molina owed all he had to Portugal—including his knowledge of Latin. [25] Francis Borgia yielded to the requests of the Portuguese province and by August, 1568, Molina had been transferred to Évora to teach theology. [26]

The University of Évora had been founded and given to the Society of Jesus in 1559 by Cardinal Henry, brother of John III and at that time Archbishop of Évora. [27] In 1561

---

[22] Rabeneck, "De Vita et Scriptis," p. 84.

Stegmüller (*Molinismus*, p. 5*) confesses: "Das Jahr der Priesterweihe Molinas ist nicht bekannt. Möglich ist, dass er sie schon während oder am Ende seiner theologischen Studien empfing, vielleicht empfing er sie auch erst im Jahr 1567 oder 1568, am Ende seiner philosophischen Lehrtätigkeit."

[23] Rabeneck, "De Vita et Scriptis," p. 2.

[24] *Ibid.*

[25] *Ibid.*, p. 93.

[26] "Augusto mense 1568 Conimbrica venerunt Ludovicus Molina et Fernandus Rebellus, Eborencis Academiae doctores valde illustres. Molina magisterium theologiae auspicaturus erat" (Stegmüller, *Molinismus*, p. 5*, n. 8).

[27] *Chronicon Polanci*, II, 377, n. 429.

For a recent history of the University of Évora, see José Maria de Queiros Velloso, *A Universidade de Évora*: elementos para a sua história (Lisboa: no publisher, 1949).

A history of the establishment of the Jesuits in Évora and the inauguration of the University is found in Francisco Rodrigues, *História da Companhia de*

there were 750 students at the University; by the spring of
1562 eighty Jesuits were living at the college of the Society
there. It was Évora which provided the platform for Molina's
most famous lectures. The buildings of this university, some
of them from Molina's day, are still in excellent condition.

Évora, the capital of the province of Alto Alentejo, has been
since Molina's day a district capital and the see of a Roman
Catholic Archbishop. With 40,000 inhabitants it is the fifth
largest city in Portugal, ninety miles from Lisbon and seventy-
five miles from Portalegre. In the sixteenth century Évora
achieved a world-wide fame in such fields as culture and art.

"The town [Évora] stretches itself along an extensive hill
of soft slopes in the plain of Alentejo. ...As it is in a high
position without having mountains near, it has a vast horizon.
Its weather is dry, the air is pure, the sky is very blue, lovely
and sunny." [28]

Molina was assigned the evening class in theology and held
that post until 1572, when he took over the morning session. [29]
A problem arose over his academic qualifications. [30] He held
only the bachelor's degree in theology and yet was preparing
students for the doctorate. After some hesitation, the General
of the Jesuits empowered the Portuguese Provincial to confer
the Degree of Doctor of Theology on Molina, which was
bestowed on April 22, 1571: "In Eborensi Academia doctoris
gradu insignitus Ludovicus Molina illius Academiae et universae
Societatis lumen fulgentissimum; coepitque moderari secundam
Theologiae cathedram, cui hactenus seu Professor extra ordinem
praeerat." [31]

Molina taught theology at Évora for fifteen years. According to the custom, he lectured on the *Summa* of St. Thomas.
Molina began by explaining the *Prima Secundae*, questions 1-76
and 98-105, which took a little more than a year. From November, 1570, to July, 1573, he treated the first part of the *Summa*.
In 1573-1574 he discussed the matter in the *Secunda Secundae*

Jesus na Assistência de Portugal (Porto: 1931) Vol. I, p. 578-585; Vol. II, pp.
303-324.

[28] Trilio Espanca, *Évora*, (Évora: Livraria Nazareth, 1971), p. 69.

[29] Rabeneck, "De Vita et Scriptis," p. 94.

[30] Suárez later had a similar problem (*Selections from Three Works of
Francisco Suárez, S.J.*, ed. James Brown Scott [2 vols.; Oxford: At the Clarendon Press, 1944], II, 7a, n. 2): "It was not until many years later that Suarez
went through the formality of obtaining a doctor's degree, and then only in
order to silence critics who pretended to feel doubts concerning his qualifications for the *prima* professorship of theology at the University of Coimbra."

[31] Stegmüller, *Molinismus*, p. 6*, n. 13.

on faith, the primacy of the Roman Church, and the authority of the supreme pontiff in 1574-1575 he covered the tract on hope and charity. Between 1575 and 1582 he taught only five full terms, devoting all of his teaching time to *De Justitia*. [32] Molina became interested in editing these lectures for print and in this desire was greatly encouraged by Claudio Aquaviva who had become General of the Jesuits in 1581. There is extant a long letter from Molina to the General in which the Évora professor detailed his plans for publishing four major works, including two tomes on justice. [33] Aquaviva approved his scheme and continued to encourage his writing efforts.

Aquaviva may have later regretted the encouragement he gave Molina, for by it he was partially responsible for the most controversial work ever published by a son of St. Ignatius [34]— Molina's *Concordia liberi arbitrii cum gratiae donis, divina scientia, praescientia, providentia, praedestinatione*. [35] Brodrick remarks on the piquant circumstance that this book, which was to raise such a storm of controversy in the Catholic schools, should have begun with the word "harmony." [36]

---

[32] *Ibid.*, p. 551.

[33] "Lo que a el presente se me offrecía representar a V. P. con toda indifferencia era que estava inclinado a hazer una pausa en la letura para imprimirse la primera parte et tomo de virtutibus theologalibus y los dos de iusticia, que son por todos quatro cuerpos de libros que tengo hechos; y tras ello el curso de artes que tengo tambien hecho" (*ibid.*, p. 555).

[34] The summary in the present chapter of the great controversy over Molina's *Concordia* relies heavily on the delightfully readable and reliable account found in Brodrick's work, *Robert Bellarmine 1542-1621* (ed., 2 vols.; London: Longmans, Green and Co., 1950), II, 1-69. (Hereafter cited: Brodrick, *Bellarmine*.)

A standard history of the controversy is Gerardus Schneemann, S.J., *Controversiarum de Divinae Gratiae Liberique Arbitrii Concordia Initia et Progress* (Friburgi Brisgoviae: Herder, 1881).

For more recent accounts, cf. Antonio Astrain, *Historia de la Compañia de Jesús en la Asistencia de España* (7 vols.; Madrid: Sucesores de Rivadeneyra, 1902-1925), IV, 115-385.

[35] Luis de Molina, S.J., *Concordia liberi arbitrii cum gratiae donis, divina praescientia, providentia praedestinatione, et reprobatione, ad nonnullos primae partis D. Thomae articulos*: Doctore Ludovico Molina primario quondam in Eborensi Academia Theologiae professore e societate Jesu autore [sic]. Adjecti sunt duo indices, rerum alter, alter eorum scripturae locorum, qui vel ex professo, vel obiter explicantur eodem autore [sic] (Olyssipone: Apud Riberium typographum regium M. D. LXXXVIII).

autor—This form of *auctor*, *auctoritatis*, etc., is used consistently throughout the printed version. No further reference to the difference in spelling will be made.

[36] Brodrick, *Bellarmine*, II, 26.

In another work the same author remarks of Molina's volume: "That

Within six years the book had gone into five editions. This small volume marks a turning point in the history of speculative theology.

> With all its obscurities of style and difficulties of matter, it was impossible for any theologian who took his business seriously to ignore it. Within a few years of its publication Molina's name was as familiar in universities, seminaries and academies and other places throughout Europe... as the name of St. Augustine himself. [37]

Molina's fame as a constructive theologian is due to his exposition of the theory of *scientia media*, [38] which he introduced to explain the infallibility with which efficacious grace obtains its effects. God's knowledge of conditioned future events is called "middle knowledge" because it embraces all objects that are found neither in the realm of pure possibility nor, strictly speaking, in the realm of reality, but partakes in a manner of both extremes. They are purely possible in the sense that they might

---

Concordance has caused more discord among theologians than anything else published since the days of Arius" (*Progress*, p. 132).

[37] Brodrick, *Bellarmine*, II, 28-29.

[38] The question of the origin of the doctrine of *scientia media* has been in much dispute. Some scholars, such as James Brodrick, attribute its origin to the Portuguese Jesuit, Pedro de Fonseca: "Studies he [Nadal] promoted with all his might, and it was owing to his encouragement that the brilliant but singularly modest Coimbra professor, Father Pedro de Fonseca, later dubbed the 'Aristotle of Portugal,' set his hand to a vast commentary on the Metaphysics of Stagyrite in which the famous theory of *scientia media* made its first innocent and trustful appearance. Fonseca, who cared nothing for the credit of a great name on earth, was not aggrieved when his illustrious Spanish pupil and brother, Louis de Molina, took over the theory, developed it, and delivered it to the theological world as his own...." (*Progress*, p. 132).

The tireless Fr. Rabeneck rejects the claims made for Fonseca and attributes the doctrine wholly to Molina. "Hinc antiqua illa legenda, secundum quam Molina ut discipulus Fonsecae ab eo scientiam mediam didicit et Fonseca saltem fundamenta 'Molinismi' jecit, in omnibus partibus suis omni fundamento caret. Molina numquam discipulus Fonsecae fuit; prior eo scientia media usus est ad libertatem arbitrii cum divina praescientia, providentia et praedestinatione conciliandam; et nulla est ratio negandi eum etiam primum auctorem illius doctrinae esse quae postea ejus nomine insignita est" (Joannes Rabeneck, S.J., "Antiqua Legenda de Molina Narrata Examinantur," *Archivum Historicum Societatis Jesu*, XXIV [1955], 326). Also Johannes Rabeneck, S.J. "Quis prior Proposuerit Doctrinam de Scientia Media, Fonseca an Molina," *ibid.*, XIX (1950), 141-145.

Cf. José de Oliveira Dias, "Em torno do duelo Fonseca-Molina: uma argumentação suicida," *Verbum*, XI, (1954), 37-63; "Fonseca e Molina: os últimos ecos dum litígio plurisecular," *Revista portuguesa de filosofia*, XI (1955), 64-67.

Severiano Tavares, "A questão Fonseca-Molina: resposta a uma crítica," *Revista portuguesa de filosofia*, XI (1955), 78-88.

but never will exist; they are actual in the sense that they would exist if certain conditions were granted. By means of this knowledge God foresees from all eternity what attitude the will of men would adopt under any conceivable combination of circumstances, and then only—though the relation is not temporal but ontological—does he decree to share his graces according to his absolute good pleasure. Efficacious grace is a grace that he foresees infallibly will be accepted. Sufficient grace differs in no way intrinsically from efficacious. It is perfectly adequate in itself for the purposes of salvation, but God infallibly foresees that those to whom it is offered will refuse it. An eminent theologian, who is neither a Dominican nor a Jesuit, observes of this doctrine:

> This doctrine is in perfect harmony with the dogmas of the gratuity of grace, the unequal distribution of efficacious grace, the wise and inscrutable operations of Divine Providence, the absolute impossibility to merit final perseverance, and lastly, the immutable predestination to glory of rejection; nay more, it brings those very dogmas into harmony, not only with the infallible foreknowledge of God, but also with the freedom of the created will. [39]

Molina's doctrine was not in harmony with what a distinguished Dominican, Domingo Bañez, had been teaching from his chair of theology at the University of Salamanca. Both men agreed on two fundamental truths: the efficacy of grace and the freedom of the will. It is only when they attempted to reconcile these truths that the two Spaniards differed. And differ they did. One of the chief points of Bañez' theory was that it placed an intrinsic and substantial difference between sufficient and efficacious grace. The one leads up to the consent but is powerless to cause it; the other causes it infallibly, and that in virtue of its irresistible might.

Bañez considered Molina's *Concordia* an open attack on his theory. Before long the two were engaged in a glorious mêlée which involved members of each man's religious order. At this distance, we can afford to look back on the struggle with a certain amount of amused detachment, but it was hardly amusing to the principals. It meant for Molina that during the last ten years of his life he was greatly harassed from nearly every quarter. If is far beyond the purpose of this chapter to record the wearying rounds of the fight that dragged on until 1608

---

[39] Joseph Pohle, "Molinism," *The Catholic Encyclopedia*, X (1913), 439-440.

when the pope as referee called it a draw. By that decision
was officially ended the greatest bout among theologians since
the early ages of Christianity.

More important for our present purpose than the controversy itself is the impetus Molina and Molinism gave to the
social-metaphysics tradition of the newly founded Society of
Jesus. [40] St. Ignatius had given the initial thrust when he wrote
his Spiritual Exercises:

> Likewise we ought not to speak of grace at such length and
> with such emphasis that the poison of doing away with liberty
> is engendered.
>
> Hence, as far as possible with the help of God, one may
> speak of faith and grace that the Divine Majesty may be
> praised. But let it not be done in such a way, above all not
> in times which are as dangerous as ours, that works and free
> will suffer harm, or that they are considered of no value. [41]

In the great conflict of the theologians over the question of
actual grace, it has been said that the Dominicans tended to
stress the omnipotence of God in producing effects with efficacious grace while the Jesuits approached the question from the
other side: all men's wills remain free under the influence
of grace. This is an obvious over-simplification but it does
spotlight two basic points of view. Gustav Gundlach has sum-
med up the Jesuit position this way: "Molinism attempts to
solve the difficult problem of how Divine Grace can coexist
with human liberty, in a manner which has always been interpreted as strongly emphasizing the autonomy of the human
creature." [42]

---

[40] This summary of the influence of Molina on the sociometaphysical tradi-
tions of the Society of Jesus is taken from the excellent study by Edgar Alexan-
der, "Church and Society in Germany: Social and Political Movements and
Ideas in German and Austrian Catholicism (1789-1950)," in *Church and Society*:
Catholic Social and Political Movements 1789-1950, ed. Joseph N. Moody (New
York: Arts, Inc., 1953), pp. 489-536.

[41] *The Spiritual Exercises of St. Ignatius*: A New Translation Based on
Studies in the Language of the Autograph by Louis J. Puhl, S.J. (Westminster,
Md.: The Newman Press, 1953), p. 161.

[42] Gustav Gundlach, S.J., *Zur Soziologie der katholischen Ideenwelt und
des Jesuitenordens* (Freiburg im Breisgau: Herder & Co., 1927), p. 96.

Cf. Anton C. Pegis, "Molina and Human Liberty" in *Jesuit Thinkers of the
Renaissance*: Essays presented to John F. McCormick, S.J. by his students
on the occasion of the sixty-fifth anniversary of his birth, ed. Gerard Smith, S.J.
(Milwaukee: Marquette University Press, 1939), pp. 75-131 and 239-241.

A recent American Jesuit traces the same Ignatian influences on Molina
but concludes that Molina's emphasis on human liberty was instinctive and

Man, in the context of Molinism, does not appear as a pas-
sively receptive object of the divine will but as an actively
cooperating subject—as God's creature who from his own will
power and decision accepts the will of God and acts as his agent.
Men become active "co-workers with God" in the dispensation
and reception of grace.

This theological concept leads to a socio-metaphysical concept which lends a strongly emphasized justification to the
social and political autonomy of man in his role as a citizen.
Man as God's co-worker, theologically speaking, becomes an
active co-worker in state and society, sociologically speaking.
One writer sums it up this way: "The concept of the working
and co-working person is the central idea of the social metaphysics of the Jesuits." [43]

The same writer stresses three characteristics of Jesuit
social metaphysics. First is the basic *realism*: Man is considered in the concrete in all his activities, with contingent
historical reality and the autonomous and independent values
of social and political life accorded full recognition. Second,
it implies a *personalism* that at all times the concrete living
person stands in the center of all studies concerning the essence

---

theological rather than rational and philosophical. "Obviously he [Molina]
thought that his indetermination of the will in choice *was* a philosophy. But
unless freedom in choice grows out of his antecedents, there is no *reason*
for asserting that choice must be free.... Still a man may be right without
knowing why. And if Molina's theology be considered correct, he was right
by his faith, without knowing, by his reason, why. If, then, Molina's theology
be admitted as true, he landed, so to say, right side up, and he lit on his
feet because of that theology and despite his philosophy." Gerard Smith, S.J.,
Freedom in Molina, (Chicago, Loyola University Press, 1966), p. 217.

"His [Molina's] faith preserved an element in liberty demanded of him
by his theology even though his reason did not succeed in rendering a philo-
sophic account of his faith." *Ibid.*, p. 219. "Given such a man, [Molina] put
him in the proper milieu, and you have the reason, in part, why he reacted
as he did. Luis de Molina was a member of the Society of Jesus, an order
whose founder, St. Ignatius of Loyola (n. 1491, ob. 1556), was a contemporary
of Martin Luther (n. 1483, ob. 1546)." *Ibid.*

"But though he was thus possessed of the prudent guidance of his chief,
[Ignatius] it was perhaps unfortunate that he [Molina] felt compelled upon
to speak." *Ibid.*, p. 221.

Father Smith's study of freedom in Molina is confined almost exclusively,
to the *Concordia*. He does not include any references to Molina's *De Justitia
et Jure*.

Also *vide* Thomas U. Mullaney, O.P., *Suarez on Human Freedom* (Baltimore.
The Carroll Press, 1950), for a strictly philosophical study of another prominent
Jesuit's teaching on the nature of human liberty.

[43] Alexander, *op. cit.*, p. 495.

and purpose of the state, society, and economy. Conversely, all political, social, and economic activity is directed towards the human personality. State and society exist through man and for man; all order of state and society, all economic activity derive their sense ad purpose from the one fact that they serve man who is both their origin and their end. Third, this social metaphysics has a *democratic* orientation which determines the role which authority will play in political and social life and yet preserves the autonomy of man. [44] Such a democratic orientation will oppose usurpation of authority by an individual or an autocracy; it also opposes usurpation of authority by a dictatorship based on mass totalitarianism.

A contemporary German Jesuit, Father Gustav Gundlach, has studied the socio-metaphysical traditions of the Jesuits and summarized them this way:

> In the Catholic world of ideas we find a democratic line principally in the doctrine of Natural Law taught by the Medieval Thomistic philosophy. This line is stressed even more strongly in the specifically Jesuit amplification of this doctrine which gives the individual a prominent place and culminates in the concepts of the social pact and the people's sovereignty. In the doctrine of the Natural Law the inalienable rights of the individual are stressed as against feudalism, absolutism and also as against the authority of the Church and the Order. We should never forget that, aside from its natural source, Christian Democracy has a supra-natural one; the equality of all saved before God, through Christ. And in general, the role Catholicism reserves for the individual contains elements that are much less hostile to the idea of democracy than is frequently inferred. The supra-national authority of the World Church through all the ages has set a brake on any undue expansion of the omnipotent and absolute state. Wherever a limit is set to state omnipotence, a larger role is reserved for the individual, the family, the vocational corporations, in short for all living forces of a democratic state built up from below. The conceptual world of Catholicism with the objective reality implied in the doctrine of Natural Law and Revelation offers indeed the basis for a sound Democracy. [45]

Molina's fame as a dogmatic theologian has all but obscured his contribution to the social sciences. This is true except in

---

[44] Peter Lippert, S.J., *Zur Psychologie des Jesuitenordens* (Freiburg im Breisgau: Herder & Co., 1923).

[45] Gundlach, *op. cit.*, pp. 73-74.

the case of economics where, in the works of Bernard Dempsey,[46] Joseph Schumpeter,[47] John Noonan,[48] and Joseph Höffner [49] Molina's importance is recognized. In the field of political science Molina's legacy is relatively unknown.[50] Granting that he has made a contribution to the field of political science, what sort of background did he have for it?

As was mentioned earlier, he spent eighteen months studying law at Salamanca and Alcalá before he joined the Jesuits. Besides the ordinary philosophical course at Coimbra he seems to have had little subsequent training in the field. Molina himself remarks on this deficiency: "I am rather amazed that anyone with so little background in moral [theology] as I had when I began the *Secunda Secundae* could produce such a finished work and arrange it so well, lecturing on the very matter I was assembling."[51]

---

[46] Bernard W. Dempsey, S.J., *Interest and Usury* (Washington: American Council on Public Affairs, 1943), pp. 118-129 and 130-147.

[47] Joseph A. Schumpeter, *History of Economic Analysis*, ed. Elizabeth Boody Schumpeter (New York: Oxford University Press, 1954), pp. 95-112.

[48] John T. Noonan, Jr., *The Scholastic Analysis of Usury* (Cambridge: Harvard University Press, 1957), pp. 222ff.

[49] Joseph Höffner, *Wirtschaftsethik und Monopole im fünfzehnten und sechzehnten Jahrhundert* (Jena: Verlag Gustav Fischer, 1941), pp. 67ff.

[50] A recent interest in Molina's political thought has been stimulated by the pioneering work of a Spanish Jesuit, José Mª. Díez-Alegría, *El desarrollo de la doctrina de la ley natural en Luis de Molina y en los maestros de la Universidad de Evora de 1565 a 1591*. Estudio histórico y textos inéditos. (Barcelona: Consejo superior de investigaciones científicas, 1951) and Manuel Fraga Iribarne's *Luis de Molina y el derecho de la guerra*. Madrid, 1947. The same author has published a Spanish translation of *De Justitia*: Luis de Molina *Los seis libros de la Justicia y el Derecho*. Madrid, J. L. Cosano, 1941-1943.

Perhaps the most extensive treatment of Molina's political thought can be found in the monograph by Johann Klenhappl, S.J., *Der Staat bei Ludwig Molina*. Innsbruck, F. Rauch, 1935. The best account in English is in a recent book by Bernice Hamilton, *Political Thought in Sixteenth Century Spain*: A Study of the Political Ideas of Vitoria, De Soto, Suárez, and Molina. Oxford, at the Clarendon Press, 1963.

[51] Stegmüller, *Molinismus*, p. 552, ll. 30-45. Letter to Claudio Aquaviva, August 29, 1582. In this and subsequent references to the letters of Molina sent to Aquaviva, it must be remembered that these letters were never meant to be seen by others. In them Molina confides his inmost thoughts to his superior. What seems vain and boastful in the cold glare of the printed page was only intimate self-revelation to one he could trust.

On this point Stegmüller (*ibid.*, p. 79*) writes: "Alles schwieg er [Molina] in sich hinein, nur dem Ordensgeneral vertraute und klagte er in kindlicher Offenheit."

The lectures that finally became *De Justitia et Jure* began as a commentary on the *Secunda Secundae* of St. Thomas. [52] He got as far as Question 62 and became dissatisfied.

> Then it seemed to me that the treatment given in the matter on justice by the theologians and principally St. Thomas was too short. The theologians on matters of government were discredited and rightly so. When questioned on many points they were at a loss for and shed little light on an answer. They were cowardly in undertaking enterprises in the service of God, expressing their conclusions, and quieting consciences— all for a lack of knowledge on moral questions, and in particular in the matter on justice (as I admit has happened to me a number of times on missions and elsewhere). Therefore I decided to drop St. Thomas from Question sixty-two up to the begining of the matter *de religione* (about fifteen questions) and do five treatises on justice in which I would say everything St. Thomas said in these questions, and a lot more he did not say. [53]

The plan of the *De Justitia* is original. Vitoria before him had not systematized his *relecciones* and the one important outlined work which preceded Molina's was Domingo de Soto's *De Justitia et Jure*. [54] The inspiration for the division of Mo-

---

[52] Rabeneck's unqualified assertion, "Opus [*De Justitia*] non erat commentarius in Summam S. Thomae...." is misleading. (Rabeneck, "De Vita et Scriptis," p. 135).

[53] Letter of Molina to Aquaviva, August 29, 1582; Ep. NN. 86, f. 283r-v (Stegmüller, *Molinismus*, 552, 10-25): "Hasta la q. 62 fui comentando a Santo Thomas como hasta allí siempre avia hecho. Despues pareciendome que estava por los theologos y principalmente por Santo Thomas muy cortamente tratada la materia de iustitia, y que estavan con razon desacreditados los theologos para cosa de govierno, y que en muchas cosas preguntados se hallavan atados y con poca luz para responder, y cobardes para acometer negocios de servicio de Dios, y dalles salida y desembaraçer conscientias, por tener corta notitia en cosas morales, maxime en la materia de iustitia (como confieso averme a mi acontecido diversas vezes en missiones y fuera dellas) determiné dexar a Santo Thomas desde la q. 62 hasta el principio de la materia de religione, que serán como quinze quaestiones, y hazer cinco tratados de iustitia, en que dixese todo lo que Santo Thomas dixo en aquellas quaestiones y mucho mas que él no tocó."

[54] Domino de Soto, *De Justitia et Jure Libri decem* (Salamanca, 1550). The ten books were divided as follows:

Books I and II: Law.
Book III: Law as the object of justice. A study of that virtue.
Book IV: Introduction to commutative justice. Ownership and restitution.
Book V: Jnjury and injustice.
Book VI: Usury and contracts.

lina's work came from the classification of justice by Aristotle. Molina divides his work into six tractates:

I. Justice in general and its classes.
II. Commutative justice with respect to external goods.
III. Commutative justice with respect to corporal goods and persons.
IV. Commutative justice with respect to the goods of honor and fame and spiritual goods.
V. Justice and execution of justice by public power.
VI. Distributive justice.

There was considerable difference between Molina's original plan, as outlined to Aquaviva in 1582, and the finished work. By 1589 the first tractate and 189 disputations of the second tractate had been completed. Molina then suspected that the second tractate would run to five hundred disputations.

The first tractate and 251 disputations of the second were printed in 1593. The next year he was still working on the next volume and informed Leonard Lessius that he would have completed it before then if he had not gone to Madrid twice that year.

In December 1594, writing from his home town, Cuenca, Molina informed Aquaviva that he had located a publisher for the second volume and that his brother had agreed to underwrite some of the printing costs. [55]

In April of the next year he was busy preparing marginal references and indices which he hoped to complete in a couple of months. Aquaviva sent along an encouraging word that he and all who had seen the first volume were eagerly awaiting the second. [56] It was 1597 before that volume was printed. [57] It contained disputations 252-575 of the second tractate. Originally it was supposed to consist of about two hundred disputations; however, as in the case of the Sorcerer's Apprentice, once

---

Book VII: Vows.
Book VIII: Oaths.
Book IX: Tithes and simony.
Book X: State and residence of prelates.

Molina is usually associated with his fellow Jesuits, Lessius and Lugo, who also wrote treatises with the same title. There was a spate of similar works with same title which became the main scholastic repository of economic thought in the sixteenth century (cf. Schumpeter, *op. cit.*, p. 5; Dempsey, *op. cit.*, p. 127; Noonan, *op. cit.*, p. 222).

[55] Stegmüller, *Molinismus*, p. 737, 11, 28-30.
[56] Rabeneck, *De vita*, p. 137.
[57] *Ibid.*

he had the second tractate going he could not turn it off until
it had flooded over into 760 disputations. The third volume
contained all the remaining disputations of the second tractate. [58]
An indication of the vast extent of this second tractate is that
it comprises all of the first three volumes printed except for
thirty-eight columns occupied by the first tractate. Rabeneck
drily observes that the subsequent tractates would likewise have
swollen in size had Molina lived to prepare them for publication.

The remaining volumes were prepared for publication by
the Jesuits of the College of Madrid. [59] It was 1609 before the
entire work was printed. [60]

---

[58] *Ibid.*

[59] "Septimo anno, cum e vita discesserat Molina, quaesitis undecumque
ejus scriptis, evulgarunt in Hispania Patres Collegii Madritani Soc. J. poste-
riorem Tomi tertii Partem, quam quidem autor absolverat, sed limare non
potuerat: quartum, quintum et sextum Tomum, quorum subinde duplex editio
curata est Moguntiae et Venetiis, 1609" (*ibid.*, p. 1176).

[60] Editions of *De Justitia*: The first three volumes were published in Cuenca
in 1593, 1597, and 1600, respectively. The fourth volume along with the fifth
were prepared for publication at Antwerp by Jesuits of the college of Madrid
in 1609. Two years later there appeared at Venice an edition of the third,
and fifth volumes. Besides the editions mentioned above, the following have
also appeared:

Vol. II	Venice	1601
Vol. I	Venice	1602
Vols. I and II	Mainz	1602
Vol. III	Mainz	1603
Vol. III	Antwerp	1609
Vols. IV and V	Antwerp	1609
Vol. V	Mainz	1613
Vol. IV	Cologne	1614
Vols. I-V	Venice	1614
Vols. I-V	Antwerp	1615
Vols. I-V	Lyons	1622
Vol. V	Mainz	1644
Vols. I-V	Mainz	1659
Vols. I-V	Cologne	1733

In the present study references to Vols. I and II will be to the Mainz
edition of 1602; Vol. III references will be to the Antwerp edition of 1615.
Vol. IV will be the Cologne printing of 1614 and Vol. V will be the Anwerp
edition of 1609.

This huge work contains the substance of Molina's political theory. It is
divided into tractates and disputations. All footnote references to this work
henceforth will be cited in this manner: e.g., II, 21, 105B, meaning Second
Tractate, Twenty-first Disputation, column 105, and the part of the column cor-
responding to the letters A-E.

A still more confusing element is introduced into the printed editions by
the use of the term "tome". Since the third volume is divided into two parts,
they are referred to as the third and fourth tomes, and the fourth and fifth
tract (though only the fifth volume) become the fifth and sixth tomes. For

It will be helpful to indicate in some detail the breakdown of the ordinary five-volume set of *De Justitia*. The first volume contains all of the first tractate (Disputations 1-13 on justice in general) and part of the second tractate (251 disputations: rights in general [1-2]; regal laws [3-20]; public law—ecclesiastical and political [21-31] containing the essentials of his teaching on Church-State relations; the laws of slavery [32-40]; ways of acquiring property: the law of prescription [60-80], the law of war [93-123], and the law of succession [124-251]).

The second volume treats contracts and quasi-contracts (Disputations 252-575).

The third volume discusses inheritance (Disputations 576-660) and tributary law (661-679), and civil, penal, and moral responsibility of acts contrary to commutative justice (680-760).

The fourth volume contains all of the third tractate and is divided into 106 disputations on penal law.

The fifth volume contains the fourth tractate on spiritual goods with fifty disputations and the fifth tractate on justice and its execution by public officials divided into seventy-three disputations.

A word about Molina's style. He has been characterized as "one of the world's worst writers who wrote one of the world's best sellers." [61] Of course the reference is to the *Concordia*. About the style of that volume, even Molina's brother Jesuits complained. Robert Bellarmine considered the work too wordy, confused and obscure. [62] The Portuguese Jesuits who were asked to review the *Concordia* before publication made the same observations. [63]

Whatever the stylistic faults of the *Concordia*, the writing in *De Justitia et Jure* is rarely obscure or confused. And the very length of the work does not necessarily imply prolixity. Molina's writings on political and ethical theory are not noticeably longer than tracts on the same subjects by such contemporary Jesuits as Suárez, Lessius and Lugo.

What does tend to exhaust the modern reader is thinking of the immensity of Molina's undertaking without the tools of modern research to assist him. Molina doggedly pursued hundreds of references and prepared copy for the printer. At

---

practical purposes, the use of the designation "tome" is unnecessary and will be omitted.

[61] Gerard Smith, S.J., *op. cit.*, p. 218.

[62] "Cum tamen ipse tam prolixe, confuse, obscure loquitur ut vix intelligi possit quid sibi velit." X. M. Le Bachelet, S.J., *Auctarium Bellarminum*, Paris, G. Beauchesne, 1913, p. 110b.

one point in August 1594, while the second volume was in pre-
paration, his provincial was urged to provide secretarial help
to expedite Molina's work. [64]   The provincial claimed he had
no one to help Molina.

Molina's work was in keeping with the trend of his day.
It was more empirical and comparative than were the works
of the earlier scholastics. [65]   For instance, he is not content to
refer to canonical sources only but cites with equal ease the
laws of Castile and Portugal. His erudition is extraordinary.
He displays exceptional familiarity with the Old and New Testa-
ments, the writings of Aristotle, St. Augustine, and St. Thomas.
Not only does he quote the earlier scholastics, he frequently
refers to works of his contemporaries such as Navarrus and
Sander. The opinion of one modern author is that in the purely
philosophical part of the treatise Molina is Aristotelian from
both the *Ethics* and the *Politics* but he adds quickly "inter-
pretandas ambas en la más pura tradición tomista." [66]   Although,
the same author continues, St. Thomas is the basis of Molina's
theological and moral teaching, many contemporary Spaniards
influenced him, such as Vitoria, Soto, and Alfonso de Castro. [67]
Vitoria, to judge by the number of citations, was his inspiration. He is cited thirty-eight times in one section alone. Luis

---

[63] "Conclusiones et parentheses nimis prolixae videntur, in probando et
refellendo crebrae et verbose repetitiones. Methodus ipsa distractis et dissi-
patis constat membris, ut vix ad unum corpus pertinere aut certum exitum habere videatur. Ordo etiam texendae cuiusque quaestionis obscurior est." Stegmüller, *Molinismus*, p. 372 ll. 21-25.

[64] "Idem eodem die (August 1, 1594) Porres Provincialem commonuit, ut
Molinae qui omni adiutore destitutus opus et utilissimum et permultis deside-
ratissimum in manibus haberet, amanuensem destinaret." Rabeneck, "De vita
et Scriptis," p. 136.

[65] "The comparative-analytical approach is obvious in every chapter of these
masters. They cite profusely not only the Roman civil law, but also the laws
of France, of Spain, of Venice, of Florence, etc. When Molina studies the
problems of slavery, he tells us about the inquiries he made about the Negro
slave trade with the ship owners and with traders, with the port authorities;
he cites the various pertinent documents in nine columns of his *De Justitia
et de Jure*" (Heinrich A. Rommen, "The Natural Law in the Renaissance Period,"
University of Notre Dame Natural Law Proceedings, II [Notre Dame, Ind.:
College of Law, University of Notre Dame, 1949], 101-102. Hereinafter cited:
Rommen, "Renaissance Period").

[66] Luis Izaga Aguirre, S.J., *El P. Luis de Molina, internacionalista* (Madrid:
Razón y Fe, 1939), p. 7.

[67] Alfonso de Castro, O.F.M. (1495-1558), former professor at Salamanca, to
whose *De Justa Haereticorum Punitione Libri Tres* and *Adversus Haereses
Libri XIV* Molina refers.

Izaga rightly concludes: "No dudariamos nostros de calificar a Molina de discípulo, pero discípulo aprovechado, de Vitoria." [68]

The range of Molina's interests amazes the modern reader. Vansteenberge says that the multitude of applications he makes of his principles is such that with the sole aid of his books a picture—broad but still accurate—of the social conditions of his time could be drawn. [69]

Besides the ordinary theological questions he discusses the slave trade, the wool trade, coinage in Spain and Portugal, taxation, money, and banking. The information he accumulated came both from those whom he consulted and those who consulted him. For instance, he conferred with the master of the mint in Cuenca on coinage. For the effect of credit on prices he consulted " one, who though not an educated man possessed great experience and good judgment; he gave as his opinion that such business was usurious and unjust." [70] Molina was always willing to credit experience. Modestly deprecating his own knowledge of economic affairs, he points out that in cases where justice is not apparent and a custom or trade practice was accepted by upright men, there is probably a valid title somewhere, for "merchants understand these things better than the doctors." [71]

But the doctors—and Molina was one of them—knew a great deal about such matters. As Molina confided to Aquaviva, jurists and men conversant with the theory and practice of law were amazed at the solid grasp of such matters that Molina had. [72] His modern readers are equally amazed at his learning in a variety of social questions. Yet perhaps what impresses the modern reader most of all is that Molina wrote and prepared his great work *De Justitia* at the very time he was being harassed from every side for his teachings in the *Concordia*. The last ten years of his life were the least tranquil. Stormed at with shot and shell he approached the valley of death. During this entire period, Molina was ill. He confided to Aquaviva

---

[68] Luis de Molina, S.J., *Los seis libros de la justicia y el derecho*, ed. Manuel Fraga Iribarne (Madrid: J.L. Cosano, 1941-1943), p. 78.

[69] E. Vansteenberge, "Molina," *Dictionnaire de théologie catholique*, X (1929), Part II, 2092.

[70] Dempsey, *op. cit.*, p. 122.

[71] *Ibid.*

[72] "Y muchos juristas doctos y exercitados en la theorica y platica [sic] del derecho que an visto de vagar mis dictados estan espentados de quanto entro en la intelligentia del derecho y doctores dél, y quan seguros pongo los piés, y no se puedan persuadir sino que oý en scuelas muchos años de derecho" (Stegmüller, *Molinismus*, p. 554).

that he was troubled with continual hemorrhaging.[73] He faced one final disappointment. In 1596 he was nominated for the position of professor of theology at the royal University of Coimbra, but his name was not acceptable to King Philip II. The job eventually went to Molina's fellow Spaniard Francisco Suárez. In 1600 Molina was sent to Madrid to teach moral theology at the Jesuit college there. Obediently he set out for his new assignment, with all his manuscripts and papers in an old sack. It was in Madrid on the twelfth of October, 1600, that he died.

---

[73] "Mi edad de sesenta años con la naturaleza tan gastada con el peso de tantos años de tan intenso y continuo estudio, de tantas y continuas indisposiciones y flaquezas y de muchos otros trabajos, y estar sin dientes y comer con enzias, y un continuo fluxo de sangre, que de ordinario tengo en tanta quantidad que admira como me quedan fuerças, y la experiencia que tengo de quanto se me augmenta con el movimiento del camino, y la interpolacion de continuar estas obras quedandome tan poco de vida para continuallas." Stegmüller, *Molinismus*, p. 739, ll. 12-20.

CHAPTER II

THE ORIGIN AND NATURE OF CIVIL SOCIETY

Sir John Robert Seeley, Regius Professor of History at Cambridge, compressed the relationship of history to political science into a well-known jingle: "History without Political Science has no fruit; Political Science without History has no root." Whereupon Ernest Barker observed, "And if this be so, history will be but philosophy—political philosophy—teaching by examples; and political philosophy in turn will be history precipitated in a patterned shape of generalities." [1]

The fundamental problem of political philosophy is the ultimate justification or explanation of the state. Every political theorist from Plato's time has turned to this problem; Molina is no exception. Before considering Molina's answer, it will be helpful to define a few terms and make a few distinctions necessary for an understanding of the problem.

First of all, it is important to distinguish between the state and civil society. Briefly, the state is not society, nor government the state. "The state," as Rommen says, "is not society, but rather public order as a living action in society." [2]

John Courtney Murray distinguishes between civil society, political society, state, and government. Civil society designates the total complex of organized human relationships on the temporal plane, whether arising by necessity of nature or by free choice of will. Civil society connotes political society, i.e., organized for the common good; this in turn connotes the state. [3]

The state is not the body politic but that particular organized function of the body politic which promotes the good of the whole. The state is not the person of the ruler; in fact,

---

[1] Sir Ernest Barker, "The Study of Political Science" in *Church, State and Education* (Ann Arbor: The University of Michigan Press, 1957), p. 176.

[2] Heinrich A. Rommen, *The State in Catholic Thought*: A Treatise in Political Philosophy (St. Louis: B. Herder Book Co., 1945), pp. 274-275.

[3] John Courtney Murray, S.J., "The Problem of State Religion," *Theological Studies*, XII (1951), 158-159.

it is not a person at all. Belonging in the category of action
rather than of substance, the state includes the notion of government.

Government is not the state, any more than government is
law. Neither is it the ruler nor the rulers. Rather, government is the ruler-in-relation-to the ruled; it is likewise the ruled-
in-relation-to the ruler. In a general sense, government—like
the state—is a natural necessity; but its forms and the actual
content and implications of the political relationships are contingent upon reason and the practical judgments it makes in
given circumstances. [4]

Molina's treatment of the question of the origin and nature
of civil society unfolds along Aristotelian-Thomistic lines.
Actually, in the passages devoted to the origin of civil society,
Molina adheres more faithfully to Aristotle than does St. Thomas
in one respect: he explicitly mentions political society as an
outgrowth of the family; but he does not overlook the special
contribution of St. Thomas. [5] Fusing Aristotle and Thomas in
a unique way, Molina submits that man has a greater need of
other men than have other living creatures of their own kind.
For this reason nature has given him a greater aptitude for
society than has been given to other creatures. The first society
towards which nature inclines him is that which he has in common with the beasts: the society of male and female for the
sake of reproduction. "For it is an innate desire of all living
creatures to leave behind them a being of the same nature as
themselves." [6]

In other words, the desire to reproduce is the *causa impul-
siva* (to use a term made popular by Samuel Pufendorf) [7] of
societas conjugalis, one of the three societies which make up
the family of men. The other two are the *societas paterna* and
the *societas herilis.* As Aristotle noted, the perfect family consists of this threefold relationship. The first is that of husband
and wife. The second is that of parents and children. The

---

[4] *Ibid.*

[5] Curiously enough, however, Molina makes no mention in this whole section of St. Thomas or (and this is even more surprising) Vitoria or Soto.

[6] "Et namque cunctis animantibus innatum desiderium, tale alterum post
se relinquendi, quale ipsum est" (II, 22, 110).

[7] Samuel Pufendorf, *De Jure Naturae et Gentium,* ed. J. B. Scott (2 vols.;
"The Classics of International Law"; Oxford: At the Clarendon Press, 1934),
I, 646.

third is that of masters and servants. From this threefold relationship arises a threefold power or authority. [8]

The first two societies in the family of men, conjugal and paternal, are established by nature. The conjugal society is contractual, although the impulse which leads to it is natural. The third, or herile, society is exclusively contractual. It is the result of the condition of fallen nature. This would not have existed in the condition of innocence—"In innocentiae statu non fuisset." Molina's conclusion is that only the paternal and conjugal societies are natural. Here, of course, he departs from Aristotle and follows St. Thomas. Up to now he has been discussing the origin of what Father Murray designates civil society.

But the natural process is far from complete. In addition to the familial associations, there is still a greater society of which man has need (*indigentia*). To this society nature inclines him and the light of intellect leads him: for these reasons he is a civil and political animal. Other animals are born requiring a minimum of guidance by the parents; each is self-sufficient from the very beginning. In addition, they are abundantly supplied with coats of hair and the means of defending themselves against enemies, with the instincts to effect their several functions. [9] In the Fifth Tract Molina returns to this point and

---

[8] "Ex hac autem societate familiae communitas, societasve, ortum habuit inter homines. Porro perfecta familia, autore Aristotele loco citato, ex tribus personarum se mutuo respicientium complicationibus coalescit. Prima est, viri cum uxore. Secunda, parentum cum filiis. Tertia, dominorum cum servis, in familiae subsidium, et obsequia necessaria assumptis. Ex his vero tribus complicationibus, quib[us] perfecta familia constat, triplex potestas oritur in familia" (II, 22, 110).

[9] "Si namque oculis ac mente caetera animalia lustres, invenies, unumquodque ita a natura fuisse productum, ut saltem modica educatione per parentes a principio adhibita, sibi ipsi sufficiant, ad necessaria vitae subsidia prout cuique est opus, comparanda: cum ab ipso naturae autore, et tegmina ad vestitum, et arma, tum ad sui defensionem, tum ad hostium offensionem, et varia instrumenta atque instinctus ad suas operationes exercendas" (II, 22, 112).

In the last section of the above quotation, Molina is paraphrasing St. Thomas, who observes: "For nature has prepared for other animals food, a covering of hair, and such defensive weapons as teeth, horns, claws, or at least speed of flight" (cited in Ewart Lewis, *Medieval Political Ideas* [2 vols.; London: Routledge and Kegan Paul, 1954], I, 175).

Juan de Mariana, a Jesuit contemporary of Molina, expressed himself in similar terms: "Thus, He who gave to other living creatures food and raiment, and who also armed some with horns, teeth and nails against external violence and bountifully supplied others with swiftness of foot so that they could save themselves from danger, cast only man bare and unarmed into the hard-

makes it very clear that he considers conjugal and paternal societies as natural and he expressly says that the power of civil society over its parts stems also from the natural law. [10]

Nature has provided in liberal measure for the subrational kingdom, but it has not been so liberal in providing for man. Only man is brought forth naked and unarmed, lacking art and instincts and requiring many things to sustain life. He needs so many things to sustain life that neither one man, nor a family unit, suffices to prepare all these things. [11] Therefore many families are necessary, and a division of labor, to supply one another with the necessities of food, clothing, shelter, medicine, and a host of other things for daily use which are necessary to sustain life. [12] Since a city is nothing else but a union of men of such a size as to be mutually self-sufficient in all things necessary for daily living, it follows that because of need man is naturally inclined to live with others in common-wealths. [13] By the term commonwealth (*respublica*) Molina says he means to include "the small neighboring towns, villages and outlying farms which surround a larger city and are necessary to its agricultural and other support." [14]

---

ships of this life, as if he had just lost all in shipwreck" (*The King and the Education of the King*, trans. George Albert Moore [Washington, D.C.: The Country Dollar Press, 1948], p. 112).

[10] *"Tractatu item 2 disp. 22* ostendimus potestates viri in uxorem, patris in filios, reipublicae cujusque in potestates ipsius, esse de jure naturali, ac proinde esse a Deo per naturae instinctum, ordinemque rebus in hoc universo earum creatione immediate ab eo constitutum ac traditum. Potestates autem dominorum in servos, licet simpliciter non fit de jure naturali; eo quod ortum non habeat ex ipsa constitutione, ordineque a Deo immediate rebus indito, neque futura fuisset in statu naturae integrae" (V, 73, 3253).

[11] "Secundo indiget etiam homo vita in plurium familiarum communitate, quoniam cum nascatur omnibus artibus, peritiaque rerum omnium vacuus, ac sine naturalibus instinctibus, quibus bruta ad nociva fugienda, quaerendaque et conficienda necessaria, sunt praedita; sane nisi in multarum familiarum communitate versaretur, neque artes addiscere, quibus ad paranda subsidia necessaria indiget (cum tamen longe plures illi essent addiscendae, eo quod aliorum opera et industria uti non posset) neque naturalium supernaturaliumque rerum posset scientiam comparare" (II, 22, 113).

[12] "Multae familiae diversis muneribus intendentes, variisque artibus pollentes, necessariae sint, ut cuique hominum, quae ad usus quotidianos vitamque transigendam necessaria sunt suppeditentur" (*ibid.*).

[13] "Cum ergo civitas non aliud sit, quam tanta hominum congregatio, ut sibi mutuo sufficiant [sic] ad ea omnia praestanda, quae, tum ad quotidianos usus, vitamque transigendam ... necessaria sunt, efficitur, ut propter indigentiam, lumine ipso intellectus id docente, ad idque instigante, naturaliter propendeat homo ad convivendum cum aliis in civitatis, Reipublicaeque communitate" (*ibid.*).

[14] "Nomine Reipublicae ac civitatis, hoc loco intellige, etiam oppida vicina,

Not only the physical structure of man, but his mental and spiritual nature as well, demand life in a political society (*socialitas*). Having considered the physical side, Molina now proceeds to the higher nature of man, which can attain its full development only within the state. Man requires life in a political community because he is born without skills and knowledge and those instincts which brute animals have. Unless man lives in such a community he would not learn the skills he requires nor acquire a knowledge of natural and supernatural matters. Finally, he could not be instructed and imbued with the knowledge and manners which are fitting to virtuous men and so friendship and the practice of many virtues would perish. [15]

And that is the reason, continues Molina, why among all living creatures only man has been endowed with speech: so that he could deal with others in a community. "And hence Aristotle in Bk. I, ch. 2 of the *Politics* concludes that man, more than the bees and other gregarious creatures, is a social animal." [16]

So far Molina has given and developed two reasons for the existence of political society: *indigentia* and *socialitas*. There is a third reason, *eventus peccati*, which will be considered in a moment. Before that is discussed, a short summary of the scholastic teaching on the point is in order.

Ewart Lewis points out that the origin of political authority was not primarily an historical question for medieval writers. Although it is not accurate to say that medieval minds were

---

pagos, ac villas circumiacentes, quibus praecipua communitas, quae caput est, ad agriculturam, aliaque subsidia indiget" (*ibid.*).

[15] "Denique instrui, imbuique non posset peritia et moribus, quae ingenuum probumque virum decent, atque ita periret amicitia, ususque multarum virtutum" (*ibid.*).

[16] It scarcely needs to be noted that Aristotle's phrase, πολιτικὸν ζῷον, is usually translated "political animal." A footnote comment from Charles H. McIlwain (*The Growth of Political Thought in the West* [New York: The Macmillan Co., 1932], p. 68, n. 4) treats the subject well: "Aristotle's phrase, πολιτικὸν ζῷον (*Politics*, Bk. I, chap. ii, 1253a) is usually translated 'political animal,' and I have retained it therefore. In the oldest Latin version, of the thirteenth century, it appears as *civile animal* and this is adopted by Victorius and later by Giphanius. Seneca speaks of man as *social animal* (De. Clem, I, 3). Saint Thomas in his *De Regimine* Bk. I, chap. i, uses the expression *animal sociale et politicum*, and both Welldon and Jowett employ the phrase 'political animal' as the English equivalent of πολιτικὸν ζῷον. There is, however, a good deal to be said against this in favor of the phrase used by Saint-Hilaire, *un être sociable*, and the use of the word 'being' rather than 'animal' as our nearest English word for Aristotle's ζῷον."

unaware of historical growth and change, they did not have an
elaborate consciousness of history. One event which they believed to be historic was often crucial to their thought; this
was the fall of man from his condition of original justice. [17]
At least from St. Augustine onward this historical event and
its consequences influenced scholastic political theory. [18] Mc-
Ilwain puts in this way:

> In the period under consideration, as always in the middle
> ages, there was a tendency to look at the institutions of
> government, servitude, and property all in much the same way,
> and as it was the fall of man that furnished the explanation
> of government's origin, by men of the middle ages the same
> general explanation was extended to slavery and to man's con-
> trol over external things. [19]

One of the problems confronting St. Thomas was how to reconcile the Aristotelian tradition of the natural origin of civil
society with the Augustinian tradition of the effects of original
sin on the origin of that same society. Aquinas made a distinction which has been incorporated into Christian political
tradition:

> Dominion is to be understood in two senses: In the first it is
> contrasted with servitude. So a master is one to whom an-
> other is subject as a slave. In the second sense it is to be
> understood in opposition to any form of subjection. In this
> sense one whose office it is to govern and control free men
> may also be called their lord. The first sort of dominion
> which is servitude did not exist between man and man in the
> state of innocence. Understood in the second way, however,
> even in the state of innocence, some men would have exercised
> control over others. [20]

What is implied, though not explicitly mentioned, is the distinction between coercive and directive rule. The rule over slaves
is coercive and has come about through sin; the rule over men
in a state of innocence is directive. In man's fallen state the

---

[17] Lewis, *op. cit.*, I, 140.

[18] There is still a great difference among scholars as to whether St. Au-
gustine held that the state has its origin in original sin. For a discussion of
St. Augustine's view, see two monographs by Otto Schilling: *Die Staats und
Soziallehre des heiligen Augustinus* (Freiburg im Breisgau: Herdersche Verlags-
handlung, 1910) and *Naturrecht und Staat nach der alten Kirche* (Paderborn:
Druck and Verlag von Ferdinand Schoningh, 1914).

[19] McIlwain, *op. cit.*, p. 160.

[20] *Summa Theologica*, I[a], qu. 96, art. 4.

coercive rule is joined to the directive rule. As St. Thomas comments elsewhere on a passage from St. Augustine: "Law ... has two essential characteristics: the first, that of a rule directive of human action: the second, that of the power to compel." [21] In the state of innocence, the former alone would have been sufficient; but in man's fallen state a coercive power has been joined to the directive power. Suárez comments on that very same passage:

> To be sure, Augustine here gives expression to the opinion that the dominion of one man other another is derived from the occasion created by sin, rather than from the primary design of nature; but he is speaking of that form of dominion whose concomitants are slavery and the condition of servitude. And Gregory the Great expresses himself more clearly with regard to the governing power; but he should be interpreted as referring to the cocercive power and the exercise thereof; since, insofar as the directive power is concerned, it would seem probabile that this existed among men in the state of innocence. [22]

Such is the scholastic tradition regarding the effects of original sin on the origin of political society. The foregoing short summary was made to bring into focus Molina's third reason for the existence of political society. He has already spoken of the first two: *indigentia* and *socialitas*.

The third reason why man requires life in a community of many families in self-sufficient commonwealths is in order that peace, security, and justice may be preserved. The power of the whole commonwealth is far greater than that of individual families and is better able to defend each person from the injuries of others and to curb and punish criminals. "Indeed, since original justice has vanished through sin, inevitably controversies and difficulties have arisen which are more easily resolved, certainly more safely and equitably, through the authority of the commonwealth that would be the case were each to be a judge of his own cause." [23]

The concluding paragraph of Molina's treatment of the origin of civil society has been the cause of dispute among commentators. Molina says:

---

[21] *Ibid.*, II* II**, qu. 96, art. 5, conclusion.
[22] Suárez, *Selections from Three Works*, II, 371.
[23] II, 23, 113.

Since indeed the senses of men as a result of sin are prone
to evil, even from youth, and so many are the depraved emo-
tions we experience, that for the most part we are ruled by
them, truly were men to live outside the political community,
and there were no superior public power which through its
might and authority could coerce and restrain them, all human
affairs would be full of killings, dissensions, plunderings, thefts,
frauds, deceits, the stronger oppressing the weaker, and far
worse would be the condition and wretchedness of mankind
than it is today among men united in separate communities. [24]

This passage and others by Molina in *De Justitia* have inclined
some scholars to the opinion that Molina conceived the state
to be simply a result of man's depraved nature following original
sin.   Representative of this opinion are J. N. Figgis and Otto
Gierke.   These two men, it should be noted, were accustomed
to survey broad areas of history and could not or should not
be expected to check their investigations in detail.   Errors do
occur by reading isolated passages out of context.   Along with
the passage included above there are two others which, if
viewed by themselves, would seem to support their conclusion.
These citations will be considered presently.

---

[24] "Cum vero hominum sensus post peccatum ad malum proni sint ab
adolescentia, totque pravi affectus, quos experimur in illis ut plurimum domi-
nentur, profecto si ita extra politicam communitatem viverent, ut nulla esset
publica superior potestas, quae sua potentia et autoritate eos coercere, ac
comprimere posset, omnia plena essent caedibus, seditionibus, rapinis, furtis,
dolis, ac fraudibus, potentiorib[us] opprimentibus minus potentes, longeque
deterior esset conditio ac miseria generis humani quam sit hodie hominibus
in Republicis distinctis adunatis" (II, 22, 114).

As the paragraph stands, it resembles a passage from Thomas Hobbes'
Leviathan (Introduction by A. D. Lindsay [Everyman's Library; New York:
E. P. Dutton and Co., 1950]: "Hereby it is manifest, that during the time men
live without a common Power to keep them all in awe, they are in that condition which is called Warre; and such a warre, as is of every man, against
every man. . . .

"Whatsoever therefore is consequent to a time of warre, where every man
is Enemy to every man; the same is consequent to the time, wherein men
live without other security, than what their own strength, and their own
invention shall furnish them withall.   In such condition there is no place
for Industry; because the fruit thereof is uncertain: and consequently no
Culture of the Earth; no Navigation, nor use of the commodities that may
be imported by Sea; no commodious Building; no Instruments of moving,
and removing such things as require such force; no Knowledge of the face
of the Earth; no account of Time; no Arts; no Letters; no Society; and which
is worst of all, continuall feare, and danger of violent death; and the life of
man, solitary, poore, nasty, brutush, and short" (Bk. 1, chap. xiii).

First of all, it should be recalled that Molina postulates three broad groups of reasons for the origin of political society: (1) *indigentia*, (2) *socialitas*, and (3) *eventus peccati*. The number is no extraordinary discovery, but Kleinhappl calls attention to the order in which these groups occur. It is to be stressed that Molina places the group of reasons which deal with the *eventus peccati* last. Kleinhappl insists that the last group is designed to indicate a contributing but not an exclusive cause of the existence of political society. [25]

Returning to the texts, the most controversial passage which both Figgis [26] and Gierke [27] cite to confirm their position that Molina regarded the state as the result of sin is the following:

> For God, as Author of nature, established the natural law, imposed and impressed upon the minds of men what they were to avoid and what they were bound to execute, what would lead to ,and bring forth greater natural and moral happiness, so they would easily recognize how to lead a happy life, especially in the sttae of perfect nature in which man was formed and placed. In which state, certainly, man required no other human laws to obtain and preserve natural happiness, especially since he then was sufficient in other gifts and means through which he was assisted to supernatural happiness. [28]

This is the first part of a rather lengthy passage and so far there is little to comment on except that Molina assumes that no human laws would have been necessary in the state of perfect nature—which, incidentally, is the theologians' "state of nature" (*status naturae integrae*) and not that of the political theorists of the seventeenth and eighteenth centuries. The remainder of the passage under consideration is the following:

---

[25] Johann Kleinhappl, S.J., *Der Staat bei Ludwig Molina* (Innsbruck, F. Rauch, 1935), p. 11.

[26] J. N. Figgis, "On Some Political Theories of the Early Jesuits," *Transaction of the Royal Historical Society*, XI (New Series) (London: Longmans, Green and Co., 1897), 102: "Salmeron, probably Molina, and others regard all government as a consequence of the fall."

[27] Otto Gierke, *The Development of Political Theory*, trans. B. Freyd (New York: W. W. Norton and Co., 1939), p. 124, n. 48.

[28] "Deus enim, ut naturae autor, legem naturalem condidit, eamque hominum mentibus indidit ac impressit, qua quid vitare quidque efficere tenerentur, quin et quid conduceret ac expediret magis ad naturalem felicitatem moralem, et subinde etiam ad contemplativam, comparandam ac conservandam facile agnosceret: maxime in statu naturae integrae, in quo hominem condere ac collocare statuit. In quo sane nullis aliis humanis legibus homo indigebat ad utramque naturalem felicitatem obtinendam ac conservandam praesertim suffultus tunc aliis donis ac mediis, quibus ad supernaturalem felicitatem adjuvabatur" (V, 46, 3025).

Nature, however, having been disrupted through sin, and the gift of original justice having vanished, and men therefore left prone to evil, their intellects darkened, subject to so many miseries and cares, and requiring so many things to sustain their mortal and laborious life, it was necessary for them to gather together and be divided into various commonwealths in order that they might help one another, and choose from among themselves either one, or more than one, to defend them from internal and external enemies, so that this way the common good of individuals and of the whole commonwealth might be better attained, advanced and preserved. [29]

At first reading there seems to be enough evidence to support the position of Figgis and Gierke. It can hardly be denied that Molina attributed a great deal of importance to the effect of sin on nature of political society. He certainly emphasizes that as a result of sin man is prone to evil; and the expression "dissoluta vero natura per peccatum" is an ever-recurring one. He stresses that man could not live without the coercive power of the state. Were this power removed, the life of man would be full of carnage and thievery. He states that in the original condition of innocence it would not have been necessary to add human laws to the dictates of the natural law. He also mentions that the divisions of commonwealths is owing to sin. He confirms these views in another controversial passage. Treating the question of the division of property and how it came about, he writes:

Although this question would chiefly have place in the treatment of dominion of property, it may also be extended to the subject of dominion of jurisdiction. For as soon as the human race fell from innocence through sin, it was necessary for a dominion of jurisdiction *with a certain coercive power* to be introduced by means of which men are kept in subjection, injuries are repelled and punished, and peace and tranquillity are preserved among them. Moreover, men having multiplied and scattered over the earth, it was also necessary for this

---

[29] "Dissoluta vero natura per peccatum, amissoque justitiae originalis dono, manenteque adeo prona ad malum, et obtenebrata quoad intellectum, totque miseriis et curis subjecta, et tam multis rebus ad transigendam mortalem hanc ac laboriosam vitam indigens, necesse hominibus fuit in varias respublicas dividi ac congregari, in quibus se mutuo adjuvarent, et in quibus ab uno aut a multis, quos sibi ad id eligerent, ab internis ejus reipublicae et ab externis defenderentur, instaurerentur, jus ipsis diceretur, et continerentur in officio, ut quam melius fieri posset, singulorum totiusque reipublicae commune bonum resultaret, promoveretur, ac conservaretur, latis ad id legibus, quae pro reipublicae qualitate ac circumstantiis concurrentibus expedirent" (*ibid.*).

form of dominion to be divided, and many rulers appointed to govern various provinces, cities and people. [30]

The words "coercive power" in the above citation perhaps furnish the key to Molina's thought on this point. When he speaks in this fashion of political society and the state, he is conceiving it as a coercive institution whose value to men in their present condition he is not inclined to underestimate. He stresses that the state preserves peace and redresses wrongs; all these things the state accomplishes with coercive power. But Molina, as a disciple of St. Thomas, is well aware of the distinction between directive and coercive power. He proves this early in his disquisition on power—lay and ecclesiastical. There he observes:

> Since indeed in a state of innocence anyone would be conceived in grace, and would be born accordingly supported by sufficient principles so that he would discover the proof of his supernatural end, and he would be instructed easily in those [principles] he would need to learn, nor would he require any coercion; certainly in that state each power, viz., ecclesiastical and lay, would be without coercive force, the superior merely directing inferior persons to their ends. [31]

There is no doubt that in the above citation Molina holds there would have been directive power in the state of innocence. What about the changes introduced into this scheme as a result of the fall? Molina replies, "Nature having been disrupted through sin, and grace having vanished, each power has joined to it a coercive force to bring subjects now requiring coercion to their ends." [32]

---

[30] "Et quamvis quaestio praecipue habeat locum in dominio proprietatis, extendi etiam potest ad dominium jurisdictionis. Etenim statim ac genus humanum ab innocentiae statu per peccatum corruit, necessarium fuit jurisdictionis dominium *cum vi quadam coercente introduci*, quo homines in officio continerentur, propulsarentur et punirentur injuriae, paxque et tranquillitas inter eos servaretur. Multiplicatis praetera hominibus, et per orbem dispersis, necesse etiam fuit ejusmodi dominium dividi, pluresque constitui rectores, qui varias provincias, civitates ac populos moderarentur" (II, 20, 98). Emphasis added.

[31] "Quoniam vero in statu innocentiae quivis conciperetur in gratia, nascereturque proinde suffultus sufficientibus principiis, ut per seipsum argumentum finis supernaturalis promeretur, facileque instrueretur in iis, in quibus eum instrui oporteret, neque ad id coactione indigeret, sane in eo statu utraque potestas, ecclesiastica videlicet et laica, esset absque vi coerciva, superioribus dirigentibus inferiores ad suos fines" (II, 21, 106).

[32] "Dissoluta natura per peccatum, ac gratia amissa, utraque potestas conjunctam habet vim coactivam, subditis coactione indigentibus, ut ad suos fines directione perducantur" (*ibid.*).

The great thinkers of the scholastic tradition have maintained that the state would have developed out of human nature
even had there been no fall from grace. As Rommen puts it:

> This doctrine was elaborated especially by late Scholasticism
> after the Reformation contended that the origin of the state
> lay in sin. It is true that the masters taught that some quali-
> ties of the state originate in sin; for instance, its coercive
> power. But they taught, too, that in the state of pure nature
> political authority would have been necessary, though only a
> directive, not a coercive one. [33]

In summary, Molina's theory of the origin of political society
unfolds along the lines of the Aristotelian-Thomistic tradition.
He holds that the family is the basic unit of political society.
The family consists of a three-fold relationship: (1) husband
and wife, (2) parents and children, and (3) master and servants.
The first two relationships flow from the natural law; the third
is the result of original sin. This threefold relationship constitutes the basic unit of political society. The structure of the
family is rooted in man's nature; man needs the stable society
of the family more than other creatures do. Molina notes that
the other creatures are provided by nature with the means of
self-defense, protective coats of hair, and the means to acquire
food and shift for themselves at an early age. Nature does not
so provide for man but instead has bestowed upon him one
invaluable gift—reason. Man is so fashioned as to make it
imperative for him to live in civil society. His reason dictates
that life in this society is proper for him. Through the repro-
ductive impulse nature provides for the institution of the family
and the continuation of the species. Through the instinctive
rational sense of need (*indigentia*) nature provides for the basis
of the state.

But it is not only man's physical structure that makes
imperative a life in civil society; his mental and spiritual nature
also require it. Man has even greater needs which can be fulfilled only in civil society. The faculties of his soul would remain
stunted were it not for the social life in a political society.
Socialitas insures the possibility of the development of the
whole man.

In the Fifth Tract, Molina distinguishes between a "status naturalis," "status innocentiae," and "status naturae lapsae" (V, 46, 3033). These three conditions will be considered in connection with the natural law in the final chapter
of this study.

[33] Rommen, *State in Catholic Thought*, p. 229.

A third reason for political society is found in the effects of original sin. Molina does not hold that political *society* is the result of original sin. Even before the fall of man the state was a natural necessity. But the *coercive* power of the state, as distinguished from its directive power, is a result of original sin. This coercive power is now needed to insure that peace, security, and justice may be preserved among me.

Molina's treatment of the positive functions of civil society has been overlooked by several commentators who cite the texts where Molina discusses at some length the coercive power of the state arising as the result of original sin. Molina bears some responsibility for the misunderstanding which has arisen concerning his position. He did emphasize the *eventus peccati* in his treatment of the matter. He can be justly accused of failing to accentuate the positive functions of civil society. Molina is prepared to consider an allied question: How does political authority originate?

CHAPTER III

THE ORIGIN OF POLITICAL AUTHORITY

The Jesuit theory on the origin of political authority has been linked with the adjective "democratic" and described as maintaining the sovereignty of the people.[1] It was Harold Laski who warned that democratic government is less a matter for eulogy than exploration.[2] The following chapter on the origin of political authority according to Molina may be called variations on the Laski theme.

The term exploration, with its connotation of traversing an area for the purpose of surveying and charting it, is a singularly apt term to describe any study of the history of political thought. The stream of Western political thought bears a striking resemblance to the Nile River. Both have been in

---

[1] For example, see Leopold Ranke, "Die Idee der Volkssouveränität in den Schriften der Jesuiten" in Vol. XXIV: *Abhandlungen und versuche* ("Sämmtliche Werke"; Leipzig: Verlag von Duncker und Humbolt, 1877), pp. 223-236, where the eminent historian maintains that there was no general theory of popular rights before the Jesuits.

Figgis ("On Some Political Theories of the Early Jesuits," *op. cit.*, p. 93, n. 2) rightly questions Ranke's sweeping generalization.

In a somewhat different context, Hilaire Belloc in his biography of *Milton* ([Philadelphia: J. B. Lippincott Co., 1935], p. 194) makes the statement, "Milton of course was familiar, as was all the educated England of his generation, with the doctrine which the Jesuits of a previous generation (especially the Spanish theologians with the great Suarez at their head) had restated. ... —the doctrine that the community is sovereign and that the prince or Civil Magistrate no more than the servant of that sovereign."

Yves Simon, *Philosophy of Democratic Government* (Chicago: The University of Chicago Press, 1951), pp. 176-177: "Among the obnoxious simplifications which fill the treatises of political science, let us single out the proposition that the divine-right theory is theocratic and the sovereignty-of-the-people theory democratic. ... Historians often described the views of Bellarmine and Suarez as expressions of the democratic theory of sovereignty; yet neither of these thinkers meant to recommended democracy. ... This point should be stressed: the transmission [translation] theory is not understood by its proponents to be distinctly democratic."

[2] Harold J. Laski, *A Grammar of Politics* (London: George Allen and Unwin, Ltd., 1925), p. 17.

the center of history for centuries. Both have been the subject
of fact and fiction. And, until recently, little has been known
about the sources of both these famous streams.

The Nile's ultimate headwaters were first explored in 1892
by Baumann; the ultimate headwaters of political thought are
still to be identified. The most striking phenomenon of the Nile
is the river's annual autumn overflow from its bed in Egypt.
A mystery to ancient geographers, it remained a mystery until
the eighteenth and nineteenth centuries when explorers such as
James Bruce and Henry Stanley discovered the reason for such
an abundant flow of water during a season when rivers are
normally low. The autumn floods and the resulting rich alluvial
deposits were traced to heavy rains in the highlands of Ethiopia
along the Blue Nile and in the Belgian Congo and Uganda on
the White Nile.

Twentieth-century political thought is the rich delta of a
long stream. The fertility of the delta is the result of the al-
luvium deposited patiently for centuries. As with the Nile, the
cause of the alluvial deposits is to be sought in the upper tributaries of the stream. The main tributaries have been known
for a long time; scholastic political thought is one of them.
What has been identified as Jesuit political thought flows into
this branch in the last quarter of the sixteenth century. Although the confluence has been noted, the stream has been little
explored. The Jesuit fork itself has many sources which are
more diversified than is generally realized. Perhaps this is best
illustrated by mapping Jesuit contributions to the theories of
the origin of political authority.

There are in general two scholastic theories concerning the
origin of political authority, both deriving from the tradition
of Greek-Medieval political philosophy—the Translation theory
and the Designation theory.[3] Both accept the same basic con-

---

[3] The summary of these two theories and the analysis of the Bellarmine
and Suárez positions is based in part on an article by Charles N. R. McCoy,
"Note on the Problem of the Origin of Political Authority," *The Thomist*, XVI
(1953), 71-81.

A more complete treatment of the subject can be found in Rommen, *The
State in Catholic Thought*, pp. 411-456.

Cf. Peter Tischleder, *Ursprung und Träger der Staatsgewalt nach Thomas
und seine Schule* (M. Gladbach: Volksverein-Verlag, 1923), pp. 201ff.

See also Gabriel Bowe, O.P., *The Origin of Political Authority*: An Essay
in Catholic Political Philosophy (Dublin: Clenmore & Reynolds Ltd., 1955),
pp. 31-67. There is some difference in terminology. The Translation theory
is usually called by that name. Fr. McCoy refers to it as the Transmission
theory. Following Rommen, this chapter will call it the Translation theory.

cepts of that tradition: the nature of man as a social and political animal, the existence of a natural law, and the establishment of political authority in response to these questions:

1. How does political authority originate?
2. In what manner is political authority in the people?

The principle of the Translation theory is that the whole people is the immediate or principal cause (though secondary and subordinate to the primary cause, which is God) of political authority in whomever it is vested. A corollary of this theory is that there is one form of government by natural institution, namely, direct democracy. Other forms of government are instituted through a transference of political authority by the people to one or several.

> There is by force of natural law no obligation on the members of the body politic to transfer political authority. Hence it is the community itself, organizing into the body politic, that holds authority and continues to do so as long as it does not transfer it to an individual or group. There is then only one constitution which exists by natural law, *viz.*, direct democracy. [4]

The Designation theory has for its principle that God is the immediate cause of political authority in whomever the people designate, and in designating their rulers the people are merely acting as an instrumental cause. The part man plays in constituting authority is restricted to designation. What man causes is simply the union of a particular person with a power not derived from man in any sense whatever. "The corollary of this theory," says Father McCoy, "is that the whole people are not constituted as a form of government by natural law." [5]

The Translation theory, at least in principle, is the older by far. Heinrich Rommen says there is little doubt that this theory is the most time honored and that the great majority of eminent doctors followed it. [6] Names of renown are counted among its defenders. Giles of Rome, Francisco de Vitoria, Domingo Soto, Luis de Molina, Robert Bellarmine, Billuart, and Suárez. [7] It has been called a Jesuit theory, though they by

---

[4] McCoy, *op. cit.*, p. 71.

[5] *Ibid.*, p. 72.

[6] Rommen, *State in Catholic Thought*, pp. 446-447.

[7] "I have made a laborious investigation of every accessible Catholic philosopher and theologian from the thirteenth to the nineteenth century. Here is the significant result: 52 writers prior to Suarez, and 87 after uphold the

no means originated it nor are all Jesuit writers on the subject
to be included among its defenders.   It would be correct to
say that Jesuits are its best-known interpreters and did the most
to popularize it.

The Designation theory was formulated as a reaction to the
Social-Contract theories of the eighteenth century because of
suspicion of a doctrinal affinity between the Translation theory
and the theory of the Social Contract of Rousseau.   Many
eminent theologians, both Jesuit and Dominican, supported the
Designation theory: Taparelli, Liberatore, Schiffini, Cathrein,
Rickaby, Meyer, and Billot of the Society of Jesus; and Man-
cini, Schwalm, and Zigliara of the Order of Preachers. [8]

Father McCoy takes the position that the principle of the
Translation theory—the whole people is the immediate cause
of political authority—is entirely compatible with the corollary
of the Designation theory—there is no one form of government
by natural right.   He feels that the Suárezian corollary of the
Translation theory is in fact an aberration from the sounder
Greek-Medieval tradition while Bellarmine's exposition upholds
that tradition. [9]   Some attempt must now be made to point
out the differences between the Suárezian and Bellarmine forms
of the Translation theory.   After the differences are discussed,
it will be time to determine with which form of the Translation
theory Molina is to be identified.

Cardinal Bellarmine's teaching on political authority appears in many of his works but it receives its most satisfactory
treatment in his *De Laicis* which was part of his *De Controver-*
siis Christianae Fidei. [10]   There Bellarmine makes it clear that
political power has its origin from God but rests immediately
"as in its subject, in the whole multitude, for the power comes
from God, and God, having assigned to it no particular man,
must have given it to the multitude." [11]   There follows a
significant passage:

---

principle that government is based on the consent of the people; 65 do not
discuss the subject at all; and only 7 Gallicans, of very doubtful orthodoxy,
reject the principle" (Alfred O'Rahilly, "Some Theology about Tyranny," *Irish
Theological Quarterly*, XV [1920], 303).

[8] Bowe, (*op. cit.*, p. 58, n. 5) gives a list of those who held the Designation
theory with the titles of their works.

[9] McCoy, *op. cit.*, p. 72.

[10] Roberto Bellarmino, S.J., *Opera Omnia* (12 vols.; Parisiis: Apud Ludovicum Vivès, 1870-1874), Vol. III.

On Bellarmine's theory, see Franz X. Arnold, *Die Staatslehre des Kardinals
Bellarmin* (Munich: M. Hueber, 1934), pp. 136ff.

[11] "Certum est politicam potestatem a Deo esse ... sed hic observanda sunt

Note, in the third place, that by the same natural law, this power is delegated by the multitude to one or several, for the community cannot of itself exercise this power; therefore it is bound to transfer it to some individual or to several, and this authority of rulers considered thus *in genere* is both by natural law and by divine law, nor could the entire human race assembled together decree the opposite, that is, that there should be neither rulers nor leaders, [12]

The importance of the above passage is manifest. Father McCoy rightly pauses to investigate the term "bound" (*tenetur*) in the key phrase "bound to transfer." [13] Bellarmine says that the transfer must be made "by the same law of nature." Father McCoy, citing St. Thomas, points out that a thing may be derived from the law of nature in two ways:

1. A thing is derived from the natural law by the determination of common principles. The example given is that the law of nature demands the evil does be punished but whether he be punished in this way or that is to be determined by the common principle. Things that are derived

---

aliqua. Primo, politicam potestatem in universum consideratam, non descendendo in particulari ad monarchiam, aristocratiam, vel democratiam, immediate esse a solo Deo, nam consequitur necessario naturam hominis, proinde esse ab illo qui facit naturam hominis. ... Secundo, nota, hanc potestatem immediate esse, tamquam in subjecto, in tota multitudine: nam haec potestas est de jure divino. At jus divinum nulli homini particulari dedit hanc potestatem: ergo dedit multitudini" (Bellarmine, *op. cit.*, III, 10-11).

[12] "Tertio, nota, hanc potestatem transferri a multitudine in unum vel plures eodem jure naturae: nam respublica non potest per seipsam exercere hanc potestatem: ergo tenetur eam transferre in aliquem unum vel aliquos paucos; et hoc modo potestas principum, in genere considerata, est etiam de jure divino et naturae; nec posset genus humanum, etiamsi totum simul conveniret, contrarium statuere, nimirum ut nulli essent princepes vel rectores" (*ibid.*).

[13] McCoy, *op. cit.*, p. 75.

For a discussion of the meaning of the phrase: "Nam respublica non potest per seipsam exercere hanc potestatem" in Bellarmine, *vide* Simon, *op. cit.*, p. 168: "All that Bellarmine demonstrates is that the transmission of political power from the multitude to the distinct governing personnel is not a matter delivered to the free choice of the multitude when, as he puts it, the republic cannot exercise such power for itself." Father McCoy questions this reading. He asks, "Does Bellarmine put it quite that way? He says not 'when', but "*Since* the republic, etc." On this point Father McCoy makes his point.

Chief Justice John Marshall in *Gibbons* v. *Ogden* (9 Wheaton [U.S.] 1) says of the grant of power made to the federal government that it "is an investment of power for the general advantage; in the hands of agents selected for that purpose; which power can never be exercised by the people themselves, but must be placed in the hands of agents, or lie dormant."

from the natural law in this way, St. Thomas says, have no other force than that of human law.[14] Bellarmine obviously does not consider the transfer of authority to be demanded by the law of nature in this sense. He insists that the whole human race gathered together could not decree otherwise.

2. The obligation may be derived from natural law in such a manner that it is contained in human law not as emanating therefrom exclusively but having some force from the natural law also. For example, St. Thomas says that *one must not kill* is derived from the principle *one should do harm to no man* which has the force of natural law itself.[15] The transfer of political power from the whole people to one or several rulers is of the natural law in the latter sense.[16]

Bellarmine is not yet finished. He points out that concrete and particular forms of government have their sanction from the law of nations and not from the natural law, for it "is obvious that it rests with the people as a whole to decide whether they shall set over themselves a king, or consuls, or other magistrates."[17] For a legitimate reason, Bellarmine continues, the people can change their government from a monarchy to an aristocracy or democracy, or the other way around. From this last sentence it is clear that the primordial institution of authority in the community does not thereby constitute a democracy. Bellarmine is considering political authority under two aspects and makes the same distinction as Vitoria—i.e., the distinction between authority in the abstract and authority in the concrete as it exists in the individual ruler. The establishment of some authority by the community is demanded by natural law. What form it will take is left to the choice of the people. So much for Bellarmine's position.[18]

What does Suárez say? The whole Translation theory is generally associated with his name, for he gave it the most elaborate exposition and, as Rommen points out, is its best-

---

[14] *Summa Theologica*, I-II, qu. 95, art. 2.

[15] *Ibid.*

[16] McCoy, *op. cit.*, pp. 75-76.

[17] "Quarto, nota, in particulari singulas species regiminis esse de jure gentium, non de jure naturae; nam pendet a consensu multitudinis, constituere super se regem vel consules vel alios magistros, ut patet; et si causa legitima adsit potest multitudo mutare regnum in aristocratiam aut democratiam, et e contrario, ut Romae factum legimus" (Bellarmine, *op. cit.*, III, 10-12).

[18] Vitoria's position will be considered later in this chapter.

known interpreter. [19]   Rommen has an admirable summary of
Suárez' views on this point and the following exposition of
Suárez' position will be based on it. [20]

First of all, Suárez holds that political authority is a necessary property of the body politic, resting with the self-organizing
political community.   Political authority does not, of its nature,
rest in any one man but in the community.   This authority in
the community is derived from God, the author of nature. [21]
Up to this point, Bellarmine and Suárez are in agreement.

Suárez has shown that it is a necessity of nature that civil
authority exists in the entire community.   Nature does not
require that it exist in any one person or in any group of persons, for this would imply that monarchy or aristocracy are
divinely instituted.   It follows that the body politic is primor-
dially democratic.

Suárez anticipates an objection: It could be argued that
neither is democracy divinely instituted, that it is not demanded
by nature, especially since both Aristotle and St. Thomas hold
democracy to be the most imperfect form of government.
Suárez argues that from the very fact that God has not immediately instituted monarchy or aristocracy, it follows that
he has given the power to the whole body politic, for there is
no other subject capable of receiving it.   Democracy is therefore divinely instituted, not in any positive way nor by any
special ordination but as a quasi-natural institution. [22]   Man's
natural reason demands neither monarchy nor aristocracy as
a necessary form of authority in political society.   They could
not be introduced (as the primordial subject of authority)
without some divine positive institution.   On the other hand,
natural reason dictates that democracy may exist without such
divine positive institution.

Suárez here introduces a further distinction.   Democracy
is of the natural law in a negative rather than positive sense, [23]

---

[19] Rommen, *State in Catholic Thought*, p. 447, and *Die Staatslehre des
Franz Suarez S.J.* (M. Gladbach: Volksvereins-Verlag, 1926), pp. 177-188.

[20] Rommen, *State in Catholic Thought*, pp. 447-450.

[21] Francisco Suárez, S.J., *Defensio Fidei Catholicae*, Vol. XXIV of *Opera
Omnia* (28 vols.; Parisiis: Apud Luis Vivès, 1856-1878), Bk. 3, chap. ll, pp. 206-212.

[22] "Ad alteram vero illationem, scil. hinc sequi democratiam esse ex divina
institutione, respondemus, si hoc intelligatur de institutione positiva, negandum
esse consecutionem, si vero intelligatur de institutione quasinaturali, sine ullo
inconvenienti admitti posse, et debere" (*ibid.*, pp. 208-209).

[23] "At vero democratia esse potest absque institutione positiva ex sola
naturali institutione, seu dimanatione cum sola negatione novae, seu positivae
institutionis" (*ibid.*).

i.e., the natural law concedes rather than commands it. [24] Although the natural law confers the power immediately upon the community, it does not demand that it shall remain there always or that the community shall always exercise it. But the power remains with the community as long as the community does not decree otherwise. Suárez therefore concludes that by natural law the civil community is free and subject to no man outside itself. If no change is introduced, it will be a democratic regime. [25] Such is Suárez' account of the origin of political authority. It is time now to hear from Molina.

Molina begins his treatment of this question by quoting his favorite authors, Vitoria and Soto. [26] They assert, he says, that by the very fact that men come together to form a body politic, the power of the whole body politic over its individual parts arises through natural law. This is for the purpose of governing them, making laws for them, and administering these laws and punishment for the breaches thereof. Since God is the author of natural law, a power of this kind is immediately from God, although the union of men in a community is a *conditio sine qua non* of this power. Continuing to quote Vitoria, Molina insists that political authority does not arise from the fact that men willingly subject themselves to it, as might happen were men to form an association for some particular

---

[24] "De jure naturali negative, non positive, vel potius de jure naturali concedente, non simpliciter praecipiente" (*ibid.*).

[25] "Sic ergo perfecta communitas civilis libera est, et nulli homini extra se subiicitur, tota vero ipsa habet in se potestatem, quae si non mutaretur, democratica esset; ... (*ibid.*).

On this point Brodrick (*Bellarmine*, I, 243, n. 1) says: "Even Suárez distinguished and most competent biographer, Père R. de Scorraille, S.J., deserted his hero's flag because, in addition to other reasons, he says: 'l'histoire nous montre que la forme démocratique est la plus rare, surtout dans les temps plus reculés et les plus voisins de l'origine des sociétés. Comment expliquer ce fait, si la forme démocratique fut toujours la forme initiale? ...' Francois Suarez t. II (1913), pp. 179-180. Suarez did not say the earliest form of government was always democratic. He was not speaking about *forms* of government at all, and he was about as much a democrat, in the modern, unpleasant sense of the word, as Père de Scorraille himself, which was very little indeed."

[26] "Victoria in relectione de potestate civili a n. 6 et Sotus 4. de justitia q. 4. art. 1. asseruerat, eo ipso, quod homines ad integrandum unum Reipublicae corpus conveniunt, jure naturali oriri potestatem corporis totius Reipubl. in singulas partes ad eas gubernandum, ad leges illis ferendum, jusque illis dicendum, et ad eas puniendum. Quare, inquiunt, cum Deus optimus maximus autor sit juris naturalis, sane hujusmodi potestas immediate est a Deo naturam instituente; tametsi hominum adunatio in unam Rempu. conditio sit, sine qua ea potestas non resultaret" (II, 22, 114).

purpose. The power of such a group is no greater than the assembled men are willing to grant. It does not have its origin from God but from men freely subjecting themselves to it. On the other hand, political power is by its very nature from God and not from men, except in the sense that a union of men in a commonwealth is presupposed as a condition without which there would be neither commonwealth nor authority.

Both Vitoria and Soto maintain, Molina continues, that, since a community of this kind is the product of nature, the community requires a power over its individual parts. Natural law forbids individual members of the community to kill malefactors, even if they themselves have suffered wrongs, and this accords with the Fifth Commandment of the Decalogue; the individual is even forbidden to punish in other ways. The commonwealth, however, is permitted to do this in accordance with both custom and Scripture. It follows, therefore, that the power which arises in a commonwealth is not from the authority of individuals but immediately from God. [27]

Political authority, then, includes the right to kill and the right to punish. Private persons are forbidden to do this by natural law. [28] Of course, nature does endow the father of a family with the right to punish his children; [29] but this is

---

[27] "Confirmat id Vitoria. Quoniam de jure naturali singulis de Republica est prohibitum interficere malefactores, esto ipsi sint, qui injuria sint affecti, idque quinto praecepto decalogi: imo eisdem etiam est prohibitum punire illos aliis poenis: cum ergo Reipublicae id liceat, ut ex ipsomet usu et ex scripturis constat, postulatque natura rei, efficitur, ut longe diversa sit potestas, quae ex natura rei consurgit in Rep. a collectione particularium potestatum singulorum, ac proinde ut eam non habeat Respublica autoritate singulorum, sed immediate a Deo" (II, 22, 114-115).

[28] Arthur K. Hesselberg ("A Comparative Study of the Political Theories of Ludovicus Molina, S.J., and John Milton" [unpublished Ph. D. Dissertation, The Catholic University of America, 1952], pp. 90-99) comments at length on this passage from Molina and states that here Molina has struck at the very heart of Locke's theory of government, anticipating all his arguments only to reject them: "It will be recalled, briefly, that Locke held that all men, before the establishment of civil society, are naturally in a state of nature, a state of perfect freedom: 'a state also of equality, wherein all the power and jurisdiction is reciprocal, no one having more than another.' ... And to insure that all men will not molest one another and invade each other's rights, 'the execution of the law of nature is in that state put in every man's hand, whereby everyone has a right to punish the transgressors of that law to such a degree as may hinder its violation.' There are two distinct rights that inhere in each person in the state of nature: (1) the right to punish crimes, 'which right of punishing is everybody,' (2) the right to take reparation 'which belongs only to the injured party.' "

[29] Jean Bodin, a contemporary of Molina, admitted a parental right to punish children and included in it the power of life and death over children:

because, during their minority, they are by nature subject to
him. [30] Adults, as free persons, may not be punished except
by properly constituted authority.

What happens in the case of primitive peoples who live in
comparative isolation, where there is no such thing as public
authority? Molina wishes to refine somewhat the views of
Vitoria and Soto. In the case of primitive peoples, the families
themselves or the heads of families possess the power of killing and/or punishing malefactors in cases where no other
superior authority has been established to which the families
might transfer their power. It is clear that Molina regards the
heads of families not as individuals but as a sort of substitute
for the better-organized political community whose functions
the head of the family performs.

The families Molina had in mind live in extremely primitive
conditions. He explains his position more fully in a later passage. [31] There he observes that a nation might be so primitive
as to have no common civil authority. He mentions a situation which then seemed to prevail in the remote regions of
Brazil where families or villages are so isolated that they have
no common superior. In these cases the heads of families are
permitted to punish wrongs inflicted by external enemies. But
private persons may not take vengeance for any wrong suffered
because these persons would tend to be partial to themselves
and easily blinded in their own cause. Molina hastens to add
that this opinion is not really in opposition to that taken by
Vitoria and Soto. First of all, it is in accordance with reason.

"In any rightly ordered commonwealth, that power of life and death over
their children which belongs to them under the law of God and of nature,
should be restored to parents. This most primitive of customs was observed
in ancient times by the Persians, and the people of Asia generally, by the
Romans and the Celts; it was also recognized throughout the New World till
the time of the Spanish conquests" (*Six Books of the Commonwealth*, [abridged
and trans. M. J. Tooley, Oxford: Basil Blackwell, n.d.], Bk. 1, p. 12).

[30] Here Molina seems to be reaching for a distinction which Yves Simon
makes in his *Philosophy of Democratic Government* (pp. 8-9) where he discusses the paternal function of authority and characterizes it as *substitutional*
and *pedagogical*.

[31] "Dubium est vero hoc loco, utrum si tam barbara sit aliqua natio, ut
superiorem non habeat, sed singulae [vel] duae familiae, aut duo pagi ita
ab invicem sint divisi, ut communem non habeat superiorem, quod in Bra-
silica regione evenire videtur, fas sit uni familiae, aut pago, propria autoritate
sumere iustam vindictam et satisfactionem de injuriis ac damnis ab altera
familia aut pago illatis. ... Licet ergo nullus privatus, etiam tunc, sumere
possit vindictam de injuria sibi illata, eo quod facile unusquisque in propria
causa posset obcaecari" (II, 100, 416-417).

Secondly, if the commonwealth were not made up of families, but of individual men, it would have the same power. Moreover, on the basis of the same line of thought, the commonwealth has power not communicated to it by the parts which comprise it. [32]

According to the eminent British historian of political thought, J. W. Gough, here is an inconsistency between implied theoretical individualism and the Aristotelian tradition that men are naturally political. Gough states that thoroughgoing contractarians avoided this difficulty by abandoning the organic view of society altogether and explaining the state completely along individualist lines. Some Spanish theologians, he says, made an interesting effort to effect a reconciliation.

> Thus the Jesuit Louis Molina follows Vitoria's account of the origin of the state, but reads into it a new interpretation. He tells us in effect that society is natural, and that the first *societas* was that of man and woman, leading to the family, and the *potestas* of husband over wife, and parents over children, master over servants. [33]

Continuing to summarize Molina, Gough says:

> But man is impelled by nature to a yet larger society, in which there can be division of labour and the production of necessaries; and being naturally prone to sin, so that a government is necessary, men must unite not in villages only, but in a complete and perfect state. Monarchy therefore was instituted. [34]

"But Molina points out," Gough observes in an especially pertinent passage, "that the authority of the state cannot have had its origin simply in the powers of individuals, for if so how could the state have the power of life and death over its citizens, which no individual rightly possesses?" [35]

---

[32] "Hac tamen solutione non obstante, placet Vitoriae et Soti opinio. Tunc quod in se consentanea sit rationi. Tum etiam quoniam, esto Respubl. ex familiis non constaret, sed ex hominibus singulis, in Republica tamen esset eadem potestas. Praeterea, quia ratione in familia ex natura rei consurgit potestas occidendi externos malefactores, quae potestas non est in singulis de familia, quatenus singulares, privataeque personae sunt, cur etiam non consurget similis potestas in tota Republica, quae a partibus, quibus constat, communicata illi non sit? profecto nulla potest reddi legitima ratio" (II, 22, 115).

[33] J. W. Gough, *"The Social Contract*: A Critical Study of Its Development (2d ed.; Oxford: At the Clarendon Press, 1957), p. 68.

[34] *Ibid.*

[35] *Ibid.*, pp. 68-69.

Some later writers, Gough continues, have concluded that
the state does not possess this power at all, but the solution
Molina offers is that the power of the state is divine. Yet men
come together of their own free will to form the state, and,
although they did not create the power of the state themselves,
this voluntary union is a necessary condition without which
it could not materialize. [36]

Sir Ernest Barker attempts to illustrate this theory of
Molina by the analogy of marriage:

> The agreement of husband and wife is necessary to the ex-
> istence of marriage. But it does not explain, or create the
> institution of marriage. The institution is an inherent part
> of the divine scheme; and the agreement of the parties is
> simply an agreement to fit themselves into that scheme, which
> exists *per se* apart from their agreement. [37]

In commenting on Suárez' theory, Barker observes appositely:

> The consenting parties who are necessary to the existence of
> a political society (just as they are necessary to the institu-
> tion of marriage) may be, as such, only an aggregate. But
> the *institution* which emerges from their act of agreement as
> a number of individuals is a part of the divine scheme. The
> distinction is fundamental and if we accept it the State is
> realliy a *corpus*. [38]

On this Gough comments that the analogy of marriage throws
light on the defects and half-truth of the social-contract theory.
Marriage, he says, has some of the features of a private contract between individuals, but it is something more than a mere
contract that can be dissolved by the wills of the parties. So
the state, while it contains elements of consent by the citizens,
which are analogous to contract, is something more than a
mere product of contractual agreements. [39]

It is time to return from examining the portage which
Molina constructed around some difficult rapids. In one sense,

---

[36] *Ibid.*

[37] Otto Gierke, *Natural Law and the Theory of Society 1500-1800*, trans.
with an intro. by Ernest Barker (3d ed.; Boston: Beacon Press, 1957), pp. 241-242.

Gough (*op. cit.*, pp. 68-69) points out that this comparison of political
obligation with the marriage tie had already been made in Beza's treatise
Du droit des magistrats sur leur sujets in *Mémoires de l'estate de France sous
Charles IX*, which appeared in the 1570's.

[38] Gierke, *Natural Law and the Theory of Society*, p. 243.

[39] Gough, *op. cit.*, pp. 68-69.

Molina is a victim of his own zeal to reconcile his political theory with what we now call anthropology. It would have been much easier for him to ignore the reports (probably coming from his fellow Jesuits) of conditions in the remote reaches of Brazil. Or, like John Stuart Mill at the beginning of his famous booklet *On Liberty*, simply state that his theory does not hold for primitive peoples, but only for highly civilized ones. But had Molina chosen to ignore the data of history, his political thought, as Sir John Seeley warned, would have no root and history would have no fruit.

All legitimate power is from God, Molina states, whether derived from the natural law or from positive law. The authority of father over children, husband over wife, commonwealth over its parts, is from the natural law. But this power of the commonwealth is not exercisable in its natural form; it must be made so by the commonwealth through its own positive law. Civil power does not exist until the commonwealth has instituted it. [40] What Molina is getting at is the distinction between state and government. Government is the channel through which the natural power of the commonwealth is exercised.

Government is necessary because the commonwealth cannot exercise this power over its parts. The light of nature teaches that it rests with the commonwealth to commit power to one person or several, as it wishes or judges expedient. "Hence there have arisen various just governments, which may be seen in diverse commonwealths, each one choosing and establishing a government for itself, granting greater or less power over itself as it chooses." [41]

---

[40] "Cum legitimae omnes potestates laicae, vel sint de jure naturali, ut potestas patris in filios, viri in uxorem, reipublicae in singulas partes, atque adeo sint a Deo tanquam ab autore naturae, vel descendant a jure naturali, constituanturque jure positivo, partim per potestatem jure naturali ad id immediate concessam, ut sunt potestates omnes supremae laicae, et si quae aliae immediate constituantur a toto corpore reipublicae; partim vero per potestatem a jure naturali mediate ad id derivatam, quales sunt potestates aliae, quas mediate constituantur a corpore toto reipubl. mediante videlicet regia, et aliis potestatibus ad ipsa creatis, et per potestatem ad id in commune reipublicae bonum illis concessam; consequens profecto est, ut legitimae omnes laicae potestates proxime vel remote sint a Deo, atque adeo juxta divinum beneplacitum et voluntatem sint constitutae" (II, 27, 125-126).

[41] "Hucusque solum ostendimus originem ejus civilis, politicaeve potestatis, quae residet in toto Reipub. corpore comparatione suarum partium. Quia vero Reipublicae secundum se totam exercere non potest potestatem hanc in suas partes (esset enim operosum, moraliterque impossibile, ad singulos hujus potestatis actus exigere, expectareque consensum singulorum de Repub. diffi-

From the foregoing it is evident that Molina belongs to
the Translation school of thought. Authority is in the community
from the natural law. But in this condition it is impossible for
the commonwealth as a whole to exercise it and therefore it
must be institutionalized and transferred to one or several. The
last sentence makes it clear that Molina belongs to the Bellarmine wing of the Translation school. It should be stressed
at once that Molina's writings antedate those of Bellarmine and
Suárez. Neither Jesuit influenced him in this regard. Very
likely, it was the other way around, though there is no attempt
here to prove the same. His mentors in this matter were the
two great Dominicans, Vitoria and Soto. And the expedition
tracing the Jesuit branch of political thought now finds its immediate source in the minds of these Spanish sons of the Spanish
Dominic.

Vitoria (1483-1556) approached the problem of the origin of
political authority in a typically scholastic fashion. [42] Analyzing
political authority according to the four causes, he holds that
the final cause is the common good and God is the efficient
cause. [43] The material cause is the body politic. [44] Since by
natural and divine law these must be some authority to govern
the state, and since there is no reason why the power should
reside in this man rather than that, it follows necessarily that
the community is sufficient unto itself. The primary grant of
power to the community takes place whether the community

---

cileque admodum tanta hominum multitudo in idem placitum conveniret) lumen
ipsum naturae docet, in Reipub. arbitrio esse positum, committere alicui, vel
aliquibus, regimen et potestatem supra seipsam, prout voluerit, expedireque
judicaverit. Hinc habuerunt ortum varia regimina justa, quae in diversis
Rebuspublicis conspiciuntur, unaquaque eligente, constituenteque sibi regimen,
tradenteque supra se majorem aut minorem potestatem pro suo arbitratu"
(II, 23, 115-116).

[42] The summary of Vitoria's views is based in part on the exposition
found in Bowe, *op. cit.*, pp. 34-37.

[43] "Efficientem vero causam hujus potestatis facile est intelligere. Si enim
publicam potestatem ordinemus constitutam jure naturali, jus autem naturale
Deum solum auctorem cognoscit; manifestum evadit potestatem publicam a
Deo esse, nec hominum conditione aut jure aliquo positivo contineri" (Vitoria,
De Potestate civili, #6, cited in *ibid.*, p. 34).

[44] "Causa vero materialis, in hujusmodi potestas residet, jure naturali et
divino, est ipsa respublica, cui de se competit gubernandi seipsam, et admi-
nistrare et omnes potestates suas in communi bene dirigere. Quod sic probatur: nam cum de jure naturali et divino est aliqua potestas gubernandi rempublicam, et sublato communi jure positivo et humano, non est major ratio,
ut potestas illa sit in uno quam in altero, necesse est ut ipsa communitas
sit sibi sufficiens et habeat potestatem gubernandi seipsam" (*ibid.*, #7, p. 35).

likes it or not. [45]   But the power thus granted does not remain in the hands of the community, for the community as such is not in a position to exercise it. [46]

For Domingo Soto (1495-1560) [47] God was the source of political authority, having provided for its establishment through the natural law which is the participation of the eternal law. [48] The first bearer of this authority is the community, but where reason dictates it, the authority must be passed on to another who can better provide for the welfare of the community. [49] Kings and princes are created by the people and not immediately by God—certain kings of Israel, of course, being exceptions.   By right, the choice of a ruler belongs to the people and this is decided by the majority. [50]   But once the ruler has been chosen he cannot be deprived of his office except for manifest tyranny. [51]

Thus the positions of Vitoria and Soto.   Gabriel Bowe aligns them this way:

> Vitoria . . . holds that the right to choose the form of government rests with the community—and this includes for him the possibility of a democracy.   On the other hand he denies that the multitude can exercise the power of itself, so that the power which the multitude initially has cannot be such as to constitute the state of a democracy right from the start. Therefore the power is only in the community in an indetermined way—according to the right of election. . . .   Soto seems to mean the same thing for he writes of the need to transfer the authority in order that the community may the

---

[45] "Constituta est enim in republica, omnibus etiam civibus invitis, potestas seipsam gubernandi" (*ibid.*, #8).

[46] "Haec potestas per ipsam multitudinem exerceri non potest (non enim commode posset leges condere atque edicta proponere, lites dirimere et transgressores punire), necesse est ergo ut potestatis administratio alicui aut aliquibus commendaret, qui hujusmodi curam gererent" (*ibid.*).

[47] The summary of Soto's views is also based on that exposition found in Bowe, *op. cit.*, pp. 37-39.

[48] "Potestatem civilem Deus per legem naturalem, quae suae sempiternae participatio est, ordinavit" (Soto, *De Justitia et Jure*, 1, 4, q. 4, cited *ibid.*, p. 37).

[49] "Per me reges regnant etc., non aliter intelligendum est quam quod ab ipso tamquam naturalis juris auctore donatum mortalibus est unaquaeque respublica seipsam regendi habeat arbitrium; ac subinde, ubi ratio, quae spiramen etiam est divini numinis, postulaverit, in alium suam transmittit potestatem, cujus legibus providentia gubernetur" (*ibid.*).

[50] "Ad hoc quod aliqua respublica Regem sibi constituat . . . requiritur publicus ejus conventus, ut saltem major pars in talem consentiat electionem" (*ibid.*).

[51] "Neque per rempublicam rex potest regni jure expoliari, nisi fuerit in tyrannidem corruptus" (*ibid.*).

more efficiently be provided for. So that the power which the people have originally is the power of election. [52]

The settlement of the fact of a transfer of authority only raises a more subtle problem which scholastic philosophers have debated for centuries. When the authority is transferred to one person or several, how is it possessed by the receiver? Is it owned outright or is it a mere delegation by the people, who retain possession? To transfer power connotes a surrender of ownership. In the Middle Ages the glossators and canonists distinguished between a *translatio* and a *concessio*. The discussion usually hinged on the interpretation of the *lex regia* of Roman law, one of the most important sentences in the whole history of political theory?: "Sed et quod principi placuit, legis habet vigorem, cum lege regis quae de imperio ejus lata est, populus ei in eum omne suum imperium et potestatem concessit." [53]

Gierke says that upon the interpretation of this dictum depended the ruler's claim to absolute power or the people's claim to popular sovereignty. [54] The dispute down through the ages was whether the transfer was revocable or irrevocable. As Gierke notes:

> One school explained this as a definitive and irrevocable alienation of power, the other as a mere concession of its use and exercise.... On the one hand from the people's abdication the most absolute sovereignty of the prince might be deduced.... On the other hand the assumption of a mere "concessio imperii" led to the doctrine of popular sovereignty. [55]

What did Molina hold on this question? As stated earlier in this chapter, he distinguishes between a power which has its origin solely in the natural law and a power which has its

---

[52] *Ibid.*, p. 38.

[53] George H. Sabine (*A History of Political Theory* [rev. ed.; New York: Henry Holt and Co., 1953], p. 171) translates the sentence this way: "The will of the Emperor has the force of law, because by the passage of the *lex regia* the people transfers to him and vests in him all its power and authority." The sentence has been translated various ways but the substantial meaning usually remains unchanged.

For some medieval interpretations of the *lex regia*, see A. J. Carlyle and R. W. Carlyle, *A History of Medieval Political Theory in the West* (6 vols.; London: W. Blackwood and Sons, 1903-1906), II, 57ff.; also Lewis, *op. cit.*, I, 252ff. and 307ff.

[54] Gierke, *Development of Political Theory*, p. 93.

[55] *Ibid.*

origin in men voluntarily subjecting themselves to it. Molina points out that "from the very fact that men gather together for the purpose of establishing a commonwealth, the commonwealth itself has power over its parts and is able to transfer this power to one, or to many, who thereupon rule it." [56] Implicit in this statement is Molina's doctrine of two powers: (1) the power which arises upon the establishment of a commonwealth and (2) the power which arises upon the establishment of a government. [57] Molina is so insistent on the distinction between the two powers that he takes exception to what he assumes to be Vitoria's position on the question. He devotes a separate disputation to a consideration and rejection of Vitoria's opinion as he interprets it. Molina seems to have misread Vitoria on this point.

> Vitoria asserted ... that kingly power is from the natural law. First, it was shown that the power of the commonwealth over its parts derives from the natural law. But this is the same power that the commonwealth transfers to the king, so that once the king has been created, there do not remain two powers, one in the commonwealth, the other in the king, but the commonwealth having divested itself of its power and transferred it to the king, there remains only the power of the king. [58]

---

[56] II, 22, 103.

[57] Bowe (*op. cit.*, p. 36) observes of Vitoria's view on this point of two powers: "Vitoria draws a distinction between *potestas* and *auctoritas* which is difficult to render in English. The latter is transferred by the people to the ruler, but not the former. This may be Vitoria's way of distinguishing between authority considered in itself or, as the scholastics put it, *ut sic*, and authority as constituted in this or that ruler. Thus the community does not create the power of the king, but it creates the king. Political authority as such is a necessary entity in human society if order is to be maintained and if the common welfare is to be taken care of. The community (which includes the king) cannot alienate from itself this authority in the sense of opting to do without it altogether—the State, to put it in topical terminology, can never 'wither away'—but it can and does concentrate, so to speak, the power in the hands of one man or group of men, and in this sense it 'transfers' the power to him or them."

[58] "Victoria in relectione de potestate civili n. 8. asseverat regiam potestatem esse de jure naturali, illi videtur subscribere Covar. de practicis quaestionibus c. 1. nu. 6. Suaderi autem id potest. Primo, quoniam potestas Reipublicae in singulas suas partes est de jure naturali, ut dispu. 22. ostensum est: sed eadem est potestas, quam respublica transfert in regem; quippe cum creato rege, non maneant duae potestates, una in Republica, et altera in rege, sed abdicante se Republica suam potestatem, eamque in regem transferente, remanet una sola potestas regis" (II, 26, 124).

Molina here seriously misreads Vitoria. Vitoria's exact words are: "Videtur ergo quod regia potestas sit non a Republica sed ab ipso Deo, ut Catholici

Therefore, Molina continues, just as the power of the Supreme
Pontiff derives from divine law but the designation of the person
who will exercise that power depends on the will and choice
of men, so the power of the king derives from natural law,
bu the delegation of it to this or that particular person who
is chosen king depends upon the free concession and choice of
the commonwealth. [59]

The content of the first argument which Molina refutes is
this: If the power which the commonwealth has from the
natural law be transferred completely to the ruler, then it would
no longer remain with the people. The ruler's power would
have its basis in natural law just as the Pope's power has its
basis in divine law. In both cases, whether through natural
or divine law, power would flow from the higher source to the
incumbents of both offices. The only part men would play
would be in choosing the persons to fill these offices. There in
its essentials is the Designation theory and it is significant that
in refuting the Designation theory Molina affirms the Translation theory. It must not be denied, Molina says, that kingly
power is immediately from the commonwealth and mediately
from God, as the commonwealth chooses for itself the type of
civil government it wishes and judges expedient. Though in
one sense kingly power may be said to come from natural law,
it is more properly a determination of human law as the commonwealth freely chooses for itself the person or persons to
whom power is granted and the type, quantity, and duration of
that power. The legislation concerning the election of the
Supreme Pontiff is a human determination, though based on
power granted the Church by divine law. In an analogous sense,
the civil government which the commonwealth chooses for itself
is a determination of human law, even though the power by
which the commonwealth acts comes from the natural law. [60]

Doctores sentiunt. Quamvis enim a Republica constituatur (creat enim Republica regem) non potestatem, sed propriam autoritatem in regem transfert,
nec sunt duae potestates, una regia, altera communitatis" (cited in Bowe,
op. cit., p. 36, n. 23). What Vitoria seems to be saying is that *potestas* remains
with the community, *autoritas* is transferred to the king. Therefore there are
not *duae potestates sed una tantum* which remain in the commonwealth.

[59] "Ergo sicut potestas Summi Pontificis est de jure divino, esto applicatio illius ad hunc vel illum, qui eligitur in Summum Pontificem, pendeat
a voluntate et electione hominum: ita potestas regis erit de jure naturali, esto
applicatio illius ad hunc vel illum, qui in regem eligitur, a libera concessione
et electione Reipublicae pendeat" (II, 26, 124).

[60] "Dicendum est ... tum regiam, tum quamvis aliam supremam civilem
potestatem, quam pro arbitratu Respublica sibi elegerit, esse immediate a Re-

Molina is quick to point out that the two cases are radically different. The power of the Supreme Pontiff was established by Christ and may not be diminished or restricted by the Church. Yet Christ did grant to the Church the power of choosing the person to whom the power should be given. But the power of the civil government is set up by the commonwealth. [61]

The analogy Molina introduces between papal and civil power is particularly apt. The Pope receives divine power directly; the papal power never rests in the whole body of the Church. Christ grants papal power to that member of the Church who is chosen to the office of Supreme Pontiff. As Hesselberg points out, if this theory were applied to the state it would mean that the sole act of positive law on the part of the state or body politic would be the selection of rulers; God would then confer power directly upon these rulers. [62] Molina insists that the commonwealth not only chooses the ruler but varies the amount of power it confers and restricts its use; this would not be possible if it were not the owner of this power. If the Designation theory were applied to the state it would also mean that the power of kings would derive immediately from natural law. One could argue that kingship has its basis in nature, as does the family. The same case would be made for the other forms of government, which brings us to the second argument which Molina attributes to Vitoria:

> Second, not only the power of the commonwealth arises from natural law, but also the committing of it to a particular per-

---

publica, et mediate a Deo per lumen naturale et potestatem, quam Reipublicae concessit, ut sibi deligeret civilem potestatem prout vellet, expedireque judicaret. Quare descendit a jure naturali, est tamen simpliciter de jure humano Reipublicae, pro arbitratu sibi deligentis, non solum personam, aut personas, quibus tribuat potestatem, sed etiam modum, quantitatem, ac durationem talis potestatis. Sicut enim leges Summi Pontificis derivantur a potestate, quam jure divino habet ad eas condendum, sunt tamen simpliciter de jure humano; ita etiam licet suprema civilis potestas, quam pro arbitratu sibi Respublica eligit, derivetur a naturali potestate, qua ad illud constituendum habet, est tamen de jure humano" (II, 26, 124-125).

[61] "Neque est eadem ratio de suprema civili potestate, ut non sit de jure humano, et de suprema Ecclesiastica potestate Summi Pontificis. Potestas namque Summi Pontificis, nec constituitur ab Ecclesia, nec ab ea variari, minui, aut coarctari potest, sed solum Ecclesiae fuit a Christo concessum, ut juxta leges, quas ipsa summi Pontifices praescriberent, facultatem haberet eligendi personam, cui potestas illa applicaretur. At vero suprema civilis potestas constituitur a Republica talis vel talis, et tanta vel tanta, hocque vel illo modo restricta et descendens ab alio aut ab aliis, pro ipsius Reipublicae arbitrio" (II, 26, 125).

[62] Hesselberg, op. cit., p. 105.

son, or persons, arises from the same light of natural law,
because the commonwealth as a whole is never able to exercise it; therefore the commonwealth chooses for itself a monarchy, or an aristocracy, or a democracy, the supreme civil
power which it chooses will always derive from natural law. [63]

In reply, Molina falls back on his scholastic training: "Concesso antecedente, neganda est consequentia." Although it is
correct to say that a ruler's commands or the punishment he
prescribes may be based ultimately on the natural law, the type
of punishment for this or that crime comes immediately from
positive law. The particular form of government which the
commonwealth selects depends on positive law; the natural law
demands that *some* form of government be chosen because the
total commonwealth cannot rule itself. [64]

Molina returns to the problem of the actual content of
authority granted. The power which the commonwealth grants
the king is far different from that which it has itself. This is
not to say that there remain two powers even after the king
has been created, either one of which can be exercised immediately and fully.

> For to the extent that the commonwealth concedes power to
> the king independent of itself in the future, to that extent
> it takes away is own power as regards its immediate use.
> Nevertheless it must not be denied that there remain two
> powers, one in the king, the other, as it were, habitually in
> the commonwealth, impeded from acting while the other
> power endures, and impeded only to the extent that the com-
> monwealth concedes power to the king independently of itself

---

[63] "Secundo, non sola potestas Reipublicae oritur ex jure naturali, sed
etiam, quod eam alicui vel aliquibus committat, proficiscitur a lumine ipso,
jureque naturali; eo quod Respublica tota nequaquam, secundum se totam, possit illam exercere: ergo sive Respublica sibi eligat regium regimen, sive Aristo-
cratium, sive Democratium, sane suprema civilis potestas, quam pro suo arbitratu elegerit, semper erit de jure naturali. Atque hoc argumento ductus
Covar. eam sibi opinionem persuasit" (II, 26, 124).

[64] "Ad secundum, concesso antecedente, neganda est consequentia. Sicut
enim de jure naturali est, quod Respublica, aut princeps jubeat, punireve
faciat malefactores; attamen, quod hac potius, quam illa poena punire faciat
hoc vel illud delictum, est de jure positivo; eo quod a libero suo arbitrio,
jureque, quod constituere ea in parte voluerit, id pendeat: ita licet de jure
naturali sit, quod Respublica aliquem vel aliquos rectores eligat, quibus regimen committat; eo quod tota non possit seipsam regere; de jure tamen positivo ipsiusmet Reipublicae est, quodcumque in singulari regimen elegerit; eo
quod ab arbitrio ipsius pendeat, hoc potius, quam quodcumque aliud eligere"
(II, 26, 125).

for the future. But this power having been abolished, the commonwealth recovers the full use of its powers. Moreover even while the king's power lasts the commonwealth can resist it, if he exceeds the limits of the power granted him. The commonwealth can also make use of whatever power it has reserved to itself. [65]

By this Molina means that the power conferred upon rulers by the commonwealth is in the nature of a *communicatio* or *concessio*. The commonwealth does not thereby divest itself of all authority. Of course, the power once granted cannot be withdrawn without weighty reasons. What the commonwealth grants is the immediate use of its power; the natural power of the commonwealth is inactive while governmental power lasts. When governmental power is abolished, the commonwealth recovers the use of its natural power. But this natural power must be institutionalized anew since it cannot be exercised in the natural state. The power of the commonwealth remains inalienable; the people cannot surrender or abdicate this power because it is natural. In establishing government the people merely relinquish the use of their natural power. Should the government be abolished, the power returns to the commonwealth—the people as a whole. [66]

---

[65] "Ad primum ergo argumentum in contrarium neganda est minor. Longe namque diversa est potestas, quam Respublica regi communicat, ab ea, quam in se habet; potestque majorem vel minorem illi communicare, ut dictum est. Ad probationem vero minoris, dicendum est, creato rege, non manere quidem duas potestates, quarum quaevis prodire possit immediate et integre in actum exercendae jurisdictionis ac regiminis in partes Reipublicae. Etenim quantum Respublica concedit regi potestatis independentis in futurum a se ipsa, tantum sibi adimit potestatem quoad immediatum illius usum; nihilominus negandum non est, manere duas potestates, unam in rege, alteram vero quasi habitualem in Republica, impeditam ab actu, interim dum illa alia potestas perdurat, et tantum praecise impeditam, quantum Respublica independenter in posterum a se Regi illi eam concessit. Abolita vero ea potestate, potest Respublica integre uti sua potestate. Praeterea, illa perdurante, potest Respublica illi resistere, si aliquid injuste in Rempublicam committat, limitesve potestatis sibi concessae excedat. Potest etiam Respublica exercere immediate quemcunque usum suae potestatis, quem sibi reservaverit" (*ibid.*).

[66] Hesselberg, *op. cit.*, pp. 106-107.

CHAPTER IV

THE RIGHT OF RESISTANCE

After Napoleon had kidnapped the King of Spain and the Prince of Asturias, the curate of a little town near Valencia wrote Admiral Collingwood, then commanding in the Mediterranean, a letter "in which he descanted at much length on the Spanish resistance to Joseph Buonaparte, and supported his arguments by various extracts from the works of Grotius and Vattel." He received in return a statement of the right of resistance: "The right of making war belongs only, it is true, to the Sovereign; but if, by taking the Spanish Princes out of the country, Buonaparte thought he had dissolved the only power which could lawfully oppose him, he was mistaken; for on the removal of the Princes, the sovereign power reverted to the source from which it sprung—the people; and the act of their delegates is legitimate sovereignty."[1]

Among the earliest monuments erected in Athens to the memory of mortal men were those set up to commemorate the first instance of an attempt to slay a tyrant.[2] Herodotus, in a passage which has been called the beginning of Greek philosophy, describes the *hubris*—the unbridled, defiant arrogance of the tyrant—in terms that later became traditional in Greek political literature.[3] Thirty-five years ago the distinguished historian, Élie Halévy, drew attention to the revival of the problem of tyranny. He suggested that the new phenomenon could best be characterized by the word tyranny—a word which came from Greek experience of a similar era—rather than the Roman word dictatorship, which originally applied to a temporary constitutional expedient.[4] Later still, Leo Strauss wrote on the failure

---

[1] The incident is described by Thomas Gilby, *Between Community and Society*: A Philosophy and Theology of the State (London: Longmans, Green & Co., 1953), pp. 286-287.

[2] Oscar Jászi and John D. Lewis, *Against the Tyrant*: The Tradition and Theory of Tyrannicide (Glencoe, Illinois: The Free Press and The Falcon's Wing Press, 1957), p. 3.

[3] W. W. How and J. Wells, *A Commentary on Herodotus* (2 vols.; Oxford: Oxford University Press, 1949-1951), I, 278.

of modern political science to recognize tyranny when confronted by it and said that one cannot understand modern tyranny before one has understood tyranny in its elementary, pre-modern form. [5]

The revival of tyranny inevitably brings with it a revival of that moral revulsion against the tyrant on which the old doctrine of tyrannicide was based. [6] Especially after the establishment of Hitler's rule, one began to hear expressions of despair and rage from the lips of kind and peace-loving people. These people were pleased rather than horrified at the statement quoted from Sir Nevile Henderson, once an apostle of appeasement: "If I were given a gun and told to take two shots, I would shoot Himmler, then Ribbentrop, and brain Hitler with the butt of the rifle." [7]

When the danger of tyranny becomes real, the problem of the right of resistance against the tyrant becomes a burning moral problem. [8] The political theorists of a moderate bent like the Jesuits and Puritans of the sixteenth century strongly insisted on the right of resistance against the tyrant as being inherent in the people. [9] The question is a delicate one, full of subtle implications, such as what precisely constitutes the people. Was the "people" only a term to designate an aggre-

---

[4] Élie Halévy, *L'ère des tyrannies*: études sur le socialisme et la guerre (Paris: Gallimard, 1938), p. 214, n. 1.

[5] Leo Strauss, *On Tyranny*: An Interpretation of Xenophon's Hiero (Glencoe, Illinois: The Free Press, 1948), pp. 1ff.

[6] Jászi and Lewis, *op. cit.*, p. viii.

[7] *The New York Times*, December 31, 1942.

[8] Two books from Germany illustrate the interest in the moral problem of resistance to Tyranny brought on by Hitler's regime. One of these studies, *Die Vollmacht des Gewissens, hrsg. von den Europäischen Publikationen*, Band I (Munich: H. Rinn, 1956), is a symposium on the right of resistance by a group of public officials, army officers, jurists, Protestant and Catholic theologians, and professors of history and philosophy. Three significant essays are noted: "Die Militäropposition gegen Hitler und das Wiederstandrecht" by Herman Weinkauff; "Der Eid nach der Lehre der katholischen Moraltheologie" by Max Pribilla, S.J.; and "Die evangelisch-lutherische Theologie und das Wiederstandsrecht" by Walter Künneth.

The other book is *Wiederstandsrecht und Grenzen der Staatsgewalt*: Bericht über die Tagung der Hochschule für Politische Wissenschaften, München, und der Evangelische Akademie, Tütsing, 18-20 June 1955..., ed. Bernhard Pfister and Gerhard Hildmann (Berlin, 1956), and is also a symposium which includes comments by noted historians, political theorists, and Catholic and Protestant theologians.

See also Max Pribilla, S.J., "An den Grenzen der Staatsgewalt," *Stimmen der Zeit, Monatsschrift für das Geistesleben der Gegenwart*, CXLII (1948), 410-427.

[9] Allen, *op. cit.*, pp. 356ff.

gate of individuals, or did the term refer to a true *corpus politi-cum*, a true organic whole which was qualitatively different from a mere aggregate of individuals? [10]

During the sixteenth century the question of the right of resistance was a burning one, with writers in all camps building their theories of resistance upon medieval foundations. Regarding the origin and nature of civil society there was remarkable similarity between the basic assumptions of the Huguenots and those of the members of the Catholic league, and those assumptions were not essentialy unlike those of the Jesuit writers. [11]

The Jesuit position on the right of resistance to tyranny is best known by its most extreme advocate, Juan de Mariana, [12] a Spanish Jesuit contemporary of Molina. Unfortunately, Mariana's notoriety has all but obscured the moderate positions of Molina, Bellarmine, and Suárez. Typical of the general neglect of Molina, the authors of a recent treatise on the subject omit all mention of him. [13]

Molina begins his study of the right of the people to resist tyrannical rulers by first considering the nature of the political relationship between ruler and ruled. It concerns the important function of making laws in a commonwealth. Here Molina opposes those who would vest all such power in the ruler. Admitting that the power to make laws is joined to the regal power, Molina insists that the ruler is not the sole legislator; the people also have a share in the law-making process. [14] He

---

[10] Rommen (*The State in Catholic Thought*, pp. 123-183) devotes an entire chapter to the organic nature of the state.

[11] The similarity between the Catholic and Protestant approaches to this moral question, which was characteristic of the sixteenth century, continues to modern times. "But the most significant fact is that, as the resistance took form toward the end of the Hitler regime, its actual leaders included both Protestants and Catholics working together. They were supporters and opponents of tyrannicide among the adherents of both creeds" (Jászi and Lewis, *op. cit.*, p. 276, n. 1).

[12] For the political theory of Mariana, see J. W. Allen, *A History of Political Thought in the Sixteenth Century* (3d ed.; London: Methuen & Co., Ltd., 1957), pp. 360ff.; John Laures, S.J., *The Political Economy of Juan de Mariana* (New York : Fordham University Press, 1928); A. Dempf, *Christliche Staatsphilosophie in Spanien* (Salzburg: A. Pustet, 1937).

Mariana's main work was translated by G. A. Moore (*The King and the Education of the King*).

There is also a short account of Mariana's political theory by the distinguished historian Leopold Ranke (*op. cit.*, pp. 230-236).

[13] Jászi and Lewis, *loc. cit.*

[14] There is a curiously faint echo of Molina's doctrine of the people sharing in the legislative process in a speech by President Franklin D. Roosevelt on

cites Alfonso de Castro, who observed that, if it is not clearly
apparent that the people reject laws they find burdensome, it
must be determined by a process of conjecture whether in the
original establishment of the ruler's power it was provided that
the king would enact laws dependent upon the approval of
the people. [15]   And if, Molina continues, it appears from usage
that such laws have no force until approved by the people,
evidently the people conceded no greater power to the kings
than to enact laws dependent upon their approval. [16]   Moreover,
even if the people do not explicitly so provide, it is to be presumed that such was their intention.

> And it is to be presumed that the king increased his power
> through force (the people not daring to resist) rather than
> to suppose that the people had diminished the power they
> had once granted him. So that it is the right of the common-
> wealth to reject laws which it finds notably burdensome, espe-
> cially if they are in no way necessary for the common good.
> And if the ruler attempts coercion, he acts unjustly. [17]

September 7, 1942, wherein he made a peremptory demand upon Congress to
repeal forthwith a certain provision of the Emergency Price Control Act:
"I ask the Congress to take this action by the first of October. Inaction on
your part by that date will leave me with the inescapable responsibility to
the people of this country to see to it that the war effort is no longer imperiled by threat of economic chaos.

"In the event that the Congress should fail to act, and act adequately,
I shall accept the responsibility, and I will act.

"The American people can be sure that I will use my powers with a full
sense of my responsibility to the Constitution and to my country... When
the war is won, the powers under which I act automatically revert to the
people—to whom they belong" (New York Times, September 8, 1942).

Aside from the fascinating theory concerning the separation of powers
implied in this remarkable address, President Roosevelt seemed to say that
he owed the transcendent powers he was claiming (in this case of their nature
legislative) to some peculiar relationship between himself and the people (see
Edward S. Corwin, The President: Office and Powers 1787-1948: History and
Analysis of Practice and Opinion [New York: New York University Press, 1948],
pp. 303-306).

[15] II, 23, 118.

[16] Molina later (see infra, chap. ix) speaks of a quasi-contract between
the ruler and people for the former's support. There is a question here of
a type of contract, pactum subjectionis, not in the sense of Hobbes and Locke,
but in that of Catholic theory. For a discussion of this point see Rommen,
State in Catholic Thought, pp. 238-245.

[17] "Si namque usus habeat, ut tales leges vim non habeant, nisi a populo
approbentur, censendum est Rempublicam non majorem potestatem regibus
concessisse, quam condendi eas leges dependenter ab approbatione populi. Veri-
simileque est, si populi ad id adverterunt, non majorem potestatem regibus
concessisse; imo esto non adverterunt, haec videtur fuisse Reipublicae intentio

Implicit in Molina's reasoning in the above passage is the sanctity of custom in the law-making process. Law is not simply a command or decree of a sovereign ruler binding at once without further question, as Hobbes would have it. [18] Rather, law is a process of growth and tradition. In case of doubt, custom must be observed. Governments of long standing without a written constitution must inevitably rely on custom, as in the United Kingdom. The warning sign of tyranny, according to Molina, is the ruler's disregard of customary law.

So far, Molina has been consistent in his doctrine of the residual power of the people, even after a grant of power to the ruler. However, if it is the custom to obey laws which are not wholly iniquitous, one must conclude that the commonwealth has yielded all its powers, which is difficult to believe. As has already been mentioned, kings are prone to extend their powers through force. Therefore "it will always be considered the right of the commonwealth to appeal against laws which are excessively burdensome by petitioning their prince either to revoke them or lessen their rigor, and he is bound to listen to the commonwealth." [19]

One of the political theorists' favorite forms of exercise is expending mental energies in jumping to conclusions. Historians are similarly addicted. Lord Acton, for example, wrote that "greater part of the political ideas of Milton, Locke, and Rous-

---

sibi regem constituentis, quando aliud non expressit, semperque est potius praesumendum regem per potentiam ampliasse suam potestatem, subditis non audentibus resistere, quam subditos restrinxisse illi potestatem semel concessam. Quare fas erit Reipublicae non acceptare leges, quae ipsam notabiliter gravent, quando ad commune bonum necessariae omnino non sunt. Quod si princeps ad id eam cogat, injustiam committet" (II, 23, 118).

[18] "The Resolutions of a monarch, are subject to no other Inconstancy, than that of Humane Nature; but in Assemblies, besides that of Nature, there ariseth an Inconstancy from the Number. For the absence of a few, that would have the Resolution once taken, continue firme (which may happen by security, negligence, or private impediments), or the diligent appearance of a few of the contrary opinion, undoes today, all that was concluded yesterday:" (Hobbes, op. cit., Part 2, chap. xix, quoted in W. T. Jones, Machiavelli to Bentham, Vol. II of Masters of Political Thought, ed. Edward McChesney Sait [2 vols.; Boston: Houghton Mifflin Co., 1950], pp. 136-137).

[19] "Si vero, inquit Castrus, usus receptus habeat, ut legibus principum non iniquis omnino pareatur, censendum est, Rempublicam omnem omnino suam potestatem regi concessisse, quod vix de aliqua credi potest. Praesertim cum, ut paulo antea dictum est, reges per potentiam suam soleant extendere potestatem, adhucque in hoc eventu fas erit Reipublicae, quasi appellare a legibus nimium eum gravantibus, principem supplicando, ut vel ab eis abstineat, vel rigorem earum minuat, oportebitque eam audire, justamne causam suae appellationis habeat: quod si sufficientem non ostenderit, tunc quidem cogi poterit, parereque tenebitur" (II, 23, 118).

seau, may be found in the ponderous Latin of Jesuits who were
subjects of the Spanish Crown, of Lessius, Molina, Mariana and
Suarez." [20]   John D. Lewis has warned against the subtle temptation to trace a direct line of descent from the *Vindiciae Contra
Tyrannos* through Milton, Harrington, Sidney, and Locke and
the theorists of the American Revolution. [21]   It is truly difficult
to establish a direct relationship between the sixteenth-century
writers on the right of resistance and John Adams, for example.
But one must note the similarity of language between Molina's
insistence on the right of the people to petition a ruler against
burdensome laws and the First Amendment of the American
Constitution: "Congress shall make no law respecting . . . the
right of the people . . . to petition the government for a redress
of grievances."

Yet, Molina cautions, once the commonwealth has granted
power to a ruler, he remains superior not only to the individual
parts but to the whole commonwealth to the extent of the power
granted him, which includes the right to punish.   Once the
power has been granted, it may not be withdrawn, diminished,
or hindered in its legitimate use.   Otherwise power granted to
a single person would not be a monarchy reducible to a single
head, but a democracy reducible ultimately to the multitude.
Should the ruler attempt to assume power not granted him,
the commonwealth indeed could resist him as a tyrant just as
if he were a foreigner bent on inflicting wrong.   The reason
for this, Molina hastens to add, is that the king in this respect
is not superior to the commonwealth, nor is the commonwealth
inferior to him.   The situation becomes just what it was before
any power was granted him. [22]

---

[20] Lord Acton, "Sir Erskine May's Democracy in Europe," in *The History
of Freedom and Other Essays* (London: Macmillan and Co., Ltd., 1909), p. 82.

[21] Jászi and Lewis, *op. cit.*, pp. 264-265, n. 21.

[22] "Concessa vero alicui per Rempublicam regia potestate, rex manet superior non solum singulis Reipublicae partibus, sed et tot [sic] Reipublicae,
quoad latitudinem potestatis sibi concessae, ita ut possit ea potestate uti,
non solum in singulis Reipublicae partes, sed etiam in totam Rempublicam,
eam, si opus fuerit, puniendo, ut Sotus et Victoria locis citatis probe notarunt.
Neque Respublica potest ab eo auferre potestatem concessam, vel eam mi-
nuere, aut legitimum usum illius impedire: alioquin regium regimen non esset
Monarchia, quae ad unum supremum caput reduceretur, sed Democratia, quae
ad Reipublicae multitudinem ultimo reduceretur. Si tamen rex potestatem sibi
non concessam vellet assumere, posset quidem Respublica ei, tamquam ty-
ranno ea in parte, resistere; perinde ac cuivis altero extraneo, qui Reipublicae
injuriam vellet inferre.   Ratio vero est, quia neque rex ea in parte est Republica superior, neque Respublica est illo inferior: sed manet, ut se habebat,
antequam illi ullam concederet potestatem" (II, 23, 118-119).

One of the features of the political theory of the *Monarcho-machs*[23] was that they regarded the king as superior to his subjects *ut singulis* but not *ut universis*. Thus the king was not regarded as superior to the whole commonwealth. He would hardly be said to rule over the commonwealth as a whole, but only over individual men. Molina rejects what Hesselberg aptly terms the atomistic concept of kingship.[24] He regards the king as superior not only to the individual parts of the common-weith, whether single individuals or entire families, but to the whole of it. The view of the Monarchomachs did not permit the king to exercise his power over the whole commonwealth; the commonwealth regarded as a whole was superior to the king and could withdraw power from him, or resist him whenever it saw fit; it could even abolish his office altogether. This theory had the effect of blurring the distinction between forms of government, reducing all essentially to democracy; it also had the effect of encouraging private persons to resist lawful authority on slight grounds. Each private person might, as an individual, feel himself inferior to the king. But what if he were a member of an aggrieved group; which regarded itself as the *vox populi*? The tyrannicides in the late sixteenth and early seventeenth centuries by private persons could be taken as a answer.

F. J. C. Hearnshaw indicts Mariana specifically by saying appearance of his *De Rege* in 1599 "coincided with a formidable recrudescence of violence."[25] Mariana taught that if the king violates the laws of the realm with respect to religion,

---

[23] For the origin of the term monarchomach see Sabine, *op. cit.*, p. 374. Sabine seems to have erred when he says that there was no objection to monarchy as such. Actually, the chief characteristic of the *Monarchomachs* was that they were haters of kings.

See also Gierke (*Natural Law and the Theory of Society*) for one of his characteristic long footnotes, which lists both Catholic and Protestant monarchomachs, including Milton and Mariana. Rightly, he does not list Vitoria, Molina, or Suárez.

R. H. Murray (*The Political Consequences of the Reformation*) [London: Ernest Benn Ltd., 1926] has a chapter entitled "The Jesuit Monarchomachs": "The Jesuits take up the ideas of Gregory VII,... Molina and Mariana, Bellarmine and Suárez are at the head of these curious monarchomachs among the Jesuits.... The secularism of these writers is only too apparent. They all, especially Mariana, write like men of the world to whom theology is almost an accident" (p. 227). The foregoing is but one in a long series of errors in Murray's prejudiced book.

[24] Hesselberg, *op. cit.*, p. 132.

[25] F. J. C. Hearnshaw, *Some Great Political Idealists of the Christian Era* (London: George G. Harrap & Co., Ltd., 1937), p. 82.

succession, taxes, or forbids or prevents the meeting of the
Cortes, he is a tyrant and should be deposed or, if necessary,
killed by anyone and in any possible fashion except by administering poison. [26]   Mariana's book was condemned not only
by the Parlement of Paris but by the Society of Jesus.   Molina
and Suárez, contemporaries of Mariana, both repudiate his doctrine without mentioning his name.

Traditional Catholic thought on the question of tyrannicide
is faithfully reflected in the political theory of Molina.   Like a
good scholastic, he distinguishes two types of tyrants.   One is
a legitimate ruler who rules wickedly and unjustly.   The other
is not a legitimate ruler but has usurped rule and oppresses
the commonwealth.   The distinction is the same that occurs
in St. Thomas' *Commentary on the Sentences*. [27]   The first is
tyrannus in exercitio; the second is *tyrannus absque titulo*. [28]
Molina warns that they are to be dealt with differently.   It is
wrong for a private person to kill a legitimate ruler who rules
unjustly.   Each person may, however, defend himself, repelling
force with force, and, within the limits of innocent safety, kill
the tyrant to defend his own life should that be necessary.   But
the leaders of the commonwealth may unite to resist him and,
having passed sentence, depose him and even punish him with
death if the common good requires it.   Molina, holding out for
due process of law, repeats that for private persons to kill a
tyrant of this type before sentence is passed is wrong, unless
it be necessary to defend their lives which the tyrant seeks to
take unjustly. [29]

---

[26] See Mariana, *The King and the Education of the King*, p. 48.

[27] *II Sentences*, XLIV, ii, 2.

[28] "Quod vero ad secundum attinet, distinguendum est. Quoniam duobus
modis aliquis est tyrannus. Uno, quia licet sit vere dominus reipublicae in
qua tyrannidem exercet, inique tamen atque injuste eam administrat. Altero
vero, quoniam non est reipublicae dominus, sed eam usurpatam habet ac op-
pressam" (III, 6, 539).

[29] "Tyrannum primo modo nefas est privatis interficere. Posset tamen
unusquisque ab eo se defendere, vim vi repellendo cum moderamine incul-
patae tutelae, eumque interficere; si ita esset opus ad propriam vitam defendendam, quam ille injuste inferre vellet. Posset item respublica ipsa quo ad
capita convenire, eique resistere, lataque sententia, deponere illum ab administratione, si id ita excessus illius, communeque bonum, efflagitarent atque
illum depositum punire. Ante latam tamen sententiam nefas privatis esset,
eum interficere, nisi quando, ut dictum est, necessarium omnino esset ad vitae
defensionem, quam injuste vellet inferre" (*ibid.*).

Suárez is of the same opinion; see *Opera Omnia*, XIV, 680-681, where he
refers to Molina's work.

Molina refers his reader to the Council of Constance's [30] condemnation of Wyclif's proposition: "Populares possunt ad suum arbitrium dominos delinquentes corrigere." [31] The same Council condemned a proposition on tyrannicide which stated that any tyrant could and should "licite et meritorie occidi per quemcumque vasallum suum vel subditum ... non obstante quocunque praestito juramento seu confoederatione factis cum eo, non exspectata sententia vel mandato cujuscunque." [32] These documents of the magisterium give important confirmatory support for Molina's reasoned opinion.

The second type of tyrant, with no legitimate title to power, may be killed by any member of the commonwealth, except when greater evils would threaten the commonwealth because of his death. In such a case it would be a sin against charity to kill him. Returning to the position he had taken on redress of war damages, Molina says that an inferior should appeal to his superior, who should come to the subject's assistance and kill the tyrant. He refers expressly to St. Thomas, where the Dominican gave the first clear-cut distinction between the two types of tyranny. [33]

Molina interjects his own agreement with the position of Marcus Tullius Cicero and St. Thomas regarding the assassination of Julius Caesar. Cicero's eloquent defense of the assassination was used by later generations as a model for justifiable tyrannicide. With obvious allusion to the death of Julius Caesar, Cicero wrote:

> What can be a greater crime than to kill a man, especially one who is an intimate friend? But is he a criminal who has killed a tyrant, even if the tyrant was his friend? It does not seem so to the Roman people, who regard this as the finest of all glorious deeds. [34]

---

[30] The Council of Constance (1414-1418) is regarded as the Sixteenth Ecumenical Council, at least in some of its decrees. A footnote in Henricus Denzinger, S.J., Clementis Bannwart, S.J., and Johannes Bapt. Umberg, S.J. (*Enchiridion Symbolorum*: Definitionum et Declarationum de Rebus Fidei et Morum [23d ed.; Friburgi Brisgoviae: Herder & Co., 1937], p. 248) puts the authority of the Council this way: "Quae hic de auctoritate Concilii CONSTANTIENSIS dicta sunt, intelligenda esse patet secundum mentem ipsius Sedis Apostolicae, quae nunquam confirmavit omnia illius decreta."

Jászi and Lewis (*op. cit.*) make no mention of the Council of Constance's condemnation of Wyclif or of the proposition on tyrannicide.

[31] Denzinger, Bannwart, and Umberg, *op. cit.*, p. 242.

[32] *Ibid.*, p. 251. Pope Paul V renewed the condemnation in a letter "Cura Dominici Gregis" of January 24, 1615.

[33] "Ita D. Th... ubi cum Tullio, approbat Julii Caesaris interfectionem,

Molina, approving of Cicero's defense, says that Caesar was a
tyrant of the second class and was waging an unjust war against
the republic. If there were no superior authority, then any
citizen could licitly kill him, especially if that be the presumed
or express will of the whole body of the commonwealth.

Heywood Broun once observed that no body politic is
healthy until it begins to itch.[35] Perhaps by this he meant the
same idea Jefferson was expressing when he wrote to Madison
that a little rebellion is a good thing and as necessary in the
political world as storms in the physical.[36] Jefferson also
wrote: "The tree of liberty must be refreshed from time to
time with the blood of patriots and tyrants. It is its natural
manure."[37] The motto on Jefferson's seal is "Rebellion to
Tyrants is Obedience to God." One can almost hear the voice
of Molina pleading for a distinction.

---

qui rempublicam Romanam tyrannice usurpaverat. Ratio vero hujus rei haec
est, quoniam, qui hoc secundo modo est tyrannus, gerit bellum cum republica,
quam tyrannice habet occupatam, et cum partibus illius; qua de causa, si
non sit superior aliquis, cujus autoritate geri debeat, quivis de illa republica
potest licite eum interficere praesertim cum ea sit praesumpta, aut expressa,
voluntas corporis totius illius reipublicae" (III, 6, 540).

[34] *De Officiis*, III, 4. Translation is that of Jászi and Lewis, *op. cit.*, p. 10.

[35] Quoted by Edward R. Murrow in "A Broadcaster Talks to His Colleagues," *The Reporter*, XIX (November 13, 1958), 35.

[36] Letter to James Madison, January 30, 1787, in *The Papers of Thomas
Jefferson*, ed. Julian P. Boyd (Princeton: Princeton University Press, 1955),
XI, 93.

[37] Letter to William Stevens Smith, November 13, 1787, in *ibid.*, XII, 356.

CHAPTER V

THE TWO SWORDS

Harold Laski was expressing but a truism when he observed that all political systems are the natural reflection of their historic development and that there has been no influential political work which was not, in essence, the autobiography of its time.[1] People in the sixteenth century, when they thought politically, were preoccupied with the problem of establishing and maintaining order; in some respects this meant establishing a new order. The Reformation forced men to consider under more or less new forms the old question of the relations of State to Church.[2] Nothing in Molina's political thought mirrors his age quite so accurately as his teaching on what are now termed Church-State relations.[3]

By 1570, the medieval unity of Christianity—*respublica christiana*—had not only been broken, it had been shattered and its sharp-edged fragments were scattered across Europe. Restoration of the Humpty Dumpty past was beyond the powers of all the popes' forces and all the kings' men. With the abdication of Charles V the last vestige of the former greatness of the Holy Roman Emperor had vanished. The papacy, long weakened by internal strife and external abuse, had been attacked in its vitals by the challenge both in Germany and England of its claim to spiritual supremacy. As one writer

---

[1] *A Defence of Liberty Against Tyrants*: A Translation of the *Vindiciae Contra Tyrannos* by Junius Brutus, Historical Introduction by Harold J. Laski (London: G. Bell and Sons, Ltd., 1924), p. 1.

[2] Allen, *A History of Political Thought in the Sixteenth Century*, p. 512.

[3] See MacIlwain, *op. cit.*, pp. 146-147: "The peculiar problem of Church and State was the greatest perturbation which has ever drawn men's thoughts about the state out of their proper political orbit, and for many ages the most powerful stimulus to all political speculation.... For the half-millenium between the eleventh and seventeenth century it is not too much to say that the bulk of the writings which we may term political was directly and primarily concerned with the great controversy between the spiritual and secular authority."

phrased it: historic *Christianitas* was no longer a problem because it was no longer a fact. [4]

At the very time of the Protestant challenge, other events
were influencing the European's concept of the unity of mankind. The impact of the discovery of the two continents of the
Americas had a profound effect on European thought, though
not as immediately evident as the religious rift in Europe. This
question will be mentioned later in this book when Molina's
view of slavery is discussed. [5]

Molina was born within two decades of the first Protestant
challenge. When he died in 1600, the new order had crystal-
lized. That year Thomas Hobbes was twelve years old but his
perceptive mind even then might have grasped the great change
which had taken place. Some years later in his *Leviathan* he
expressed strikingly the picture that must have appeared to
many contemporaries: "And if a man consider the originall of
this great Ecclesiastical Dominion, he will easily perceive, that
the *Papacy,* is no other, than the *Ghost* of the deceased *Romane
Empire,* sitting crowned upon the grave thereof." [6]

The concept of an independent spiritual authority having
claims and a sphere of its own, distinct from the claims and
sphere of the secular state, was unknown to pagan jurisprudence. Christianity was the first religion to make real the
distinction between the two powers, the spiritual and the
temporal; but, as James Brodrick remarks, Christianity succeeded in obtaining recognition for the reality of the distinction only after a stern struggle in which the blood of her
martyrs was her argument. [7] Naturally enough, princes and
politicians have never been fond of the distinction and at times
have striven to obliterate it altogether. The Middle Ages wit-
nessed many such struggles but the Church, far from losing her
independence, was able, under a succession of strong popes from
Gregory VII to Boniface VIII, to dictate terms and to lay down
the law to a half-dozen powerful kings and emperors. Ironically, the hard-won recognition of duality tended to disappear
under the theory of "direct power" which claimed to reduce
to a single papal origin the jurisdiction of State and Church.

---

[4] John Courtney Murray, S.J., "St. Robert Bellarmine on the Indirect
Power," *Theological Studies,* IX (December, 1948), 509.

[5] Ernest J. Burrus, S. J., "The Impact of the New World Discovery upon
the European Thought of Man" from J. Robert Nelson (editor) *No Man Is
Alien*: Essays on the Unity of Mankind. (Leiden: E. J. Brill, 1971), pp. 85-108.

[6] Hobbes, *op. cit.,* p. 614.

[7] Brodrick, *Bellarmine,* I, 252.

The wheel had come to a full circle; its motion had caused values to tumble like kaleidescope pieces. Molina, living during the down-turn of the new cycle, attempted to catch patterns as the pieces whirled by.

A recent writer has said that "the very thing which renders the history of the sixteenth century so tragic is the fact that the medieval conceptions of a united Christendom survived at a time when national policy was veering more and more decisively towards independent and secular aims." [8]

Differences Between the Two Powers

Molina begins his study of relations between Church and State early in the Second Tract. Since *dominium* in general was the subject of the first part of the Second Tract, he discusses the power of jurisdiction in the Twenty-first Disputation. If jurisdiction is understood, he says, the title of property will be more easily understood. First of all, he defines power (*potestas*) as a faculty of someone who has authority and superiority over others to rule and govern them. [9] Such power is divided into lay and ecclesiastical, each distinguished according to its ends—the former ordained to a natural and the latter to a supernatural end—which are mutually subordinate: "Quod fit ut hae duae potestates distinguantur ex parte finium diversorum adinvicem subordinatorum." But Molina says in effect the noble eminence of ecclesiastical power gives it precedence over law power. [10]

The ecclesiastical power which resides in the supreme pontiff as the head of the Church is then distinct from the lay power as Gelasius says in his famous "Two Swords" statement. These two powers, as mentioned above, differ by reason of their ends. Since the natural end of the state is ordered to the supernatural, [11] it follows that the supreme pontiff can order secular

---

[8] Joseph Lecler, S.J., *The Two Sovereignties*: A Study of the Relationship Between Church and State (London: Burns Oates & Washbourne, 1952), p. 66.

[9] « Est facultas alicujus autoritatem et eminentiam super alios habentis ad eorum regimen et gubernationem" *De Justitia et Jure*, II, 21, 105.

[10] "Cum vero nobilitas et eminentia cujusque facultatis ex objecto et fine potissimum pensanda sit, sane pro quantitate excessus supernaturalis finis ad naturalem, salutisque spiritualis animae ad temporalia commoda, pacificumque ac tranquillum hujus vitae statum, judicanda erit nobilitas et eminentia potestatis ecclesiasticae supra potestatem laicam" (II, 21, 106B).

[11] Cf. Francis P. Canavan, S. J., "Subordination of the State to the Church According to Suarez," *Theological Studies*, XII (1951), 354-364. Unlike Molina, Suárez did not hold that the state was ordered to a supernatural end. Father

rulers who are subject to the Church to accommodate themselves to the supernatural end if in their government they have
deviated from it. [12] These two powers also differ as to their
effects, the one supernatural and the other natural. [13] The
third difference between the two is that the ecclesiastical power
was established by Christ by positive divine law while the civil
power of rulers belongs to the realm of human law. [14] They
differ also in that the power of the Supreme Pontiff is the same
throughout the world while the power of secular rulers differs
from country to country. [15] Concerning this difference Molina
quotes a famous figure of speech by Innocent III:

> As God... established two great lights in the firmament of
> the sky... so in the firmament of the universal church...
> He established two great dignities, the greater to rule souls
> as the sun rules the days, the lesser to rule bodies as the
> moon rules the nights; and these are the pontifical authority
> and the royal power. Moreover, as the moon derives her light
> from the sun and is inferior to it in size and quality, in sta-
> tion and in effect, so the royal power derives from the pontifical
> authority the splendour of its dignity.... [16]

Canavan concludes that subordination of the state to the Church is, in Suárez
doctrine, an extrinsic relation, contingent upon the fact of baptism and incor-
poration into the Church and the one society. "It is not a relation flowing
from the nature of the State as such. In other words, for Suárez, the State
is by its nature secular and not ordered to a religious end" (p. 364).

[12] "Habemus deinde, eandem Summi Pontificis potestatem differre a potestate principum secularium sibi subditorum. Primo, ex parte finis: illa namque respicit finem supernaturalem, et media illi proportionata; haec vero respicit finem naturalem, et media ed eum accomodata. Quare cum finis naturalis ad supernaturalem ordinetur: et facultas, quae finem superiorem respicit,
praecipere et ordinare ei facultati debeat, quae inferiorem ac subordinatum
finem respicit; efficitur, ut ad Summum Pontificem spectet praecipere et ordinare secularibus principibus sibi subditis (hoc est iis, qui intra gremium Ecclesiae sunt) ut fini supernaturali se accomodent, quando in suo regimine ab eo
deviant" (II, 21, 109C).

[13] "Differt secundo, quod potestas Summi Pontificis supernaturalis est, ad
supernaturales effectus se extendens: potestas vero principum secularium est
mere naturalis" (ibid.).

[14] "Tertio, potestas Summi Pontificis, non ab Ecclesia, sed a Christo in
Ecclesia est instituta; tametsi illius applicatio ad hanc vel illam personam ex
electione Ecclesiae pendeat: quare de jure divino est positivo. Potestas vero
laica principum secularium de jure est humano, a Republ. ipsa instituta, et
collata principi, ut disputatione sequenti erit manifestum" (II, 21, 109D).

[15] "Quarto differt, quia potestas Summi Pontificis est una in universo orbe:
potestas vero principum secularium, nisi jure belli, aut legitima successione vel
consensu ipsarummet Rerumpublicarum, multae unum communem principem
habeant, multiplicatur pro diversitate Rerumpublicarum sibi principem eligen-
tium" (ibid.).

[16] Carlyle, op. cit., V, 518.

Direct Temporal Power of the Pope

In the Twenty-ninth Disputation Molina takes up the problem of papal power in temporal matters. First of all, he examines the question historically and cites the authors who held the position that the pope had supreme temporal as well as spiritual jurisdiction. According to the theory, the prince's power was a type of delegated authority, an emanation of the papal *magisterium*. Among the authors who held this view were *multi ex jurisperitis*—Panormitanus,[17] Antoninus,[18] Henry of Segusio,[19] Augustinus Triumphus de Ancona.[20]

Molina lists this as an "extreme" position and by no means the common opinion of theologians. Otto Gierke differs with Molina here and contends that "from Gregory VII onwards the Popes and their supporters were unanimous in holding that, so far as the substance is concerned, the Temporal as well as the Spiritual Power belongs to the Chair of Peter and that the separation which is commanded by divine law affects only the Administration, not the Substance."[21] It is a mistake, Gierke continues, to represent the great popes as proclaiming, and the

Lewis (*op. cit.*, II, 629, n. 95) rightly remarks that Innocent III dit not deduce from this analogy a theory of the derivation of the temporal from the spiritual power, but the passage was so interpreted by the canonists. Dante's refutation of Innocent's analogy is translated in part by Lewis (pp. 591-592).

[17] Nicholas de Tudeschis (Panormitanus), a Benedictine who was a pupil of Zabarella, and later professor of canon law at the Universities of Siena and Parma. As Archbishop of Palermo he took a prominent part in the proceedings of the Council of Basel. His great work was *Commentaria in Decretales*. He died in 1453.

[18] Antoninus, St. (1389-1459), Archbishop of Florence, papal theologian to the Council of Florence.

[19] Hostiensis, Henry (Blessed Henry of Segusio, d, 1271), Cardinal-bishop of Ostia, Italian canonist.

[20] Augustinus Triumphus of Ancona was born in 1243, became an Augustinian and studied at Paris. Ewart Lewis describes him as one of the most important intellectual defenders of the *plenitudo potestatis papae*. "He was the author of many theological works, including commentaries on the *Sentences* of Peter Lombard and the *Metaphysics* of Aristotle, and of a number of publicistic works, of which the most important was his *Summa de Potestate Ecclesiastica*, variously dated 1320 or 1324-28 and dedicated to John XXII. It was a systematic and comprehensive exposition, in rigorous scholastic form, of the extreme doctrines already outlined by Aegidius Romanus and James of Viterbo; it was widely read in his own day and printed several times before the sixteenth century" (Lewis, *op. cit.*, II, 384-385).

[21] Otto Gierke, *Political Theories of the Middle Age*, trans. with an Introduction by Frederic William Maitland (2d ed.; Cambridge: At the University Press, 1951), pp. 107-108.

common opinion of the later Middle Ages as accepting, only
that sort of indirect power in temporal affairs which was
claimed for the Apostolic See by later theorists. Gierke piles
text upon impressive text which prove, according to him, that
such was the common opinion of theologians of the later Middle
Ages. Among the authorities cited are some of those whom
Molina lists. [22]

Molina follows this exposition of the extreme papalist claim
with what he terms some suasive reasons. These reasons and
Molina's refutation of them will be included together. The first
argument advanced to support the above opinion is that Christ
as man is lord of the earth and has supreme temporal jurisdiction. All lay powers are subject to him and he may depose
rulers at will. This power Christ could communicate to whom-
soever he willed and Christ left this power to the supreme
pontiff. [23] Molina disposes of the argument trenchantly: The
power Christ had was *excellentiae*, i.e., it belonged to him as
man by reason of his pre-eminent dignity and was not communicated to the supreme pontiff. [24]

The second argument contends that Christ instituted a perfect society in founding the Church and such a perfect society
demands that, even in temporal affairs, secular rulers must be

---

[22] *Ibid.*, pp. 105-118.

[23] "Quoniam Christus, quatenus homo, est dominus orbis, aut, ut nos disputatione praecedente ostendimus, habet supremam potestatem in temporalibus,
ita ut non solum potestates omnes laicae illi omnino subjaceant, possitque illas
pro arbitratu deponere, sed etiam res omnes creatae illi omnino subsint, ita
ut absque cujusquam injuria, possit eas concedere cui voluerit: sed Christus
vicario suo reliquit potestatem, quam habuit: ergo tam latam potestatem in
temporalibus habet, quam latam illi tribuunt authores citati" (II, 29, 136E).

[24] "Ad primum negandum est minor: potestas namque illa Christi circa
temporalia fuit excellentiae in Christo, quam proinde negandum est reliquisse
Summo Pontifici" (II, 29, 149A).

[25] Credit for the figure of the two-headed monster probably belongs to
the famous canonist Henry de Segusio (Hostiensis) who, in his *Summa super
Titulis Decretalium* (quoted by Lewis, *op. cit.*, II, 527), had stressed the need
for one ultimate head: "For since we are one body in Christ, it would be
a monstrosity that we should have two heads."

McIlwain (*op. cit.*, p. 237) observes of this author: "The complete and final
exposition of these newer views [on full temporal jurisdiction of the pope] in
their most developed forms is to be found in the famous *Summa super
Titulis Decretalium*, popularly known as the *Summa Aurea*, of Henricus de
Segusio, Cardinal of Ostia (Hostiensis) who died in 1271, one of the most
famous of all the glosses on the canons, of which some eleven editions appeared
after the invention of printing."

Carlyle prints some of these glosses with helpful commentary (*op. cit.*, V,
325-332).

subject to the one supreme head; otherwise the Church would
be some monstrous body (*monstruosum corpus*) [25] with more
than one head. [26] The presupposition of this argument would
seem to be that a perfect society is one which includes every
other society. The classic definition of a perfect society is one
which has within itself all the means necessary for it to attain
its end. Molina inclines to this definition in his reply. [27] He
states that all the argument really proves is that temporal rulers
are subject to the supreme pontiff, inasmuch as the supernatural
end demands it. In that sense the state is subordinate to the
Church and is, as it were, included within it. He concludes
with an important sentence: "Looked at in itself, the state is
a complete society, whose highest authority is the temporal
ruler." [28] The third argument is less theoretical and more
historical. It is divided into three sections. The first historical
event cited is the transfer by the supreme pontiff of the empire
from the Greeks to the Romans, at which time he gave seven
German princes the right to elect an emperor subject to his
approval. [29] In his reply Molina justifies the transfer as neces-

---

[26] "Secundo, Christus instituit Rempublicam Ecclesiae perfectissimam, quae
tamquam monarchia ad unum dumtaxat supremum caput reduceretur: ergo
potestates laicae in temporalibus subjectae omnino sunt Summo Pontifici, non
minus, quam optimates suo Regi subjecti sunt; alioquin si in temporalibus
Summo Pontifici non subjicerentur, regimen Reipublicae Ecclesiasticae non ad
unum supremum caput, sed ad plura, tamquam monstruosum corpus reduceretur » (II, 29, 136E-137A).

[27] J. Neville Figgis "Political Thougth in the Sixteenth Century," *The Cambridge Modern History*, ed. A. W. Ward, G. W. Prothero, and Stanley Leathes
[New York: The Macmillan Co., 1905], III, 756-759) maintains that the theory
of the Church as a *societas perfecta* began in the age of Molina. This view,
he says, was not the same as the medieval,, which identified the Church with
the hierarchy and in any case contemplated a single polity with diversities
of function, known as temporal and spiritual. A view of the Church as a
respublica perfecta, Figgis continues, can be found in Bellarmine, Molina, and
Suárez: "The concept of the Church as a *societas perfecta* like the State admits the view that each has its own orbit, its own principles and its own
methods; and they need not collide with one another... Molina, in whom
both views jostle one another, says that the State is imperfect without the
Church" (p. 758).

[28] "Ad secundum dicendum est, solum probare, potestates laicas omnino
subjici in temporalibus Summo Pontifici, quantum necesse est ad finem supernaturalem. Eatenus namque Respublica temporalis subordinatur Reipublicae
spirituali Ecclesiae, et in ea quasi includitur: secundum se autem Respublica
temporalis integra quaedam Respublica in se est, cujus potestas summa est
Princeps temporalis" (II, 29, 149A).

[29] In Disputation 24 of the Second Tract, Molina had discussed the origin
of the imperial dignity (II, 24, 119E-122B).
The complex question of the origin of the Holy Roman Empire is pain-

sary for the conservation of the Church. Since it was Germany which assumed the office of defender of the Church and offered its resources for that end, it was only right that the selection of the emperor be made by German princes and approved by the pope. The agreement was such that without legitimate cause neither party could deprive the other of its rights in this case. [30]

The second historical instance involved the deposition of an emperor already elected and crowned, as happened when Innocent IV deposed Frederick II. [31] Molina's reply to the complex question was boldly simple; it belongs to a pope to depose an emperor for a just cause because of the plentitude of power which he possesses over those matters which concern the supernatural end. Also by an exceptional right which was unique he could depose because of the nature of the right of approval, coronation, and anointing [32] which the pope had in the case of the German emperor. A final reason why the pope could depose an emperor was that the office of the emperor was instituted to defend the Roman and universal Church and the office of

---

stakingly treated by Walter Ullmann, *The Growth of Papal Government in the Middle Ages*: A Study of the Ideological Relation of Clerical to Lay Power (London: Methuen & Co. Ltd., 1955), pp. 44-86.

[30] "Translationem illam Imperii licuisse Summo Pontifici, quatenus id ad conservationem Ecclesiae erat necessarium. Cum autem Germania munus illud Imperatoris, defensorisque Ecclesiae, assumeret, viresque suas ad id offerret, recta ratio postulabat, ut electio Imperatoris ad Germanos optimates pertineret: quare quasi pactum quoddam fuit tempore Ottonis tertii, ut electio ad optimates illos, approbatio vero et confirmatio Imperatoris ad Summum Pontificem pertineret: et ob id, neque Summus Pontifex, absque legitima causa, potest illos privare jure illo, neque a Summo Pontifice tolli potest jus, quod habet ad confirmandam et approbandam electionem" (II, 29, 149B).

[31] For a discussion of this famous case cf. Carlyle, *op. cit.*, Vol. V, *passim*, but especially pp. 293-317.

Cf. also J. B. LoGrasso, *Ecclesia et Status*: Fontes Selecti Historiae Juris Publici Ecclesiastici (Roma: Apud Aedes Pontif. Universitatis Gregorianae, 1952), pp. 191-192, for a reprint of Frederick's deposition by the Second Council of Lyons.

[32] Ullmann (*op. cit.*, p. 68) links the anointing to the office of the emperor as defender of the Church: "We should take note that whenever the pope referred to the unction [anointing] in his letters, he invariably employed a phrasing which revealed the purpose, the telos, the finis, of the papal unction: the employment of conjunctive terms, such as the final 'that,' 'in order to' ('ut') or 'for the sake of' ('ad') are expressions characteristic of papal phraseology as well as papal ideology: Pepin was anointed '*in order* to defend the Roman Church' or 'for the sake of defence' or of liberation—these are standing phrase in the papal letters.... In short, then, the Frankish king, by virtue of the papally conferred office ... was to be the defender and protector of the Roman Church."

the emperor made its tenant a sort of an assistant to the pope, exercising the sword of temporal power at the will of the pope. [33]

The third historical event which Molina mentions is a classic—Pope Zacharias' deposition of Childeric, [34] King of the Franks, because he was useless to the realm, and the pope's conferring of the crown on Pepin, father of Charlemagne. This event, famous in itself, has added interest because it was cited as a precedent by Gregory VII in his action against Henry IV. [35] Writing to the Bishop of Metz in March, 1081, Gregory said:

> Another Roman Pontiff, Zacharias, deposed the king of the Franks from his kingdom, not so much because of his crimes, as because he was not suitable to exercise such great authority; and he set up in his place Pippin, father of Charlemagne the Emperor, and absolved all the Franks from the oath of fidelity which they had taken to the previous king. [36]

Ullmann remarks that Zacharias' action, though much distorted by Gregory, was perfectly justifiable from the point of view of

---

[33] "Imperatoris depositionem ex justa causa pertinere ad Summum Pontificem. Tum pro potestate plenissima, quam in temporalibus habet ad omnia, quae spirituale bonum, finisque supernaturalis postulat. Tum etiam, quoniam jure peculiari ad eum spectat approbatio, coronatio, et unctio Imperatoris. Tum denique quoniam munus Imperatoris ad defendendam Romanam universalemque Ecclesiam institutum est, quasi Imperator tanquam minister Summi Pontificis sit, gladium jurisdictionis temporalis Summi Pontificis ad illius nutum sua potentia exercens" (II, 29, 149C).

[34] Ullmann makes a distinction between deposition and excommunication. Writing in the context of the investiture controversy, he says: "Secondly, formal *deposition* of a reigning king must, in theory, be distinguished from his excommunication. Whilst the latter was the consequence of a purely religious or moral disobedience and could be inflicted upon any member of Christian society, deposition was the consequence of the king's uselessness. He was no longer useful, because as a consequence of his disobedience to papal orders, he did not execute *justitia* laid down by the pope. Hence he was to be deprived of his title to rule. And we may recall that, according to Gregory, Childeric was deposed by Zacharias, not because he was iniquitous, but because he was useless. Incapacity to govern was the effect of excommunication. Deposition, on the other hand, concerned the title-deed, the basis, of the king's position: it was this which was taken away and he therefore had no longer any right to rule.... Excommunication concerned Henry the Christian, deposition Henry the king. Exercise of rulership was, according to hierocratic ideology, an honour or a privilege, and this must be lost if the ruler tries to follow his own views of government to the detriment of the whole body" (*op. cit.*, p. 301).

[35] It is interesting to note that Molina never cites the Gregory VII-Henry IV controversy.

[36] *Church and State Through the Centuries*: A Collection of Historic Documents with Commentaries, ed. Sidney Z. Ehler and John B. Morrall (Westminster, Md.: The Newman Press, 1954), p. 34.

papal ideology. Since Childeric was useless, and according to papal ideology usefulness (or uselessness) could be judged only by the criterion which papal ideology itself supplied, modern absolute criteria will only blur the issue. [37]   Molina's answer, in the light of our present knowledge of history, is less than satisfactory. He simply states that the papal action was necessary for the spiritual good of the kingdom. As if conscious of its inadequacy, he concludes: "And besides, in both cases there was the consent and request of the nobles and people of these countries." [38]

In the final suasive argument which Molina brings forward, he includes two papal pronouncements; one is the letter of Nicholas II and the other is Boniface VIII's *Unam Sanctam.* [39] Admitting that Boniface's claims are much clearer, Molina confines himself for the most part to a study of them. This bull is one of the most important church documents of all time and rates top billing in any study of Church-State relations. It must be remembered here that Molina is discussing and refuting arguments for the opinion that the pope has supreme direct temporal jurisdiction in the world. McIlwain's observation is very much to the point:

> However sweeping its demands, there is in the bull no explicit clai mto a direct power in temporal matters. This is very significant but no one can doubt it who reads the whole bull with attention. [40]

Molina must have read it with attention, for he quite agrees with this estimate and says that all the *Unam Sanctam* proves is that the supreme pontiff has supreme power in temporal affairs only when such power is necessary to the spiritual good and that such is all the two popes wished to express. With this Molina concludes his exposition and refutation of the opinion that the pope has direct supreme temporal jurisdiction.

---

[37] Ullmann, *op. cit.*, p. 35.

Cf. H. Büttner, "Aus den Anfängen des abendländischen Staatsgedankens," in *Historisches Jahrbuch der Görresgesellschaft*, LXXI (1952), 77-90.

[38] This assertion of Molina would seem to be gratuitous. For a factual account of the matter see L. Halphen, *Charlemagne & l'empire carolingien* (Paris: A. Michel, 1947), pp. 21ff.

[39] For a well-developed discussion of the entire period and the *Unam Sanctam* in particular, see Carlyle, *op. cit.*, V, 374-440; also Joseph Lecler, S.J., "L'argument des Deux Glaives dans les controverses politiques du moyen age: ses origines et son développement" in *Récherches de science religieuse*, XXI (1931), 299-339; XXII (1932), 151-177 and 280-303.

[40] McIlwain, *op. cit.*, p. 246.

He refers the reader who wants further arguments "minoris momenti" to John of Paris' *De Potestate Regia et Papali* [41] and to Navarrus. [42]

After proposing the extreme papalist claims and refuting their arguments one by one, Molina deftly introduces the opposite point of view. This opinion is that the sovereign pontiff has no jurisdiction at all in temporal affairs but only in spiritual matters. [43] The reason alleged to support this position was that Christ gave Peter the keys of the kingdom of heaven, which is not an earthly kingdom. The successors of Peter, therefore, have no power at all in temporal affairs. Although Molina cites no authors who held this opinion, he refers the reader to one of the best-known writers in the field for further arguments: "Rationes alias, earumque solutiones lege apud Turrecrematam." [44]

---

[41] The section to which Molina refers his readers is entitled "Premittuntur preambula ad solutionem predictorum et ad intelligendum quam auctoritatem Papa habeat a Christo in temporalibus, et primo ponuntur auctoritates Petro et Apostolis a Christo commissae" (Jean Leclerq, O.S.B., *Jean de Paris et l'ecclésiologie du XIII° siècle* [Paris: Librairie Philosophique J. Vrin, 1942], p. 173).

[42] Navarrus is the name by which Martin Aspilcueta, a famous Spanish canonist and moral theologian, is known. Born in the kingdom of Navarre in 1491 he lived to the patriarchal age of 95. He studied at Alcalá, taught canon law at Toulouse, Salamanca, and Coimbra. His best-known work is *Manuale sive Enchiridion Confessariorum et Poenitentium* published about 1568. He was still alive when Molina wrote much of the *De Justitia* (see Hugo Hurter, *Nomenclator Literarius Theologiae Catholicae*: Theologos Exhibens Aetate, Natione, Disciplinis Distinctos [Innsbruck: Wagner, 1906], I, 124-127).

[43] "Quidam in extremam sententiam abierunt, nempe Summum pontificem nullam omnino habere potestatem in temporalibus, sed in spiritualibus dumtaxat" (II, 29, 137E).

John of Paris begins his preface by stating that there are two errors about the authority of the Church. The first, that of those who call themselves Waldensians, is that the pope has no lordship in temporal affairs nor can he possess worldly goods: "Nam error Waldensium scilicet papae et prelatis ecclesiasticis repugnare dominium in temporalibus nec licet habere divitias temporales" (Leclercq, *op. cit.*, p. 173).

[44] II, 29, 138A.

John of Turrecremata (Torquemada—not to be confused with his famous fellow-Dominican Thomas Torquemada [1420-1498], Inquisitor-General) was a Spanish Dominican born in Valladolid in 1388. He was present at the Council of Constance in 1415 and in 1431 was made Master of the Sacared Palace by Pope Eugene IV. His support of the papal cause at the Council of Basel was rewarded by the cardinalate in 1439. He died in 1468. Among several theological works the most important was his *Summa contra Ecclesiae et Primatus Apostoli Adversarios*.

"Modern political thought, as distinct from medieval, begins not with Gerson or Nicolas Cusanus but with John of Torquemada's *De Potestate Papae*. In this work the arguments for monarchy are to be found set forth very much

Between these two extreme opinions, Molina continues, a middle course should be followed. This course is marked clearly by some conclusions in which the following agree: Vitoria, [45] Soto, Navarrus, Turrecremata, Henricus, [46] Albertus Pighius, [47] Peter Paludanus, [48] Thomas Waldensis, [49] Sander, [50] Ca-

---

as they were to be quoted for a couple of centuries. Of course much of his argument is concerned with Petrine texts. Yet it may be doubted whether the Divine right of monarchy ever had a more efficient defender" (Figgis, "Political Thought in the Sixteenth Century," *op. cit.*, p. 736).

A more recent writer says that the *Summa* "may be taken as the most authoritative statement of the principles of the papalist reaction of the fifteenth century" (Lewis, *op. cit.*, I, 239).

[45] For a study of the influence of John of Paris on Vitoria, cf. Beltrán de Heredia, O.P., "Doctrina de Francisco de Victoria sobre las relaciones entre la iglesia y el estado y fuentes de la misma," *Ciencia Tomista*, LVI (1937), 27-39.

[46] Henry of Ghent (Henricus Gandavensis, *ca.* 1217-1293), *Doctor Solemnis*, Dutch theologian and scholastic philosopher. Molina refers to his *Quodlibeta*, vi. 23.

[47] Albertus Pighius (1490-1542), Belgian controversialist and mathematician. The work Molina refers to is *Hierarchiae Ecclesiasticae Assertio*.

[48] Pierre de la Palu (Petrus de Palude or Paludanus, 1274-1342), French Dominican theologian, Archbishop, Patriarch of Jerusalem, who wrote a commentary on the *Sentences*.

[49] Thomas Waldensis (Thomas Netter) was born about 1380 at Saffron Walden, Essex, whence he is often called Walden or Waldensis. He entered the Carmelite Order in London. In 1409 he attended the Council of Pisa. He opposed the Lollards, Wiclif and Hus, his chief work being *Doctrinale Fidei Ecclesiae Catholicae contra Wiclevistas et Hussitas*. First published in 1426, it was reprinted in part in Salamanca in 1556-1557 and reprinted as a whole in Venice in 1571 (cf. Charles Lethbridge Kingsford, "Thomas Netter," *The Dictionary of National Biography*, ed. Sir Leslie Stephen and Sir Sidney Lee [22 vols.; London: Oxford University Press, 1937-1938], XIV, 231-234).

[50] Nicholas Sander (Sanders) was born in England in 1530. Educated at Oxford, he left England in 1559 and became professor of theology at Louvain where he wrote his great work *De visibili monarchia ecclesiae*, published in 1571. It is to this work that Molina refers. Sander was considered one of the chief leaders of the English Catholic party in exile. Summoned to Rome in 1572, he went to Spain the next year and from there to Ireland, where he died in 1581. Father Pollen says of him: "He belonged to the first group of English exiles, who, never having lived in England during the persecution, never realized how complete Elizabeth's victory was. He believed, and acted consistently in this belief, that strong measures, like war and excommunication, were the true remedies for the great evils of the time; a mistaken policy, which though supported by the popes of that day, was subsequently changed" (J. H. Pollen, S.J., "Nicholas Sander," *The Catholic Encyclopedia*, XIII [1913], 435-436; also J. H. Pollen, S.J., "Dr. Nicholas Sander," *The English Historical Review*, VI [1891], 36-47).

Allen (*op. cit.*, p. 203, n. 1) says that in England Sanders was nicknamed "Slanders," "but his work is no more slanderous or inaccurate than that of other fervid partisans."

jetan, [51] Durandus, [52] and John of Paris. [53]   The last name, by
far the most important on the list, is followed by this cautionary
sentence: "John of Paris, however, restricts papal power in
temporal matters somewhat more than is proper in favor of
the secular princes." [54]

Another caution follows.   Molina warns his reader that in
the following discussion he is not referring to the temporal
jurisdiction of the pope in the papal states.   "In these states
the sovereign pontiffs have supreme temporal jurisdiction just
like other rulers in their own areas." [55]   St. Thomas makes the
same exception.   Generally Thomas defends the traditional
Gelasian principle of the distinctive character of the two swords,
which is to be preserved unless, as in the case of the papal states,
secular power is combined with spiritual authority. [56]

---

[51] Cardinal Cajetan (Thomas de Vio, 1469-1534), Italian Dominican theologian, philosopher, and scripture exegete, one of the most famous commentators on the works of St. Thomas.   Molina refers to his *Opuscula Omnia*.

[52] Durandus (Guilelmus a Sancto Porciano), French Dominican philosopher
and theologian who died in 1334.   Molina's reference is vague but it would
seem to be to his *De Jurisdictione Ecclesiastica et de Legibus*.

[53] Jean Quidort, or Jean Le Sourd, was born about 1269, probably in Paris.
He joined the Dominican Order after 1290.   His writings show the influence
of Aquinas' works.   He died at Bordeaux in 1306.   For a careful analysis of
his political theory, cf. John C. Murray, S.J., "Contemporary Orientations of
Catholic Thought on Church and State in the Light of History," *Theological
Studies*, X, 177-234.

[44] "Tametsi Joannes Parisien. nonnihil in favorem principum secularium
plus justo potestatem summorum Pontificum ad temporalia restringat" (II,
29, 138B-C).

Bellarmine later expressed a similar reserve about classing John of Paris
with the proponents of the middle position.   Concerning John, he wrote:
"Quoniam incidit in tempora turbulenta ob discordiam inter Bonifacium VIII
pontificem et Philippum regem Gallorum, et ipse Parisiis agebat et docebat,
videtur propensior fuisse erga regem quam erga pontificem" (Leclercq, *op. cit.*,
p. 157).

Of John of Paris' middle position, Leclercq (*ibid.*, p. 160), writes: "Mais
par là se manifestait aussi la complexité de sa doctrine, et la modération qui
la caractérise: il était difficile de classer Jean de Paris parmi les théoriciens
extrémists; ... Heureusement, de bons juges ne s'y étaient pas trompés: Turrecremata et Victoria n'avaient pas craint de l'utiliser largement, Molina et Bos-
suet de l'approuver, et S. Bellarmin de lui faire prendre rang parmi les con-
tinuateurs fidèles de la doctrine de saint Thomas, avec ceux qui soutiennent
l'opinion commune des théologiens."   He continues: "Mais d'est la *via media*
inaugurée par Jean de Paris qui S. Bellarmin reconnaitra plus tard 'l'opinion
commune des théologiens catholiques'" (p. 164).

[55] "In ejusmodi namque terris Summi Pontifices habent supremam potestatem et jurisdictionem temporalem, non secus ac reges in suis propriis. ...
Quare in illis utrumque habet gladium plenissime" (II, 29, 137D).

[56] Nisi forte potestati spirituali etiam saecularis potestas conjungatur sicut

Although Molina excepts the papal states from the discussion, he leaves little doubt as to what he would consider the
ideal situation. It is wrong, he says, for ecclesiastics, especially
prelates, to get so involved in temporal affairs that their spiritual
duties suffer. The spiritual care of the Church is not compatible
with administrative rule in temporal affairs. [57]

Pope Is Not Lord of the World

The first conclusion Molina draws after these preliminaries
is that the pope is not lord of the world in temporal matters;
neither is he emperor or king, nor is the power of jurisdiction
exercised by temporal rulers derived from him. [58] Temporal
power is totally different from papal power. The former is
derived ultimately from God but immediately by the consent
and election of the commonwealth choosing a ruler. The papal
power comes from God through Christ who instituted it to
govern His Church for its supernatural end only. [59]

Molina supports his first conclusion by citing a number of
authorities: Pope Nicholas' letter to the Emperor Michael, Gelasius, Pope John, Innocent III, Pope Miltiades, St. Bernard.
Furthermore, he says, the pope's power in temporal affairs could
not be greater than his spiritual power and yet the latter is
limited to the baptized and he has no jurisdiction over infidels. [60]

---

in Papa, qui utriusque potestatis apicem tenet, scilicet spiritualis et saecularis"
(*Commentary on Sentences of Peter Lombard*, II D. 44, qu. 2, art. 3). Cf. also
McIlwain, *op. cit.*, p. 236, and Carlyle, *op. cit.*, V, 352.

Cardinal Bellarmine has some acute observations on this passage in *De
Romano Pontifice*, Vol. V, cap. v.

[57] "Quamvis inquam, haec ita sint, nihilominus nefas est Ecclesiasticis,
praesertim praelatis, plus se immiscere curis et negotiis temporalibus, quam
postulat recta ratio, et quam patiatur eorum cura et munus in spiritualibus,
cui ante omnia incumbere tenentur. Quia ergo cura in spiritualibus Ecclesiae
universalis non compatitur secum regimen, et administrationem imperii in temporalibus" (II, 29, 138E).

[58] "Summus Pontifex neque ita habet potestatem jurisdictionis in temporalibus, ut sit dominus orbis, aut ut nomen regis vel Imperatoris sibi possit
vendicare, neque ita ut ab eo dominium jurisdictionis temporalis ad reges
derivetur" (II, 29, 139B).

[59] "Sed potestas regalis est omnino diversa a papali, quae a Deo, mediante
consensu et electione Reipublicae regem sibi ad administrationem in temporalibus, finemque naturalem constituentis, habet ortum: papalis vero ortum habet
a Deo per Christum eam instituentem ad regimen per comparationem ad finem
supernaturalem dumtaxat" (*ibid.*).

[60] "Praeterea, non majorem potestatem habet Summus Pontifex in temporalibus, quam in spiritualibus: sed in infideles nullam potestatem habet in
spiritualibus" (II, 29, 140E).

Therefore, he is not lord of the world. Even though Christ possessed all temporal power by way of excellence, he did not communicate this power to the supreme pontiff.[61] As a consequence of the above, Molina goes on to say that ordinarily it does not belong to the supreme pontiff to appoint kings or to depose them but this power belongs to political societies, always supposing right reason and a just cause.[62]

It is a good idea to consult the supreme pontiff, Molina continues, when there is a matter of dispute and he can settle the matter with greater justice to all; but especially it belongs to the pope to intervene when, as is often the case, the spiritual good of a country is at stake and he may impose proper penalties upon those who would block his decision.[63] Although he does not mention it, Molina would seem to have in mind the Bull of Alexander VI, "Inter Cetera," of 1493 assigning zones of influence to Spain and Portugal.[64] According to Lecler, it is still a matter of dispute among historians whether the papacy was claiming the right to divide the New World between two colonial powers, or whether it had only in view the organization of its missionary apostolate.[65] Molina's position as a Spaniard in Portugal was rather delicate and he can readily be excused from mentioning by name the papal action he seems to be describing.

The rulers of the world do not depend for their power on the supreme pontiff as do the bishops of the world, whom the

---

[61] "Potestas autem illa ad temporalia, quam disputatione precedente ostendimus esse in Christo, est in eo excellentiae, quam proinde, sicut neque potestatem excellentiae in spiritualibus, quibus illum praeficiebat, Summo Pontifici non communicavit" (II, 29, 141C).

[62] "Ad Summum Pontificem via ordinaria, cessanteque fidei causa, et exigentia, non qualicumque, sed admodum per comparationem ad finem supernaturalem, neque pertinere creare Reges et alias potestates laicas, neque etiam eas deponere, sed id pertinere ad Respublicas ipsas, quarum, ut est Reges sibi constituere, sic etiam est eos deponere, postulante id recta ratione, occurrente justa et urgente causa" (II, 29, 141E).

[63] "Optimum tamen consilium est, ut quando dubii alicujus potest esse suspicio, et quando non tota Respublica, sed major illius pars consentit, consulatur Summus Pontifex, ut ejus interveniente authoritate id fiat, in majorem causae justificationem: praesertim cum, ut plurimum, bonum spirituale commune Reipublicae inde pendeat, quo dato, ad Summum Pontificem spectat suam interponere authoritatem, bonumque commune censuris et aliis modis juvare comprimendo eos, qui id impedire contendunt" (II, 29, 141E).

[64] The text of the bull is printed in LoGrasso, op. cit., pp. 239-243.

An English translation is contained in Church and State Through the Centuries, pp. 155-159

[65] Lecler, The Two Sovereignties, p. 66.

pope can create and remove at will; however, he should not remove even them without cause. [66] Nor does there exist a type of feudal dependence upon the supreme pontiff. [67]

The next section is somewhat confusing. [68] Bringing up the case of the German emperors, he says there is a *greater dependence* on the supreme pontiff than would be the case with other rulers of the Christian world, since the Emperor's position is dependent on the approval and confirmation of his election by the supreme pontiff. [68] Perhaps the terminology is unfortunate.

---

[66] "Non ergo eo modo Reges pendent a potestate Summi Pontificis, quo Episcopi constituti per diversa loca, quos et creare et amovere potest tamquam supremus in spiritualibus Ecclesiae pastor ac moderator: tametsi sine rationabili causa eos amovere non debeat" (II, 29, 142A).

[67] "Neque pendent ab eo perinde ac optimates Regni pendent a Rege, ac perinde atque Reges, vel alii Principes, ab Imperatore non exempti, ab eo pendent, esto ab Imperatore amoveri nequeant" (II, 29, 142B).

[68] The following observation seems pertinent. Professor A. L. Lilley, writing of another Jesuit political thinker of the same period as Molina, remarks: "If the process of his [Suárez] argument seems to us often tortuous and not infrequently to lead to conclusions which are in violent contrast with the general principles from which he set out, that may be after all less his fault than ours. We can deal directly with facts as history gives them to us and frame whatever theory fits them independently of the prescriptions of past theory. ... And therefore we find it difficult to be fair to those thinkers of the past whose interpretation of changing fact had to be made to conform somehow to the requirements of a sacrosanct theory. That was roughly the position of the Jesuit thinkers of the later sixteenth century in as far as they aimed at being political theorists, as indeed it was of all the orthodox Christian publicists of the time whether Catholic or Reformed. The facts with which they had to deal were novel facts, and they were by no means unconscious of their novelty. But they held themselves bound by a theory which corresponded naturally only to a very different set of facts. In attempt to be true both to the altered fact and to the authoritative theory they seem to us either confused or evasive where to themselves they seemed only to be making the necessary distinctions" ("Francisco Suarez," *The Social and Political Ideas of Some Great Thinkers of the Sixteenth and Seventeenth Centuries*, ed. F. J. C. Hearnshaw [London: George C. Harrap & Co., Ltd., 1926], pp. 93-94).

The author's implication is that Suárez and the other Jesuit writers of the sixteenth century were theologians but not philosophers. This, of course, is not true—they were eminently both. E.g., Molina's greatest claim to fame rests on his *Concordia* in which he relates a dogma of theology (actual grace) to a conclusion of philosophy (freedom of the will).

[69] "Quodammodo vero major est dependentia Imperatorum Germanorum a Summo Pontifice, quam aliorum Regum catholicorum: eo quod Germanum Imperium ... creatum sit dependenter ab approbatione, et confirmatione Summi Pontificis" (II, 29, 142B).

The origin and history of the Imperial dignity was discussed by Molina in a separate article: "De ortu Imperatoriae dignitatis et quatuor illis praecipuis orbis imperiis, de quibus Daniel 2. Et num juste fuerint comparata" (II, 24, 119E-122B).

A phrase such as "certain dependence" might have conveyed his meaning more precisely.

Molina draws a second inference from his first conclusion that the sovereign pontiff is not lord of the world in temporal jurisdiction. The inference is that there is no power in the pope *directly* to settle disputes, quarrels, and contentions among secular rulers nor can those civil laws which do not deviate from the supernatural end be invalidated by the supreme pontiff. [70] Although the latter has power to legitimize children in those areas which pertain to ecclesiastical discipline, such as receiving of Holy Orders, he has no power to legitimize those children when it pertains to the civil and temporal order such as hereditary succession in which illegitimate children are licitly prohibited by civil law. [71] What Molina has just affirmed he seems to deny in the next sentence. If the common spiritual good demands it, he may, even without the consent of the secular ruler, use his power to legitimize children even in those areas which pertain to temporal administration. [72] It follows, he says, that secular rulers and their courts in the temporal administration of the state are exempt from the power of the supreme

[70] "Secundo infero, in Summo Pontifice non esse potestatem judicandi directe causas, litesque et contentiones temporales inter Principes, neque item posse Summum Pontificem infirmare eas leges civiles Principum secularium, quae a supernaturali fine non deviant" (II, 29, 142C).

[71] "Et quamvis legitimare possit quocumque ad spiritualia, ut ad ordines suscipiendos, ad beneficia Ecclesiastica obtinenda, et universim ad ea, quae ad Ecclesiasticam jurisdictionem spectant: non tamen potest legitimare ad ea, quae ad jurisdictionem civilem et temporalem pertinent, ut ad successionem in haereditate, et alia, quae legibus civilibus licite filiis illegitimis sunt prohibita" (*ibid.*).

Molina mentions expressly Innocent III and the decretal *Per venerabilem* in which Innocent refused to legitimize the sons of a French count for secular inheritance. As Lewis (*op. cit.*, II, 525) points out, the pope "incidentally asserted a papal right to exercise jurisdiction on such matters as the legitimization of heirs 'casually,' 'on investigation of specific cases,' especially if a petitioner, like the king of France in a similar case, was subject to no secular lord. The legitimation of bastards, he maintained, was an instance of a case in which ecclesiastical and civil jurisdiction overlapped, 'in which, if there is anything difficult or ambiguous, recourse should be had to the judgment of the apostolic see.' This *obiter dictum* became the classic reference for the whole theory of casual jurisdiction: i.e. an abnormal jurisdiction which would come into play in specific cases, as contrasted to the 'ordinary' jurisdiction of a normal superior."

The letter of Innocent may be found in LoGrasso, *op. cit.*, pp. 170-174.

[72] "Nisi forte Principes seculares consentirent, ut Summus Pontifex ea etiam in parte legitimaret; vel nisi bonum commune spirituale id in aliquo eventu postularet; tunc enim, invito etiam Principe seculari, legitimare posset in iis quae secundum se ad jurisdictionem pertinent secularem" (II, 29, 142C).

pontiff except in those matters which pertain to the supernatural end, if there has been a deviation from it, or when
something is altogether necessary for the common spiritual
good. [73]

The second conclusion Molina draws is that the pope has
universal jurisdiction over, but not ownership of, the temporal
goods of the Church. He is not free to dispose of anything at
will but only for a reasonable cause. If he acts otherwise, such
a disposition is invalid and he is bound to make restitution to
the Church. Citing both Turrecremata and Cajetan, Molina says
this is the common opinion among theologians. The reason
given is that the possessions of the Holy See and of individual
sees belong to the dioceses themselves and not to the one who
happens to be governing them. [74]

Up till now Molina has been discussing *direct* power of the
pope to intervene in temporal affairs. His vacillating position
leaves much to be desired. He seems to hold firmly to the position that there is no direct power of the pope in temporal
affairs, then subtly inserts his escape clause—unless it is absolutely necessary for the spiritual common good. Following
this, for the first time he introduces the notion of *indirect*
power. "Indirectly also, by way of fraternal correction, both
he and other prelates can intervene in secular affairs and controversies among rulers." [75] Here he drops the matter, except
to cite some historical examples, with the promise that he will
treat fraternal correction in the Fifth Tractate. [76] Molina is

---

[73] "Haec omnia ex eo sunt manifesta, quod Principes seculares eorumque
tribunalia in temporalis Reipublicae administratione, exempta sunt a potestate
Summi Pontificis, praeterquam in iis, quae ad finem supernaturalem pertinent,
si quando ab eo deviarent, aut quando aliquid omnino necessarium esset ad
bonum spirituale commune, ut dicemus" (II, 29, 142D).

[74] "Licet Summus Pontifex jurisdictionem universalem habeat in temporalia
bona Ecclesiae, non tamen est illorum dominus, sed dispensator ac gubernator,
qui proinde non ad libitum de illis potest disponere, sed solum ex rationabili
causa. ... Ratio vero illius est, quoniam hujusmodi bona non sunt collata
Summis Pontificibus, aut aliis praelatis Ecclesiae, sed quaedam Ecclesiae Ro-
manae, quaedam vero particularibus Ecclesiis" (II, 29, 143C).

[75] "Indirecte etiam, per modum correctionis fraternae, possunt, tam ipse,
quam alii praelati inferiores, se intromittere in rebus secularibus, et in con-
troversiis principum" (II, 29, 142C).

[76] In the first disputation of the Fifth Tractate Molina discusses fraternal
correction but sheds little light on the question here of indirect power of the
pope in temporal affairs. "Discrimen inter correctionem fraternam et judicia-
lem. Et quarum virtutum actus sit judicium, justitiaeque exequutio per potestates publicas, materia scilicet ad objectum hujus quinti de justitia tractatus,
ad quod caetera, de quibus in eo est sermo, attributionem habent" (V, 1,
2737B-2739C).

now in a position to present his views on the indirect power theory. A brief review of its antecedents is in order.

The Theory of Indirect Power

The theory of indirect power rose during the period following the appearance of national states. [77] Shortly before that period, St. Thomas had pointed out in commenting on Aristotle's *Politics* that the government of pagan kings, because of its natural origin, remained even after the coming of Christ. In some passages he recognized the diverse ends which Church and State possessed. [78] Yet on this question the thought of St. Thomas is inconclusive. [79]

> Strangely enough, Aquinas himself must be added to the list of those whose comments on the relation of the spiritual and secular authority were fragmentary and inconclusive. He has, indeed, often been claimed by modern commentators as one of the first champions of papal supremacy over the temporal power; but as Bellarmine observed in the sixteenth century, "as for St. Thomas, what he thought is not so certain." [80]

Bellarmine, [81] however, classed St. Thomas with the precursors of his own theory and modern scholars who have studied both men incline to agree with him.

It was John of Paris in his *De Potestate Regia et Papali*, who, relying on the principles of Aquinas regarding the natural origin of the state, surpassed him in precision. John taught that political society is subordinate to the spiritual society but explained in his own way what this involves in case of a clash between the two. Ecclesiastical jurisdiction, he insists, is only spiritual and cannot directly inflict any but spiritual penalties. [82]

---

[77] The following short summary of the history of the indirect power theory is based in part on Lecler, *The Two Sovereignties*, pp. 71-76.

[78] *Summa Theologica*, 2. 2, qu. 12, art. 2c; 2. 2, qu. 147, art. 3c; 2. 2, qu. 60, art. 6, ad 3.

Commentar. In II. Sent. dist. 44, qu. 2, art. 3, ad 4.

[79] See, for example, Carlyle, *op. cit.*, V, 348-354; E. Kurz, O.F.M., *Individuum und Gemeinschaft beim Hl. Thomas von Aquin* (Munich: J. Kösel & F. Pustet, 1932), p. 155; M. Grabmann, *Die Geschichte der katholischen Theologie seit dem Ausgang der Väterzeit* (Freiburg im Breisgau, Herder & Co., 1933), pp. 97-98.

[80] Lewis, *op. cit.*, II, 522.

[81] Cf. Jakob Gemmel, S.J., "Die Lehre des Kardinals Bellarmin über Kirche und Staat," *Scholastik*, V (1930), 357-359.

[82] As an appendix to his *Jean de Paris et l'ecclésiologie* (pp. 173-260) Leclercq has included an edited text of *De Potestate Regia et Papali* from which the following excerpt is taken: "De potestate vero correctionis seu censur[a]e eccle-

It has certainly the right to intervene in temporal matters in
the event of a moral fault.   Even in this case, however, the
Church's coercive powers would not enable her, except in an
indirect and incidental manner, to do more than inflict spiritual
censures. [83]

In the sixteenth century, the theory of indirect power was
modified somewhat by Molina's predecessors, Vitoria and Soto.
The former had said, "When he has a spiritual aim in view,
the Pope possesses a real temporal authority over kings and
emperors." [84]   Molina never quite states his theory in those
terms, but he does not expressly reject them as did Bellarmine. [85]
As the first Jesuits writing in the field, both Molina and Bellarmine in taking John of Paris' theory, modify it in a distinctive
fashion to fit the conditions of the sixteenth century.   Sabine
says that the special purpose of the Jesuits was to reformulate,
in the light of political conditions that came to prevail in the
sixteenth century, a moderate theory of papal superiority upon
lines suggested by St. Thomas.   "It was the dream of the Jesuits
to win back the seceders and, by conceding the fact of independence in secular matters, to save for the pope a sort of spiritual
leadership over a society of Christian states." [86]   But let Molina
speak for himself:

> The spiritual power of the Pope, relative to the super-
> natural, involves as a necessary accompaniment full and su-
> preme power of temporal jurisdiction over all temporal rulers,
> as over all others belonging to the Church.   This, however,
> only inasmuch as it is needed for the accomplishment of a
> supernatural end or purpose, which is the very reason for the
> existence of his spiritual power.   Wherefore, if need be for
> the attainment of this supernatural end, he can dethrone kings,
> deprive them of their realm, adjudicate their temporal affairs
> and mitigate their laws, just as he can investigate for cor-
> rection all other matters pertinent to Christian life and living
> and pertaining to this supernatural end and to the common
> spiritual good, which he, not by an arbitrary decision but by

---

siastic[a]e sciendum est quod non nisi spiritualis directe, quia nullam penam
in foro exteriori potest imponere nisi spiritualem, nisi sub conditione et per
accidens" (p. 214).

[83] *Ibid.*, p. 216: "Ex quibus predictis apparet quod tota censura ecclesiastica est spiritualis scilicet excommunicando, suspendendo, interdicendo, nec aliquid ultra potest ecclesia nisi indirecte et per accidens ut dictum est."

[84] *De Potestate Ecclesiastica*, quoted by Lecler, *The Two Sovereignties*,
p. 75.

[85] *Ibid.*

[86] Sabine, *op. cit.*, pp. 386-387.

prudent judgment, might deem to be in need of such action. Moreover, he can enforce this power not only by ecclesiastical censures but also by actual punishment, by force and by arms, as might be done by any other temporal ruler.... [87]

These measures may seem somewhat unsuitable, a point which Molina concedes, for he continues:

Such a means, however, would probably have better results if put into execution by the secular rulers rather than by the Pope himself. Wherefore, it may be said that the Pope is possessed of a double-edged sword of spiritual and of temporal power. Let it be noticed, however, that since this supreme power of temporal jurisdiction, which the Pope possesses, pertains ultimately not to the temporal as such, but to a supernatural end, it is not merely a temporal but rather a spiritual power, because of the end to which it is directed (*ex parte finis*). And again, in order to distinguish this particular power from the purely spiritual power inherent in it, it is best designated, not as a secular or laical, but as an ecclesiastical power, with temporal jurisdiction. [88]

---

[87] "Potestas spiritualis Summi Pontificis ad finem supernaturalem, adjunctam quasi ex consequenti habet supremam et amplissimam potestatem jurisdictionis temporalis super omnes principes et reliquos, qui sunt de Ecclesia; praecise tamen quantum postulat finis supernaturalis, ad quem spiritualis potestas ordinatur. Quare, si id exigat finis supernaturalis, potest Summus Pontifex deponere reges, eosque regnis suis privare. Potest leges infirmare, et reliqua omnia inter Christianos omnes exequi, quae ad supernaturalem finem salutemque communem spiritualem, non utcumque, sed simpliciter prudentis arbitrio judicata fuerint necessaria, idque non solum censuris ad id cogendo, sed etiam poenis externis, ac vi, et armis, non secus, ac quivis alius princeps secularis: ..." (II, 29, 143E-144A).

[88] "Tametsi ut plurimum expediens sit Summum Pontificem non per se, sed per principes seculares id exequi. Atque hac ratione vere Summus Pontifex dicitur habere utrumque gladium, supremamque potestatem temporalem et spiritualem. Observa tamen, supremam hanc potestatem jurisdictionis temporalis, quae in Summo Pontifice residet, cum non ad temporalia ipsa, sed ad supernaturalem finem ordinetur, non esse mere potestatem temporalem, sed esse spiritualem ex parte finis. Quo fit, ut appellanda non sit potestas laica, sed Ecclesiastica, jurisdictionis tamen temporalis, ut illam distinguamus a potestate mere spirituali, quae illam annexa habet" (*ibid.*).

[89] Cf. Rommen, *Die Staatslehre des Franz Suarez S.J.*, p. 361.
The concept of necessity expressed by Molina is found in Turrecremata, *Summa de Ecclesia* II, c. 113: "Quantum necesse est pro bono spirituali ... sive quantum Ecclesiae necessitas exigit aut debitum pastoralis officii in correctione peccatorum exposcit" Vitoria, *Relectio de Potestate Ecclesiae*, V, n. 12; Soto, *Comm. in Sent.*, dist. 22, qu. 2, art. 2.; Bellarmine, *De Potestate Pontificis*; V, c. 6: "...si id necessarium sit ad animarum salutem"; Suárez, *Defensio Fidei*, III, c. 23, n. 10.

It is obvious that Molina here concedes much more power to the supreme pontiff than does John of Paris. Where the latter would limit the pope's retaliatory power to spiritual censures, Molina grants him the right of armed force if necessary, [89] though he is quick to suggest that such an action might be better executed by a secular ruler acting in the pope's name. He wavers between calling the power full and supreme temporal jurisdiction and spiritual power with temporal jurisdiction.

Molina explains his conclusion. The Church, presided over by the pope, and a state presided over by a Christian ruler are not two different societies as are the kingdoms of Spain and France, but they are subordinate to one another so that one is included in the other. The purpose of any state, since it is imperfect, is ordered to the supernatural purpose which is under the Church's care. [90] When two artisans are subordinate so that the purpose of one is ordered to the other, the superior artisan prescribes rules and operations to the lower as the superior end demands. The pope, who is in charge of the supernatural end, has the right to prescribe and give orders to secular rulers and other Christians insofar as the supernatural end requires. Certainly Christ would have provided insufficiently for his Church if he had not made all Christian rulers and the rest of the faithful subordinate to the supreme pontiff, granting him the fullest power to coerce them to do that which, in virtue of his office, he thinks is necessary for the supernatural end. By the very fact that Christ committed the supreme care of the Church to Peter and his successors, it follows that he granted them the power of which there is question. God provides all things necessary. In government he grants those things without which it could not survive.

Yet Molina insists that the power of the temporal ruler, looked at in itself, is independent of the pope in its own sphere and as a result, the pope cannot interfere in the affairs of secular rulers in questions that pertain to the natural end of the state. However, because a Christian ruler can deviate from the supernatural end and because in this area his rule is dependent on

---

90 "Primo, quoniam Ecclesia Christiana, cui Summus Pontifex jure divino caput et supremus rector praeficitur, et quaecumque alia Respublica secularis cujusvis Christiani principis non sunt duae diversae Respublicae, perinde atque Respublicae Hispanorum et Gallorum; sed sunt adinvicem subordinatae, ita ut una in alia includatur, finisque naturalis cujusque Reipublicae secularis, tamquam inperfectus, ordinatur, ad finem supernaturalem quem respicit Ecclesia" (II, 29, 144B).

the pope, the ruler can be compelled to do what is ordered. In other words, since the pope is universal shepherd, he must recall all erring sheep of whatever dignity. Not only does the pope have temporal jurisdiction when the need arises but, as Vitoria observed, bishops have temporal jurisdiction within their dioceses for the same reason. The bishops can punish not only by censures but even by external punishments, provided they do not act from greed but of necessity and for spiritual profit. [91]

Furthermore, Molina continues, both the pope and bishops have power to demand from secular rulers who are subject to them the proper subsidy needed for spiritual administration. Just as the secular ruler when urgent need arises, can exact subsidies from his subjects, so the supreme pontiff has the same power. [92] But, as both Vitoria and Soto warn, the pope in the cases cited must be careful to wield his temporal sword well. He should first use the spiritual power he has. For his

---

[91] "Observat optime Victoria relectione de Indis Insulanis par. 1. nu. 29. Potestatem ad temporalia, quatenus spiritualia exigunt, non solum residere in Summo Pontifice comparatione omnium, qui sunt de Ecclesia, sed etiam in quocumque Episcopo comparatione suorum subditorum: Episcoposque posse eodem modo punire et cohibere peccata secularia, non solum censuris, sed etiam poenis exterioribus, pecuniariis, et exilii, ac aliis: modo tamen id non faciant ex avaritia, et ad quaestum, sed ex necessitate, et ad commodum rerum spiritualium" (II, 29, 147D).

From the title *De Indis Insulanis* it is to be presumed that Molina is using the first edition of Vitoria's *Relectiones Theologicae XII* printed at Lyons in 1557, because in the second the work is entitled *De Indis Recenter Inventis* and the third and subsequent editions have the title *De Indis Noviter Inventis*. The reference to the first *Relectio de Indis*, n. 29, is to be found in the second section of the 1696 edition published at Cologne by Johan George Simon, a photographic reproduction of which is printed in *De Indis et Jure Belli Relectiones*, trans. John Pawley Bate and ed. Ernest Nys (Washington: The Carnegie Institution of Washington, 1917), p. 242. (Cited hereinafter as *De Jure Belli*). The first section is divided into twenty-four parts. The citation referred to here is the fifth of the second section, which would be the twenty-ninth section of the first *Relectio de Indis*.

[92] "Ulterius Summus Pontifex, et in suo ordine et gradu caeteri Episcopi, potestatem habent exigendi a secularibus sibi subditis debitum subsidium pro administratione spiritualium, eosque ad id cogendi: cum vero ejusmodi causa finem respiciat spiritualem, ad forum Ecclesiasticum spectat. Item quemadmodum rex, orta necessitate urgente Reipublicae secularis, potestatem habet exigendi a subditis subsidia, quibus necessitati illi subveniat, quando aliter non potest sufficienter illi subveniri: sic arbitror Summum Pontificem, orta urgente necessitate Ecclesiae universalis, cui aliter non possit commode subveniri, habere potestatem exigendi a principibus Christianis, et a caeteris suis subditis, subsidia et auxilia ad id necessaria, eosque cogendi ad illam praestandum" (II, 29, 147E).

ordinary method of action is by use of his spiritual power to
which the temporal is joined as an auxiliary. The sword of
temporal jurisdiction is not to be unsheathed except when,
after trying, it is found that the power of the spiritual sword
is insufficient. [93]

Clerical Exemption

One of the areas of joint jurisdiction where friction may
arise concerns the position of clerics in the state. If Molina's
rules are taken before the exceptions, it should be noted that
clerics are bound by all civil laws passed for the efficient administration of the state and which are not contrary to the
liberty of the Church. [94] The examples he uses have modern
counterparts: food price control (*pretia frumenti*), zoning laws
(*quibus prohibetur talis ratio aedificandi*), inheritance laws (*aliquid statuitur circa succedendi modum in haereditate*). Clerics
are bound because they are members of the state. [95] If,
for example, a cleric would sell grain for more than the established just price, he incurs moral guilt the same as any layman
and is bound to restitution. [96]

When it comes to the question of clerical exemption Molina
distinguishes between governments. Clerics who reside in non-
Christian lands are bound in conscience to pay taxes which are
levied for the common good and defense of that country. [97] In
areas ruled by men who are Christian, there are two types of
exemption, one from divine and one from human law. In purely
ecclesiastical matters, clerics are not subject by divine law to
legislation which would hinder the selection of priests and
bishops, division of dioceses and parishes, and so on. [98] By
divine law also Molina would exempt the person of the supreme
pontiff from jurisdiction of any secular court. He is hesitant
on this conclusion and does not press it far. The proof he al-
leges is rather curious. First of all, except in the case of heresy,
the supreme pontiff cannot be punished or deprived of his office
or judged by any earthly power. Second, not only may the

---

[93] II, 29, 148B.
[49] II, 31, 155E.
[95] II, 31, 155E.
[96] II, 31, 155E-156A.
[97] II, 31, 155B.
[98] II, 31, 151B.

sovereign pontiff not take his own life, but he may not give any person such a power [99] and therefore, no matter what the crime, he may not be executed for it. Thus he is exempt from all temporal jurisdiction and criminal prosecution. [100]

All other exemptions for all clerics arise from the human, not divine law. Exemption of clergy from secular prosecution would seem fitting (*maxime consentaneum*). It seems to Molina that there would be something unbecoming for a bishop to have to appear before a judge who was subject to him in spiritual matters. Such an action would be lacking in the proper reverence due churchmen. Actually, he says, clerics were exempt from civil suits by the positive law of the Empire and states like France and Spain. Therefore he would conclude that the existing exemption arose from human law.

Molina is willing to concede, however, that such exemption is not absolute. If the safety of any state were imperiled by clerical exemption, the government may take steps to prosecute even exempt clerics. The reason for this is that "a state is self-sufficient and by its own authority may defend itself... even against ecclesiastics." He would limit this power to the supreme ruler and not local officials, though even they may defend their jurisdictions against unjust actions by clerics.

Conclusions

Molina's observations on Church-State relations leave much to be desired. He vacillated between a rejection of the "direct power" theory and an acceptance of John of Paris' view. Molina was apprehensive that the Church, though admittedly a perfect society, could hardly exist—in crises at least—without some means of direct temporal power. The concept of emergency powers for the ecclesiastical society played an essential role in Molina's thought just as the concept of emergency power for political society played an essential role in the history of Germany's Weimar Republic. It is ironic that Molina's reasoning on indirect power reached, in practice, the same conclusions

---

[99] "Pontificemque ipsum, quemadmodum non potest seipsum interficere, ita nec facere alteri potestatem, ut eum interficiat, eaque ratione a nemine pro quocumque crimine posse interfici, esto propria sponte se aliorum judicio velit subjicere" (II, 31, 153C).

[100] "Summum Pontificem arbitror jure divino esse omnino exemptum ab omni universim terrena potestate" (II, 31, 152E).

as the rival theory of direct power. His theory, like the other, permits the pope to intervene directly in secular affairs and even to depose the ruler in virtue of a type of *raison d'Église* which has some analogy with the *raison d'État*.

The study of Church and State is essentially the study of a *relation*, at least one of whose terms—the state—is in a continual process of evolution. Each change produces a new relation. Abstractly, it might be profitable to discuss the relation of *a* church with *a* state. But this alone will never solve the problem of Church-state relation. Concretely the visible Kingdom of Christ exists in the world with varied relations to varied states. To regard any single relationship as the ideal or the ultimate is to miss the essential dynamism of both societies.

Perhaps it is unreasonable to expect anyone to have solved the Church-State question in the sixteenth century. Any attempt to stop the stream of history and judge its contemporary flow is a hazardous occupation. Who can ever assimilate enough history, political science, and sociology, canon law and theology to effect the needed synthesis of Catholic thought in its historic and doctrinal dimensions on the problem of Church and State?[101] Molina attempted to do so. We are grateful for his effort and for the light it shed on the conditions of his day. If at times his position seems obscure, it but reflects in a glass darkly the confused conditions of the sixteenth century.

---

[101] John Courtney Murray, S.J., "Reversing the Secularist Drift," *Thought*, XXIV (1949), 45-46.

CHAPTER VI

MOLINA'S INTERNATIONALISM: *JUS AD BELLUM* [1]

Don Quixote said it is vain to look for birds in last year's nests and many historians of political thought must have agreed with him. Otherwise it is difficult to understand their almost universal neglect of Molina. Difficult as this is to understand of his political theory in general, it is completely incomprehensible when one studies Molina as an internationalist. The revived interest during the present century in the Spanish origins of international law left Molina's works undisturbed. James Brown Scott [2] and John Eppstein [3] omit all reference to him. Vanderpol at least makes mention of Molina, although erroneously on a number of points. [4] Luis Izaga did pioneer work some forty years ago in a series of articles on Molina as an internationalist, refuting and correcting Vanderpol. [5] Another Spanish Jesuit, R. S. de Lamadrid, [6] edited the first lectures of Molina on war and two French Jesuits, Robert Re-

---

[1] There are two sections of the body of international law which treat of war or relate to it. The first deals with the recourse to war and forms the *jus ad bellum*. The second group is comprised of all the rules for which the outbreak of war is the *conditio sine qua non*. This entire group of rules forms the *jus in bello* which regulates the belligerency of the two contending parties. The present chapter deals with Molina's treatment of the *jus ad bellum*; the following chapter will deal with his treatment of the *jus in bello*. On the importance of this distinction see Lothan Kotzsch, *The Concept of War in Contemporary History and International Law* (Genève: Librairie E. Droz, 1956), pp. 83-126.

[2] James Brown Scott, *The Spanish Origin of International Law*: Francisco de Vitoria and His Law of Nations (Oxford: Oxford University Press, 1932).

[3] John Eppstein, *The Catholic Tradition of the Law of Nations* (Washington: Catholic Association for International Peace, 1935).

[4] Alfred Vanderpol, *La doctrine scolastique du droit de guerre* (Paris: A. Pedone, 1919), pp. 257, 261-264, and 271-272.

[5] Luis Aguirre Izaga, S.J., "El P. Luis de Molina, internacionalista," *Razón y Fe*, CX (1936), 43-55, 192-206, and 491-513.

[6] R. S. de Lamadrid, "Luis de Molina S.J.—*De Bello*: Commentario a la 2.2, Q. 40," *Archivo teológico granadino*, II (1939), 155-231; see also Kleinhappl, *op. cit.*

gout [7] and Yves de la Brière, [8] devote a few pages to Molina in their respective works. A Spanish Augustinian, Lucas Gracia Prieto, [9] has done the most to bring Molina's contributions to the attention of scholars. His volume, published during the Second World War, [10] raised Molina to a long-awaited niche in the international-law hall of fame. Ironically, Prieto's timely volume on Molina and war, because of the war, received little notice in this country. [11]

Yet, in spite of the neglect by historians and the late recognition of his worth, the twenty-six disputations on war in the Second Tract on *Justice* are still Molina's best-known contributions to political thought. These disputations first appeared in printed form in 1593 as a commentary on the Fortieth Question of the *Secunda Secundae* dictated to his pupils at Evora in the school year 1574-1575. [12] These lectures contain

---

[7] Robert Regout, S.J., *La doctrine de la guerre juste de Saint Augustin à nos jours* (Paris: A. Pedone, 1935), pp. 250-261.

[8] Yves de la Brière, S.J., *Le droit de juste guerre*: tradition théologique adaptations contemporaines (Paris: A. Pedone, 1938), pp. 41-43.

[9] Lucas Garcia Prieto, O.S.A., *La Paz y la Guerra*: Luis de Molina y la escuela española del siglo XVI en relación con la ciencia y el derecho internacional moderno (Romae: Pontificium Institutum Utriusque Juris, 1944).

[10] During the war several articles on Molina and war were written by an Italian Jesuit, B. Anselmo: "La guerra difensiva nella dottrina di Ludovico Molina, S.J.," *Civiltà Cattolica*, II (1943), 354-363; "La guerra offensiva nella dottrina di Ludovico Molina, S.J.," *ibid.*, III (1943), 270-281; "La guerra offensiva e l'autorità necessaria nella dottrina di Ludovico Molina, S.J.," *ibid.*, IV (1943), 25-38; "Gli elementi di una giusta pace nella dottrina di Ludovico Molina, S.J.," *ibid.*, IV (1943), 307-316.

See also Manuel Fraga Iribarne, *Luis de Molina y el derecho de la guerra* (Madrid, 1947); and Luis Sánchez Gallego, "Luis de Molina, internacionalista," *Anuario de la asociación F. de Vitoria*, V (1932-33), 41-69.

[11] A recent author on war in contemporary society has written "There have been nearly a thousand books published in the different countries in the post-war [World War II] years dealing with the various aspects of war, strategy, weapons and arms control. And a comprehensive bibliography on these subjects would easily fill a volume as long as this book." Alastair Buchan, *War in Modern Society*: An Introduction (New York: Harper and Row, Publishers, 1968).

For the specific issue of the morality of modern warfare see Robert Tucker, *Just War and the Vatican Council*: with commentary by George C. Higgins, Ralph Potter, Richard H. Cox and Paul Ramsey (New York: The Council on Religious and International Affairs, 1966) and Paul Ramsey, *The Just War*: *Force and Political Responsibility* (New York: Charles Scribner's Sons, 1968). An extensive bibliography on the subject can be found in *Morality and Modern Warfare: The State of the Question* edited by William J. Nagle (Baltimore: Helicon Press, 1960), pp. 151-168.

[12] J. A. Aldama, S.J., "Luis de Molina, S.J. De Spe: Comentario a la 2ª 2ᵃᵉ. 17-22," *Archivo teológico granadino*, I (1938), 111-112.

in embryo the printed version and, when compared with the final text, afford an interesting study in the evolution of Molina's ideas.

At first there appears to be a vast difference between the lectures in manuscript and the printed version. St. Thomas divided his study on war into four articles [13] and Molina's lectures had four divisions also. The printed version had twenty-six disputations (98-123 of Tract II). But the difference between the two versions is more apparent than real as the following outline will reveal. The disputations are fitted on a framework of the original four articles. [14]

1. De bello cur hoc loco dicendum (Disp. 98)
2. Utrum bellum sit licitum aliquando (Disp. 99)
3. Quae requirantur ad bellum licitum (Disp. 100-107)
   a. auctoritas (Disp. 102-106)
   b. causa recta (Disp. 102-106)
   c. intentio recta (Disp. 107)
4. De militibus et caeteris cooperantibus ad bellum (Disp. 108-123)
   a. de episcopis et clericis pugnantibus (Disp. 108-110)
   b. de licitudine insidiarum et pugnae in die festo (Disp. 111)
   c. de caeteris cooperantibus (Disp. 112-116)
   d. de actis licitis in bello et in pace (Disp. 117-123)

Between the manuscript lectures and the published text there are changes in style and phraseology and a certain tendency to more concise and clearer propositions. [15] But it is

---

[13] St. Thomas divides his treatment of war in the following manner:

Quaestio 40, De bello. Art. I, Disp. 1^a: Utrum sit licitum christianis bellare. Disp. 2^a: Quae requirantur ut bellum sit licitum. Disp. 3^a: De militibus et caeteris cooperantibus ad bellum. Disp. 4^a: Quantum liceat in bello justo.

Art. II: Utrum clericis et episcopis licitum sit pugnare

Art. III: Utrum in bello justo fas sit uti insidiis

Art. IV: Utrum liceat diebus festis pugnare.

As was pointed out in the introductory chapter of this study, Rabeneck's statement that Molina's *De Justitia* is not a commentary on the *Summa* of St. Thomas is misleading. In a letter to Aquaviva, Molina expressly states that he began his work as a commentary on the the the *Secunda Secundae*. "The five remaining years (after lecturing briefly on the matter *de prudentia*—just enough to complete what I had already said on the *Secunda Secundae*) I spent on the matter of justice. Up to Q. 62 I went on commenting on St. Thomas just as I had been doing" (Stegmüller, *Molinismus*, letter of Molina to Claudio Aquaviva, August 29, 1582, p. 552).

For further excerpts from this letter, *vide supra*, chapter 1.

[14] This scheme, slightly modified, is modeled on one which appears in Lamadrid, *op. cit.*, p. 156.

[15] Following is an example of the type of refinement of style and conciseness that is noticeable between the two versions:

enough for our purpose to have noted the modifications. There
are further examples of them in Lamadrid's article. It is time
now to consider Molina's doctrine.

Molina begins his treatment of war on the defensive. He
sets out to justify his consideration of the entire problem in
the general framework of his loss and gain of ownership. Since
men lose ownership by means of war, the study of war comes
naturally at this part of his Tract.[16] Although St. Thomas
included war under his investigation of the virtue of charity,
the study really belongs to a treatise justice because "multo
magis cum justitia pugnat, et tam justum, quam injustum bel-

I

Petes quando duae integrae republi-
cae ac regna habent immediate idem
commune caput, eundemve regem, ut
regnum Castellae et regnum Arago-
niae regem Hispaniarum, possit unus
adversus alterum, absque facultate
communis regis, movere bellum. Et
patet, ex dictis, respondendum negative. Nam tota facultas cuiusque regni ad movendum bellum est in rege.
Quare neuter, sine consensu communis regis, movere poterit bellum, nisi
propter necessitatem, quando rex ne-
gligeret punire, aut non auderet punire regnum, quod alteri regno iniuriam
inferret, ut de ducibus et civitatibus
ejusdem regni dicebat Vitoria (ibid.,
pp. 171-172).

II

Petet aliquis, utrum quando duae integrae respublicae, aut regna, unum
habent commune caput, ut hodie habent regna omnia Hispaniarum, possit unum adversus alterum movere
bellum absque facultate communis regis. Ex dictisque facile constat, non
posse eo quod tota authoritas utriusque ad movendum bellum sit penes communem principem. Excipitur
quando supervenisset ea necessitas,
quae de civitatibus et magnatibus eius-
dem regni paulo antea explicata est
(II, 100, 418).

On the changes in style and brevity and clarity of expression, Molina himself notes: "Porque aunque deseo toda limpieza en el stilo, y para ello ser
aiudado de otro (aunque no faltan personas doctas, que digan que para cosas
scholasticas basta mi stilo) deseo que esta limpieza sea sin quitarse nada de
la clareza, brevedad, niervos y recato, con que cumple vaian hechas cosas
scolasticas" (Stegmüller, Molinismus, letter of Molina to Claudio Aquaviva,
March 6, 1583, p. 562).

Figgis ("On Some Political Theories," op. cit., p. 99) refers to the "clear
and analytic Molina." He goes on to say that some of the Jesuit writers had
a much wider scope than the resolving of politico-ecclesiastical problems and
it is as one element in the general system that the problem appears. "But
it is generally discussed with exhaustive completeness even when it forms
but a part of the writer's subject. Many of them take the form of Commentaries on the 'Summa' of St. Thomas, or rather of collections of disputations on that part (I. 2, qq.xc.sqq), which treats of law. Indeed, after perusing
them one finds St. Thomas refreshingly brief" (p. 100).

[16] "Id tamen quod amplius licet, hoc commune habet cum acquisitione et
amissione dominii in poenam, quod jure belli semper dominium comparatur
contra voluntatem ejus, qui illud amittit" (II, 98, 410).

lum, ex principiis justitiae longe majori ex parte, quam ex principiis charitatis, exprimendum examinandumque est."[17]

Having erected his scaffolding, Molina follows his predecessors and begins his climb with the fundamental question: Is it permissible to wage war?

St. Augustine, Gratian, and St. Thomas had all answered the question affirmatively.[18] Vitoria, writing in the age of the Lutheran heresy,[19] had treated the question also. The Dominican rather caustically remarks that "Luther, who left nothing uncontaminated, denies that Christians[20] may take up arms

---

[17] "Porro licet bellum injustum cum charitate quadam ex parte pugnet, eaque de causa de eo disseruit D. Thomas ... Quo circa ad hunc potius locum quam ad materiam de charitate spectat disputare de bello; longeque plures sunt, qui in materia de justitia, quam qui una cum charitate de eo disserant" (*ibid.*).

Molina confided to Aquaviva that it seemed to him the treatment given to the matter *de justitia* by the theologians and principally by St. Thomas was very short (see Stegmüller, *Molinismus*, p. 552).

See M.-D. Chenu, O.P., "L'Evolution de la théologie de la guerre," *Lumière et Vie*, XXXVIII (1958), 76-97, where he traces the development of the doctrine ot the morality of war. St. Thomas summarized the doctrine of Augustine in the context of his own treatment of charity. The scholastic theologians, introducing the question of juridical rights and considering peace as the work of justice, under took the rationalization of peace and war and took these terms beyond the confines of the Gospel spirit of Christianity into a far more rational sphere. Vitoria and his followers brought back into focus the emphasis of the Gospel. They did not destroy the rational categories of the earlier views but combined the two—the evangelical note of charity and the rational theme of justice—into an admirable synthesis that was the foundation of all later developments.

Suárez, following St. Thomas, includes his treatment "De Bello" in the third part of his "De Charitate" which is a part of his *De triplici virtute theologali* (*Opera omnia*, XII, 737-759).

[18] *Vide* Vanderpol, *op. cit.*, pp. 18-27, for a summary of the Augustinian answer to the question; *ibid.*, pp. 308-312, for St. Thomas' position.

[19] Leo X in the Bull "Exsurge Domine," June 15, 1520, condemned the following proposition as one of the errors of Martin Luther: "Proeliari adversus Turcas est repugnare Deo visitanti iniquitates nostras per illos" (Denzinger, Bannwart, and Umberg, *Enchiridion Symbolorum*, 774, p. 277).

[20] Vitoria's question was whether Christians are permitted to wage war. Molina's phrasing is more universal but there is little difference between the two questions. Garcia Prieto on this point remarks: "En realidad y sustancialmente non existe diferencia alguna, puesto que Vitoria puso la susodicha restricción a su enunciado en cuanto que solamente a los cristianos les había sido negado el derecho a recurrir a las armas, y, una vez probada la falsedad de esta negativa, quedaba establecido el principio universal de la licitud de la guerra" (*op. cit.*, p. 114).

The literature on Vitoria and the law of war is vast and there will be no attempt here to give even a representative sampling. On Domingo Soto, see Venancio Carro, O.P., *Domingo de Soto y el derecho de gentes* (Madrid:

even against the Turks, and he relies ... on the fact that if the
Turks attack Christendom, it is the will of God, which may not
be resisted. Herein, however, he had not as much success as
his other dogmas in imposing on the Germans, who are born
soldiers. " [21]

There is a striking resemblance between Molina's answer
to the question and Vitoria's. Paragraph by paragraph, citation
by citation, the replies are almost identical. Molina does spend
much more time than did Vitoria in refuting the position of
Luther. Basically his answer is founded on the petition of the
Litany of the Saints: "A peste, fame et bello, libera nos, Domine." If Christians are expected to seek means against famine
and disease, by which God also visits and punishes his people,
why is it wrong for Christians to defend themselves against the
scourge of war waged by the Turks? [22]

Once the right to wage war is established, Molina is in
a position to discuss the problems of war in his day. It has
been observed that in the sixteenth century many people regarded war as a means of change and progress; in the twentieth
century, chief interest lies in peace as the hope of a new epoch
and a new unity. The sixteenth and seventeenth centuries were
periods of disruption of a unity which was felt to be retro-
gressive and oppressing; while the wars of that same time were,
broadly speaking, less of an evil than those of the present
world. [23]

The accent now lies on the injustice of aggressive war and
the means of preventing it. In the sixteenth century, on the

Revista de las Españas, 1930) and *Domingo de Soto y su doctrina jurídica*
(Madrid: Imp. Hijos E. Minuesa, 1943).

For Bañez' position on the law of war, see Regout, *op. cit.*, pp. 236-242.

A summary of Mariana's views may be found in *The King and the Education of a King*, pp. 289-301.

The literature on Suárez is also large. The best treatment of his law
of war will be found in Rommen, *Franz Suarez*, pp. 270-305, and L. Vincente
Pereña, *Teoría de la guerra en Francisco Suárez* (2 vols.; Madrid: Consejo
Superior de Investigaciones Científicas, Instituto 'Francisco de Vitoria,' 1954).

[21] Vitoria, *De Jure Belli*, Appendix B, pp. xlix-1.

[22] "Quod si Lutheri fundamentum alicujus esset ponderis ac momenti, sane
neque famis, pestis, aliorumque morborum ac infortuniorum tempore, fas esset
media quaerere adversus ea mala; cum non minus hisce malis visitet nos
Deus, ac puniat iniquitates nostras, quam Turcarum bello.... Etenim, qui fame,
aut morbo laborans panem aut medicinam non sumeret, cum posset ac spe-
raret ea se ratione mortis periculum declinare posse, lethaliter peccaret"
(II, 99, 413).

[23] Sir Geoffrey Butler and Simon Maccoby, *The Development of International Law* (London: Longmans, Green and Co., Ltd., 1928), p. 3.

other hand, the accent was on the justification of war as an instrument of law. In a real sense, the justification of war had preoccupied scholastic theologians from Augustine's time. After the radical pacifism of earlier teachers such as Origen and Tertullian, St. Augustine settled the basic question of the lawfulness of war by teaching that war is an evil and can only be resorted to in order to attain justice and peace. Even then it would only be waged in an extreme necessity when no other means were left and only for a just cause: "Justa bella definiri solent quae ulciscuntur injurias." [24]

Most authors followed Augustine's footsteps by distinguishing between various types of lawful wars and giving separate considerations to the war of defense. Suárez was the first to draw a sharp line between natural law and positive international law. He regards wars in self-defense to be permitted by the natural law while the other *bella justa* find their justification in positive law.

Defensive war was taken in a wider sense than the military interpretation prevailing today. Suárez divides *bella defensiva et aggressiva* according to whether the wrong is being done or is already accomplished. The notion of war includes the war of assistance to a state which is the victim of an actual injustice. [25] Vitoria states this very clearly in the *Relectio de Indis*. A grave offense against innocent subjects, e. g., the religious sacrifice of adults and children and even the existence of tyrannic, barbarous laws providing for such atrocities is good enough motive for a just, defensive war. [26]

The justification of offensive war is the real core of the scholastic doctrine of *bellum ex justa causa*. It is of this war that St. Augustine said, "Bellum geritur ut pax acquiratur." [27] He did not mean peace in the sense of the mere absence of war —that would be a truism—but in the wider fundamental notion of *omnium rerum tranquillitas ordinis*, the peace as an *opus justitiae* and the *ordo* as a creation of justice.

The term *bellum offensivum* was introduced into scholastic thought about Vitoria's time to express what earlier writers had

---

[24] For a documented history of the development of the Christian ethics of war see Vanderpol, *op. cit., passim*. The treatment of St. Augustine's position may be found on pp. 17-99.

[25] Suárez, *Opera Omnia*, Vol. XII, Sec. I, n. 6.

[26] Vitoria, *De Jure Belli*, Apendix B, Sec. III, No. 15.

[27] St. Augustine, *Ad Bonifacium*, VI, and *De Civitate Dei*, XIX, 13, from J. P. Migne (ed.), *Patrologiae Cursus Completus*, Series Latina (218 vols.; Paris, 1844-1855), Vols. XXXIII and XLI. Cited hereinafter as *PL*.

meant by *indicere vel movere bellum*. Vitoria used the division
of offensive and defensive war—for him defensive war was one
undertaken to recover what had been taken by another; offensive war was solely punitive, to administer a sanction for
a injury received. [28]

Molina, retaining the terminology, gives the words another
meaning. He distinguishes offensive and defensive war not only
according to their purpose but also according to the operations
of war. Offensive war is one of attack, one in which the ini-
tiative is taken. Defensive war is limited to resistance to aggression. Offensive war is of two types:

> Unum quod infertur ad ultionem sumendam de injuria illata,
> sive simul intendamus recuperare nostra, resarcireque damna,
> nobis illata, sive non. . . . Alterum genus . . . ad occupandum
> nostra, eave, quae nobis debentur quando ignorantia invincibili
> detinentur . . . ad tale bellum necesse non est praecedat culpa. [29]

---

[28] Vitoria, *De Jure Belli*, No. 1: "Quarto probatur etiam de bello offensivo,
id est in quo non solum defenduntur, aut etiam repetuntur res, sed ubi petitur
vindicta pro injuria accepta.... Probatur etiam quinto de bello offensivo:
quia bellum etiam defensivum geri commode non potest, nisi etiam vindicetur
in hostes qui injuriam fecerunt aut conati sunt facere...." No. 13: "Item
bellum offensivum est ad vindicandam injuriam, et ad animadvertendum in
hostes..., sed vindicta esse non potest ubi non praecessit culpa et injuria."

[29] II, 102, 422.

The problem of the definition of aggressive war remains unsolved. Julius
Stone (*Legal Controls of International Conflict* [New York: Rinehart and Co.,
Inc., Publishers, 1954], pp. 330-334) devotes a full chapter to the subject with
copious references to the attempts made to solve the problem.

See also C. A. Pompe, *Aggressive War*: An International Crime (The Hague:
Martinus Nijhoff, 1953), pp. 85-115, for an analysis of proposed definitions;
W. Komarnicki, "La Définition de l'agresseur," *Recueil des cours de la acadé-
mie de droit international*, LXXV (1949), 5-110. All subsequent references to
this periodical will be shortened to: *Recueil des cours*; Philip C. Jessup, "The
Crime of Aggression," *Political Science Quarterly*, LXX (1947), 1-10; J. Maktos,
"La Question de la définition de l'agression," *Revue de droit international de
sciences diplomatiques politiques et sociales*, XXX (1952), 5-9; D. Sidjanski and
S. Castanos, « L' 'agresseur' et l' 'agression' au point de vue idéologique et réel,"
Revue de droit international de sciences diplomatiques politiques et sociales,
pp. 44-45; G. Amado, « La question de la définition," *Revue de droit inter-
national de sciences diplomatiques politiques et sociales*, pp. 147-155.

Quincy Wright, "The Concept of Aggression in International Law," *American
Journal of International Law*, XXIX (1935), 373-395; Clyde Eagleton, *The Attempt
to Define Aggression* ("International Conciliation," No. 264; New York: Carnegie
Endowment for International Peace, 1950); L. Kopelmanas, "The Problem of
Aggression and the Prevention of War," *American Journal of International Law*,
XXXI (1937), 244-257; Louis Le Fur, "La Convention de Londres et la définition
de l'aggression," *Revue de droit international de sciences diplomatiques poli-*

Luis Izaga makes note of the clear opposition in terminology between Vitoria and Molina.[30] For the former, war undertaken "ut repetantur res" is always defensive; for Molina, such a war is offensive. Molina was the only one among the classical authors of this day to use this terminology.[31] A fuller explanation of Molina's position will be made under the title of a just cause for a war later in this chapter. Molina gives three essential elements of a just aggressive war: (1) competent authority, (2) just cause, and (3) right intention. By far the longest treatment is given to the second essential element; Molina covers the first and third elements in comparatively brief fashion. For this reason, *competent authority* will be considered first; *right intention* will be treated second. The rest of this chapter will be devoted to *just cause*.

Authority to Declare War

By-passing the easier question of defensive war, Molina begins with the more difficult case of an aggressive (*offensivum*) war: "Prima conditio necessaria, ut bellum offensivum justum, licitumque sit, est, authoritas in inferente."[32] Such authority, he

---

tiques et sociales, XI (1933), 176 ff.; H. Thirring, "Was ist aggression?" *Oesterreichische Zeitschrift für öffentliches Recht*, V (1952-53), 226-242.

See John Courtney Murray, S.J., "Theology of Modern Warfare," An address to the 31st Annual Conference of the Catholic Association for International Peace, Washington, D.C., October 24, 1958, reprinted in the *Catholic Messenger* (Davenport, Iowa), November 6, 1958, pp. 7-8. Father Murray outlined the traditional teaching on the morality of war as stated and interpreted by Pius XII. The first principle of this teaching he said, is that all wars of aggression fall under the ban of moral proscription. Father Murray says that this principle enunciated by Pius XII represents an important modification in the traditional doctrine of war. The reason for banning even a just war of aggression is the immeasurably increased violence of war today, and the fact that to continue to admit the right of war as an attribute of national sovereignty would seriously block the progress of the international community towards the establishment of an international organization capable of outlawing all war. A defensive war against aggression is morally admissible both in principle and fact. This principle, far from being a contradiction of the basic Christian will to peace, is the strongest possible affirmation of this will. There is no peace without justice, order and law. The conditions under which such a war is just, he added, are that it be made necessary by an obvious and extremely grave injustice and that it be the last resort.

30 Izaga, *op. cit.*, p. 195.

31 Prieto, *op. cit.*, p. 75: "Además de estas divisiones, figuran en nuestro Autor y en los clásicos españoles del siglo XVI otras de menos importancia y cuyo solo nombre las define, como *la guerra de religión, de civilización, de colonización, de conquista, de independencia nacional, de intervención.*"

32 II, 100, 415.

continues, is in a sovereign person or state: "Porro ejusmodi authoritas est in principe, qui superiorem in suo principatu non recognoscit." [33] The authority to declare war also resides in a free republic such as Venice and Genoa. But rulers who recognize a superior rule to their own do not possess such authority—e. g., the Duke of Braganza in Portugal, the Duke of Alba in Castile, the cities of Lisbon and Toledo. Molina includes an impressive list of authors of similar views: St. Thomas, Caietan, [34] Adrian, [35] Vitoria, [36] Covarrubias, [37] Castro, [38] Soto, [39] Gabriel, [40] Panormitanus, [41] Bartolo, [42] St. Isidore, [43] and S. Augustine. [44]

---

[33] "Eadem ratione est in republica libera, quae superiori non est subjecta, quales sunt Venetorum, Genuensium, et similes aliae Reipublicae.

"Alii vero domini temporales, qui superiorem recognoscunt, et quorum dominium pars est alicuius integri principatus, ut dux Brigantius in hoc Lusitaniae regno, Albanus in regno Castellae, et alii similes, nec non civitates, quae partes sunt alicujus integrae Reipublicae, ut Olyssipo, Toletum, et aliae similes, authoritatem non habent movendi bellum offensivum absque suorum principum facultate" (*ibid.*).

The Tuscarora Indian tribe of New York state, part of the Iroquois group, is reported as having declared war on Germany in 1917 as an "independent people." The Tuscarora tribe, however, never offered to smoke the peace pipe with a German representative during peace negotiations and therefore a technical "state of war" with Germany still exists (see *New York Times*, May 12, 1941, p. 1).

[34] St. Thomas and Cajetan's commentary are linked together under one citation: *Summa Theologica*, II^a and II^{ae}, qu. 40, art. I.

[35] Adrian VI (1459-1523), last non-Italian pope, native of Utrecht, eminent theologian. His *Quaestiones in IV Sententiarum*, published at Louvain in 1516, is cited three or four times in Molina's treatise on war.

[36] Vitoria, *De Jure Belli*, nos. 5 ff.

[37] Diego Covarrubias (1512-1577), writer on theology and jurisprudence at Salamanca and Oviedo. His treatise on war is to be found in his "Relectiones in Regulam Peccatum...," Pars II, par. 9, no. 1, *Opera Omnia* (Lugduni, 1586). Cited sixteen times by Molina.

[38] Alfonso de Castro, O.F.M., is cited by Molina eight times. The reference at this point is to the first work, lib. II, cap. xiv.

[39] Soto, *op. cit.*, lib. V, q. 3, art. 5.

[40] Gabriel Biel (1425-1495), one of the better known theologians of his time. His treatise on war is contained in his *Collectorium seu Epithome in Magistro Sententiarum Libros Quatuor*, in which work the present reference is lib. IV, disp. 15, q. 4, art. 5. He is cited by Molina nine times.

[41] Panormitanus (Nicholas de Tudeschis), O.S.B. (1386-1445), a celebrated Sicilian author who was referred to *supra* in the chapter on Church-State relations. The reference here is to his *Lectura in Decretales*, II^a in II^{um}, "De Jurejurando," Capit. *Sicut*, no. 7 ff.

[42] Bartolo de Sassoferrato (1312-1357 [?]) famous civil lawyer and professor at Pisa, known to the Spaniards as "el grande comentador." His work *Tractatus Repressaliarum* and *Commentaria in Secundam Digesti Novi Partem*

Quincy Wright devotes a chapter to the problems of sovereignty and war in which he points out that modern international law took form in the sixteenth century while princes were claiming and in some places maintaining a monopoly of violence in territories larger than the feudal domains and smaller than Christendom. The distinguishing feature of international law was its assertion of the sole competence of the sovereign state to make war. Sovereignty has been considered a major cause of modern war. [45] According to Arnold Brecht, "There is a cause of wars between sovereign states that stands above all others—the fact that there are sovereign states, and a very great many of them." [46] Quincy Wright muses that perhaps it would be no less accurate to attribute war to the fact that there are no sovereign states but a great many that want to be. [47]

Bodin defined sovereignty in Molina's lifetime, insisting that it is the "distinguishing mark of the sovereign that he cannot in any way be subject to the commands of another, for it is he who makes law for the subject, abrogates law already made, and amends obsolete law." [48]

Bodin conceived of sovereignty as a relation between a personal ruler and his subjects and gave only casual attention to the relations of such rulers *inter se.* Grotius would later give detailed attention to these relationships but thought of them as relationships between individual monarchs. Both Grotius and Bodin were aware of the medieval tradition that conceived society as an organic hierarchy of governing individuals. They modified this concept in the light of changing conditions by giving extraordinary emphasis to one state in the hierarchy which they term "sovereignty." [49]

---

are cited by Molina six times in this section. The present reference is to the second work, "De Cap. et Postlim. Reversis," *v. hostes.*

[43] St. Isidore of Seville (570-636), whose *Etymologiarum Libri XX* was a veritable encyclopaedia of knowledge right up to Molina's time. He treated war in the first chapters of Book XVIII, to which Molina refers in this place.

[44] St. Augustine, *Contra Faustum,* lib. XXII, cap. 75.

[45] Quincy Wright, *A Study of War* (2 vols.; Chicago: The University of Chicago Press, 1942), II, 895-922.

[46] Arnold Brecht, "Sovereignty" in *War in Our Time,* ed. Hans Spier and Alfred Kähler (New York: W. W. Norton, 1939), p. 58.

[47] Wright, *Study of War,* II, 896.

[48] Bodin, *op. cit.,* p. 28. Another aspect of the question of sovereignty will be seen later in this chapter when the right of conquest and colonization of public-held natural resources is treated by Molina as a possible just cause of war.

[49] Wright, *Study of War,* II, 899.

When Dante wrote his *De Monarchia*, he was convinced
that there could be but one "monarch" in the world; he was
thinking, of course, of the Christian world. Two centuries later
Machiavelli located supreme power, or at least the competence
to strive for it, in the hundreds of princes, dukes, counts, and
republics continually waging war on each other. Quincy Wright
is of the opinion that the shift in the locus of supreme power
may not have been as great as the above citations suggest. [50]
It is true that there were warring baronies in the fourteenth
century and aspirations for unity in the sixteenth century, but
there is more ground for attributing sovereignty to the many
in the later than in the earlier period. [51]

The theologians and canonists of the Middle Ages inquired
whether the wars of princes and barons were "private wars"
or "public wars." They agreed that the war against the infidel
authorized by the pope and conducted in the Crusades was a
public war, but with respect to other wars they differed. According to the theory of time, a public war could only be authorized by a ruler who had legal characteristics which later
would have been called sovereignty. Some thought the emperor or the pope alone had all these characteristics. Others
recognized that certain kings had these powers and they all
assumed that the right to make war was prior to the fact of
waging war. Because one was fighting or even fighting successfully did not prove that he had the right to fight. [52]

The age of science reversed this order. Instead of inquiring
who can wage a just war, writers began to ask: "Whom does
the army obey?" He whom the army obeyed actually made
war, whatever be his title or his morals. In both the ages, war
power was associated with sovereignty but in the Middle Ages
the war power flowed from the legal title of the monarch.
During the Renaissance legal titles flowed from successful war-
making.

---

[50] *Ibid.*, p. 901.

[51] On this point, J. Neville Figgis (*From Gerson to Grotius, 1414-1625* [Cam-
bridge: Cambridge University Press, 1916], p. 23), remarks, "With all reserva-
tions there remains a broad difference between the self-sufficing unit of International Law, and the spoke in the wheel of Christendom. The closer we look
the more we see that it is the resemblance which is superficial, and the differences that are profound, between medieval and modern notions."

[52] Wright, *Study of War*, II, 902.

For a summary of the medieval scholastic position on this point, *see*
Regout, *op. cit.*, p. 31.

In the late sixteenth century the juristic conception of sovereignty could be applied to territorial princes with less doubt
than in either the fourteenth or the fifteenth century.   On
the one hand, the papacy had lost prestige and the Empire
had lost its shadowy titles to land outside of Germany and
northern Italy.   On the other, many of the minor princelings
had been united by force of arms, so that Bodin could "tidy
up Europe" by distinguishing a moderate number of sovereigns
who deserved the title according to his juristic definition. [53]

Molina places in his text a famous quotation from Augustine:
"Ordo ille naturalis mortalium paci accomodatus hoc poscit, ut
suscipiendi belli authoritas atque consilium penes principes sit."
In this text Augustine is considering an absolute monarch but
Molina extends its meaning to cover the free commonwealths
of his own day, for he expressly refers to his earlier treatise on
the origin of civil authority where he taught that any authority
practised by an executive is derived from the commonwealth
which never wholly yields all its authority. [54]

By way of parenthesis, Molina disposes of an opinion of
Bartolo which held that any member state in the Holy Roman
Empire needed the Emperor's consent to declare and wage war.
Whatever it meant in Bartolo's day, it certainly, according to
Molina, did not refer to the Spanish kingdoms, France, Italy,
and some others who need no consent of the Emperor to wage
war. [55]

The reason authority to wage war resides in a sovereign
ruler is based on Aristotle's dictum that a perfect society is
self-sufficient.   Therefore it may take any means, even the sword,
to recover what has been taken unjustly from its subjects and
punish those who have inflicted injuries on them.   If the commonwealth as a perfect society has this power, the ruler to

---

[53] Wright, *Study of War*, II, 903.

[54] "Idem de Republica libera intelligens.   Ut enim disp. 23 et 26 ostensum
est, authoritas quae est in principe aut rege, a Republica in eum derivata est,
eamque proinde retinet Respublica, quae alio regiminis genere seipsam gubernat" (II, 100, 415).

[55] "Cum jura quaedam Caesarea, ut l. hostes. ff. de captivis et postlim.
revers. et l. hostes, ff. de verb. signif. docent, bellum inferri non posse absque
Imperatoris consensu, intelligendum id esse, de subditis Romani Imperii, ut
tempore, quo jura illa condita fuere, subdita erat pars magna orbis.   Iam
vero hodie paucissimae provinciae illi subsunt: reliquae autem, ut Hispanicae
omnes, Gallicae, Italicae, et pleraeque aliae, eo consensu non indigent" (II,
100, 416).

whom it has been transferred ("in quam proinde suam transtulit potestatem") may exercise this power. [56]

The reason a ruler who has a superior may not wage war
on his own authority is that he can petition from his superior
for redress of damages and injuries received. [57]   Although

---

[56] "Ratio quare authoritas bellum inferendi resideat in principe, qui superiorem non habet, et in Republica libera, reddita est in disputatione praecedente. Unaquaeque enim integra Respublica sufficiens sibi esse debet, ut Arist. 3.
Politicorum docet, eaque de causa, propter rationes disputatione praecedente
redditas, stringere potest gladium, etiam in externos malefactores, repetendo,
quae injuste a sibi subditis abstulerunt, et injurias suis illatas vindicando:
porro quae authoritas est in Republica libera, eadem est in principe, quem
sibi in caput supremum elegit, in quem proinde suam transtulit potestatem:
eadem quoque est in principe, qui belli jure legitimum Reipublicae alicuis [sic]
dominium comparavit" (II, 100, 416; II, 99, 412).

Corwin (op. cit., p. 210) uses the "perfect society" reasoning in discussing
the powers of the United States in foreign affairs. "It must follow, then,
that the Constitution, instead of being the *immediate* source of external powers
of the National Government, is only their mediate source, and confers them
simply in consequence of having established a nation which is truly sovereign
in relation to other nations. Or in other words, the power of the National
Government in the diplomatic sphere, while susceptible of limitation by the
Constitution when the restrictions which it imposes upon all power apply,
is an *inherent* power, one which owes its existence to the fact that the American people are a sovereign entity at international law."

Justice Iradell in *Penhallow* v. *Doane* (3 Dallas 54 [1795]) advanced the
theory that sovereignty originally belonged to the states in external as well as
the internal field, but that upon the establishment of the Constitution their
sovereignty in the former field passed to the national government. Justice
Paterson, in the same case, took the position that external sovereignty of the
national government as to foreign relations was an inheritance from the Continental Congress and this latter theory is adopted by the Supreme Court in
the case of *United States* v. *Curtiss-Wright Export Corporation.*

Justice Sutherland maintained (299 U.S. 304, [1936], 316-317): "As a result
of the separation from Great Britain by the colonies, acting as a unit, the
powers of external sovereignty passed from the Crown not to the colonies
severally, but to the colonies in their collective and corporate capacity as
the United States of America. Even before the Declaration, the colonies were
a unit in foreign affairs, acting through a common agency—namely, the Continental Congress, composed of delegates from the thirteen colonies. That
agency exercised the powers of war and peace, raised an army, created a
navy, and finally adopted the Declaration of Independence. Rulers come and
go; governments end and forms of government change; but sovereignty sur-
vives. A political society cannot endure without a supreme will somewhere.
Sovereignty is never held in suspense. When, therefore, the external sovereignty of Great Britain in respect of the colonies ceased, it immediately passed
to the Union."

[57] "Ratio quare magnates, qui superiorem habent, et civitates, quae partes
sunt integrae Reipublicae, jus non habent inferendi bellum propria authoritate,
haec est. Quoniam petere possunt justam vindictam, et compensationem damnorum ac injuriarum coram suo superiore" (II, 100, 417).

Molina seems to agree with Vitoria in this matter, he actually takes a stricter stand than his Dominican mentor. Vitoria would permit a right of prescription for certain dependent regions and cities. [58] Molina is less willing to admit such customs, especially regarding the then-dependent areas of Germany and Italy, but admits it is too difficult to make any general rule: "Quam rem, qui absentes sumus, commode definiri non possumus." [59]

Vitoria allowed a reason of necessity to confer the power of waging an aggressive war on a dependent ruler:

> For if within one and the same realm one city should take up arms against another, or one of the dukes against another duke, and the king should neglect or should lack courage to exact redress for the wrongs that have been done, the aggrieved city or duke may not only resort to self-defence, but may also commence war. . . . [60]

Molina, having cited this opinion of Vitoria, betrays his own reluctance to accept it by the following observations: "Non tamen auderem facultatem hanc multum extendere." [61]

Molina finds no difficulty in agreeing with Panormitanus that a ruler who is subject to another may, within his own jurisdiction, wage war against rebellious citizens. [62] This same right is acknowledged today in the United States where every state governor is empowered to call out the militia in times of emergency. However, instead of being considered part of power to make war, it is generally conceded to be an act of the police power to restore order . Strictly speaking, it is not an exception to Molina's rule. [63]

---

[58] "As, however, these matters are for a great part governed by the law of nations or by human law, custom can give power and authority to make war. And so if any State or prince has obtained by ancient custom the right to make war of itself or himself, this authority cannot be gainsaid, even if in other respects the State be not a perfect one" (Scott, *op. cit.*, Appendix B, p. liii).

[59] II, 100, 418.

[60] Scott, *op. cit.*, Appendix E, p. liii.

[61] II, 100, 418.

[62] "Panorm. c. sicut, 3. de jure jurando, quem multi alii sequuntur, affirmat, magnatem, qui superiorem agnoscit, posse pro quantitate jurisdictionis, quam ad sibi subditos puniendos habet, movere bellum adversus suos rebelles et iniquos, intra limites effectuum, ad quos sua jurisdictio sese extendit. Id quod nulli potest esse dubium" (*ibid.*).

[63] Stone (*op. cit.*, p. 304, n. 40a) points out that in the case of civil war, which is not international war, insurgents not recognized as a government

Molina asks wheter two sovereign kingdoms who have one head may war on each other without the consent of their mutual head. [64] Molina cites the example of Spain and Portugal during his day united under the single crown of Philip II. Molina denies these two states the right of independent war. In this he differs (without mentioning the fact) from Vitoria. [65] The Dominican carries the Aristotelian principle to its logical conclusion and says that two such commonwealths could wage war without the consent of their common superior. [66]

Molina concludes the disputation with a discussion of the rights of the Roman Pontiff regarding war. Not only in his capacity as prince of the patrimony of Peter and the estates of the Church may the Roman Pontiff wage war; but also because of the authority he has over all rulers to promote the supernatural end may he wage war and, if necessary, delegate his power to another. [67]. Here Molina has returned to the posi-

---

may, by recognition of their "belligerency," be accorded a limited status under war-law.

See W. L. Walker, "Recognition of Belligerency and Grant of Belligerent Rights," *Transactions of the Grotius Society*, XXIII (1938), 177-210.

[64] "Petet aliquis, utrum quando duae integrae Respublicae, aut regna, unum habent commune caput, ut hodie habent regna omnia Hispaniarum, possit unum adversus alterum movere bellum absque facultate communis regis. Ex dictisque facile constat, non posse: eo qoud tota authoritas utriusque ad movendum bellum sit penes communem principem. Excipitur, quando supervenisset ea necessitas, quae de civitatibus, aut magnatibus ejusdem regni paulo ante explicata est" (II, 100, 418).

[65] Prieto (*op. cit.*, pp. 133-135) has a rather lengthy discussion of this difference between Molina and Vitoria. Elaborate explanations do not seem to be necessary if one considers the uniquely delicate situation Molina found himself in as a Castilian teaching in a Portuguese university. There were tensions enough between the two temporarily united kingdoms without encouraging them.

[66] "A perfect State or community, therefore, is one which is complete in itself, that is, which is not a part of another community, but has its own laws and its own council and its own magistrates, such as is the Kingdom of Castile and Aragon and the Republic of Venice and others.... For there is no obstacle for many states and principalities and perfect States being under one prince" (Scott, *op. cit.*, Appendix B, p. liii).

[67] "Illud superest admonendum cum communi Doctorum sententia, quando persona Ecclesiastica supremum dominium temporale alicujus Reipublicae obtinet ad eum spectare authoritatem movendi bellum, sive illud per se sive per alium, juxta ea quae inferius dicenda sunt, debeat exercere. Summus autem Pontifex, non solum tamquam princeps patrimonii Divi Petri, terrarumque in Ecclesiae bonis contentarum, movere potest bellum, non secus ac alii principes temporales, sed etiam, pro potestate, quam in omnes laicas potestates ad finem supernaturalem habet, poterit vel bellum movere, vel facultatem illud movendi aliis concedere, oblata justa aliqua occasione ac causa, juxta ea quae disp. 29 dicta sunt" (II, 100, 418).

tion he had explained in the treatise on Church-State relations. Soto earlier and Suárez later recognized a similar right of the Supreme Pontiff. [68]

In the following disputation [69] Molina completes his teaching on the authority necessary to wage war. His teaching is that those who without proper authorization undertake to wage war, even when they think their cause is just, sin gravely against both charity and justice and are bound to repair all injustices committed against their opponents.

Such is the doctrine of Molina concerning the first essential condition for a just war: competent authority. Molina is cited in this matter by Suárez, [70] Valentia, [71] Vazquez, [72] and St. Alphonsus Liguori. [73] It should be remarked that Molina's use of the "princeps" has a rather elastic meaning as is evident from treatment in the preceding disputation, where he insists that legitimate custom can determine that others than the heads of state can have the power to wage war. Modern interpretation of Molina's principles would depend in part on the particular constitutional arrangements of each state. [74]

The Right Intention

The medieval writers had included right intention among the conditions necessary for a licit war. St. Thomas expressly lists it among the requisites: "Tertio requitur ut sit intentio bellantium recta, qua scilicet intenditur vel ut bonum promoveatur, vel ut malum vitetur." [75] Molina, devoting a brief disputation to the question, begins with the statement: "Tertia

---

[68] Prieto, *op. cit.*, p. 135.

[69] II, 101, 418-420.

[70] Suárez, *De Charitate*, Disp. XIII, sec. IIa.

[71] Gregory de Valentia, S.J., *Commentariorum Theologicorum ... 2ª 2ᵃᵉ D. Thomae* (Lugduni, 1609), Tomus III, qu. 16, ad 2ᵘᵐ.

[72] Gabriel Vazquez, S.J., *Commentaria in 1ᵃᵐ 2ᵃᵉ S. Thomae* (Venetiis, 1600), qu. 19, art. VI, Disp. 64, 2-3.

[73] St. Alfonso de Liguori, *Theologia Moralis*, Vol. II, Bk. 2 (2 vols.; Taurini: Marietti, 1872), Tract. 4, chap. i.

[74] For a collection of the relevant constitutional provisions see Boris Mirkin-Gutzévitch, *Les constitutions européennes* (Paris: Presses Universitaires de France, 1951), pp. 205ff.

On the position in the United States see Alfred H. Putney, *Executive Assumption of the War Making Power*, Sen. Doc. No. 39 (Washington: Government Printing Office, 1928).

[75] *Summa Theologica*, qu. 40, art. 1.

conditio necessaria ut bellum sit licitum est ut debita fiat intentione." [76]

St. Thomas, viewing war as an evil opposed to the virtue of charity, states that a war undertaken without this third condition is illicit—i. e., contrary to the virtue of charity. Molina, treating war under the formality of the virtue of justice, also holds that a war undertaken without this third condition (presupposing the other two) would not be unjust but illicit; [77] Cardinal Cajetan had earlier defended the same doctrine. [78]

Molina, with St. Thomas and St. Augustine, insists that war may not be waged from a motive of hatred but only for the promotion of the common good, or to recover what has been unjustly taken. [79] Enlargement of empire and fame are not sufficient motives for war. Occasions of war must not be sought. To this general principle Molina subjoins a curious exception. If a war will redound to the good of the nation against which it is being waged, or to the Church so that many will be converted and the Faith spread, it is permissible to wage war in the hope that a just cause be found. [80] This exception seems inadmissible. St Paul warns: "Non sunt facienda mala ut eveniant bona." [81]

Just Causes of War

The second condition which is required for a just war is a just cause. In the language common to the theologians and jurists this is generally comprehended by the term *injuria* in the sense of the violation of a right. Molina takes up this

---

[76] II, 107, 437.

[77] "Ratio est quoniam peccatum ejusmodi bellum illicitum inferentium non est contra justitiam, sed solum contra caritatem (pugnant namque juste, sed non bene ex parte intentionis), obligatio autem restituendi non oritur ex culpa contra charitatem, sed contra justitiam" (II, 107, 439).

[78] Prieto, *op. cit.*, p. 204.

[79] "Necesse est ergo, ut bellum non procedat ex odio, sed vel intuitu boni communis, vel recuperandi, quod ad bellum moventem pertinet, vel justae vindictae, aut alterius justae causa belli" (II, 107, 437).

[80] "Illud addiderim, quando bellum cederet in majus bonum nationum quibus inferretur, necnon Ecclesiae, quia ea via converterentur ad fidem, propagaretur Ecclesia, cessarent a peccatis, multique eorum vitam aeternam consequerentur fas esse, utendo nostro jure, id efficere, unde futurum speramus, ut detur nobis justa causa belli, esto alioquin id non essemus facturi, et esto simul intendamus commodum nostrum temporale" (II, 107, 438).

[81] Romans 3:8.

question in the next disputation. [82]   He begins by citing St. Augustine, [83] St. Thomas, [84] and Vitoria. [85]

Vanderpol protests it is unfortunate that Vitoria and Suárez departed from St. Thomas' definition of a just war: "On peut de même regretter que Victoria et Suarez n'aient point conservé pour la définition de la cause juste de la guerre la formule donnée par saint Thomas, et qui résume toute la doctrine." [87]   Later he says:

> Malheureusement, Victoria et Suarez, comme nous l'avons vu plus haut, ne la conservèrent pas intégralement dans sa forme nette et concise; nous disons "malheureusement," car, s'il est contestable et démontré par le contexte qu'ils avaient sur la cause juste absolument les mêmes idées que saint Thomas qu'ils commentaient, les définitions qu'ils ont données étaient moins précises, et avaient le désavantage de ne pas contenir le mot *faute*; de sorte qu'isolées du reste de leurs ouvrages des explications complémentaires qu'ils donnaient, ces définitions pouvaient prêter à des interprétations différentes, et préparer les modifications dans la doctrine que l'on constate dans les auteurs qui les suivent. [88]

The key word in Vanderpol's mind is *faute* (*culpa*), which St. Thomas includes but Vitoria omits from the definition of war.   It is a question of some importance because on its solution rests the answer to another question: Can a war be just on both sides? [88]   And it is especially pertinent to this study since Molina is expressly indicted by Vanderpol as one who

---

[82] Although Ernest Nys says, "Les causes de juste recours aux armes furent étudiées et scrutées (au Moyen Age) comme elles ne le furent plus depuis" (*Le droit de la guerre et les precurseurs de Grotius* [Bruxelles: Librairie Européene C. Muquardt, Merzbach et Falk, Editeurs, 1882], pp. 71-72), one must agree with Prieto (*op. cit.*, p. 140): "Por nuestra parte, podemos afirmar que a nadie cuadran mejor que a nuestro Autor, pues, entre todos los clásicos, es, sin duda alguna, el que más ampliamente trató le presente cuestión, a la que dedicó cinco de sus Disputaciones (102-106), ricas en principios humanitarios y en las que destaca, mejor que en ninguna otra parte, como pensador profundo e independiente."

[83] "Justa bella definiri solent quae ulciscuntur injurias" (St. Augustine, *Questionum in Heptateuchum*, Lib. VI, qu. 10; *PL*, XXXIV, 781).

[84] "Secundo requiritur causa justa ut scilicet illi qui impugnantur propter aliquam culpam impugnationem mereantur" (*Summa Theologica*, II^a II^{ae}, qu. 40, art. 1).

[85] "Unica est sola causa justa inferendi bellum injuria accepta" (Vitoria, *De Jure Belli*, no. 13).

[86] Vanderpol, *op. cit.*, p. 253.

[87] *Ibid.*, pp. 259-260.

[88] *Ibid.*, pp. 261-263.

deviated from the traditional doctrine by following this definition.

Since right and duty are correlative terms, a real absolute
right to an object necessarily excludes another real absolute
right to the same object in the same order. Otherwise one
would be affirming and denying the same thing about the same
subject in the same respect and at the same time. Before
Vitoria's time, since *culpa* was always required before a war
could be just, the scholastic writers did not admit that a material injustice (one without fault) could be admitted as a just
and sufficient cause of war. This proposition had one exception
—invincible ignorance—and the exception was confirmed by a
classic case in the Old Testament. The Israelites were commanded by God to seize the land of the Amorrhites in Canaan. [89]
The Amorrhites, invincibly ignorant of God's command to the
Israelites, defended their territory against what they considered
to be an unjust aggressor. [90] On their side, the war was materially just; on the side of the Israelites, it was both materially
and formally just. [91]

Molina cites [92] this classic case from the Old Testament and
argues that taking the land was not the only object of the
Israelites, otherwise they could not have slaughtered all the
people they did in that campaign. He says that God ordered
the Israelites to wipe out these tribes because of idolatry and
other serious sins. They acted therefore as ministers of God's
justice. [93]

---

[89] Josue 10:8-43.

[90] See Vanderpol, *op. cit.*, pp. 48-50, for a list of the theologians, including
St. Augustine, who held the possibility of the exception noted.

[91] II, 102, 421.

[92] "Observa tamen, ad bellum justum sufficere interdum injuriam materialiter, hoc est absque peccato. Eo namque ipso, quod Deus concesserat
filiis Israel terras Chananaeorum, et Amorraeorum, jus habebant expellendi
bello gentes illas repugnantes, ut, quod suum Dei donatione erat, occuparent,
esto gentes illae donationem a Deo factam ignorarent, eaque de causa absque
peccato resisterent, retinereque vellent terras illas, ac proinde solum materialiter injuriam filiis Israel facerent. Hac ratione Abulen. Josue 11 affirmavit,
bellum illud ex utraque parte fuisse justum. Ex parte quidem filiorum Israel
materialiter et formaliter: ex parte vero illarum gentium formaliter solum,
quatenus, invincibiliter ignorantes donationem et voluntatem Dei, absque peccato se resque suas tuebantur" (II, 102, 421).

[93] "Attente tamen, filios Israel non habuisse solum hoc jus, ut bellum
illud moverent; alioqui nefas illis profecto fuisset, interficere omnes gentes
illas, quae nullum peccatum adversus eos commiserant, atque adeo ex eo
titulo solum illis licuisset ea efficere, quae omnino necessaria erant, ut de
illorum potestate extraherent, quae sibi a Deo erant donata, et nihil amplius.
Ultra illum autem titulum, hunc etiam habebant, quod propter idololatriam

Molina retains the principles of the scholastic authors un-changed, adding an important distinction which by no means constitutes the doctrinal deviation which made Vanderpol so unhappy.

First, Molina says that for a just war material injury suf-fices. [94] This material injury is of two types. The first type is the result of invincible ignorance, for example, when in in-vincible ignorance something is retained which really belongs to another. [95] Even though, because of the invincible ignorance, there is no moral fault involved, the retention of what belongs to another is an injury which suffices to justify war. [96] The second type of material injury is that by which, through the same invincible ignorance and thereby without moral fault, an injury is inflicted though the person inflicting the injury does not gain anything. [97] There is no obligation, therefore, of re-turning anything since nothing is gained, although injury has been inflicted, and no right of recovering anything since nothing is lost. Thus this second type of material injury does not justfy war. [98]

Now Molina is in a position to distinguish two types of offensive war. The first type of war is undertaken because of an injury received; whether at the same time the object is to recover what rightly belongs to the party injured does not matter. For this war to be just, there must be a previous fault

---

et gravissima alia peccata, quae gentes illae in Deum commiserant, jusserat Deus filiis Israel, ut eas interficerent, ac delerent; eaque de causa, tamquam Dei ministri, authoritate et jussu Dei puniebant eorum peccata interficiendo homines illos, terrasque et eorum bona occupando. Quia tamen gentes illae hoc quoque invincibiliter ignorabant, absque peccato seipsos defendebant, et contra impugnantes bellabant" (*ibid.*).

[94] "Observa tamen, ad bellum justum sufficere interdum injuriam mate-rialiter, hoc est, absque peccato" (*ibid.*).

[95] "Dixi paulo antea, ad bellum justum sufficere interdum injuriam mate-rialiter: quoniam duplex est materialis injuria. Una, qua sine peccato propter ignorantiam invincibilem, detinetur, quod revera alteri debetur, ita quod obli-gatio id tradendi est ex parte ipsius rei, excusat tamen a culpa ignorantia invin-cibilis" (*ibid.*).
422).

[97] "Altera vero, qua ex eadem ignorantia, ac proinde sine culpa damnum aut injuria infertur, inde tamen, qui injuriam infert, non fit locupletior, atque adeo neque ex parte rei acceptae consurgit obligatio quicquam tradendi, neque ex parte injustae acceptionis: eo quod ignorantia a culpa excuset" (*ibid.*).

[98] "Posterior vero non item: eo quod neque in poenam possit juste inferri, cum nulla praecesserit culpa, neque ad obtinendum, quod bellum inferenti debeatur; cum nihil, quod ad eum pertineat, detineat is, cui bellum infertur" (*ibid.*).

(*culpa*) on the part of the enemy. It is of this type of war
that Augustine, Aquinas, and Vitoria are speaking. [99]

The second type of offensive war is undertaken to recover
what belongs to a party which is now, as the result of invincible ignorance, being retained by another and there is no other
way to get it back. In this type of war a material injury suf-
ficies; it is not necessary that there be previous moral fault.
Since the enemy is not guilty of formal fault, only that which
is necessary to recover what has been taken is allowed. Anything beyond that results in injustice and he, in turn, would
be bound to restitution. [100]

Molina is quick to subjoin that not all injuries, either
material or formal, present cause for a just war. To justify
a war the injury received must be judged a grave one. Just
as criminals are not punished with severest penalties for each
and every violation of the law, so neither for just any injury
from an external enemy may war be waged which involves so
much slaughter and devastation. [101]

Molina likewise warns that a ruler who wages war can be
as unjust against his own country as against that of his enemy.
If in the judgment of a prudent person a war would be gravely
detrimental to his own commonwealth because it lacks the resources to win; or, with a minimum possible good resulting,
he exposes his subjects to great dangers and hardships, to in-

---

[99] "Juxta hactenus dicta, possumus distinguere duplex genus belli offensivi.
Unum, quod infertur ad ultionem sumendam de injuria illata, sive simul intendamus recuperare nostra, resarcireque damna nobis illata, sive non. Atque,
ut hoc justum sit, necesse est praecedat culpa in hostibus, et de hoc tantum
videntur locuti Augustin. D. Thomas, et Victoria locis citatis, dum ad justitiam ejusmodi belli culpam praerequirunt in hostibus" (*ibid.*).

[100] "In hoc secundo belli justi genere, cum nulla sit culpa ex parte
hostium, solum licet facere adversus eos, quod necessarium est ad extrahen-
dum de ipsorum potestate, quae injuste materialiter detinent: etiam si sit
cum eorum interitu ac caede conjunctum . . . quod si aliquid amplius fiat, injustitia committitur cum onere restituendi" (*ibid.*).

[101] "Illud est animadvertendum cum Victor. loc citatio nu. 14. et aliis, non
quamcunque injuriam vel materialem, vel simul etiam formalem, esse sufficientem, ut bellum juste inferatur, sed oportere esse prudentis arbitrio gravem,
et dignam, ut propter eam tantum malum, quantum est bellum, inferatur.
Ratio est, quoniam sicut non licet pro quacunque culpa exsequi graves poenas, ut mortis, abscissionis membri, et flagellorum, in internos malefactores:
ita non licet pro quacumque injuria ab externis illata bellum adversus eos
movere, quo tot caedes, direptiones, incendia, vastationes, et similia alia gravissima mala inferuntur. Etenim juxta delicti quantitatem esse debet plaga-
rum modus. Unde pro levioribus injuriis, et causis, concedi solent repraesalia
[sic], quae vocant, de quibus infra erit sermo" (II, 102, 423).

creased taxes, and so forth, then a ruler who wages such a war would be guilty of grave injustice. "A commonwealth does not exist for the ruler but the ruler exists for it, to defend, administer and govern it not according to his own whims and desires but for the good of the commonwealth." [102]

Can A War Be Just on Both Sides?

The question of the possibility of a war being just on both sides was no problem to the Romans or the pagans in general. Suárez points out that they believed might makes right. [103] Christian morality soon developed the fundamental distinction between a just and an unjust war; war could not be just on one side without being unjust on the other. St. Augustine makes that clear in his *City of God*. St. Thomas does not treat the subject explicitly, but his answer to the question lies in his definition of a just war: "Causa justa, ut scilicet illi qui impugnantur propter aliquam culpam, impugnationem mereantur." [104]

Vitoria asks the question whether it be enough cause for a just war that a prince believes himself to have a just cause.

---

[102] "Illud etiam est animadvertendum, Principem in bello inferendo non minus posse esse injustum adversus suam Rempublicam, quam adversus alienam, cui illud inferre parat. Eaque de causa, non solum esse illi attendendum, an habeat justam belli causam adversus alienam Rempublicam, sed etiam, an injustus sit adversus suam ejusmodi bellum movendo. Etenim si prudentis arbitrio tale bellum futurum est in detrimentum maximum suae Reipublicae, quia vires non habet ad superandum, vel quia cum modico suae Reipublicae, bonique communis emolumento, subditos suos maximis periculis et detrimentis exponet, reditus publicos in eo insumet, Rempublicam novis tributis et exactionibus gravabit etc. sane culpa erit lethalis, contra justitiam adversus suam Rempublicam, ejusmodi bellum suscipere, si commode ab eo possit abstinere.

"Respublica namque non est propter Regem, sed Rex propter Rempublicam, ut illam defendat, administret et gubernet, non ad suum arbitratum, vanitatem, et commodum, sed ad Reipublicae commune bonum, quo fine adductae gentes praefecerunt sibi Reges ac Principes, atque eis ad id jus, quod habent, potestatemque tribuerunt" (*ibid.*).

[103] Suárez, *Opera Omnia*, Vol. XII, Disp. XIII, Sectio Quarta: "Fuit error Gentilium qui putaverunt regnorum jura esse posita in armis, licereque bella indicare solum ad nomen ac divitias comparandas: quod etiam in ratione naturali est absurdissimum.

"Leges civiles ex hac parte videntur processiones ex injusto modo, quo tunc bella gerebantur. Nam credebant Romani bella, quae gerebant contra hostes reipublicae, justa esse ex utraque parte; ut enim quas tacito pacto volebant mutuo pugnare, ut qui vinceret dominus evaderet. Inde ergo putabant omnia bona hostium fieri capientium" (*ibid.*, Sectio Septima, par. 9).

[104] *Summa Theologica*, II^a II^{ae}, qu. 40, ad 2um.

His reply is that such a belief is not always enough. Even in matters of lesser moment it is not enough for a private person to believe he is acting justly. His error may be vincible and deliberate and his opinion is not enough to render the act good, but it must come up to the standard of a wise man's judgment. Otherwise, Vitoria continues, the result would be that very many wars would be just on both sides. It is not a common occurrence for princes to wage war in bad faith; they nearly always think theirs is a just cause. In this way all belligerents would be innocent and it would not be licit to kill them. Were it otherwise, even the Turks and Saracens might wage just wars against Christians—for they think they are thus rendering service to God.

Molina agrees with Vitoria that it is not sufficient cause for a just war if the ruler thinks he has a just reason, for in such a case the wars of the Turks and Saracens against the Christians would be just. When there is doubt, it is necessary to make a diligent inquiry and seek the advice of learned and prudent men in order to make a mature judgment. Also, one must listen to the reasons of the other side sincerely and without deceit. The ruler who wages war is in the position of a judge. Since not only the art of war is involved in his decision, but also the slaughter of many innocent people, the ruler must explore carefully all the reasons for and against before he decides on such an important matter. [105] It is easy to make a mistake in a moral question, especially when the welfare of the person judging is affected. If he decides carelessly and in a partisan manner, he is responsible morally for all that follows. [106]

---

[105] "Ut bellum ex parte causae justum, licitumque sit, non satis est, Principem, qui illud movet arbitrari se habere justam belli causam: sic enim et Turcarum, et Saracenorum adversus nos bella essent justa; sed opus etiam est, ut, quando res dubia esse potest, pro rei pondere, gravitate, ac difficultate diligens prius inquisitio fiat, adhibito eorum sapientium et presidentium consilio, de quibus merito credendum sit, syncero et maturo judicio, passioneque semota ea de re judicaturos, veritatemque inventuros. Audiendae etiam sunt adversariorum rationes, modo syncere, et sine fraude agere velint. Etenim princeps, qui bellum movet, rationem judicis subit circa adversarios in re gravissima, in qua, non solum agitur de re, propter quam bellum movetur, sed etiam de caede multorum, gravissimisque aliis malis alteri Reipublicae inferendis; quae proculdubio multos etiam innocentes, contingent; judex autem non, nisi sufficienter prius explorata et perspecta causa, potest licite sententiam ferre, et multo minus eam executioni mandare, eoque plus illi est trepidandum, videndumque num causa perspecta satis explorataque sit, quo de re graviori agitur" (II, 103, 423-424).

[106] "Cumque in re morali difficile verum ac justum attingatur, praesertim quando de commodo judicantis agitur, sane si negligenter et cum passione

When a dispute arises between rulers over the lawful possession of something, it is necessary to distinguish and determine (1) whether one or the other is in legitimate possession and (2) whether right of ownership is claimed in good faith. [107]

Where there is doubt of ownership, with one party in possession, the party in possession is not obligated to surrender what he holds either wholly or in part; on the other hand, the contending party may not resort to war or attempt to seize it. He may only advance his claims and the other party is obligated not only to listen to them but diligently to inquire whether the disputed possession is his. [108] Molina cites the dispute between Charles V and John III of Portugal over the rightful possession of the Molucca Islands and as an example of such a contention and how it should be settled. [109]

---

haec examinentur, facile errabitur, neque error a gravissima culpa, et restitutionis onere Principem et consiliarios excusabit" (II, 103, 424).

[107] "Quando inter Principes aliquod oritur controversia circa rem aliquam, distinguendum est. Quoniam vel unus eorum erat in legitima possessione illius, ita quod bona fide, absque dubio quin ad se pertineret, coepit illam possidere, . . ." (*ibid.*).

[108] "In primo eventu, interim dum certum non est, ad quam res pertineat sed dubium, et rationes sunt pro utraque parte, neque qui est in possessione, tenetur tradere totum, aut partem, neque qui est extra possessionem, potest, vel bellum movere, vel quicquam rei illius occupare; sed rationibus dumtaxat potest experiri jus suum; aliusque non solum tenetur eas audire, sed etiam moralem adhibere diligentiam, ut sciat, an res ad se, vel ad alium pertineat, si via aliqua occurat unde id possit deprehendi" (*ibid.*). Molina refers at this point to Vitoria: "Ita Victor. de jure belli a nu. 25" (*ibid.*). The reference is inaccurate. It should be no. 27.

[109] "Exemplum habemus accomodatum in Insulis Malucis, antequam Regnum hoc Lusitaniae cum Regno Castellae conjungeretur. Cum enim Johannes 3. Lusitaniae Rex in pacifica esset illarum possessione, dubium oriri coepit tempore Caroli V. an, juxta divisionem illam orbis occidentem et orientem versus authoritate Alexandri 6. inter Reges Castellae, et Lusitaniae factam, insulae illae ad eam partem orbis pertinerent, quae ad Reges Castellae, an vero ad aliam, quae ad Reges Lusitaniae spectat. Qua in re dico. Interim dum certum non erat, ad quam partem pertinerent, neque Regem Lusitaniae teneri tradere eas, aut partem earum, neque Regem Castellae licite potuisse movere bellum, aut partem earum occupare, sed rationibus tantum negotium fuisse transigendum, ut re ipsa peractum fuit, antequam lis ad certum tempus pro certa aureorum summa inter Carolum V. et Johannem III. componeretur. Regem tamen Lusitaniae teneri moralem facere diligentiam, ut sciret, ad quam partem pertinerent" (*ibid.*).

Sir Hugh Charles Clifford ("The Malay Peninsula," *The Encyclopaedia Britannica*, 11th ed., XVII, 469) confirms Molina's account: "Meanwhile the Spanish government was considering whether the Moluccas did not fall within the Spanish sphere of influence as defined by the Treaty of Tordesillas in 1494; and in August 1519 an expedition commanded by Ferdinand Magellan ... sailed from Seville to seek a westward passage to the archipelago. After losing the

If the contending party could, while in doubt of his title, resort to war against the one who holds possession, it would follow that since the claim was being pressed by both parties war would be just on both sides: "Id autem concedere, sane esset concedere justum bellum formaliter et materialiter ex utraque parte, *quo nihil absurdius affirmare potest.*" [110] The last phrase completely refutes Vanderpol's claim that Molina taught that a war could be just on both sides. [111]

There are some, Molina says, who hold that if doubt remains and certitude cannot be established, the one in possession must divide what he has with the other party. [112] If he refuses, then

---

commander in the Philippines and discovering Borneo, the two surviving ships reached the Moluccas late in 1520. One vessel returned to Seville by the Cape route, thus completing the first voyage round the world; the other attempted to return by the Pacific, but was driven back to Tidore and there welcomed by the natives as a useful ally against the Portuguese. Reinforcements from Spain arrived in 1525 and 1528; but in 1529 a treaty was concluded between the emperor Charles V. and John III. of Portugal, by which, in return for 350,000 gold ducats, the Spanish claim to the Moluccas was withdrawn. The boundary between the Spanish and Portuguese spheres was fixed at 17° E. of the Moluccas, but by a geographical fiction the Philippines were included within the Spanish sphere. Further disputes occurred from time to time, and in 1542 a Spanish fleet came into conflict with the Portuguese off Amboyna; but after 1529 the supremacy of each power in its own sphere was never seriously endangered."

See also Kenneth Scott Latourette, *A Short History of the Far East* (3d ed.; New York: The Macmillan Co., 1957), p. 288.

[110] "Praeterea, si is qui est extra possessionem, posset in dubio movere bellum adversus eum, qui possidet, sequeretur, existente eadem cognitione in utroque bellantium de justitia utriusque partis dari bellum justum ex utraque parte ... id autem concedere, sane esset concedere justum bellum formaliter et materialiter ex utraque parte, quo nihil absurdius affirmari potest" (II, 103, 425).

Prieto (*op. cit.*, p. 155, n. 35) says that Molina's position is the same as that of Vitoria, Soto, Covarrubias, Bañez, Suárez, John of St. Thomas, and the Salamanticenses. He cites pertinent verse and number for each.

[111] Wright (*Study of War*, pp. 878-879) perpetuates Vanderpol's error: "Even churchmen like Victoria and Molina, who clung to the medieval tradition that war could be just only on one side, modified this tradition in fact by the doctrine of 'invincible ignorance.' This doctrine held that if the side in the wrong remained ignorant of the unjustness of its cause after due study, the war should be treated as just on both sides."

See also William Ballis, *The Legal Position of War*: Changes in Its Practice and Theory from Plato to Vattel (The Hague: Martinus Nijhoff, 1937), pp. 85-86.

[112] Domingo Bañez, O.P. (*Scholastica Commentaria in Primam partem necnon in Secundam Secundae Summae Angelici Doctoris Sancti Thomae* [Lyon: S. Michael, 1638], "De Fide," qu. 40, art. 1, 1359-1362) expressly defends the position that if one of the parties to the dispute refuses to examine the other's

the party not in possession may resort to war. This was the opinion of Pope Adrian, but no other classical authors held it [113] and Molina also disagrees with it. Basically his reason is the well-known dictum: "Melior est conditio possidentis." [114]

Arbitration

Julius Stone reminds us that arbitration in its central essence of third-party decision can be found in some form throughout historical times. [115] It was known among the Greeks in a form approximating the international. [116] Neither was it uncom-

---

reasons, the latter need not delay but may resort to war. Molina implicitly admits Bañez' position.

Cf. Carro, *Domingo de Soto y su Doctrina Jurídica*, p. 330.

Yves de la Brière (*op. cit.*, pp. 42-43) has a neat summary of the general positions of Bañez and Molina on the law of war: "Ce qui pourtant différencie Bañez de Molina est que Bañez considère comme normalement acquise la culpabilité morale du prince qui détient un bien étranger et, par conséquent, le caractère punitif de la guerre dans laquelle le légitime propriétaire revendique son propre droit par la force des armes.

"Au contraire, Molina est soucieux de distinguer l'injustice d'un adversaire *coupable*, de l'injustice, d'ailleurs réélle et certaine, d'un adversaire *qui se trompe* de bonne foi. Dans ce dernier cas, le recours à la force des armes, comme moyen ultime, à défaut de tout autre, de recouvrer son propre droit et son propre bien, n'a pas et ne doit pas avoir le caractère d'une expédition punitive, tendant à châtier un coupable.

"Mais c'est par un contresens que plusieurs attribuent à Molina l'opinion, répudiée par lui, d'après laquelle une guerre pourrait être objectivement juste des deux côtés à la fois ou d'après laquelle la légitimité d'une guerre se déduirait de considérations arbitrairement empruntées au probabilisme ...;

"Chez Molina, il y aurait peut-être plus d'*esprit de finesse*. Chez Bañez, plus d'*esprit de géométrie*."

[113] "Sunt qui dicant in eventu, de quo disputamus, si re diligenter examinata, major sit verisimilitudo, quod pertineat ad eum, qui non possidet, quam ad eum, qui possidet, non tamen res certo constet, sed semper maneant dubia, eum qui possidet, teneri eam dividere cum eo, qui non possidet, pro quantitate dubii, ita ut majorem partem illi tradat, et minorem sibi retineat. Quod si opere id non praestet, posse alterutrum movere bellum tamquam adversus injustum detentorem" (II, 103, 425).

[114] "Mihi vero longe probabilius est contrarium. Quoniam interim dum res est dubia, ita ut absque ambiguitate non constet ita pertinere ad alterum, ut integre sit illi tradenda, melior est conditio possidentis, ac proinde nec totum, nec partem, existente dubio tenetur tradere" (*ibid.*).

[115] Stone, *op. cit.*, p. 75.

[116] J. H. Ralston, *International Arbitration from Athens to Locarno* (Stanford: Stanford University Press, 1929), pp. 153-298.

Karl Strupp, "Le droit du juge international de statuer selon l'équité," *Recueil des cours*, XXX (1930), 347-348, gives a basic historical survey from the ancient world to the General Act of 1928.

mon in medieval times, although medieval arbitrations were
based on rather different assumptions.[117]   One of the first effects of the emergence of the modern state system was to undermine any existing arbitral traditions.   The period immediately
following Molina's death was one of repeated and protracted
wars with but rare resort to arbitration.   Modern international
arbitration is usually traced back to Jay's Treaty of 1794, and
is considered to have developed in four stages : first, from Jay's
Treaty to the "Alabama" case of 1872; second, from 1872 to
The Hague Convention in 1899; third, from 1899 to the establishment of the Permanent Court of International Justice in
1921; and, fourth, the contemporary stage.[118]

The decline of arbitration as a means of settling disputes
in the seventeenth and eighteenth centuries spotlights Molina's
treatment of the subject.   Yves de la Brière contends "il est
exact que Molina incline plus expressément que ses contempo-
rains vers le réglement des litiges internationaux par conciliation ou arbitrage, en raison même des causes d'incertitude ou
d'erreur qui gouvernent les jugements respectifs de adversaires
en présence."[119]

When a dispute arises between two heads of state, Molina
says, one of them must propose to the other his reasons and
the other is bound to listen.   The matter in dispute must be
examined without fraud or deceit and the examination must
continue until there is no more hope of light to be gained from
its continued study or from the advice of the experts in the
field.[120]   Sometimes it helps to send emissaries to negotiate
the matter; sometimes, too, it helps for the parties in dispute
to meet with their advisers ("missisque viris doctis et peritis")
to settle the matter, as happened in the above-mentioned dispute

---

[117] On the medieval period see Baron M. de Taube, "Les origines de l'arbitrage international," *Recueil des cours*, XLII (1932), 5-114.

On the role of the Roman Pontiffs as arbitrators see G. Goyau, "L'église
catholique et le droit des gens," *Recueil des cours*, VI (1925), 162-178.

[118] Stone, *op. cit.*, p. 76.

[119] La Brière, *op. cit.*, p. 43.

[120] "Quando inter duas Respublicas, Principesve diversarum Rerumpublicarum, controversia oritur circa aliquam rem, ut quondam inter Joannem III.
et Carolum V. circa Insulas Malucas, hoc pacto res est peragenda, antequam
ad arma veniatur. Pacifice Princeps unus proponere debet alteri rationes,
ac jus totum, quod circa eam rem habet, vicissimque audire tenetur rationes,
et jus totum alterius, sicque ultro, citroque datis rationibus, et responsionibus,
res sine technis, fraudibus, ac subdolis dilationibus examinari debet, quousque verisimile sit, nihil plus lucis ex eo examine, consiliisque peritorum ea de
re posse haberi" (II, 103, 426).

about the Moluccas. [121]   Suppose, Molina asks, that after all
these efforts have been made the matter remains in dispute?
The person in possession retains possession as long as he is in
good faith, and the other party may not wage war. [122]   If neither
party has clear title, a division should be made between them
according to the claims advanced. [123]   In the case which may
arise where both parties are certain that the object belongs
to them, one is in error due to invincible ignorance.   A resulting war would then be just on both sides: "... sed ex una formaliter simul et materialiter, ex altera parte vero formaliter
tantum.   Tunc vero consilium esset optimum, ut litem transac-
tione componerent, vel ut judices eligerent arbitros, quorum
judicio starent." [124]

Regarding the role of the Roman Pontiff as arbiter, [125]
Molina returns to the position of an earlier disputation in which
he taught that the Supreme Pontiff may intervene in a dispute
between Christian rulers and render a decision "if he judges it
expedient for the good of the Church and the promotion of
the supernatural end." [126]   Ordinarily, however, it is much bet-

---

[121] "Fieri autem id poterit, vel legationibus utrinque missis, vel conventu
aliquo celebrato in confiniis Regnorum, missis utrinque viris doctis et peritis,
ut factum fuisse fertur, quando controversia illa fuit circa Insulas Malucas,
vel quovis alio modo, qui Principibus placuerit" (*ibid.*).

[122] "Re autem ita examinata, si res utrinque ita dubia maneat, ut judicio
utriusque partis certo, semotove omni dubio, non constet ad quem pertineat,
tunc si alter eorum erat bonae fidei possessor, illi omnino est relinquenda,
quousque aliud constet; neque potest quicquam ab eo exigi, nisi forte ille velit
cum alio transigere, ut remittat in futurum jus totum, quod circa eam rem
poterit obtendere.   Neque item potest ullum bellum adversus eum moveri"
(II, 103, 427).

[123] "Quod si neuter erat bonae fidei possessor, res est dividenda inter
utrumque pro dubii quantitate, ut dictum est" (*ibid.*).

[124] "Quod si partes judicio discordent, et utraque judicet semoto dubio
ad se pertinere; tunc una sane decipitur, sed si invincibiliter erret, quia moralem adhibuit diligentiam, secutaque est judicium peritorum, ac timoratorum,
erit bellum justum ex utraque parte; sed ex una formaliter simul et materialiter, ex alter vero formaliter tantum.

"Atque hac ratione potest saepe esse bellum justum formaliter ex utraque
parte.   Quamvis semper timendum sit, ne, saltem pars altera, sit in culpa,
quod non quantum oportet, aut non sine passione velit rem expendere, et
examinare" (*ibid.*).

[125] Cf. Suárez (*De Bello*, sec. II, no. 5) and Vitoria (*De Jure Belli*, II,
no. 16) for their treatment of this matter.

Eppstein (*op. cit.*, pp. 149-223) presents, with documentation, an historical
survey of the role of the Roman Pontiffs as arbitrators.

See also Goyau, *op. cit.*, pp. 162-178.

[126] "Quamvis autem, quando lis est inter principes Christianos, et judica-
retur bono Ecclesiae, finique supernaturali expedire omnino, ut Summus Pon-

ter that he not do this. [127]   The obvious reasons are that the
party against whom the judgment is rendered may take that
occasion of refusing obedience to the Holy See. For this reason
rarely, if ever, does the Roman Pontiff intervene in disputes
among Christian rulers by using his fullness of jurisdiction.
Rather, does he as a father warn the disputants to compose
their differences and avoid war. [128]

Declaration of War

International war is a relation of one or more governments
to at least one other government, in which one of such governments no longer permits its relations with the other or others
to be governed by the laws of peace. Involved in this statement, as has been wittily observed, is the assumption that while
it takes two to make a quarrel, it takes only one government
to make a war. [129]   According to Lord Stowell:

> A declaration of war by one country is not ... a mere chal-
> lenge to be accepted or refused at pleasure by the other. It
> proves the existence of actual hostilities on the one side at
> least, and puts the other party also into a state of war, though
> he may, perhaps, think proper to act on the defensive only. [130]

To constitute a war in the sense of international law, the hostile
intention must at least be directed by one government against
another government, or some authority which for the purpose
of hostilities has the status of a government. [131]

---

tifex rem definiret, posset pro plenitudine potestatis, quam ad finem supernaturalem habet, se intromittere, causamque ad se avocare, eamque sententiam
definire, et censuris, ac aliis viis rebellem compescere, ut disp. 29. dictum est"
(II, 103, 427).

[127] "Ordinarie tamen expedientius est, ne id faciat. Quoniam id occasio
esse posset gravissimorum malorum; dum, qui damnaretur, facile in odium
Summi Pontificis exardesceret, arbitraretur que passione ductum, aut re non
bene perspecta, sententiam contra se tulisse, indeque sumere posset occasionem
denegandi obedientiam Summo Pontifici, tum in aliis, tum etiam ea in re,
tam perspectumque obtenderet esse jus suum, ut diceret se etiam adversus
Summum Pontificem posse bellum movere" (ibid.).

[128] "Atque hac de causa raro aut numquam solet se intromittere in litibus
Principum Christianorum utendo plenitudine hac suae potestatis; sed solum
tanquam pater solet eos monere, ut seipsos componant, et a bello abstineant"
(ibid.).

[129] Stone, op. cit., p. 304.

[130] Ibid., p. 305.

[131] In the case of a civil war which is not an international war insurgents
not recognized as a government may, by recognition of their "belligerency,"

In spite of its obvious importance, before The Hague Convention No. 3 of 1907 no modern rules appear to have regulated the preliminaries of war relative to the opening of hostilities. The old Roman fetial law offered analogies for modern international law. [132] Down to the sixteenth century it was customary to give notification of an intended war by letter of defiance (*diffidatio*) or by heralds—variations of Roman fetial practice.

Although no formal law governed the actual declaration of war in Molina's day, there is no doubt that he and the classical authors would demand such a declaration before the outbreak of hostilities. Once the whole question has been explored sufficiently, Molina says, and the intention to wage war is made known to the enemy, if the enemy remains pertinacious it is lawful to wage war against him. [133] But Molina immediately subjoins the proviso that if the state against which war is declared offers to make satisfaction for the injuries committed, the first ruler must cease and desist from his war-like efforts. Augustine had said, "Bellum non est voluntatis, sed necessitatis." [134]

---

be accorded a limited status under war-law. On this matter Stone (*ibid.*) observes that "*vis-à-vis* governments recognizing the belligerency of General Franco's insurgent government, that government became entitled to visit and search merchant ships and impose the penalties allowed by international law for contraband and the like; and was correspondingly bound by the duties of a State at war. The civil war became, for such purposes, an international war. So, also, though the Republic North Korea was not recognized as a State by the United Nations and its Members, the hostilities which broke out in 1950 constitute international war at least to the extent that both sides have acknowledged themselves to be bound by the rules of war."

See Walker, "Recognition of Belligerency," *op. cit.*, pp. 177-210.

[132] For the history of the *jus feciale* see Coleman Phillipson, *The International Law and Custom of Ancient Greece and Rome* (2 vols.; London: Macmillan and Co. Ltd., 1911), and Isidoro Ruiz Moreno, *El derecho internacional público antes de la era cristiana* (Buenos Aires: Facultad de derecho y ciencias sociales, 1946).

Stone (*op. cit.*, p. 305) says that the main contributions of Roman private law to the origins of international law were indirect and not through the *jus feciale*.

See A. Nussbaum, "The Significance of Roman Law in the History of International Law," *University of Pennsylvania Law Review*, X (1952), 678-687.

Also Celestino Farrera, *El derecho internacional en la antigüedad y en la edad media* (Caracas: Lit. y. tip. Varbas, 1927), pp. 192-197.

[133] "Belli causa explorata et cognita sufficienter, hostibusque proposita, ut cedant, sufficienterque satisfaciant, si rebelles fuerint comperti et pertinaces, poterit moveri bellum adversus eos" (II, 103, 428).

[134] "Si hostes, antequam bellum inchoatum sit, et utrinque dimicari sit caeptum, offerant sufficientem satisfactionem, ita ut non solum parati sint

Molina now asks whether the one who is in the position to wage a just war must accept the conditions laid down by his enemy to call off the hostilities. [135] He replies affirmatively that as long as the enemy offers satisfaction he may not wage war on him. Also, a war cannot be materially and formally just on both sides. Yet it is difficult to see how the party who committed the injury and now offers satisfaction cannot defend himself if the party to whom satisfaction is offered refuses to accept it and wages war. [136] The war would then become unjust on the part of the one who refuses to negotiate. This is especially true in the case of material injury only. If full compensation is offered for the injury and the injured party refuses to accept, he will be acting unjustly. [137] However, if among his enemies certain persons are guilty of death because of their actions, Molina says the offended party would not be sinning against *justice* in demanding their execution as the price of peace, but he would be sinning against *charity* if he refused to accept other compensations in their stead. [138]

Once the war has begun, the authorities say that the party waging a just war is not bound to cease even if his adversary

---

compensare injurias et damna illata, reddereque omnia, quae ad bellatores spectant, sed etiam solvere omnes belli expensas factas, teneri Principem desistere a bello, quod movebat. Ratio est, quoniam authore August. Epistol. 205 ad Bonif. et habetur cap. Noli. 23 quaest. 1. Bellare non est voluntatis, sed necessitatis" (*ibid.*).

[135] "Dubium est. Utrum usque adeo, qui justam belli habet causam, teneatur acceptare competentem satisfactionem, et desistere a bello, quando tuto ante praelium coeptum offertur, ut nisi eam acceptet bellum ex parte ipsius sit deinceps, non solum illicitum, quia contra charitatem, sed etiam injustum, ac proinde restituere teneatur damna, quae dederit" (II, 103, 429).

[136] "Secundo, bellum non potest esse justum formaliter et materialiter ex utraque parte: sed durum admodum est concedere Rempublicam, aut Principem, qui peccarunt, et offerunt competentem satisfactionem, non posse licite se defendere, si adversa pars eam non acceptat, bellumque inferat: ergo bellum erit tunc injustum ex parte ejus, qui non vult desistere" (*ibid.*).

[137] "Ergo quando adversarius condignam satisfactionem offert, desinit alius Princeps procedere ut judex, publicave authoritate, ac proinde peccat contra justitiam, teneturque restituere damna quae intulerit" (*ibid.*).

[138] "Quando vero aliqui in particulari digni essent morte propter injuriam illatam, esto de numero eorum esset Princeps Reipublicae, adversus quam bellum geritur, non credo peccaret contra justitiam, si desistere non vellet a bello, nisi offerrentur, qui digni sunt morte, aut fugissent de ea Republica: et cum in reliquis competens satisfactio offerretur, integrum jus ei relinqueretur interficiendi malefactores illos ubicumque deprehendere eos potuisset. Peccaret tamen contra charitatem, si postulante id recta ratione, et bono utriusque Reipublicae, non acceptaret competentem satisfactionem oblatam in rebus aliis" (*ibid.*).

offers satisfaction. [139]   Molina says these authors are speaking of one being bound by the obligations of the virtue of justice but they are not speaking of the virtue of charity.   He who prosecutes a just war is more strictly bound by the law of charity to cease from the war-like intentions from the beginning of hostilities, when compensation is offered, than he is when compensation is offered after hostilities have begun. [140] The rigor of vindictive justice always permits full satisfaction for the injury committed unless due compensation is proffered. [141]

Some Particular Causes of War

Molina devotes one disputation to the types of war justified from examples in the Scriptures. [142]   Since each of these examples particularizes a principle he has already explained, they will not be detailed here.   Even Garcia Prieto admits that these examples add little to our knowledge: "La única novedad, que nuestro Autor aporta a la presente materia, es la de haberla confirmado con su competente autoridad." [143]

The next disputation does add to our knowledge, for Molina expressly departs from a position taken by his master, Vitoria, regarding immigration and colonization. [144]   Vitoria taught that the Spanish had the right to travel to other areas and settle there as long as they did not injure the natives. [145]   The Spanish,

---

[139] "Postquam autem bellum coeptum est, et caedes aliquae intervenerunt, dicunt authores citati eum, qui juste bellum infert, non teneri ab eo desistere, esto adversarii debitam offerant satisfactionem" (II, 103, 430).

[140] "Hinc credo hoc Doctores non loqui de obligatione ex justitia, sed solum ex charitate. Plus namque lege charitatis tenetur, qui justam belli habet causam, a bello abstinere, ab exequendove rigore justitiae vindicativae iura belli exequendo, quando rationabilis compensatio offertur antequam praeliari sit coeptum, quam quando compensatio post praelium incaeptum offertur" (*ibid.*).

[141] "De justitiae vero rigore semper licet exequi totam vindictam ad illud usque tempus pro injuria illata commeritam, nisi illa eadem compensatio, quae de justitiae rigore debetur, offeratur" (*ibid.*).

[142] "De causis quibusdam particularibus justi belli, Scripturarum exemplo roboratis. Disput. 104" (II, 104, 430).

[143] Prieto, *op. cit.*, p. 179.

[144] "De aliis justi belli causis, quarum quaedam probantur, quaedam rejiciuntur, aliae in locum alium remittuntur. Disput. 105" (II, 105).

[145] Vitoria, *De Jure Belli*, sec. III, 1-2: « Primus titulus potest vocari naturalis societatis et communicationis. Et circa hoc sit prima conclusio: Hispani habent jus peregrinandi in illas provincias, et illic degere, sine aliquo tamen nocumento barbarorum, nec possunt ab illis prohiberi."

likewise, have the right to the use of the water, rivers, and harbors in those areas. [146]   They are also free to carry on trade with the Indians so long as they do no harm to their home country, nor may the Indians prevent the Spaniards from communication and participation in those things which they treat as common alike to natives and strangers. [147]   All these rights, Vitoria maintains, flow from the *jus gentium*. [148]

Molina, as was said above, takes a position here that is expressly opposed to Vitoria's—"At nobis contrarium videtur verum."   He grants that in one sense Vitoria is correct: As long as a stranger is in grave necessity, he may not be prevented from taking whatever is needed.   The law of charity demands that, even without the owner's consent, a stranger to the country may take and use whatever he needs. [149]   Once there has been a division of goods and each one possesses something of his own, then that owner can licitly forbid all others to use it as long as they are not in grave necessity.   The same process works in the commonwealth.   The ruler of a state can licitly forbid all strangers to use those things which belong to all citizens as long as they are not in grave need.   He may also forbid all trade with them and does not thereby commit an injury.   Much more may foreigners be forbidden trade benefits and harbor facilities if thereby they would wax stronger. [150]   A country may

---

[146] "Jure naturali communia sunt omnium, et aqua profluens, et mare, item flumina et portus" (*ibid.*).

[147] "Licet Hispanis negotiare apud illos, sine patriae tamen damno, puta importare merces, quibus illis carent, et adducentes illinc vel aurum vel argentum, vel alia, quibus illi abundant, nec Principes illorum possunt impedire subditos suos ne exerceant commercia cum Hispanis, ne contrario Principes possunt prohibere commercia cum illis" (*ibid.*, no. 3).

"Si quae apud barbaros communia tam civibus quam hospitibus, nec licet barbaris prohibere Hispanos a communicatione et participatione illorum. Ex. gr., si licet aliis peregrinis vel effodere aurum in agro communi, vel ex fluminibus, vel piscare margaritas in mare" (*ibid.*, no. 4).

[148] "Si barbari vellent prohibere Hispanos in supradictis a jure gentium.... Hispani possunt se defendere ... et si acceperint injuriam, illam auctoritate Principis bello prosequi, et alia belli jura agere" (*ibid.*, no. 6).

[149] "Etenim, licet illa omnia gentium jure in hoc sensu fas sint cuique extraneo, quod interim dum ab habitatoribus non prohiberentur, licitum sit cuique illa efficere; et praeterea, quod dum extraneus aliquo illarum rerum usu extreme vel graviter indigebit, non possit licite prohiberi; eo quod, et lex charitatis id postulet, et rerum divisio praejudicare non potuerit quominus unusquisque, etiam invitis dominis, ea re utatur, qua extreme indiget" (II, 105, 433).

[150] "Nihilominus, cum post rerum et provinciarum divisionem non minus propria sint cuivis Reipublicae, quae ab ea possidentur in commune, et quorum dominium tota Respublica habet, quam sint cuiusque de Republica, quae

grant the use of its raw materials to some foreigners and not to others since this is each country's prerogative.[151] And it certainly cannot be denied that harbors, rivers, and mining rights come under the jurisdiction of the country where they are located. Jurisdiction in territorial waters[152] belongs to that country which is nearest and for this reason it is able to regulate the right to fish[153] therein and prohibit others from fishing in those waters.[154]

---

ab eo tanquam propria possidentur, sane quemadmodum quicunque particularis interdicere licite potest omnibus aliis ne rebus ipsius utantur quando graviter, aut extreme, his non indigebunt, et licite etiam potest nullum cum aliis commercium admittere: sic etiam Respublica moderatorve illius, licite prohibere poterit omnibus extraneis, ne rebus propriis Reipublicae, quae communes sint civibus omnibus, utantur interim dum illis extreme aut graviter non indigebunt; licite etiam poterit velle nullum cum illis habere commercium; neque in his ullam eisdem faciet injuriam" (*ibid.*).

[151] "Quod autem provincia aliqua usum quarundarum rerum suarum communium quibusdam extraneis concedat, sane ab ea libertatem non adimit, quo minus similem usum peregrinis aliis denegare possit: cum integrum cuique sit concedere, cui libuerit, rerum suarum usum; eoque aliis interdicere" (*ibid.*).

[152] The position defended by Molina is, of course, an accepted part of international law today. Most nations claim sovereignty over their territorial waters. The claims extend from three to twelve miles. Hans Weigert *et al.* (*Principles of Political Geography* [New York: Appleton-Century-Crofts, Inc., 1957], pp. 100-101) say that a majority of countries claim a zone three miles wide. The Scandinavian countries claim a four-mile limit while the remaining countries, including the Soviet Union, claim a twelve-mile belt: "The United States, on September 28, 1945, proclaimed that it would regard the 'natural resources of the subsoil and the sea bed of the continental shelf beneath the high seas but contiguous to the coasts of the United States as appertaining to the United States, subject to its jurisdiction and control'.... This assertion of rights, which is based on the geological unity of the shelf and the adjacent land, received legislative sanction by the Outer Continental Shelf Act of August 7, 1953. A number of states, most of them in the Americas and around the Persian Gulf, have followed the American example and claimed certain rights over the continental shelf. Australia followed suit in 1953, by proclaiming sovereignty over her entire continental shelf reaching in places more than two hundred miles off her coast. The Japanese were thus precluded from fishing for pearl shell in the waters off Australia's northern coast.... The present situation is confusing and gives rise to international conflicts in many oceanic boundary areas. The International Law Committee of the United Nations is therefore attempting to clarify the problems involved by emphasizing that a coastal nation exercises sovereignty over the continental shelf, but subject to the principle of the freedom of the seas" (*ibid.*, p. 101).

[153] Fishing rights in adjacent areas remain a problem for international law. Japan, for example, has been involved frequently in international conflicts arising out of actual and alleged violations of foreign waters by her fishing vessels.

A case in point is the fishing issue between Japan and the Republic of Korea, which accused Japan of violations of the so-called Rhee Line, a uni-

9

There is opposition between Vitoria and Molina on this
question, even though Luis Izaga does not admit a real difference: "En resumen, une a los dos maestros absoluta comu-
nidad de doctrina; los separa una mera discrepancia en la reso-
lución de un caso práctico: admite uno, rechaza el otro, algu-
nas razones aducidas para justificar la entrada de España en
América. No creemos que sea indefensible la posición de
Molina." [155]

There is much more than a mere discrepancy between the
two Spanish theologians. García Prieto agrees, but modifies
his opinion by the rather naive conclusion: "Es cierto que am-
bos Doctores admiten la justificatión de la conquista de América por parte de su Patria." [156] Far from being certain, it is
the real point in question. Basing his position on the law of
nations, Vitoria reaches the logical conclusion that the state
which violates this right commits an injustice; against that
state war may licitly be declared. Molina, on the contrary, basing his case on the right of public property which is already
under the jurisdiction of some state, denies a juridical obligation to concede its use to foreigners. Consequently, the state
which denies the use of its public property to foreigners is not
guilty of an injustice and there is no question of a right to
wage war, except in case of extreme need or some impediment
to the preaching of the Gospel. García Prieto admits that
historically the principles of Molina have prevailed in the field
of modern international law. [157] Considering the problem from

laterally set water boundary extending more than sixty miles from the Korean
coast (see Weigert, *op. cit.*, p. 526).

Another example occurred when some Japanese were fishing in United States
territorial waters near the Pribilof Islands and were fired upon. The ruling
in this case was that the guard could lawfully fire on these poachers (see
Charles Joseph Bonaparte to the Secretary of State, April 15, 1908, in Pressed
Copies of the Opinions of the Attorney General, [National Archives, Washington,
D.C.], XXXV, 375-381.

On this point see [n.n.] Bittremieux, *Lessius et le droit de guerre* (Bruxelles: Dewit, 1920), pp. 111.

[154] "Negari etiam non potest, portus, flumina, et fodinas auri et argenti
ad eorum dominium pertinere, quorum est provincia, in quibus sunt: Quin
et maritima unda continenti adhaerens ad eos solos pertinet quorum est provincia, eaque de causa usurpare sibi possunt jus ibi piscandi, caeterisque pisca-
turam eo loco prohibere." (II, 105, 433).

[155] Izaga, *op. cit.*, p. 197.

[156] Prieto, *op. cit.*, p. 183.

For a general discussion of the topic see Joseph Höffner, *Christentum und
Menschenwürde*: Das Anliegen der spanischen Kolonialethik in goldenen Zeitalter (Trier: Paulinus-Verlag, 1947).

[157] *Ibid.*, p. 183.

the point of view of ethics, Vitoria would seem to have the more solid arguments buttressed by the concurring opinions of a long series of authors including Soto, Bañez, and Suárez. The whole question turns on the concept of the natural society of nations. In Molina the concept of sovereignty is more accentuated than it is in Vitoria. [158] Venantio Carro points out that "las diferencias proceden de las causas señaladas por nosotros al principio de este capítulo, y que se concretan en el distinto concepto del Derecho de Gentes e Internacional. Descendiendo más, añadiremos que las divergencias se explican por el distinto concepto de la soberanía." [159]

The principles of Molina are in perfect harmony with the practice of modern international law, representing a type of "closed door" policy which bars the freedom of emigration and immigration. Vitoria's internationalism provides a remedy for some of the evils which afflict international society today, among which is the vast abyss in living standards between the "have" and "have not" nations. Soto [160] and Suárez [161] are in Vitoria's camp on this question.

---

[158] Fraga, *Los seis libros,* Appendix: "La doctrina de la soberanía en el P. Luis de Molina."

[159] Carro, *Domingo de Soto y su doctrina jurídica,* p. 320.

Vitoria's position has been exhaustively examined in a series of lectures collected into a volume of the *Anuario de la asociación Francisco de Vitoria* (Madrid), Vol. I, 1927-1928:

Three articles by Camilo Barcia Trelles: "Las 'Relecciones' de Vitoria—El problema de la conquista de América," pp. 187-197; "La autoridad universal del Emperador," pp. 197-213; "La ocupación como medio adquisitivo de la soberanía," pp. 229-269.

Aniceto Sela y Sempil, "Vitoria y los medios de aquirir la soberanía territorial," pp. 213-229.

Manuel Lasala y Llanas, "Conceptos y principios fundamentales del derecho de gentes, según la doctrina del P. Vitoria," pp. 269-305.

Isidoro Beato Sala, "Examen de los títulos 2º. y 4º. de la 'Relectio prior de Indis,'" pp. 305-329.

Joaquín Fernández Prida, "Ultimos títulos justificantes de la soberanía," pp. 329-345.

[160] Domingo Soto, *De Justitia et Jure,* Lib. IV, qu. 3: "Ex quo fit non solum divisionem in genere, verum et quod istae nationes hanc regionem possideant, et aliae aliam, esse de jure gentium. Contra quam Cajetan. 2.2. q. 66. art. 2. opinatus est.... Quarta conclusio. Complura manserunt communia jure naturae, quorum dominia jus gentium dispertiri nequivit: Puta locus, ut ait illic Arist, nempe civitas, itinera, etc. Et (ut refertur eodem Insti.) elementa: videlicet aër, aqua, littora, et portus, pisces, ferae, aves, etc. jure enim naturali, et permissione juris gentium, piscatio et venatio communes sunt: licet jura postea civilia, forsan non tam aequitate quam licentia et consuetudine, plus nimio interdictae sint."

Molina admits that Christians have the right of world-wide evangelization, of sending missionaries and protecting them and enforcing their right to preach. If certain nations or kings refuse to grant this privilege, then force may be used to punish any injury committed against the Faith and the Gospel. It would be better, however, before any use of force, to negotiate with them about sending protection for the missionaries' lives.[162] St. Thomas treated the problem, stating that pagans could in no way be forced to embrace the faith because to believe is an act of the will. Yet the missionaries could compel them to cease from blasphemy. It frequently happens, the Angelic Doctor says, that Christians make war on pagans not to force them to be baptized but to force them to cease from impeding the spread of the Gospel.[163] Duns Scotus admits a right of the Church to force pagans to profess the Gospel, as long as they had been sufficiently instructed in it.[164] A real controversy broke out after the discovery of the Americas regarding the juridical condition of the Indians respecting Spain. Vitoria,[165] Soto,[166] Bañez,[167] Suárez,[168] and Luis de Leon[169] agree with Molina's position as outlined above.

---

[161] Suárez, *De Bello*, sec. IV, no. 3: "Alterum genus injuriarum si neget communia jura gentium, sine rationabili causa, ut transitus viarum, commune commercium etc."

[162] "Cum vero Christiani jus habeamus denunciandi Evangelium ubique terrarum, concionatores ad quoscumque infideles deferendi, eos protegendi, cogendique infideles, non quidem ut Evangelium suscipiant, sed ne impedimento sint... si vero gentes aliquae, aut Reges, et dynastae contrarium effecerint, fas nobis sit bello illos coercere, injuriamque fidei et Evangelio ea in parte illatam punire...; possumus cum navibus ad eos eo fine accedere, tamdiuque et cum ea potentia in eorum portibus et terris commorari, quamdiu et quantum necesse erit, ut haec tuto fiant, eaque ratione commercium aliquod, vel ipsis invitis, cum eisdem exercere" (II, 105, 434).

[163] "Utrum infideles compellendi sint ad fidem. Respondeo dicendum quod infidelium quidam sunt qui nunquam susceperunt fidem, sicut gentiles et judaei: et tales nullo modo sunt ad fidem compellendi ut ipsi credant: quia credere voluntatis est; sunt tamen compellendi a fidelibus, si adsit facultas, ut fidem non impediant vel blasphemiis, vel malis persuasionibus, vel etiam apertis persecutionibus. Et propter hoc fideles Christi frequenter contra infideles bellum movent, non quidem ut eos ad credendum cogant, quia etiam si eos vicissent, et captivos haberent, in eorum libertate relinquerent an vellent credere; sed propter hoc ut eos compellant, ne fidem Christi impediant" (*Summa Theologica*, IIᵃ II, qu. 10, art. 8).

[164] Prieto, *op. cit.*, p. 186.

[165] Vitoria, *De Jure Belli*, sec. II, no. 13.

[166] Soto, *De Justitia et Jure*, Lib. IV, qu. iv, art. 2; Lib. V, qu. iii, art. 5.

[167] Bañez, *De Fide, Spe et Caritate*, qu. 10, art. 10.

Or a well-documented account of the three Dominicans' positions see Carro, *op. cit.*, pp. 285-320.

Neutrality and Armed Intervention

A recent writer has observed that—despite the long line of visionaries from the Hebrew prophets through the Church Fathers, the great St. Thomas, the Spanish jurist-theologians, and Grotius himself—war as an institution of international law still stands rock-like amid the waves of controversy. [170] Neutrality as a status is largely the obverse aspect of the nature of war as a legal relation. With the failure of the just-cause-of-war doctrine to establish itself, the status of neutrality and its legal consequences moved correspondingly to the center of the war-like stage. [171] The duties of third states had to be defined by some other standard. That other standard is neutrality.

The traditional law of neutrality confronts the third states with only two choices, either to join in the war or to observe the duties of neutrality. The problem of neutrality in the modern sense was just emerging in Molina's day. As Kotzsch says, the concept of neutrality started to take shape as a legal status in international law after the Peace of Westphalia in 1648. [172] Before that time the third-state decision was usually confined to the question of whether to join in the war. It is under this aspect that Molina treats the question.

First of all, he sets down the principle that it is never allowed to assist a state which is waging an unjust war. Secondly, it is permitted to intervene in favor of a state which is involved

---

[168] Suárez, *De Bello*, sec. V.

[169] Marcelino Gutiérrez, O.S.A., *Fray Luis de León y la filosofía española del siglo XV* (El Escorial: Real Monasterio de ll Escorial, 1929), I, 333-334.

[170] Stone, *op. cit.* p. 380.

For a history of the development of the concept of neutrality see Philip Jessup and Francis Deák, *Neutrality*: Its History and Economic Law, Vol. I: *The Origins* (New York: Columbia University Press, 1935); also Philip Jessup, "The Birth, Death and Reincarnation of Neutrality," *American Journal of International Law*, XXVI (1932), 789ff.

For an etymological account of the development of the word neutral see Ernest Nys, *Études de droit international et de droit politique* (Bruxelles: A. Castaigne, 1896).

There is an historical development of the question of neutrality from the Middle Ages to early modern times in T. Boye, "Quelques aspects du développement des règles de la neutralité," *Recueil des cours*, LXIV (1938), 161-165.

[171] On the point that neutrality is a product of international anarchy thriving only under the dogma of sovereignty see Nicolas Socrate Politis, *La neutralité et la paix* (Paris: Hachette, 1935).

[172] Kotzsch, *op. cit.*, p. 129.

in a just war, providing one has that state's expressed or tacit permission. [173]

What about eliciting the help of non-Christians? All admit, Molina says, that it is permitted to assist infidels in a just war and to enter into alliances with them against other infidels. [174] On the question of asking infidels to assist in a war, presumably against Christians, Molina walks a tight rope. "Per se ... nullis allis circumstantibus spectatis licitum id esse" for the reason outlined above concerning a just war. [175] *Per accidens*, by reason of the possible scandal and injury to the Church and Christians if the infidels should invade a Christian land it is illicit. [176]

A Word About Molina's Critics

As was mentioned earlier, historian Alfred Vanderpol laments that the traditional Catholic teaching on the law of war, which had been preserved intact by the medieval writers, was contaminated toward the end of the sixteenth century by scholastic writers who introduced certain modifications and additions to the traditional teaching. Vanderpol says that these writers introduced the principle of probabilism and admitted a material injustice as a sufficient cause of war. The consequence of the latter is that a war can be just on both sides. [177]

Among the writers of the sixteenth century whom Vanderpol indicts, Molina is first. Taking up the charge that Molina admitted the principle of probabilism, one must reply that Vanderpol is simply in error. Molina expressly rejects the opinion

---

[173] "Consequenter dicendum est de adjuvantibus ad bellum. Et primo: quando de justitia belli constat. Et quidem ex dictis praesertim disp. 105 facile patet licitum esse non solum de expresso, sed etiam de praesumpto consensu eorum, quos constat bellum justum gerere, partes eorum agere, ipsosque adjuvare: quoniam id non aliud est, quam cooperari ad id quod bonum, justumque est, accepta ad it auctoritate ab eo, qui illam potest conferre. Quin si illi periclitarentur, adversus quos bellum injustum infertur, possetque quis eos sine notabili suo detrimento eruere ab interitu, teneretur id efficere sub reatu lethalis culpae" (II, 112, 450).

[174] "In primis nullus dubitat fas esse adjuvare infideles in bello justo, quod adversus alios infideles habeant. Itemque inire foedus cum illis adversus alios infideles" (*ibid.*).

[175] "Eo quod ut quivis conducere licite potest milites infideles ad juste se defendendum, regnumque suum, vel sua recuperandum; sic etiam vocare in suum adjutorium potest principem infidelem" (*ibid.*).

[176] "Per accidens tamen ratione scandali et damnorum, quae Ecclesiae inde possent provenire ... foedissimum id regulariter esse et illicitum" (*ibid.*).

[177] Vanderpol, *op. cit.*, pp. 254-275.

that a leader in doubt of the justice of his position may wage war: "Mihi vero longe probabilius est contrarium."[178]   It is true that Molina admits probabilism in the case of doubts on the part of subjects who are commanded to engage in war. But this is not introducing probabilism into the question of the just causes of war.   To follow a division made earlier, Molina demanded certitude regarding *jus ad bellum*; he admitted that combatants in doubt about the justice of the cause they were fighting could continue if they had a *probable* opinion that the cause was just.

The second charge, that Molina admitted a material injustice as a sufficient cause of war, is true.   The consequence Vanderpol draws that a war could be just on both sides should be distinguished: materially and formally just on both sides, *negatur*; materially and formally just on one side, and formally just only on the other, *conceditur*.   As was pointed out, *supra*, this is not a new opinion with Molina.   The classic case from the Old Testament had been considered by all the writers since Augustine's time.   They all admitted it as an exception to the general rule.   Molina, arguing *ab esse ad posse valet illatio*, admitted the possibility.   It should be noted that Molina himself observes the possibility itself would be rare, if the norms he lays down in Disputation 103 are observed.[179]

It has been said that Molina reduced war to commutative justice, removing it from the area of vindictive or punitive justice.   Molina expressly treats of the subject.   Vindictive justice is very close to commutative justice, he says, and may be reduced to it at times inasmuch as it demands satisfaction according to arithmetic proportion.[180]   However, it differs from

---

Cf. Franziskus M. Stratmann, O.P., *Weltkirche und Weltfriede*: Katholische Gedanken zum Kriegs-und-Friedenproblem (Augsburg: Haas und Grabherr, 1942).

For a discussion of the charges by Vanderpol and Stratmann in relation to Suárez' teaching see Rommen, *Suarez*, pp. 301-302.

[178] II, 103, 425.

[179] "Observa tamen, quod si, antequam bellum inferatur, ea serventur, quae disputatione sequenti dicenda sunt deberi servari, raro eveniet, quin culpa sit saltem praesumpta ex parte adversarii, ac proinde quin puniri possit, exigique ab eo possint expensae belli, ex parte illius, qui bellum intulerit formaliter et materialiter justum" (II, 102, 422-423).

[180] "Justitiam vindicativam esse quidem valde affinem justitiae commutativae, ad eamque reduci, quatenus ad aequalitatem secundum proportionem arithmeticam poenam exigit ac imponit pro delicti, injuriaeque quantitate" (I, 12, 25).

commutative justice inasmuch as the penalty which is imposed because of the injury does not repair the damage but only sees that the guilty party is punished. [181]

---

[181] "Nihilominus deficere a perfecta ratione justitiae, quatenus poena, quae pro injuria et delicto sumitur, damnum illatum non resarcit, sed solum patitur reus, quantum justum est ipsum pro delicto pati, cum tamen damnum integrum perseveret" (ibid.).

Cf. La Brière, op. cit., pp. 71-72.

CHAPTER VII

MOLINA'S INTERNATIONALISM: *JUS IN BELLO*

A nation's wars, whatever else they may represent, can be taken as wide-screen, three-dimensional projections of the underlying and overt ills and virtues of a period. One writer has observed that in United States history this rule-of-thumb judgment is most applicable to the Civil War. [1]

The writer was reviewing a book about the Reconstruction period in the South—a period whose bitter memories haunt this country a century later. [2] The causes of the War Between the States have been discussed at exhausting length in a never-ending stream of books and journals detailing personal reminiscences of battles and barracks. In the context of the preceding chapter the *jus ad bellum* aspect of this conflict has been explored. This is far from true about the *jus in bello* which, though regulating the actions of belligerents, extends beyond the duration of the war itself. In one sense interest in Civil War history is shifting from the *jus ad bellum* to the *jus in bello*. An enormously successful best-seller recounted the horrors of Andersonville Prison in Georgia where tens of thousands of Union prisoners were confined under conditions so terrible that over twelve thousand died. [3] A century's perspective has enabled historians to point out that the American Civil War was a prototype of modern total war. [4] Characteristic of both

---

[1] Jean Holzhauer in a review of *The Angry Scar*: The Story of Reconstruction by Hodding Carter, in *The Catholic Messenger* (Davenport, Iowa), February 12, 1959, p. 11.

[2] "It is essential," Carter writes, "for those who are not inheritors of bitter fact and legend to know something of the tenure and employment of the Yankee bayonet in the South of Reconstruction; something of the nature and duration of the civil governments which rules [sic] the Southern States; something of the response of many men, white and black, Yankee and former Rebel, Republican and Democrat, to the vast national opportunity for public plunder" (*ibid.*).

[3] MacKinlay Kantor, *Andersonville* (Cleveland: World Publishing Co., 1955).

[4] Bruce Catton, "The Civil War—First Modern War," Gaston Lecture at Georgetown University, December 9, 1957 (copy in Georgetown University Ar-

was a perceptible breakdown of the traditional regard for the *jus in bello*.[5]

The idea of "total war" has grown out of the premise about war taught by Clausewitz, which was itself derived from features of Revolutionary-Napoleonic practice. Reasoning in the abstract, Clausewitz postulated the striking premise that "to introduce into the philosophy of war a principle of moderation would be absurd. War is an act of violence pursued to the utmost."[6] With the rise of totalitarian states, this philosophical military conception was given a sociological connotation and introduced into the province of politics. Once total war was justified by ideological principles, then total disregard of traditional laws— *ad bellum* and *in bello*—was the logical result.

---

chives): "For the Civil War, archaic as it may look now, was the first of our really modern wars.... It was a modern war, to begin with, in the weapons that were used and in the way these affected the fighting.... But it was more than just a matter of weapons. Much more important is the fact that the mental attitude of the two governments involved—which of course is to say the mental attitude of the opposing peoples themselves—had that peculiar, costly, ruthless cast which is the great distinguishing mark of modern wars. By this, I mean that neither side in the Civil War was prepared to stop anywhere short of complete victory. They were shooting the works. In the old days wars had been formalized; two nations fought until it seemed to one side or the other that it would not be worth while to fight any longer, and then some sort of accommodation would be reached—and, in the last analysis, nothing would have been changed very much. But in the Civil War it was all or nothing."

Basil Henry Liddell Hart (*The Revolution in Warfare* [New Haven: Yale University Press, 1946], p. 58) remarks of the Civil War that "the devastation of Georgia by Sherman, and of the Shenandoah Valley by Sheridan, were designed to undermine the resistance of the Confederate armies by destroying their homes, as well as their sources of supply. The 'anti-civil' operations proved more effective than Marlborough's devastation in Bavaria, for they were decisive in producing the collapse of the Confederacy. The end appeared to justify Sheridan's argument for the means: 'Reduction to poverty brings prayers for peace more surely and more quickly than does the destruction of human life, as the selfishness of man has demonstrated in more than one great conflict.'"

[5] The summary in this chapter of the breakdown of the concept of *jus in bello* is based in part on Kotzsch, *op. cit.*, 116-126.

"La guerra total, como existe hoy, no es una consecuencia de los regímenes totalitarios: es el resultado de la combinación del progresso técnico en las armas y un cambio en la manera de conducir la guerra" (Rubio Leandro Garcia, "La población civil y la guerra aérea moderna," *Revista española de derecho internacional* [1953], p. 338).

Joseph L. Kunz, "Chaotic Status of the Laws of War and the Urgent Necessity of Their Revision," *American Journal of International Law*, XLV (1951), 41.

[6] Liddell Hart, *op. cit.*, p. 55.

At the same time there was an increased reliance on the *jus necessitatis* in international law. [7] In general, the law of necessity was said to flow from the right of self-preservation. These two, however, are not to be identified; the distinction between them lies in the principle involved: self-preservation excuses the repulse of a wrong while the law of necessity justifies the invasion of a right. The latter tends to disregard the binding force of the rules of warfare between belligerent parties. [8]

Speaking of the moral order and the law of war, John Courtney Murray says that the traditional doctrine on war became irrelevant during World War II.

> There is no argument against the traditional doctrine. The Ten Commandments do not lose their imperative relevance by reason of the fact that they are violated. But there is place for an indictment of all ... who failed to make the traditional relevant. [9]

Later in the same address the author suggests that the classical doctrine of war needs more theoretical elaboration in order to relate it more effectively to the unique conflict which agitates the world today. This is in contrast with the older historical conflicts upon which the traditional doctrine sought to bear, and by which it in turn was shaped.

---

[7] For a discussion of this development see William Vincent O'Brien, "Military Necessity: The Development of the Concept of Military Necessity and Its Interpretation in the Modern Law of War" (unpublished Ph. D. dissertation, Georgetown University, 1953).

For a further discussion of this problem see Max Huber, "Die kriegsrechtlichen Verträge und die Kriegsraison," *Zeitschrift für Völkerrecht*, VII (1913), 351ff.; Paul Weiden, "Necessity in International Law," *Transactions of the Grotius Society*, 1939, pp. 105ff.; Burleigh Cushing Rodick, *The Doctrine of Necessity in International Law* (New York: Columbia University Press, 1938); and Joseph L. Kunz, "Individual and Collective Security in Art. 51 of the Charter of the United Nations," *American Journal of International Law*, XLI (1947), 872 ff.

[8] Quincy Wright summarizes this result: "War during the last four centuries tended to involve a larger proportion of the belligerent states' population and resources and, while less frequent, to be more intense, more extended, and more costly. It has tended to become less functional, less intentional, less directable, and less legal. In the most recent period the despotic states have attempted a more efficient utilization of war as an instrument of policy and have led the nations to a more complete organization of the states' resources, economy, opinion, and government for war even in time of peace. States have become militaristic and war has become totalitarian to an unparalleled extent" (*Study of War*, I, 248).

[9] Murray, "Theology of Modern Warfare," *op. cit.*, pp. 7-8.

In any case, another work of the reflective intelligence is even more badly needed. I shall call it a politico-moral analysis of the divergent and particular conflict-situations that have arisen or are likely to arise in the international scene as problems in themselves and as manifestations of the underlying crisis of our times. It is in these particular situations that war actually becomes a problem. It is in the midst of their dense materiality that the *quaestio juris* finally rises. To answer it is the function of the moralist, the professional or the citizen moralist. His answer will never be more than an act of prudence, a practical judgment informed by principle. But he can give no answer at all to the *quaestio juris* until the *quaestio facti* has been answered. From the point of view of the problem of war and morality the same need appears that has been described elsewhere in what concerns the more general problem of politics and morality. I mean the need of a far more vigorous cultivation of politico-moral science. [10]

In the light of Father Murray's challenge, a study of the classical doctrine of war is the first step to a more theoretical elaboration of it in order to relate it to the conflcts of today. One of the initial efforts towards that goal will be a presentation of Molina's doctrine of the *jus in bello*.

Before the actual presentation of Molina's views on this matter. it may be helpful to consider a problem of conscience regarding the lawfulness of war. As was outlined above, [11] the leader of a commonwealth has the obligation, before deciding to resort to war, of examining all the reasons to determine whether the war he would wage is just. Molina requires careful soul-searching in such a person. If a doubt about the justice of his cause remains, he may not act until the doubt is resolved.

A different problem exists for the citizen-soldier who, not having access to all the information, must still decide his own problem of conscience regarding whether the war be just. Molina lays the foundations for his solution on two general principles. [12]

---

[10] *Ibid.*

[11] See *supra*, chap. VI.

[12] Prieto (*op. cit.*, p. 160-166) treats this feature of Molina's treatise under the consideration of the just causes of war, though Molina himself seems to consider it as belonging to the *jus in bello*. Prieto explains his plan: "No obstante, para dar mayor unidad a la materia, para completarla de una vez y no tener que volver sobre ella, juzgamos oportuno interrumpir el orden sistemático de Molina y tratar en este lugar el problema propuesto, notando que nos autorizan también a ello Vitoria, Bañez, Suárez, y Los Salmanticenses, los quales a continuación de la certeza o conocimiento, que de la causa justa

The first principle states that if the war is certainly unjust, then all who take part in it sin seriously and are held to restitution for all damages committed. [13]

The second principle is the converse of the first: If the justice of the war is evident, it is licit to take part in it; if there is a command from the sovereign to take part, the subjects are bound to obey. [14]

The two general principles cover clear-cut cases: the war is either manifestly just or unjust. What is one to do when the justice or injustice is not immediately discernible? To answer this question Molina distinguishes various categories and assigns the responsibility of each.

The first is composed of the sovereign's council. These men must diligently examine all the aspects of the question and render their opinion. If, because of their negligence or malice, unjust war results, they also are responsible with the sovereign for the damage caused. [15]

The second category, made up of the ordinary citizens, is not obliged to examine all the aspects of the question, but may safely rely on the judgment of the sovereign and his council. [16] Molina warns that there will be occasions when the injustice will be so manifest that even the ordinary soldier will be aware of it. Reliance on the judgment of others is no excuse in such cases. The soldiers who, under Pilate's command, crucified Christ are by no means to be considered free of guilt. [17]

---

debe tener el Soberano, se ocupan inmediatamente de los súbditos y extranjeros frente al mismo problema" (p. 161).

[13] "Quando de injustitia belli constat, tunc, qui ad illud vel pugnando, vel quovis alio modo adjutorium praestant, et peccant lethaliter, et tenentur restituere damna omnia inde secuta, ut ex se est manifestum, affirmatque communis doctorum sententia" (II, 115, 454-455).

"Unde merito infertur, eos milites, qui parati sunt sequi ad bellum quemcumque vocantem, non curando an bellum sit justum necne, in status esse damnationis, neque posse absolvi" (II, 114, 453).

[14] II, 112, 450.

[15] "Qui ad principis consilium, vel vocantur, vel admittuntur, inquirere et examinare tenentur justitiam belli, adeo, ut si eorum malitia, aut culpabili negligentia bellum injustum inferatur, restituere *teneantur* damna omnia inde secuta " (II, 113, 451).

[16] "Minores de Republica non tenentur examinare causam belli, sed tuto pugnare possunt committentes se judicio, aut definitioni Principis, et eorum, qui Principi sunt a consiliis.... Tam aperta vero esse possent indicia injustitiae belli, et tales de eo rumores, ut non solum sapientes, sed etiam communes milites tenerentur rem examinare, aut de ea aliis inquirere" (*ibid.*).

[17] "Tertia vero probatur, quoniam quando ejusmodi adessent indicia et rumores de injustitia belli, haec ipsa suadent subditos non debere se committere Principis definitioni, sed debere aliunde inquirere et perscrutari rem,

The third is composed of those who are in doubt about the morality of their participation in a war. Henry Davis describes the doubtful conscience as the conscience of one who, antecedent to action, has reasons for thinking that a certain line of action is morally correct, although he is aware at the same time that there are also reasons for thinking it is not. [18] In the analysis of moral action, the speculative judgment precedes the practical dictate of reason. The speculative judgment is an intellectual act which weighs and ponders reasons for and against an action; not being able to arrive at certainty, it arrives at probability only. [19]

To make up one's mind in respect to certain lines of action is not always an easy matter, if speculative judgments alone are considered. What is one to do? If a person acts in doubt as to the rectitude of an action, he is acting in bad conscience; but if he goes on weighing reasons he will never act. Consequently, in order to be able to act conscientiously and without unreasonable delay, it is important to formulate some guiding principles of action. One such set of guiding principles is Probabilism. [20]

In its ultimate analysis, Probabilism is common sense; it is a system used in practical doubt by the majority of mankind. [21] The development of Probabilism as a system was a slow process, having traces of its presence far back in theological speculation and in the writings of the Fathers. [22] The

---

prout quisque commode posset: alioquin ignorantia esset quasi affectata nolentis intelligere, ut bene ageret: quae sane nec a culpa, nec a restituendi onere excusaret. Possumusque id confirmare, quoniam aliter Turcae, et Saraceni sequentes Principes suos in bello contra Christianos, et milites, qui ad Judaeorum et Pilati imperium Christum comprehenderunt, injuriis affecerunt, ac crucifixerunt, excusarentur a culpa quod nulla ratione est dicendum" (*ibid.*).

[18] Henry Davis, S. J. (*Moral and Pastoral Theology in Four Volumes* [6th ed.; London: Sheed and Ward, 1949], I, 78-112) treats the matter of the doubtful conscience and the principles of Probabilism. The short summary here is based in part on Davis.

[19] *Ibid.*, pp. 78-79.

[20] *Ibid.*, pp. 80-81.

[21] *Ibid.*, p. 91.

[22] For an excellent study of Probabilism see Th. Deman, O.P., "Probabilisme" in *Dictionnaire de théologie catholique*, Vol. XII, cols. 417-619. Deman gives an extensive list of Molina's contemporaries, including Vitoria, Soto, Bañez, Toletus, Gregory of Valentia, Vasquez, Suárez, Ledesma, and Lessius, who are considered Probabilists. Molina's name is not mentioned.

Pierre Bouvier, S.J. ("Jesuites: La théologie morale dans la Compagnie de Jésus," in *Dictionnaire de théologie catholique*, Vol. VIII, col. 1085) says

theory was first clearly formulated by the learned Dominican, Bartholomew Medina, a contemporary of Molina. [23]

In Molina's answer to the question of whether a person in doubt about the lawfulness of war could participate, there is one of the earliest applications of the nascent system of Probabilism. This is clear not only from the arguments Molina uses but also from the fact that the historians of Probabilism cite as an example a passage from Vitoria which is identical with a passage from Molina. [24]

Both men concentrate on rejecting an opinion of Adrian of Utrecht, who held that a citizen in doubt about whether the alleged cause for declaring war is sufficient may not serve in such a war even at the command of the sovereign, because he would thereby expose himself to the danger of mortal sin. Vitoria highlights the cause of Adrian's mistaken opinion:

> Now, Adrian's mistake seems to be in thinking that, if I am in doubt whether this war is just for my prince or whether there be a just cause for this war, it immediately follows that I am in doubt whether or not I ought to go to this war. I admit that I am in no wise justified in doing what my conscience doubts about, and that, if I am doubtful about the lawfulness of doing any given thing, I sin if I do it. But any doubt of mine about the justice of this war does not necessarily involve a doubt whether I ought to fight or serve in this war. Nay, it is quite the other way about. For although I may doubt whether the war is just, yet the next point is that I may lawfully serve in the field at my prince's command. It is precisely the same as with a lictor who has his doubts whether the judge's decree is just, it does not follow there-from that he has doubts whether or not be ought to carry it into execution; he knows he is bound to carry in into execution. [25]

---

that "Molina ne traite nulle part la question mais se montre d'accord avec les probabilistes sur des points importants."

Albert Schmitt, S.J. (*Zur Geschichte des Probabilismus* [Innsbruck: F. Rauch, 1904], p. 105) makes the same observation.

[23] For a history of the development of Probabilism in Molina's day see J. Ternus, *Zur Vorgeschichte des Moralsysteme von Vitoria bis Medina* (Paderborn: F. Schoningh, 1930); J. de Blic, "Barthélemy de Medina et les origines du probabilisme," *Ephemerides Theologiae Lovaniensis*, 1930, pp. 46-83 and 264-291; and J. de Blic, "A propos des origines du probabilisme," *Revue des sciences religieuses*, 1930, pp. 460-464.

[24] Deman, *op. cit.*, col. 459.

[25] Vitoria, *De Jure Belli*, Appendix B, p. lx.

Molina develops the same argument:

> In the matter we are discussing there is a speculative doubt
> whether the war which my sovereign wages is just or not.
> The practical doubt is whether, while I am in doubt about
> the justice of the war, I may assist my sovereign at war. We
> say that, even while the prior doubt remains, it is certainly
> lawful to take part in such a war. It is just like the speculative
> doubt whether what I have up to this point retained in good
> faith, I may continue to retain. Since in doubt, *sit melior
> conditio possidentis*, it is certain that I may retain it, so also
> a citizen not only may but should assist his sovereign as long
> as the war is not manifestly unjust. [26]

Having disposed of his cases of conscience about partici-
pating in the war, Molina is prepared to discuss in detail what
may be done. To begin his study of the *jus in bello* Molina
poses several questions, the answers to which he handles in turn.
The first one asks if it is permitted to use ambushes in fighting
the enemy. [27] Although it is illicit to lie in dealing with the
enemy, it is lawful to conceal strategy and use diversionary
tactics to deceive the other side. [28]

The second question asks if it is required to keep one's
word. Yes, replies Molina, but if the enemy first breaks a
promise, one is no longer bound by it. Quoting Augustine,
Molina says that faith must be kept even with the enemy aginst
whom war is waged. [29] But if the enemy breaks his word, e.g.,
on a truce, then one is free from the obligation of observing

---

[26] "In re autem, de qua disputamus, dubium speculativum est, utrum bellum, quod meus Princeps gerit, justum sit. Practicum vero, utrum dum de
justitia hujus belli dubius sum, fas sit adjuvare meum Principem. Quod vero
nostra conclusione asseveramus, est, manente priori dubio, fas esse subditis
adjuvare in eo bello, ac proinde non esse dubium, sed certum, id licere. Sicut
enim insurgente dubio speculativo, an quod hactenus bona fide possedi, meum
sit, necne, possum licite illud retinere; quia cum in dubio, sit melior conditio
possidentis, simul cum eo dubio est certum licite me illud retinere: sic etiam,
cum subditus suae Reipublicae ac Principi sit divinctus, bonumque illius prae-
ponere debeat bono cujusvis alterius, sane interim dum illi non constat de
injustitia suae Reipublicae, debet illi favere, eamque adjuvare" (II, 113, 452).

[27] "In bello an liceat uti insidiis. Hosti quousque fides sit servanda. An
liceat pugnare in die festo. Et meditationes bellicae quousque liceant. Disp.
III" (II, 111, 448).

[28] "Quod ad primum attinet, breviter dicendum est. Licet nefas sit mentiri hostibus in bello justo, fas tamen est uti insidiis, occultare consilia, dissi-
mulare, ac simulare multa, quibus hostes decipiantur, capiantur, et vincantur"
(*ibid.*).

the same. [30]   A pact of this type has the tacit condition—"Modo tu vicissim omnia serves." [31]

What about fighting on feast days? It is permitted in urgent necessity or when the occasion arises to take advantage of a situation and win the war. [32]   Since it is permitted to fish on feast days, it is far more lawful to fight on those days when there is a possibility of achieving peace. [33]   When with necessity one engages in war on a feast day he would not be guilty of serious sin, as long as he was present at Mass that day.   Tournaments and military games are permitted since the danger of death or serious injury is usually remote. [34]

In all of Molina's responses there is evidence of the Christian tradition which regulated conduct in war. William Stubbs writes of that tradition:

> Let papal Rome, as the law-giver of the Medieval Church, have all the credit of her great achievements; however based, on law or on idea, her position was a standing protest against brutal force, a standing offer of peace and goodwill to those who could pay for it; a great office of incipient diplomacy, a great treasury of legal chicanery, but still a refuge against overbearing violence. [35]

---

[29] "Quod vero attinet ad secundum, dicendum est. Nefas est frangere fidem hostibus, non stando juste promissis, justeve cum eisdem constitutis. Unde Aug. ad Bonifacium ca. Noli. 23. qu. 1. Fides quando promittitur, etiam hosti servanda est, contra quem bellum geritur" (*ibid.*).

[30] "Quod si adversarius promissis cum eove constitutis non staret, neque nos stare tenemur. Verbi gratia, si induciae, quas *treguas* [sic] vocant, ad tempus essent constitutae, et adversarius eas non servaret, neque nos servare eas teneremur, esto juramento essent confirmatae" (*ibid.*).

[31] "Quoniam pactum semper habet tacitam illam conditionem, modo tu stes ... quoniam semper habent tacitam illam conditionem, modo tu vicissim omnia serves" (*ibid.*).

[32] "Quod ad tertium attinet dicendum. Non solum urgente necessitate, sed etiam occurrente occasione melius pugnandi, consequendique victoriam, fas esse pugnare diebus festis" (II, 111, 448-449).

[33] "Si namque ad capiendos pisces, qui certis quibusdam temporibus adveniunt, fas est piscari in die festo, ut in eo ca. conceditur, longe majori cum ratione fas erit pugnare in die festo occurrente occasione id tunc efficiendi, consequendique victoriam in tantum Reipublicae bonum" (*ibid.*).

[34] "Meditationes bellicas, ludosve militares, ut sunt hastiludium, torneamenta, equestris ludus mutua arundinum jaculatione, etc. si ita fiant, ut ex illis non immineat ut plurimum periculum mortis, mutilationis, vel notabilis vulneris, esto raro aliquando horum sequatur, licitos esse" (*ibid.*).

[35] William Stubbs, *Seventeen Lectures on the Study of Medieval and Modern History* (Oxford: Oxford University Press, 1886, p. 216).

The Fourth Lateran Council in 1179 formally established the Truce of God.

"Treguas a quarta feria post occasum solis, usque ad secundam feriam

Using the question-and-answer technique, Molina lays down a number of principles to be followed in conducting a war.

First principles—In a just war it is lawful to do everything necessary far one's own defense and the common good. This means that the fortresses of the enemy may be destroyed, trenches may be built, ammunition and ships seized, as long as these actions are required to attain peace and preserve public order. [36] For the same reasons hostages may be taken. Returning to his favorite analogy from commutative justice, Molina says that hostages are justified on the grounds that in domestic disturbances the judge not only demands the guilty person give satisfaction for the injury caused but may even force him to leave the city if it is feared he might commit another crime. [37] However, Molina quotes the proviso of Vitoria approvingly—that if a city or fortress has been taken in war for a particular purpose it must be restored to the enemy once the war is over. [38]

---

in ortu solis, ab adventu Domini, usque ad octavas Epiphaniae, et a Septuagesima usque ad octavas Paschae, ab omnibus inviolabiliter observari praecipimus" (Prieto, *op. cit.*, p. 216, n. 15).

[36] "In bello justo in primis fas est facere omnia, quae ad defensionem propriam, bonique communis necessaria fuerint judicata. Eaque ratione fas est diruere arces hostium, erigereque propugnacula propria in eorum terris, et capere ab eis arma et naves, quantum satis sit ad pacem ac securitatem conservandam" (II, 117, 459).

[37] "Quo fit, ut si necessarium, expediensve fuerit judicatum, fas etiam sit exigere ab eis ad eum finem obsides. Confirmarique hoc potest, quoniam si civis injuriam alicui alteri intulit, magistratus non solum cogit eum satisfacere injuriam passo, sed etiam, quando juste timetur ne ulterius pergat facere injuriam, cogitur vel satisdare, vel recedere ab urbe, et denique facere id omne, quod necessarium fuerit judicatum, ut vitetur periculum: ergo idem licebit adversus extraneos Reipublicae hostes, quando justam belli causam adversus eos habemus" (*ibid.*).

[38] "Victoria loco citato, num. 56, recte admonet, quando arx, civitas, aut quodvis aliud, necessitate belli esset occupatum solum ob finem aliquem, de quibus praecedente conclusione habitus est sermo, et non ob causas, de quibus sequenti conclusione dicetur, tunc rebus compositis, belloque omnino peracto, ita ut nihil timendum jam sit ab hostibus, restituendum illis esse. Cum enim solo eo fine occupare, retinereque id liceret, sane cessante fine, restituendum continuo est" (II, 117, 460).

Stone (*op. cit.*, p. 434) summarizes modern international law on the points discussed by Molina: "First of all, public property, whether it consists of movables or immovables or ships of war or other public vessels of an enemy State, whether found by the belligerent on the belligerent's own territory, or on the field of battle, or on the high seas, is confiscable by that belligerent. On the other hand, enemy public property on the enemy's own territory under a belligerent's occupation is subjected to more complicated rules. The fate of enemy *private* property is affected, in the first place, by the ambiguity of

Second principle.—In a just war one may take everything belonging to him together with just compensation from the goods of the enemy for any damage suffered and also the costs of waging the war. [39] Molina says he means that not merely the fruits of conquest may be taken but also a just return for the labor undergone and the danger to which the winning side had been exposed, insofar as the fruits of war were insufficient to satisfy this claim. It is likewise allowed to punish the enemy for their crimes—even executing them, if necessary, according to the gravity of the crime committed. [40] In this matter the ruler, prosecuting a just war, acts as a judge in relation to those to be punished. [41]

Molina insists that this second principle is applicable only when there has been formal guilt in the enemy; material guilt

---

the term 'enemy.' When taken by a belligerent at sea or otherwise as a maritime prize it is confiscable. When found by him within his own territory, its former confiscability has been mitigated in modern times, especially by the practice of requisition or sequestration in lieu of confiscation. When found on the enemy territory, whether occupied by him or not, it is again governed by rules which do not lend themselves even to an accurate generation indication."

See "Report of the Committee on Effect of War on Enemy Property," *Reports of Conferences of the International Law Association*, XXXV (1932), 245-247.

Also see A. Martin, "The Treatment of Enemy Property under the Peace Treaties of 1947," *Transactions of the Grotius Society*, XXIV (1949), 77-97; F. A. Mann, "Enemy Property and the Paris Peace Treaties," *Law Quarterly Review*, LXIV (1948), 492-518.

[39] "Secunda conclusio. Deinde fas est in bello justo occupare ea omnia, quae ad nos pertinent, accipereque de bonis hostium compensationem damnorum omnium, quae intulerunt, necnon impensas omnes belli. Impensarum nomine intelligendo, non solum sumptus belli, sed etiam justam mercedem pro laboribus, quos subierunt, et periculis, quibus se exposuerunt, quatenus belli sumptibus non fuerunt haec persoluta. Item fas est sumere de hostibus justam vindictam pro delictorum quantitate, capite, si ita fuerit opus, plectendo eos, qui delicta patrarunt, eorumne fuerunt causa, justasque alias poenas imponendo, ut tributa pro quantitate culpae, vel alias similes poenas" (II, 117, 460).

[40] "The peacetime redress for a legal wrong by protest and claim for compensation of the aggrieved state can rarely be effective between belligerents. No belligerent, even if it admits the wrong, is likely to pay damages to its enemy. At the war's end, indeed, the question might become practical, and in the present century the practice has grown for the victors to require not only monetary reparations, but the punishment of individuals in respect of violations of international law" (Stone, *op. cit.*, p. 356).

[41] "Sed princeps aut Respublica, quae justam belli causam habet adversus aliam Rempublicam, judicis rationem subit comparatione illius ad illam puniendam, exequendumque id omne, quod justum fuerit: ergo illa omnia fas sunt in bello justo" (*ibid.*).

does not permit the victor to inflict punishment. Garcia Prieto
reminds his readers that the second principle is in perfect harmony with the traditional doctrine both before and after
Molina's period and has been incorporated into positive international law. [42]

Third principle.—If something is taken in a war otherwise
just which exceeds the compensation due for the damage caused,
then it must be restored. [43]   This is the teaching of Vitoria,
Gabriel Biel, Mayor, and Silvester all cited (by Molina) and of
Covarrubias, Bañez, Soto, and Suàrez.   Molina justly notes that
the longer the war is protracted, the greater are the expenses
involved in prosecuting it, and the injured party is entitled to
exact compensation for the cost of war. [44]

Fourth principle.—Moveable goods captured in a just war
belong to the captors according to the law of nations even if
what is taken exceeds the compensation due for damages.   This
principle is valid not only for moveable goods but even for
persons captured.   If Christians are captured by Christians, they
by custom are released. [45]

---

[42] Prieto, *op. cit.*, pp. 222-223.

[43] "Tertia conclusio.   Si aliquid amplius usurpetur bello, alioquin justo,
quam quae duabus praecedentibus conclusionibus commemorata sunt, quasi
vel poena excedat culpam, vel recompensatio excedat quantitatem damnorum,
earumque rerum, quae ad juste bellantes pertinent, obnoxium est restitutioni"
(II, 117, 460-461).

[44] "Observa tamen, quo plus bellum justum perseverat, hostibus repugnan-
tibus, damnaque inferentibus, aut inferre attentantibus, eo plus accrescere belli
impensas, damna, injuriam ac delicta, eaque ratione eo plus fas esse postea
accipere in compensationem ac poenam justam" (*ibid.*).

[45] "Sit nihilominus 4. conclusio.   Mobilia capta bello justo gentium jure
sunt capientium, etiamsi excedant compensationem damnorum.   Intelligendum
id est, non solum de aliis rebus mobilibus, sed etiam de hominib. bello justo
captis, qui manicipia capientium fiunt.   Si tamen Christiani ab aliis Christianis bello justo capiantur, consuetudine inter eos praescripta, quae vim legis
habet, liberi manent" (*ibid.*).

Stone (*op. cit.*, pp. 651-652) remarks that a humanitarian attitude towards
prisoners of war and captives did not develop generally until after the middle
of the nineteenth century.

For a brief summary of the history, see Lassa F. Oppenheim, *International
Law*: A Treatise, ed. H. Lauterpacht (7th ed.; London: Longmans, Green and
Co., 1948-1952), II, 366; G. Werner, "Les prisonniers de guerre," *Recueil des
cours*, XXI (1928), 6-24.

The question of enslaving prisoners of war will be discussed later in this
chapter.

Justified Killing in War

In the actual fighting, in the storming or defense of a city, while the danger lasts it is permitted to kill enemy belligerents without discrimination. [46] The reason for this is that whoever fights a just war cannot hope to achieve victory unless those opposing him are removed. Therefore, he may kill even those on the other side who are fighting in good faith as long as he judges their deaths necessary to attain victory. [47] Of course, if it is possible, he should spare their lives. [48] Molina observes that the killing he refers to is necessary for one's own defense and the common good. [49]

The second conclusion is that, once victory is achieved, it is permitted to punish those guilty of crimes which deserve death. [50] The one who prosecutes a just war becomes a type

[46] "In conflictu belli, oppugnatione, aut defensione civitatis, vel castri, et denique quando res est in periculo, licitum est interficere indifferenter omnes e contrario pugnantes. Probatur, quoniam qui justum bellum gerunt, non possunt commode bellum expedire, victoriam, securitatem, et pacem consequi, nisi ex adversa parte dimicantes de medio tollant" (II, 122, 474-475).

[47] "Quo fit, ut, etiam quos scirent innocentes, utpote excusante eos ignorantia, aut simul praecepto principis a peccato pugnandi, possent interficere, quantum judicarent necessarium ad victoriam comparandam, et periculum, quod ex eis immineret, vitandum" (II, 122, 475).

[48] "Si quem tamen horum innocentum possent commode servare, tenerentur eum non interficere, juxta ea quae disputatione 119. dicta sunt" (*ibid.*).

[49] "Hoc loco observa, interfectionem innocentum, de qua loquimur, esse in defensionem propriam ac boni communis, atque ad occupandum, quae ad nos pertinent, ac ipsi impediunt" (*ibid.*).

Stone (*op. cit.*, p. 352) is of the opinion that, though The Hague Convention provided that the means of injuring the enemy is not unlimited, many writers in the field, including British, American, and German, hold a state is privileged, in title of self-preservation, to violate its ordinary duties under international law.

See Wieden, "Necessity in International War," *op. cit.*, pp. 105-132; also W. G. Downey, Jr., "The Law of War and Military Necessity," *American Journal of International Law*, XLVII (1953), 251-262.

[50] "Secunda conclusio. Parta victoria, rebusque jam extra periculum constitutis, ex se fas est interficere nocentes, hoc est, eos qui prudentis arbitrio crimen morte dignum commiserunt. Probatur, quoniam, qui bellum justum intulit, subit tunc rationem judicis ad hostes puniendos, ut supra non semel ostensum est" (II, 122, 475).

Stone (*op. cit.*, p. 356, n. 43) points out that prior to 1914 there was a long-standing practice of granting to the ex-enemy State, and to its citizens and soldiers an amnesty in respect of all breaches of war-law and peace and thus ending all recriminations. The Treaty of Versailles, Arts. 227 and 288, began the modern trend by requiring the surrender by Germany for trial of persons in her forces or employment charged with violation of the laws and customs

of judge to punish his enemies and therefore may do whatever a judge can do legally. [51]

The Right of Reprisals

Historically, the root of reprisals [52] as an instrument of international law can be traced to the Middle Ages, when reprisals were considered as a legitimate resort to force by private persons. [53] The exercise of reprisals meant forcible seizure of goods and, in exceptional cases, of persons. Reprisals were only to take place after the so-called *lettres de requête* had been disregarded. The aggrieved party was then to obtain *letters of marque and reprisal* which would authorize him to make reprisals until he had recovered property equal in value to that which had been forcibly taken from him.

In the course of the eighteenth century, [54] reprisals by pri-

---

of war, as well as the trial of the German Kaiser for a supreme offense against international morality and sanctity of treaties.

[51] "Ergo sicut quicunque judex in sua Republica licite, quantum est ex se, interficit malefactorem sibi subditum, quem morte dignum comperit: sic, quantum est ex se, fas erit interficere ex hostibus quotquot morte dignos invenerit" (*ibid.*).

In this whole section Molina has been paraphrasing Vitoria, *De Jure Belli*, no. 46.

Vitoria, *De Jure Belli*, no. 45: "In ipso actuali conflictu praelii, vel in oppugnatione, aut defensione civitatis, licet indifferenter occidere omnes, qui contra pugnant: et breviter quando res est in periculo."

Soto, *op. cit.*, lib. V, a. I, art. vii; Suárez, *Opera Omnia*, Vol. XII, Sec. VII, nos. 6, 7, and 17.

[52] "In modern international law, a reprisal has been defined as a measure of self-help taken by the injured State in reply to an act contrary to the law of nations on the part of the offending state, *after summons which proves unavailing*. Its effect is to suspend temporarily the observance of a particular rule of the law of nations in the relations between two states. It is *limited* by the experience of humanity and by the rules of good faith, applicable in international relations. *It would be illegal if a previous act, contrary to international law*, had not provided its justification. Its object is to compel the offending State to make reparation for the injury, or to return to legality, avoiding further offences" (Kotzsch, *op. cit.*, pp. 146-147).

[53] For a succinct summary of the history of reprisals, see Simon Maccoby, "Reprisals as a Measure of Redress Short of War," *Cambridge Law Journal*, 1924, pp. 60ff.

[54] On August 18, 1787, James Madison in the Constitutional Convention submitted a list of powers for the proposed Congress. Among the powers was the right "to grant letters of mark and reprisal" ("Debates of the Federal Convention of 1787 as Reported by James Madison" in *Documents Illustrative of the Formation of the Union of the American States*, ed. Charles C. Tansill

vate persons as conceived under the legal title of *letters of marque and reprisal* became more and more modified from the original meaning and were instead regarded as being tantamount to war. Thomas Jefferson, as Secretary of State, represents the legal thought of his time in this matter:

> It is undeniable that at present general letters of marque and reprisal are war to all intents and purposes; that they are never granted but in consequence of an existing war or as a way of making war without formal declaration. [55]

The Declaration of Paris in 1856 led to the abolition of privateering, though the Declaration does not prohibit the creation of voluntary navies consisting of private vessels under the control of a state, such as that used in the Second World War in the evacuation of Dunkirk. [56]

With his usual thoroughness Vitoria deals with the problem of reprisals of his day. He takes up maritime conflicts in the form of reprisals, where there has been a refusal to restore property wrongfully taken.

> There is, accordingly, no inherent injustice in the letters of marque and reprisal which princes often issue in such cases, because it is on account of the neglect and breach of duty of the other prince that the prince of the injured party grants

---

[Washington. Government Printing Office, 1927], p. 564). Madison's proposals were referred to the Committee of Detail and emerged from the Committee (after an orthographic change) as Clause 11 of Section 8 of Article I of the Constitution: "To declare War, grant Letters of Marque and Reprisal, and make Rules concerning Captures on Land and Water."

See *The Constitution of the United States of America Analysis and Interpretation*: Annotations of Cases Decided by the Supreme Court of the United States to June 30, 1952, ed. Edward S. Corwin (Washington: Government Printing Office, 1953), pp. 279-298; see also John Bassett Moore, *A Digest of International Law* (7 vols.; Washington: Government Printing Office, 1906), VII, 122.

[55] Moore, *op. cit.*, VII, 122.

See also A. Messineo, S.J., "Le rappresaglie nella dottrina degli antichi," *Civiltà Cattolica*, I, (1941), 101-119.

See La Brière (*op. cit.*, pp. 135-146) for a treatment of the question from the point of view of modern Catholic teaching; also the same author's *La communauté des puissances*: D'une communauté inorganique à une communauté organique (Paris: Beauchesne, 1932), pp. 142-194.

[56] For a history of the problem of reprisals in the present century, especially in relation to the Covenant of the League of Nations and the Charter of the United Nations, see Kotzsch, *op. cit.*, pp. 154-175.

him this right to recoup himself from innocent folk. These
letters are, however, hazardous and open the way to plunder. [57]

Molina treats reprisals incidentally as a confirmatory argument
to his fourth conclusion mentioned above. He includes an involved description (if not definition) of reprisals which almost
defies translation into readable English and will be for that
reason repeated here in Latin:

> Confirmari vero hoc potest ex communi Doctorum sententia ...
> asserentium licitas esse represalias (impignorationes caste lo-
> quentes appellant, marches etiam nonnulli vocant) quando ali-
> quis, aut aliqui de aliena Republica damnum intulerunt, et
> neque ipsi volunt satisfacere, neque princeps supremive mode-
> ratores Reipublicae admoniti cogunt illos satisfacere: eo nam-
> que ipso Respublica, in suo principe aut moderatoribus, cul-
> pam contrahit, fasque proinde est Principi, cui subditus est
> is, qui injustitiam est passus, concedere illi, aut aliis suis sub-
> ditis ut faciant represalias, seu impignorationes in bonis sub-
> ditorum alterius Reipublicae usque ad debitam compensatio-
> nem, esto illi, quorum bona occupantur, in culpa non fuerint. [58]

The ruler whose failure to right the injury was the cause
of the reprisals must make restitution for damages caused to
the property of his innocent citizens. [59]
Molina cautions that the right of reprisals should not be
granted for a light reason, especially if the depredation is likely
to involve property owned by persons who are innocent in relation to the original injury. [60] The authority to grant the right
of reprisals belongs to one who has the right to declare war.
But he must first inform the ruler of the other commonwealth
about the fault. While awaiting his reply, the ruler may detain
merchants of that commonwealth who happen to be in his ter-

---

[57] Scott, *op. cit.*, Appendix B, p. lxiv.

[58] II, 121, 473.

[59] "Quo loco adverte, Principem aut supremos illius Reipublicae modera-
tores, qui in culpa fuerunt, ut represaliae illae concederentur, teneri restituere
innocentibus suae Reipublicae bona, quibus ita spoliati sunt" (*ibid.*).

[60] "Licet autem minor causa sufficiens sit, ut represaliae concedantur, quam
ut bellum indicatur; requiritur tamen non levis causa, saltem quando bona,
quae sunt usurpanda, non ad eum, qui nocuit, pertinent, sed ad alios de
eadem Republica. Cum enim usurpatio facultatum eorum hominum, qui non
nocuerunt, odiosa sit, facileque occasionem injuriarum ac scandalorum praebere
soleat, profecto neque facile, neque levi ex causa represaliae sunt conceden-
dae" (*ibid.*).

ritory.[61] However, their gods may not be taken until it has been determined that *lettres de requéte* are being ignored.[62]

William O'Brien points out that pillage, which has been formally excluded from modern war,[63] was apparently a normal and necessary element of Medieval and Renaissance wars.[64]

> Much of the soldiers' maintenance was supplied through pillage and their morale depended on its rewards. The Scholastics permitted pillage when military necessity required it.

---

[61] "Ad quem pertinet bellum movere, ad eum solum spectat concedere represalias. Prius autem tamen admoneri debet supremus moderator alterius Reipublicae de culpa, in qua est, quod non cogat satisfacere, quam adversus eam represaliae concedantur. Si tamen post injuriam acceptam adessent mercatores Reipublicae, quae illam intulit, periculumque esset, ne, dum satisfactio petitur, illi recederent, neque speraretur posse postea recuperari facile damnum illatum, credo fas esse eos detinere, bonaque eorum secrestare expectando rei eventum" (*ibid.*).

[62] "Nefas tamen esset, vel bona eorum omnino eripere, vel injuriam aliam illis irrogare, antequam de negligentia et culpa Reipublicae, cujus illi sunt membra, constaret" (*ibid.*).

[63] Article 23 (b) of The Hague Regulations forbids the destruction or seizure of the enemy's property unless such destruction or seizure be imperatively demanded by the necessities of war. More specific and detailed prohibitions as to occupied territory are now contained in Article 53 of the Geneva Civil Persons Convention of 1949, protecting all real or personal, individual or collective, state, public or cooperative property; Article 147 forbids extensive destruction of property not justified by military necessity and carried out unlawfully and wantonly (Stone, *op. cit.*, pp. 559-560).

The customary right to take booty is not expressly embodied in modern treaty law but it is implied in the qualification to the prohibition in Article 23 (g) of The Hague Regulations. By analogy with Article 23 it is generally assumed that postwar compensation must be paid in case of private property but not of state-owned property. See H. A. Smith, "Booty of War," *British Yearbook of International Law*, XXIII (1956), 227-237; see also W. G. Downey, Jr., "Captured Enemy Property: Booty of War and Seized Enemy Property," *American Journal of International Law*, XLIV (1950), 488-504; D. H. Lew, "Manchurian Booty and International Law," *American Journal of International Law*, XL (1946), 584ff.

Article 244, Annex 1 (2) of the Treaty of Versailles required Germany to pay damages for the carrying away, seizure, injuring, and destruction of all property belonging to allied civilian population wherever situated, with the exception of naval and military works and materials.

[64] Prior to modern developments, the law of war, though barbarous, had already been tempered both by Christian ideals and by the idea of medieval chivalry. The Christian ideal was slow in asserting itself, while the chivalrous spirit of the Middle Ages was too artificial to survive. Yet under those two influences barbarous practices, such as killing and torture of prisoners and the sacking of towns taken by assault, came to be frowned upon (Stone, *op. cit.*, p. 335).

See Goyau, *op. cit.*, VI (1925), 142-161 and 179-194.

However, the military necessity had to be proportionate to the cause and nature of the war. [65]

Molina teaches that, if it is necessary to expedite the war and to raise the spirits of the troops—and to terrify the enemy, it is not illicit *per se* to hand over even a Christian city to be sacked. [66] *Per accidens* it could be illicit because of the slaughter of innocent persons, the raping and molestation of women, [67] the profanation of churches, and the like which soldiers are wont to indulge in. [68] The leaders should forbid wild injustices, but Molina adds, realistically, "Quantum commode potuerint ea impedire." [69]

Juridical Situation of Noncombatants [70]

The right of life.—It is always wrong, even in a just war, to intend directly to kill an innocent person. [71] Citing Vitoria

---

[65] O'Brien, *op. cit.*, pp. 65-66.

[66] "Quare si judicetur necessarium ad expediendum bellum, incendendos animos militum, et deterrendos hostes, fas erit civitatem, etiam Christianorum, tradere interdum militibus in praedam, esto verisimile sit milites aliquos sua culpa similia flagitia commissuros" (II, 122, 474).

[67] Under the 1949 Civilian Persons Convention persons in occupied territory are entitled in all circumstances to respect for their honor, family rights, religious convictions, manners, customs, and to humane treatment and immunity from insults and public curiosity. Protection of feminine honor is particularly enjoined by Article 27, 2. See Stone, *op. cit.*, p. 74.

[68] "Quamvis per accidens nefas esse soleat, praesertim quando civitas est Christianorum, idque propter caedes et cruciatus innocentum, stupra, adulteria, et oppressiones aliarum foeminarum, quae milites in similibus eventibus committere solent, necnon propter templorum spoliationes, et saeva alia, ac injusta, quae solent accidere; nihilominus per se non esse illicitum" (II, 122, 474).

[69] "Duces tamen, quando civitas in praedam traditur, tenentur prohibere ejusmodi saeva et injusta, et quantum commode potuerint ea impedire" (*ibid.*).

[70] "Noncombatants" is the closest modern term for Molina's "innocentes." O'Brien (*op. cit.*, p. 61) uses the term in this sense.

[71] "Per se et ex intentione, nefas est bello, quantumvis alioquin justo, interficere innocentem" (II, 119, 469).

Cf. Vitoria, *De Juri Belli*, no. 35; Soto, *op. cit.*, V, qu. 1, art. VII; Bañez, *op. cit.*, qu. 40, art. 1; and Suárez, *Omnia Opera*, Vol. XII, sec. VII, no. 15.

In the text Molina cites John Driedo (1485-1535), Flemish professor at Louvain and author of *De Libertate Christiana*. The reference is to the second part, chapter six, of this work.

Besides Vitoria and Driedo, Molina cites John Mair (Mayor 1470-1550), Scotch theologian, author of *Commentarium in Libros Sententiarum Petri Lombardi*; Silvestre Mazzolini (1460-1523), Dominican, author of a famous work known as the *Summa Sylvestrina* to which Molina refers eighteen times in his treatise on war.

Covarrubias, *op. cit.*, Part II, pars. 3 and 4; Biel, *op. cit.*, Dist. 15, qu. 9, art. 1.

at once, it is presumed that Molina agrees with the Dominican's reason: "Fundamentum justi belli est injuria, ut supra ostensum est; sed injuria non est ab innocente; ergo non licet bello uti contra illum."

Continuing to cite Vitoria, Molina agrees that it is wrong to kill the women and children of the Turks and Saracens. But if, as happened in the war against the Moors at Granada, the women are also heretics and apostates, then they may be killed for their religious crimes. [72] The women campfollowers ("Quae vel comitantur hostes. . . .") are not considered to be free of guilt, Molina adds wryly, because of the help they afford the enemy ("solere adjuvare hostes"). [73] Vitoria also notes that the children of heretics are not be killed for the supposition that they will grow up to be heretics: "Neque enim facienda sunt mala, ut eveniant bona." [74] Foreign visitors in the area are considered innocent, as are the clergy and religious. [75]

Outside of these general classes it is difficult, Molina says, to distinguish the innocent. For that reason it is lawful to kill

---

[72] "Hinc infert Victoria, nec in bello adversus Turcas aut Saracenos fas esse interficere infantes. Addit, imo neque foeminas: quia praesumuntur innocentes, nisi contrarium constet. Imprimis observa, si bellum esset adversus haereticos aut apostatas, ut fuit praeteritis annis in Regno Granatensi adversus illos ex Saracenorum progenie, qui rebellarunt, et de quibus tam evidentia erant argumenta omnes esse apostatas, eaque potissimum de causa rebellare, fas proculdubio esse, foeminas adultas interficere ob haeresis et apostasiae crimen" (II, 119, 469).

[73] "Adde, foeminas adultas, quae vel comitantur hostes, vel intra urbem, quae obsidetur, cum eis sunt, non solere immunes esse a culpa, sed solere adjuvare hostes. Quare licet tutius sit eas vivas reservare, dum de illarum culpa non constat, non sunt tamen in eodem innocentum gradu cum infantibus computandae" (*ibid.*).

[74] "Ut vero probe notat Victoria loco citato numero 38. non est justa causa ad interficiendos pueros filios hostium infidelium, quod verendum sit ne, cum adoleverint, sequantur vestigia parentum, pugnent contra Christianos, et eis nocumenta inferant. Neque enim facienda sunt mala, ut eveniant bona. Neque fas est punire pro peccato, quod patrandum timetur, neque adhuc est commissum" (*ibid.*).

[75] "Qui non sunt de ea Republica, ut peregrini, et ii mercatores, qui in ea non habent domicilium, sed ibi hospitantur et sunt quasi in transitu, innocentes reputandi sunt, ut bene ait Caietanus in summa verbo bellum. ... Clerici et religiosi non reputantur Reipublicae partes, quod attinet ad bella: et idcirco reputandi sunt innocentes, nisi contrarium aliunde constat, nefasque est eos interficere, ut communiter tradunt Doctores" (II, 119, 469-470).

Suárez (*Opera Omnia*, Vol. XII, Sec. VII, no. 10) summarizes his teaching neatly: "Innocentes sunt quasi naturali jure pueri, mulieres, et quicumque non valent arma sumere; jure gentium legati; jure positivo inter Christianos religiosi, sacerdotes etc. c. 'Novimus' ['innovamus'] de treuga et pace et in cap. 'Illi qui' 23, a. 4."

a person unless it is certain he is innocent either because he is a country bumkin (*rusticitas*) or is mentally retarded (*stoliditas*). [76]

It is permitted to kill innocent persons while intending only the death of the guilty, as when a city is justly under attack and it is known that the innocent and guilty are together within. In such a case it is permitted to connonade the city ("mittere in eam globos") or set fire to it ("ignem illi supponere") even if it is understood that some innocent persons may be killed. [77] Turning to naval warfare, Molina applies the same

---

[76] "Inter reliquos Reipublicae, cum qua justum geritur bellum difficile ... est discernere, an aliqui sint innocentes: eaque de causa fas est singulos interficere, nisi de aliquo in particulari constet, illum innocentem esse, vel propter nimiam suam rusticitatem aut stoliditatem, vel alia de causa: hos enim tenerentur milites servare, si possent" (II, 119, 470).

Molina later gives an insight into what he means by the term rusticity. Anticipating an objection against his doctrine about the general right of reprisals as being contrary to the decree *Innovamus* of the Lateran Council in which farmers are protected from depradations by the enemy, he replies that the prohibition applies only in war among Christians: "Neque in ea prohibetur, ne ullo pacto rustici suis bonis spolientur, sed solum praecipitur, ut quando ad agriculturam egrediuntur, aut regrediuntur, vel in agris commorantur, tam ipsi, quam animalia, quibus arant et semina portant, congrua securitate laetentur" (II, 121, 474).

[77] "Secunda conclusio. Per accidens, intentione nocentes interficiendi, fas est, etiam scienter, innocentes interficere. Ut quando arx, aut civitas juste oppugnatur in qua constat innocentes aliquos permixtos esse cum nocentibus, fas est mittere in eam globos, aut ignem illi supponere, vel quodvis aliud facere ad illam capiendam, esto intelligatur per accidens, hoc est, praeter intentionem id efficientium, interficiendos esse aliquos innocentes" (II, 119, 470). Here, of course, Molina is invoking the well-known principle in moral science of the "double effect."

Davis (*op. cit.*, I, 13-14) summarizes the principles involved and gives some apposite examples: "It is permissible to set a cause in motion, in spite of its foreseen evil effect, provided that the act which produces the evil effect is not itself a morally wrong act; secondly, provided that a good effect also issues from the act, at least as immediately and directly as the evil effect, that is to say, provided that the evil effect does not first arise, and from it, the good effect; thirdly, provided that the agent has a justifying and sufficient reason for acting, one that is commensurate with the evil effect, foreseen and permitted.

"On these principles, and prescinding from international agreements, it would be permissible, in war, to sink a neutral ship carrying munitions to the enemy, provided that the mere capture and confiscation of the munitions were not possible. In this case the gun or torpedo discharged has for its first, immediate, and intended effect, the disabling and sinking of the ship; the second effect, not so immediate and not intended on its own account, is the destruction of neutral property and the lives of non-belligerents; the sufficient and justifying reason is self-defense, for we may rightly defend ourselves against all hostile acts, even those that are constructively hostile."

principle to the bombardment (*bombardarum*) of Turkish galleys which are known to have Christians aboard. In such circumstances there is no obligation of restitution for the damages caused *per accidens* to the innocent. [78]

The Right of Liberty

Molina, influenced by the *jus gentium* and the custom of his day, admitted that even noncombatants could be enslaved if captured in a just war. The condition he laid down was that they must be citizens of the commonwealth at war. [79] Molina considers personal liberty as a good of fortune ("cum libertas inter fortunae bona computetur") and the victor is entitled to despoil the conquered of their gods of fortune. He repeats his earlier warning that this does not apply to Christians captured by Christians. [80] He extends his earlier conclusion even to the children of the enemy; by taking the children captive, one is able to punish the parents. He expressly says that Vitoria concurs in this conclusion. [81]

Molina's generally harsh position on prisoners of war needs some comment. First of all, he is giving an exposition of the accepted practices of his day according to the *jus gentium*. [82]

---

[78] "Quando in triremibus Turcarum scitur permixtos esse remiges Christianos, fas est mittere in eos globos bombardarum quibus subvertantur, pugnareque adversus illos, esto intelligatur ejusmodi remiges una cum Turcis esse perituros. Neque in similibus eventibus consurgit obligatio restituendi ejusmodi damna innocentibus per accidens illata" (II, 119, 470).

[79] "Quamvis nefas sit interficere eos innocentes, qui partes sunt Reipublicae, cum qua bellum est justum, fas tamen est servituti eos subjicere. Dixi, qui partes sunt Reipublicae: quoniam hospites aut peregrini, qui partes non sunt Reipublicae, quemadmodum nulla ratione sunt hostes, si culpa vacant, nec proinde spoliari possunt bonis suis, aut ullum aliud jus belli potest per se adversus eos exerceri: ita neque servituti possunt subjici" (II, 120, 471).

[80] "Est etiam excipiendum a conclusione, quando bellum est Christianis cum aliis Christianis" (*ibid.*).

[81] Vitoria, *op. cit.*, no. 42: "Eodem modo licet ducere innocentes in captivitatem sicut licet spoliare illos, quia libertas et captivitas inter bona fortunae reponuntur: unde quando bellum est talis conditionis, quod licet spoliare indifferenter omnes hostes, et occupare omnia bona illorum, etiam licet ducere in captivitatem omnes hostes sive nocentes sive innocentes."

Bañez, *op. cit.*, col. 1379: « Licitum est in bello juste expoliare, et in captivitatem ducere innocentes, etiam illos, quos scimus esse innocentes."

Suárez, *op. cit.*, Sec. VII, no. 12: "Dico quinto: Si necessarium sit ad plenam satisfactionem, licet privare innocentes suis bonis, etiam libertate."

[82] Molina discusses the problem of slavery at some length earlier in the Second Tract, Disputations 32-41. Silvio Zavala (*La filosofía política en la*

Modern practices have modified this custom and modern readers
are sometimes astonished by the opinions of great Catholic
theologians regarding the rights of victors in war. [83]. On this
very point of modification of practice of the *jus gentium*, Vitoria
says:

> Secondly, I say that the law of nations can well be abrogated
> in part, though not entirely, just as the law of nations is that
> those taken in a just war may be made slaves; but Paludanus

---

conquista de America [Mexico City: Fondo Cultura Económica, 1947], pp. 110-
111) summarizes Molina' position: "Por tanto, siendo así que estos etíopes
ni son esclavos por su nacimiento, ni por sí mismos, o por sus padres fueron
vendidos por causa de urgente necesidad, ni han sido condenados a la servi-
dumbre por sentencia de legítimo juez, ni pueden ser considerados como
cautivos en guerra justa—ya que sus bárbaros reyezuelos guerrean entre sí
por mero antojo o por causas insiñificantes; más todavía después de que los
europeos establecieron aquel comercio, las más de las veces hacen le guerra
sólo por coger hombres para venderlos, como claramente se ve por las mismas
historias de las portugueses, ingleses y holandeses (de los cuales los últimos
dedícanse con gran empeño a tal comercio); síguese que esa esclavitud, como
expresamente scribió Molina, es del todo injusta e inicua, a no ser que los
Ministros Regios a quienes les está encomendado este asunto tengan noticia
del justo título que la haga lícita en casos particulares y den testimento acerca
del él; sobre todo si consideramos que en los reinos de Angola y del Congo,
en la Isla de Santo Tomás y en otros lugares hay muchísimos cristianos que
son hechos cautivos por los infieles y que no es lícito a los cristianos com-
prarlos."

An interesting item about the Portuguese Jesuit colleges is furnished by
Manuel Fraga Iribarne in Molina's *Los seis libros de la justicia y el derecho*;
I, 92: "Más aún, en los mismos Colegios portugueses de la Compañía de Jesús
solía haber dos o tres esclavos para el trabajo doméstico. Los Generales siempre recomendaron que se prescindiese de ellos; pero los Provinciales se resis-
tían, alegando el ejemplo de los demás monasterios religiosos. San Francisco
de Borja los prohibió terminantemente en 1569; pero es significativo que esta
prohibición hubiera de repertirse por Everado Mercuriano en 1576, y por el
P. Aquaviva en 1584."

[83] See Eppstein, *op. cit.*, p. 407: "The third and even more widely accepted
cause of slavery ... was the supposed right to enslave men taken captive in
war. An adroit and uncharitable application of the traditional doctrine of
the conditions of just war was sufficient to provide the consciences of the
colonial adventurers with a pretext for annexing vast areas of Africa and the
Americas, and regarding the whole of the inhabitants as the guilty enemy who
could legitimately be killed, or reduced as prisoners to servitude. The
astonishing rights allowed to the victor in a just war by Suárez, not to speak
of less reputable theologians, show the extent to which the Schoolman of
the Renaissance yielded to the temptation of exalting the military practice
of his day into a theory—a theory which only the perfect (and therefore
most improbable) use of charity by the conqueror could prevent from opening
the floodgates in Roman custom, certainly recognized the right to enslave
prisoners of war cannot be denied: that it should ever have been sanctioned
by any Christians is the tragedy."

says that this does hold among Christians. For if the Spaniards capture Frenchmen in a war, the Frenchmen are captives, but not slaves, because they are able to appear in a court of justice and do other things of that sort, which nevertheless could not be permitted if they were slaves. The acts of a French captive are valid, and a Christian could not sell him at all. Behold here the *jus gentium* is in part violated, for by the *jus gentium* those taken in a just war are to be made slaves. [84]

On the point that liberty is a good of fortune, one must be cautious in contrasting it with twentieth-century views of liberty as a substantive right. Molina was writing in the context of the law of war, as were Vitoria, Bañez, and Suárez. The reason liberty was viewed as a good of fortune was that in primitive times the enemy was to be put to the sword when captured. The extreme right of killing was sometimes renounced in order that the prisoners taken might serve as slaves. Finally, the occasional practice became the general rule. Hence liberty, in the circumstances of a prisoner of war, was viewed as one of the goods of fortune, depending on the decision of the captor.

The Right of Property [85]

Molina divides his study into four conclusions which will be considered in turn.

First conclusion.—It is permitted to despoil noncombatants, even foreigners and those merely visiting the area, of any property which could be used by the enemy to prosecute the war. This means not only taking weapons, ships, money, food, horses, and the like, but also devastating the fields if that is considered

---

[84] Vitoria: "De Jure Gentium et Naturali," quoted from Scott, *op. cit.*, Appendix E, pp. cxiii-cxiv.

[85] Nys (*Le droit de guerre*, p. 115) observes that the theory of the just war provided the occasion for very extreme practices regarding property, both private and public, as being at the mercy of the invaders: "Au Moyen Age, la guerre rempt tous les liens qui ont pu exister entre les adversaires. C'est le principe du droit romain: dès l'ouverture des hostilités la personne de l'ennemi peut être saisie et ses biens peuvent être capturés; aucune différence n'est faite entre la propriété privée et la propriété de l'Etat. Durant les hostilités tout commerce est prohibé entre les sujets des belligérants. Les ressortissants de l'ennemi sont ennemis et comme tels à la merci des combattants. Les déclarations de guerre sont conçues en ce sens."

necessary to defeat the enemy. [86]   Molina says this is but an extension of the above-mentioned principle of double effect. [87]

Second conclusion.—After despoliation, there is no obligation (in justice, that is) for restitution to be made unless they took more than was needed ("facti essent locupletiores").

Third conclusion.—If the property seized belongs to the Church or ecclesiastics, then it must all be restored to its owners. [88]

Fourth conclusion.—Property taken from noncombatants in enemy territory may be retained for the reason that the whole commonwealth is considered as the enemy. [89]   For this same reason reparations may be imposed upon all members of the enemy commonwealth, even mortgaging the future citizens. [90]

* * *

Molina began his study of war in the general framework of the loss and gain of ownership.   It is fitting that the present exposition of Molina's internationalism end on this note.   That

---

[86] "Fas est spoliare innocentes quoscunque, etiamsi advenae sint, et peregrini, iis bonis et rebus, quibus hostes usuri sunt adversus nos, quibusve adjuvari possunt ad bellum sustinendum. Ut fas est sumere arma, naves, pecuniam, frumentum, equos, et id genus alia, eaque ipsa, necnon agros devastare, quantum judicatum fuerit expedire ad hostium vires minuendas, eosque superandos" (II, 121, 471-472).

[87] "Probari autem potest, quoniam si fas est interficere per accidens innocentes, hoc est, non intentione eis, sed hostibus nocendi, quando id postulat belli status, expedireque judicatur ad victoriam comparandam, ut disputatione 119. ostensum est, longe majori cum ratione fas erit ea omnia efficere, quae commemorata sunt, quando id postulat belli status, necessariaque sunt ad victoriam comparandam, indeve hostes sumere, vel conservare possunt vires ad bellum sustinendum" (II, 121, 472).

[88] "Tertio conclusio. Si ejusmodi bona sunt Ecclesiarum, aut Ecclesiasticorum innocentum, aut aliorum innocentum qui partes non sunt Reipublicae, adversus quam justum geritur bellum, peractoque bello manserint, aut, qui justum bellum gerunt, scientes esse ejusmodi innocentum, illa consumpserint in suos usus, aut his utendo adversus hostes, aut quavis alia ratione, vel ea destruxerint plusquam belli status postularet, tenentur illa propriis dominis restituere" (*ibid.*).

[89] "Quarta conclusio. Spoliare possunt bonis externis eos innocentes, qui sunt partes Reipublicae cum qua gerunt justum bellum, eaque sibi retinere" (*ibid.*).
"Ratio est, quoniam, ut disputatione praecedente dictum est, tota Respublica reputatur hostis, fasque est eam punire in omnibus suis membris, quatenus partes illius sunt, quoad externa et fortunae bona" (II, 121, 473).

[90] "Ea etiam de causa fas est imponere tali Reipublicae tributum ab omnimus suis partibus solvendum, imo et ab omnibus successoribus, quatenus futuri sunt partes ejusdem Reipublicae, esto cooperati non fuerint ad Reipublicae delicta" (*ibid.*).

his contribution is important is apparent from the fact that Hugo Grotius expressly refers to Molina twenty-one times in his *De Jure Belli et Pacis*. [91] Modern students of internationalism and the law of war would do well to follow Grotius' example.

Molina's treatise on war and the rules of war blossomed in the high summer days of the development of a just war theory. In the four hundred years since his writing a dramatic change has taken place in the approach to the moral questions surrounding the issues of war.

As one writer has phrased it: "When we come to appraise the traditional Christian positions with regard to the ethic of war we must bear in mind that the situations in confrontation with which they were originally conceived no longer exist." [92]

It is not so much that Christian morality has rejected the just war theory; rather it finds it inapplicable to the conditions of warfare in the last half of the twentieth century. The just war theory was a valid system by which the conflicts of Molina's day could be judged. The just war theory is simply not adequate for the problems posed by the nuclear age.

The Second Vatican Council while not rejecting the just war theory dramatically illustrates the changing attitudes of Christians.

> All these considerations compel us to undertake an evaluation of war with an entirely new attitude. The men of our time must realize that they will have to give it a somber reckoning for their deeds of war. For the course of the future will depend largely on the decisions they make today.
>
> With these truths in mind, this most holy Synod makes its own condemnations of total war already pronounced by recent Popes, and issues the following declaration:
>
> Any act of war aimed indiscriminately at the destruction of entire cities or of extensive areas along with their population is a crime against God and man himself. It merits unequivocal and unhesitating condemnation.
>
> The unique hazard of modern warfare consists in this: it provides those who possess modern scientific weapons with a kind of occasion for perpetrating just such abominations. Moreover, through a certain inexorable chain of events, it can urge men on to the most atrocious decisions. That such in

---

[91] Hugo Grotius, *De Jure Belli ac Pacis Libri Tres*, trans. Francis W. Kelsey *et al.*, for *The Classic of International Law*, ed. James Brown Scott (Oxford: At the Clarendon Press, 1925).

[92] Roland H. Bainton, *Christian Attitudes Toward War and Peace*, A Historical Survey and Critical Re-evaluation (New York: Abingdon Press, 1960), p. 230.

fact may never happen in the future, the bishops of the whole world, in unity assembled, beg all men, especially government officials and military leaders, to give unremitting thought to the awesome responsibility which is theirs before God and the entire human race. [93]

Rather than attempting to justify war which was the effort of the just war theorists like Molina the Second Vatican Council moved in a different direction: "It is our clear duty, then, to strain every muscle as we work for the time when all war can be completely outlawed by international consent." [94]

One has a feeling Molina would have welcomed this challenge.

---

[93] Walter M. Abbott, S.J., General Editor, *The Documents of Vatican II*, with Notes and Comments by Catholic, Protestant and Orthodox Authorities (New York: The American Press, 1966), pp. 293-294.

[94] *Ibid.*, p. 295.

CHAPTER VIII

SLAVERY—RED AND BLACK

"Slavery has no birthday. In the annals of history the slave is present from the beginning, inglorious and unexplained, as though he had sprung, complete with his manacles and misery, from the serpent's head, when Paradise was lost."[1]

Though slavery has no birthday, it did experience growing pains in the era of discovery, the period in which Molina lived.

Molina was born in Spain within fifty years of Columbus' first voyage to the New World. He lived in Portugal during the century of that small country's amazing development of an overseas empire. The impact of these events on Molina's thoughts must have been enormous. When scholars and statesmen began to realize the consequences of Columbus' voyages they wrote, "This is the greatest event since the birth and death of Christ."[2]

In reaching for parallels to understand these events one is tempted to associate the discovery of the New World with the landing of the first men on the Moon. Yet Ernest Burrus warns of this very temptation:

> Hundreds of millions of people watched on television as Armstrong and Aldrin emerged from the space capsule almost at the very instant they made their historic move. ...It would be all to easy for us moderns to imagine something similar in regard to the discovery of two vast continents—a truly New World. Closer study, however, shows that precisely because the discovery was such an unexpected and overwhelming event, it took several generations to grasp its real significance. But, for the very reason that it took Europeans so long to realize its full import, its effects were all the more profound, extensive, and enduring.[3]

---

[1] O. A. Sherrard, *Freedom from Fear: The Slave and His Emancipation* (New York: St. Martin's Press, 1959), p. 11.

[2] Burrus, *No Man Is Alien*, p. 85.

[3] *Ibid.*

Molina lived the last years of his life in the United Kingdom of Spain and Portugal with Phillip II as his sovereign.
The ethical problems concerning the treatment of the natives
of the New World and the treatment among the natives of Africa
in the developing slave trade were of great concern to him.
Molina's response to these relations among the natives of both
continents will be the subject of this chapter.

The plan of this chapter will be to consider Molina's
principles on the slavery issue, to apply them to the question of
the American Indians and then to the larger question of the
African slave trade.

Before beginning the discussion of the moral principles of
slavery, the reader should be alerted that one of the most controversial aspects of Molina's political thought concerns his
writings on slavery. David B. Davis in a recent work wrote
in critical fashion that "Molina believed that in a just war even
the innocent members of an enemy population might be enslaved as a way of punishing the entire state." [4] Later in the
same study Davis cited the Spanish Council of Indies' appeal
to Luis de Molina in defense of the legitimacy of the African
slave trade. [5] Somewhat earlier another scholar charged Molina
with the belief that children of the enemy population might
be enslaved in order to punish the parents. [6]

A distinguished Spanish scholar evaluates Molina's teaching
on slavery somewhat differently. Francisco Mateos, S.J. concludes that the portion of Tract II dealing with slavery is "un
estudio maravilloso de los lugares donde estaba más extendida,
y los modos con que los esclavos venían a poder de los portugueses, fundado en informes directos de los mismos navegantes
que ejercían el comercio, y más todavía de los misioneros jesuí-
tas que eran testigos de cuanto pasaba en el continente negro." [7]

Bernice Hamilton considers Molina's treatment fascinating:
"Molina, in his long fascinating discussion on the ethics of
slavery, based on detailed information gathered from many
countries, followed the new factual and historical approach to
politico-moral matters inaugurated by the Dominican reports
from the New World." [8]

---

[4] David Brion Davis, *The Problem of Slavery in Western Culture* (Ithaca:
Cornell Universtiy Press, 1966), p. 108.

[5] *Ibid.*, p. 191.

[6] Johann Kleinhappl, *Der Staat bei Ludwig Molina* (Innsbruck: 1935), pp.
145-146.

[7] F. Mateos, "El Padre Luis de Molina y la Trata de Negros," Miscellanea
Antonio Pérez Goyena, *Estudios Eclesiásticos*, XXXV (1960), p. 209.

[8] Hamilton, *Political Thought in Sixteenth Century Spain*, p. 7.

Having noted the controversial nature of Molina's slavery teaching, it would now seem appropriate to consider in some detail what Molina held on slavery and later in the chapter to review the allegations against him.

Molina treats slavery in at least two places in *De Justitia*. Reference has already been made to his position regarding prisoners of war and slavery. In Tract II, Disputations 32-36, Molina specifically treats the slavery question.

At the beginning of the first disputation Molina plunges boldly into a question of Aristotle's [9] teachings on slavery. [10] Aristotle, he says, speaks of slaves in two senses. The first sense refers to a type of person who by his natural gifts and aptitudes is more suited to be governed than to govern. This type of subjection is improperly called slavery. [11] There is another type of subjection which Aristotle calls civil and legal slavery. Persons captured in war are *manicipia*. [12] They are called *servi*

---

[9] In the sixteenth century, citing Aristotle's *Politics* was a crutch for those who favored Indian slavery. The passage referred to by Molina is in the *Politics*. For Aristotle, true slavery derived from an innate deficiency in the beauty and inner virtue of the soul. "From the hour of their birth some are marked out for subjection, others for rule" (*Politics* I, 1254a). Molina gives a benign interpretation to this passage. So does Alonso de la Vera Cruz, an Augustinian friar, pupil of Vitoria and friend of Las Casas who is less well known than, but no less important, than the other two. Lewis Hanke, *Aristotle and the American Indians* (London. Hollis and Carter, 1959), treats the background of this issue which was the heart of Las Casas vs. Sepulveda debates in Valladolid in 1550-1551. For Sepulveda's numerous citations of Aristotle see Angel Losada (ed.). Juan Ginés de Sepúlveda, *Demócrates Segundo o De las justas causas de la guerra contra indios* (Madrid: Instituto Francisco de Vitoria, 1951). They are summarized in Juan Friede and Benjamin Keen (eds.), *Bartolome de las Casas in History*: Toward and understanding of the Man and His Work (De Kalb: Northern Illinois University Press, 1971). Ernest J. Burrus, S.J. (ed.), *The Writings of Alonso de la Vera Cruz*. IV vols. (Rome: Jesuit Historical Institute, 1968-1972), Vol. II, p. 72. "Vera Cruz dared not reject the overwhelming authority of the Greek philosopher; he would show that a more humane interpretation could be given to his theory of natural superiority and natural inferiority of men. . . . It is true that there is such a passage in the first book of Aristotle's *Politics* but when the sum total of what the Greek philosopher had to say on natural superiority and natural inferiority is taken together, I do not think that it is possible to defend Vera Cruz's benign interpretation."

[10] II, 32, 156B.

[11] The definition of slavery is a problem to his day. David Brion Davis, *The Problem of Slavery in Western Culture*, discusses the issue, p. 35: "No single definition has succeeded in comprehending the historical varieties of slavery or in clearly distinguishing the institution from other types of involuntary servitude."

[12] In this treatise Molina does use the general word *servitus* (slavery) and *servus* (slave), but his most common word to designate what he is discussing

from *servando* because they are saved from death by the mercy
of the captor who commuted their lawful death sentence into
life-long servitude.[13] This type of slavery is permitted because
perpetual servitude is a lesser evil than loss of life.

This type of slavery is just, but just only so long as the
titles by which the slaves are held are legitimate.

In the next disputation he treats the methods by which a
person can legitimately be subjected to such a servitude. There
are four legitimate titles by which a bound servant may be held:
as a captive, as a criminal, as one who sold himself, as one who
was born a slave.

The law of nations permits those captured[14] in a just war[15]
to have the death penalty[16] commuted to the condition of per-

---

is *mancipium* (bond servant) for which there is no exact English equivalent.
One common English word which comes from the same Latin root as *mancipium* is *emancipation*, which, of course, is the process of setting free or
liberating slaves. *The Oxford English Dictionary* (Vol. IV, p. 109) lists some
other words from the same root, *mancipate*, *mancipation*, and *manciple*. The
latter term, which means a bondslave or servant or a steward or purveyor,
as for a college or Inn of Court, would be the closest English equivalent,
etymologically. Since *manciple* is not in common use, this author has chosen
to use *slave* to translate *mancipium*, realizing that the term is inadequate and
has certain unpleasant connotations.

[13] The ancient attitude toward a prisoner taken in war was well expressed
in the definition given by Winston Churchill in the debate on the Korean War
on July 1, 1952: "What is a prisoner of war? A prisoner of war is a man
who has tried to kill you and, having failed, asks you not to kill him." Quoted
in F. J. P. Veale, *Advance to Barbarism*: The Development of Total Warfare
from Serajevo to Hiroshima (New York: The Devin-Adair Company, 1968),
p. 56N.

[14] An in depth study of the practices of warfare (especially in France) in
the period immediately preceding Molina's may be found in M. H. Deen's,
The Laws of War in the Late Middle Ages. (London: Routledge & Kegan Paul,
1965), see in particular his treatment of prisoners of war, pp. 156-164.

[15] II, 33, 158A. As late as 1750 military prisoners were being shipped to
the British colonies as indentured servants. See Abbot Emerson Smith, *Colonists in Bondage*: White Servitude and Convict Labor in America 1607-1776
(Chapel Hill, University of North Carolina Press, 1947), pp. 152-203.

[16] "To a hunting community, a prisoner of war is merely an extra mouth
to feed. He is an encumbrance to be retained, if at all only long enough
to provide diversion by torturing him to death. Generally prisoners taken in
battle would be disposed of summarily with a stone club. But as soon as
a state of civilization had been reached in which there were fields to be tilled,
walls, temples, palaces, and tombs to be built, and mines to be worked, a
prisoner of war ceased to be merely an extra mouth to feed, and came to
possess a definite economic value as a slave. Professor M. R. Davie expresses
the opinion that the mitigation of war received its greatest impetus from the
institution of slavery which put an end to slaughter and alleviated torture
in order not to impair the efficiency of the captive as a worker." Veale,

petual bondage. An exception is made for Christians. Custom
has decreed that Christians may not be so bound to service
when captured by other Christians. [17] Those of the enemy who
are innocent, such as women and small children and others,
though not subjected to death when captured in a just war,
are subject to mancipation. [18]

Molina sees no problem regarding this type of slavery, *pro-*
viding all the conditions were met to make the circumstances

Advance to Barbarism, pp. 55-56. Veale also points out a consequence of the
introduction of slavery which gives this issue an ironic twist. Slavery resulting
from prisoners of war relieved a section of the community from the necessity
of taking part in any form of manual labor. Thus there arose for the first
time in history of mankind a leisured class not dependent on its own exertions
for maintenance and with little to do but take part in war. Work was equivalent to sinking to the level of a slave. The only form of work which a
member of the leisured class could undertake without loss of dignity was
connected with warfare, since from such work slaves were naturally debarred.
"Once implanted, this idea continued to flourish unchallenged in influential
circles in most countries down to 1918." Veale, *loc. cit.,* pp. 56-57.

[17] The great Grotius, writing fifty years after Molina, supports the same
view. Hugo Grotius, *The Law of War and Peace: De Jure Belli et Pacis Libri*
Tres. Books I-III translated by Francis W. Kelsey (Indianapolis: The Bobbs-
Merrill Company, Inc., 1962), pp. 232-233. Grotius cites Luis de Molina no less
than 20 times in his *Law of War and Peace* published about twenty-five years
after Molina's death. On the prisoner of war issue and resultant slavery
Grotius writes: "In those places where custom sanctions the captivity and
slavery of men, this ought to be limited primarily, if we have regard to moral
justice, in the same way as in the case of property; with the result that, in
fact, such acquisition may be permitted so far as the amount of either an
original or derivative debt allows unless perhaps on the part of men themselves there is some special crime which equity would suffer to be punished
with loss of liberty. To this degree, then, and no further, he who wages a
lawful war has a right over the captured subjects of the enemy, and this right
he may legitimately transfer to others." Grotius, *The Law of War and Peace,*
p. 761. For a discussion of Grotius and slavery see Russell Parsons Jameson,
Montesquieu et L'Esclavage: Étude sur les Origines de l'Opinion Antiesclavagiste en France au XVIIIe Siècle (Paris, Librairie Hachette et Cie, 1944), pp.
147-152).

[18] Life-long servitude of this type, a common practice in Molina's day, has
been long rejected by international accords, but persons captured in modern
war are still held as prisoners (the right to hold such persons is recognized
in the Geneva Laws of War).

International concern with the humane treatment of prisoners of war was
manifested in Articles 4-20 of the Hague Regulations of 1899 and 1907 and
firmly established in the Geneva Convention of July 27, 1929. The Geneva
Convention of 1949, to which forty-eight states were parties, is designed to
replace the 1929 Convention. For excerpts of pertinent articles of this Convention see: Herbert W. Biggs (ed.), *The Laws of Nations*: Cases, Documents
and Notes (2nd edition). (New York: Appleton-Century-Crofts, Inc., 1952),
and Notes (2nd edition). (New York: Appleton-Century-Crofts, Inc., 1952), pp.
1008-1012.

just—for instance, that these persons had been captured in a just war by a legitimate ruler. He cites the common opinion of the civil and canonical jurists in addition to many citations from Holy Scripture.

The second legitimate title by which persons may be held in mancipation is by punishment of a crime. Molina then cites some instances in ecclesiastical discipline which he says confirms this practice.

He also refers to the Spanish practice in the war with the Saracens in the kingdom of Granada. On this point he is not certain, but rather indulges in an examination of the pros and cons of this position. [19]

Basically, Molina agrees with the measures taken by Philip II. The history of Christians and Moslems in Spain is a complex one and beyond the scope of this study. It was much more a political question than is generally realized. The author of a standard work on the subject warns the student:

> It has been the fashion to regard the war of the Reconquest, through which Spain was gradually won back from the Moslems, as a war of religion. ...In fact, however, the medieval history of Spain shows that in the long struggle there was little antagonism either of race or religion. [20]

The third title is the sale of one's self or one's children into slavery.

What are the conditions for selling oneself? The person must be: (1) 21; (2) free; (3) willing; (4) paid; and (5) aware of his condition. The buyer must realize he is buying a free

---

[19] "Molina is, as usual, rather harsher to infidels and especially apostates. He draws his examples from the war again[st] Granada. 'Note, he says, commenting on Vitoria's remark that women may not be slain unless they are proved guilty, that if (as in times past when there was a war against the descendants of the Saracens in the kingdom of Granada) one were fighting heretics or apostates who had revolted, and were quite evidently apostate, and if apostasy were evidently the cause of the rebellion, it would without doubt be right to kill grown women for the crime of heresy and apostasy. I may add that grown women who march with the enemy or are beside them in a besieged town are usually not free from blame, but are as a rule helping the enemy. For this reason they are not to be considered as having the same degree of innocence as children, though it is safer to leave them alive when their guilt is not established. We know that the women of Granada marched with their rebellious menfolk and gave them such help as to be virtually fighting, so it is no wonder that history also tells us that they were slain, especially when the signs of their apostasy were so evident." Hamilton, *op. cit.*, p. 153.

[20] Henry Lea, *The Moriscos in Spain: Their Conversion and Expulsion* (Philadelphia: Lea Brothers & Co., 1901), p. 1.

man. The simultaneous presence of all five conditions would make such a transaction legitimate. The absence of one of these conditions would nullify its legitimacy. [21]

What about parents selling their children in grave necessity? This phrase—*in grave necessity*—is a classical one from moral theology. A twentieth century text on moral theology defines it this way: "A person is in *grave need*, when he is in probable danger of death, or is in manifest danger of some serious misfortune, such as severe sickness, amputation of some member, long and bitter imprisonment, insanity, loss of good name, reduction from wealth to poverty, destruction of home by fire, etc." [22]

For his opinion, Molina relies heavily on Diego de Covarrubias y Leyva's [23] *Variarum ex jure resolutionum*, first published

---

[21] II, 33, 161A.

[22] John A. McHugh, O.P. and Charles J. Callan, O.P., *Moral Theology: A Complete Course Based on St. Thomas Aquinas and the Best Modern Authorities*, 2 vols. (New York: Joseph F. Wagner, Inc., 1958), I, 501.

[23] Covarrubias was a Spanish jurist who wrote on the question of the Spanish conquest of America. Born in Toledo in 1512, he studied at the University of Salamanca, graduating in civil and canon law. He became a professor at Salamanca and served at various times as a judge in Burgos and Granada and as a member of the Council of Castile. From the days at Salamanca as a student of Francisco de Vitoria he had a great interest in the Indies. He lectured at Salamanca on the Indian problem, participated in the commission that was asked to pass judgment on *Demócrates segundo* of Gines de Sepúlveda, and referred to the subject in several writings. "Covarrubias, opposing the imperialistic thesis of Sepúlveda, proclaimed the thesis of natural liberty, for which he sought philosophical foundations in Roman law, Greek philosophy and Holy Scripture, and theological bases in Thomas Aquinas and Juan de Torquemada. He refuted the Aristotelian doctrine, which served Sepulveda as the basis for his own thesis. For Covarrubias the natual law was superior to all human laws, and by nature all men were born free. Slavery originated as the law of history; it was the humane and just way to guarantee peace and restore justice if there was no other way. He based his theory on the colonization of America on that principle. It was not a question of aggression but of intervention on behalf of the barbarians to save them and integrate them in the community of civilized peoples." J. Malagon-Barcelo, "Covarrubias y Leyva, Diego de." *New Catholic Encyclopedia*. 15 vols., vol. IV (New York: McGraw-Hill Book Co.), p. 401. Later he was a bishop with a somewhat roving way. He was named bishop of Santo Domingo but never took over the see. In 1560 he was consecrated bishop of Ciudad Rodrigo and in 1565 moved to the See of Segovia. He was bishop-elect of Cuenca, Molina's home town, at the time of his death in Madrid in 1577.

Covarrubias also held that prisoners captured in a just war could be enslaved. Jameson says of him: "En premier lieu, il accepte sans hésitation que, dans une guerre juste, les prisonniers deviennent esclaves.... Pour Covarrubias, l'esclavage paraît dépendre uniquement de la guerre; c'est là une juste punition de ceux qui troublent la paix des nations. Cependant il y a

at Salamanca in 1552.   He also cites Arius Pinellus. [24]   Molina
spends almost no time describing what he considers a grave
need to be.   The whole opinion may seem startling to modern
readers, but Molina's contemporary, Jean Bodin (1530-1596), the
French political philosopher, went even further by maintaining
that parents should have restored to them the absolute power
of life and death over their children. [25]

When Molina discusses the actual conditions of slave trading, he will have more to say on this subject.

Molina turns at this point to the question of whether a
person who is justly condemned to death may be sold into
slavery.   The issue was raised as a result of reports from Africa
and Brazil either of cannibalism practiced on prisoners of war
or criminals.   Molina says slavery is permitted as an escape
from cannibalism or death.   May a person unjustly condemned
to death sell himself into slavery?   Under certain circumstances
Molina would permit it.   His treatment of this particular question will be discussed briefly later in this chapter.

The fourth title for legitimate slavery is by birth from a
female slave.   Independent of the status of the father, the person born to a female slave is a slave, *"quia partus sequitur ven-
trem,"* a dictum of Roman law. [26]   Molina says this is a common teaching.   The only authority he cites is Panormitanus. [27]
Though he does not cite St. Thomas Aquinas by name, he is
following his opinion. [28]

---

une réserve à faire; les chrétiens qui sont faits prisonniers par d'autres chrétiens ne deviennent pas esclaves." Russell Parsons Jameson, *Montesquieu et
L'Esclavage*: Estude sur les origines de l'opinion antiesclavagiste en France
au XVIIᵉ Siècle (Paris: Librairie Hachette et Cⁱᵉ, 1911), pp. 87-88.

[24] Arius Pinellus was an obscure contemporary of Molina who had published a work concerned with the question of maternal succession in Salamanca
in 1564.   See Antonio Palau y Dulcet, *Manual del Librero Hispanoamericano*
(Barcelona, Librería Palau, 1961), XIII, p. 255.

[25] "Examples from the practice of the Romans and early people demon-
strate that a well-ordered state requires parents to have over their children
the power of life and death, which both the law of God and that of nature
assigns to them.   Unless this power is restored to the parents, we can never
hope to see revival of the good customs, honour, virtue, and splendour of
ancient states." *Masters of Political Thought* (edited by Edward McChesney
Sait), 2 vols. (Boston: Houghton-Mifflin Company, 1950), II, 56. For a discussion of Bodin and slavery see Russell Parsons Jameson, *op. cit.*, pp. 138-143.

[26] For a discussion of this Roman concept, its application in medieval
Europe and in the Americas, see David B. Davis, *op. cit.*, pp. 38-40, 96-97, 277-278.

[27] II, 33, 165A.

[28] David Brion Davis is of the opinion that Aquinas' belief brought him
"perilously close to a belief in the natural inferiority of slaves.... It was
accepted doctrine that in physical generation the father supplied the form and

After surveying Molina's treatment of the legitimate titles to hold slaves, we can briefly discuss the question of slavery for the natives of the New World.

On the question of Indian slavery Molina writes generally and academically. In contrast, Vitoria's lectures, *De Indis*, spring hot from the crisis of settlers' behavior in the New World. Generally speaking, by the time Molina was writing, some forty years after Vitoria, the theoretical question of the rights of the Indians had been settled.

From 1500 to 1570 the Indians had tireless protectors in at least three outstanding champions of their rights: Bartolomé Las Casas, [29] Francisco de Vitoria, [30] and Alonso de la Vera Cruz. [31]

It is in the disputations on war as noted in Chapter VI that Molina touches on the rights of the conqueror and the

---

the mother supplied the matter; and since the being of a thing depended primarily of its form, how could it be held that the son of a free man and a bondswoman should be a slave? 'We observe,' answered St. Thomas, 'that in animals born from different species the offspring follows the mother rather than the father; wherefore mules born of a mare and an ass are more like mares than those born of a she-ass and a horse. Therefore it should be the same with men.' Moreover, the woman's womb had the same relation to a man's seed as a plot of land, had claim to all produce. Finally, bondage was a condition of the body, it was she who transmitted the condition of slavery. While these arguments did not add up to a theory of inferiority, it is not surprising that Aquinas' followers, Ptolemy of Lucca and especially Egidius Colonna, appeared to accept the Aristotelian view that some men were slaves by nature." Davis, *The Problem of Slavery in Western Culture*, pp. 96-97.

[29] The literature on Las Casas is extensive. A convenient summary of his work and influence can be found in Lewis Hanke's *Aristotle and the American Indians*. (London: Hollis and Carter, 1959). This work contains helpful bibliographical information.

[30] Vitoria's approach to the Indian question is more theoretical. Unlike Las Casas and Vera Cruz, he never visited the Indies but relied on reports from missionaries and public officials to prepare public lectures at the University of Salamanca. All three men have tremendous influence. Their broad scholarships and cogent reasoning had a profound effect on European thinkers in general and on Spanish lawgivers in particular. Burrus, *op. cit.*, p. 98. A bibliography on Vitoria can be found in Bernice Hamilton, *op. cit.*, pp. 189-190.

[31] Vera Cruz, an Augustinian Friar, pupil of Vitoria and friend of Las Casas, is less well known but no less important than the other two. Ernest Burrus, S.J. has published *The Writings of Alonso de la Vera Cruz*. 4 vols. (Rome: Jesuit Historical Institute, 1968-1972). The same author has published some studies of Vera Cruz. "Alonso de la Vera Cruz's, *Defense of the American Indians* (1553-1554)" in *The Heythrop Journal*, vol. IV, no. 3 (Oxford, 1963, July), pp. 225-253. "Las Casas and Vera Cruz: Their Defense of the American Indians Compared" in *Neue Zeitschrift für Missionswissenschaft*, vol. XXII (Backennied, Switzerland, 1966), pp. 201-202.

natives in the new land. Molina believes that Christians have
the right to preach the gospel to the natives:

> As Christians we have the right to preach the gospel through-
> out the world, to send missionaries to any infidels, to protect
> the missionaries, and to force the infidels, not of course to
> accept the Gospel, but to create no obstacles against the mis-
> sionaries' preaching and against the hearing, accepting and
> following of the Gospel message by their subjects. If any
> peoples, kings or powers do create such obstacles, we may
> rightfully coerce them by war and punish the injury done to
> the faith and to the Gospel in that land. ... Since this is so,
> I hold that even if the infidels are unwilling, we can for this
> particular purpose go with ships and stay in their harbours
> and in their land for as long as, and with such force as,
> may be necessary to accomplish this aim safely. If however,
> it could conveniently be done and were advisable, we could first
> discuss the matter with them through envoys, and send the
> missionaries alone or with just a few soldiers, rather than
> enter with such forces as would provide complete military
> control and safeguard the missionaries. [32]

He also declares that refusal to accept the faith is no cause
for war.

Further it is not justifiable to seize possessions of pagans
simply because they are infidels, for it would be just as much
an act of robbery as it would be if it were done to Christians.

Molina says there is nothing to hinder infidels from being
masters of their own things and possessing things as private
persons. Jurisdiction and ownership are common to the entire
human race. They are not based on faith and charity but arise
directly or indirectly from the very nature of things and their
first foundations. [33]

Again, he denies that a nation may be subjugated "because
of its utter barbarity." If this were true there would be good
reason "for the Brazilians and all other inhabitants of the New
World—even the Ethiopians too—to be conquered and brought
into slavery like slaves, acquiring property only for their masters, deprived of their lands and all their belongings"—and there
is certainly no truth in this. [34]

A much discussed reason for the conquest of the Indians
was the so-called crimes of the natives. Molina quotes a number

---

[32] II, 105, 434A. The translation is Hamilton's, *op. cit.*, p. 112.
[33] V, 73.
[34] II, 105, 435B.

of Spanish authorities who do believe that the subjection of
the Indians to Spain by war was justified by their idolatry and
refusal of the faith and a further list of authorities who believe
that infidels may be punished for unnatural vice on the authority
of the Pope or the emperor. But Molina, along with Vitoria,
disagrees—with the understanding that innocent persons are
not being harmed. Their own rulers may of course stop the
pagans from committing such crimes.

Christian princes may wage war on natives because of cannibalism and human sacrifice, for this war would be to protect
the innocent.

> It is quite proper to end by force the atrocities and cruel
> behaviour due to wickedly unjust laws, if necessary by a dec-
> laration of war and using all the rights of war, even to depos-
> ing wicked rulers and if necessary appointing others. It does
> not matter if the barbarians [rulers] and their subjects are
> in favour of such customs and sacrifices and do not want
> outsiders to attack them, for everybody has the right to save
> a man who is being unjustly killed, even if the victim does
> not want to be saved, as in the generally-agreed case of a
> man trying to hang himself or to commit suicide in some
> other way. [35]

Such an intervention should not be used as an excuse for
continued war.

> One condition must be noted: this kind of war is not for
> the purpose of recovering one's own property nor of avenging
> a personal injury; it is purely to help the innocent who look
> to the invaders as neighbors. It is therefore not right for
> the invaders to take more of their enemies' property than
> will pay the cost of the war, cover any loss and damage
> suffered during it, and be a fair payment for the trouble and
> labour involved. For the invaders are not obliged to risk
> their lives and expend their energies without reward: the
> enemy who by their unjust acts gave cause for such a just
> war are obliged to defray these expenses themselves. Any
> possessions left over are the rightful due of the innocent peo-
> ple for whose sake the fighting was started and whose cause
> is being upheld, for they could have justly begun a war to
> defend themselves and to save themselves from injury. [36]

---

[35] II, 106, 437C. The translation is Hamilton's, *op. cit.*, pp. 128-129.
[36] *Ibid.*, p. 130.

Hamilton points out that Molina here is less liberal than Vitoria and more inclined to the letter of the law. [37]

Having completed his examination of the titles by which slaves may legitimately be acquired Molina proceeds to discuss the practical aspects of the situation. It is one of his typical searches of the existential order. He engages in an extensive review (twelve long columns in the printed text) of the association of Portugal with the locales where the slave trade was then in progress. His method is historical. First he recounts the history as objectively as he can [38] (Disputation 34), then he applies the principles he has outlined (Disputation 33) to the concrete historical situation (Disputation 35). The complete study is, as Bernice Hamilton has noted, fascinating. [39] It would be much too long a detour to detail the facts contained in Molina's history of the areas of Africa where the Portuguese were involved in slave trading. Disputation 34 is a little known account of race relations in the West and Southeast Coasts of Africa. As far as can be determined, Francisco Mateos' and Joseph Höffner's studies are the only ones to have examined it in print. [40] Mateos's is an excellent summary of Molina's exposition. What is needed, in addition, is a complete critical editing of Disputation 34. The present writer is not prepared to do this at this time. What will be attempted is a listing of some geographical and historical references Molina has assembled and the checking of certain of these against the accounts of later historians.

---

[37] *Ibid.*

[38] "Hujus rei fidelem historiam," II, 35, 177B; "Facta autem diligenti inquisitione, dicam paucis, quod de hac re comperire potui," II, 34, 166B.

"What Dr. Freeman-Grenville has lately said of East Africa is true of almost all precolonial history of Africa: That 'we are only at the beginning of its serious study, and there is a vast field for research in the collections of oral traditions and of documents in private hands, as well as for the classification and study of documents in libraries scattered all over the globe'." Quoted in Basil Davidson's *The African Slave Trade: Precolonial History 1450-1850* (Boston: Little, Brown and Co., 1961), p. 293.

"Of the history of the Portuguese in West Africa during the sixteenth century singularly little is known. They had by this time become much more interested in their possessions in India, and most students of Portuguese expansion dwell upon India and Brazil rather than upon West Africa, which gradually became merely a source of slaves for Brazil." Elizabeth Donnan, *Documents Illustrative of the History of the Slave Trade to America*, 3 vols. (New York: Octagon Books, Inc., 1965), vol. I, p. 6.

[39] Hamilton, *op. cit.*, p. 7.

[40] F. Mateos, "El Padre Luis de Molina y la Trata de Negros," *op. cit.*, pp. 203-222.

Cape Verde Islands

He begins his study with the Cape Verde [41] Islands mentioning São Tiago (*earum praecipua Divi Jacobi*) [42] in particular. He notes that these islands were uninhabited until the Portuguese arrived. [43] He further notes that this area of Africa in general is divided into upper and lower Guinea [44] and even mentions an alternate spelling, *Guiné*, which is the Portuguese form to this day. [45] He identifies the natives as Jolofs. [46] From

---

[41] "The key links to Portuguese control over Western Africans were the Cape Verde Archipelago and São Tomé. In the 1460's the Cape Verdes, São Tiago in particular, were colonized and developed into a base for trade in slaves and other commodities with the adjacent mainland... São Tomé also became important to the Portuguese trade, particularly as a depot for slaves bound for Brazil." R. H. Chilcote, *Portuguese Africa*. (Englewood Cliffs, N.J.: Prentice Hall, Inc., 1967), p. 85.

[42] II, 34, 165C.

[43] "The crescent-shaped archipelago of the ten Cape Verde islands lying off the west coast of Africa was uninhabited until the Portuguese first arrived in the fifteenth century." Chilcote, *op. cit.*, p. 85.

[44] "The exact geographical definition the Gulf of Guinea is, like all such definitions, bleak but clear: 'A large open arm of the South Atlantic in the angle of West Africa and including the Bight of Benin and the Bight of Biafra.' The term 'Guinea Coast' was customarily applied to the shoreline bordering this gulf, but the coast itself was considered to begin at the Senegal River —sixteen degrees north of the equator—and to curve down and away to South Angola, sixteen degrees south of the equator. 'Upper Guinea' stretched from Senegambia to the Cross River on the Slave Coast, 'Lower Guinea' from that river to the Congo and Angola, including the Spanish island of Fernando Po. By the eighteenth century this coast-line had by long usage been subdivided in European minds. First of all, running from north to south, came the area known as the Rivers of the South; then the Grain Coast (where the malaguetta pepper was obtained); the Ivory Coast (source of elephant tusks); the Gold Coast and the adjacent Slave Coast (both named for obvious reasons); and on down past the lands bordering the Bight of Biafra to Gabon and Angola. Naturally enough these European trade appellations did not mean that the West African shore-line was neatly compartmented in the fashion of a supermarket and its shelves. Gold could be purchased on the Grain Coast, ivory and pepper on the Slave Coast—although in point of fact slaves were easily the chief product of the Slave Coast, and of the marshy regions east of the Volta River." James Pope-Hennessy, *Sins of the Fathers*: A Study of the Atlantic Slave Trade 1441-1807 (New York: Alfred A. Knopf, 1968), p. 38.

[45] " 'The Gulf of Guinea,' 'the Guinea Coast'—there are certain words or phrases which cannot only be heard and seen, but tasted and smelt. I would put those amongst them. The names have sounded down the centuries with the tantalizing ring of the guinea coins of purest yellow gold first minted for the Royal African Company by order of King Charles II. Visually, the words conjure up a low, hot, green shore-line, hazy with vapour, and forever beseiged by the monotonous breakers of the South Atlantic. Taste the words on your palate and you get the pricking of space, or the cloying flavour of the mango. The scent is that of the hibiscus and of the deep mould of tropical

this area imports are gold, amber, civet cats, wax and leather
"but above all an enormous number of slaves." [47]

---

forests steaming after rain. Then there is the traditional hint of risk and
adventure about almost everything to do with Guinea, whether it be the
'Guineamen,' high masted sailing ships West Africa bound, or even the 'Guinea
merchants' who sped them keeling on their way. Of course the prefix 'guinea'
has other more pedestrian connections—guinea-grain or malaguetta, which the
Portuguese sought upon the Coast before they found the true pepper of the
East; guinea-grass; and the guinea-fowl, sophisticated cousin of some of the
wild fowl of West Africa. Chaffing Roderigo for his despairing love for Desde-
mona, Iago refers contemptuously to Othello's wife as 'a guinea-hen.' But
from the days of the first Portuguese explorers who brought back alive,
Negroes and Negresses as trophies for the Court, Guinea became to the ordinary, stay-at-home people of Europe an established and persistent myth.
Besides the exotic landscapes and costumes of the West Africans, there was
the added thrill of the 'savage' and the unknown. 'None of us Europeans
ever go to Guinea,' wrote a seventeenth-century trader 'but we are apt at our
return to make horrid pictures of the manners and vices of the blacks.'"
ibid., p. 37.

[46] "The Jalloffs, Jolloffs, or Yalofs, were negroes of the Senegambia, neigh-
bors of the Foulis." Donnan, *Documents Illustrative*, II, p. 422N.

"The kingdom of Jalofo, however, was quite well known to the Portuguese. It does not seem to have been a political unit. There were a large
number of small potentates, each the lord of a tribe, like the subjects of
King Boudoniel, and like the Barbacini and the Serreri, who were perpetually
at war with one another. Nor were the Jalofos a very rich people. Yet
they gave the Portuguese a fair welcome, so that treaties were made and a
flourishing trade developed between blacks and whites." J. W. Blake, "European Beginnings on the West Coast" in *Africa from Early Times* (edited by
P. J. M. McEwan), (London: Oxford University Press, 1969), p. 218.

[47] II, 34, 165D; Several times in his historical narrative Molina makes
reference to the volume of slave traffic. Although the full extent of the traffic
is difficult to judge, some attempt has been made by recent authors to
estimate it. See Philip D. Curtin, *The Atlantic Slave Trade*: A Census (Madison: The University of Wisconsin Press, 1969), pp. 15-49, 95-126.

"We do not have enough information to be able to state exactly how
many African slaves were carried across the Atlantic to America. However,
on the basis of the information we do possess, it seems likely that the number
of slaves imported into America, from the time the trade began in the sixteenth century until it was eventually brought to an end in the nineteenth
century, was at least fifteen million, and unlikely to have been much greater
than twenty million. It should be noted that these figures are for the slaves
landed in America. The number *leaving Africa* must have been considerably
greater, since it was rare for a slave ship to complete a voyage without death
from disease of at least part of its human cargo. It seems reasonable from
what we know of the mortality on slaving voyages to assume that *on the
average* at least a sixth of the slaves shipped from Africa never lived to see
America. On occasions, the mortality was very much higher than this. Thus
in all probability somewhat between eighteen and twenty-four million Africans
were carried away from West Africa by the European slave trade." J. D. Fage,
"The Slave Trade (i)" from *Africa from Early Times to 1800* (edited by P. J. M.
McEwan) (London: Oxford University Press, 1969), p. 271.

The Portuguese did not wage war with the Africans of Guinea. On the contrary, they continuously, "as I've been told," pressure the slave buyers of Cape Verde, not to give the natives any reasons for beginning hostilities, lest the lucrative business dealings be curbed. Consequently, the slaves were not the result of just wars between the Portuguese and the Africans. Rather do the various black tribes of Guinea oppose each other "without right or justice" in internal strife. "Thus, when the Portuguese ships drop anchor somewhere along the coast or in a river, the Africans themselves are intent on looting the neighboring villages in order to have slaves to be used in bartering for goods." [48]

In addition, Portuguese businessmen, "who are called Tangosmaos," [49] reside there along the coast. As soon as the arrival of Portuguese ships is imminent, these dealers go into the interior of the country, accompanied by Africans, in order to acquire slaves on the slave markets. These unfortunates, "covered with chains," are then driven to the ships "in public" and sold to the shipmasters. [50]

It is further reported that in those areas it is customary to hold court over the populace under a certain tree. The chief of that specific area is the judge. A few elders vote and decide the sentence. In this manner many are sentenced to life-long slavery instead of death, while on occasion some are still executed. It is customary there to impose the death sentence or life-long slavery for the most trivial cases of theft, perhaps for stealing a chicken. Molina was told that one of these chiefs sentenced his own son, who had been caught in a minor robbery, to be punished by a life of slavery with the Portuguese. Those savages are so barbaric, that on occasion, an entire clan,

---

[48] II, 34, 165D.

[49] "In upper Guinea, which may be roughly defined as the region between the River Senegal and Cape Palmas, Portuguese traders and exiled criminals frequented many of the rivers and creeks, often penetrating a considerable distance into the interior. Many of them settled in the Negro villages, where they and their Mulatto descendants functioned as principals or intermediaries in the barter-trade between the Africans and Europeans. Those of them who went completely native, stripping off their clothes, tattooing their bodies, and speaking the local languages, and even joining in fetishistic rites and celebrations were called *tangos-maos*, or *lançados*.... Through the medium of these *lançados* and *tangos-maos*, Portuguese became and for centuries remained the *lingua franca* of the coastal region of Upper Guinea." C. R. Boxer, *Race Relations in Portuguese Colonial Empire*, 1415-1825, p. 9.

[50] II, 34, 165D.

all its descendants and relatives, might be wiped out or sold
into slavery because of the guilt of the father. [51]

The Portuguese dealers were not in the least concerned
about the reasons for the slaves' loss of freedom. "Whatever
is offered them, they buy, so long as they can reach agreement
on the price." [52] They explained that they could ascertain nothing about the background of the slaves, no matter how hard
they tried. Besides that, they claimed the Africans found it
unpleasant to be asked where they procured their slaves.

> I have spoken with a few slave-traders who had bought
> such slaves in Africa and were delivering them here. They
> all confirmed my explanation. As much as I was able to learn
> from them, they pursue only one goal in this entire trade,
> namely their own profit and advantage. They are actually
> surprised when anyone suggests unscrupulous actions [are in-
> volved in their dealings], and say that the Africans who are
> bought and taken away are treated quite well. After all, in
> this manner we lead them to Christianity and to a far better
> life than they enjoyed previously among their own people,
> where they ran around naked and had to be satisfied with
> miserable sustenance. [53]

Molina asked the dealers further whether it did not happen
that slaves were occasionally shipped who had apparently or
probably been kidnapped. They answered, "That happens sometimes, but not very often."

To his question, "How could they reconcile such business
with their consciences?" one of the dealers responded: "If we
don't buy them, they are murdered on the spot by the slave-
hunters, so that their activities will not become public and
they themselves be killed by their own people because of this
deed." The chiefs demanded that a black interpreter be present
at the conclusion of each sale. It was hoped to prevent the
kidnapping of slaves in this manner. If anyone did not observe
these rules, he would endanger himself and the entire slave-
trade. [54]

At this point Molina injects the grisly note of cannibalism
which he reports is practiced among the Africans of Upper
Guinea with whom the Portuguese are trading.

---

[51] II, 34, 167A.
[52] *Ibid.*
[53] *Ibid.*
[54] *Ibid.*

These were the titles and the methods by which the Portuguese slave merchants bought their cargo. Concerning this
trade and these titles there did not seem to be any scruple in
the mind of the bishop of Cape Verde nor in the mind of the
priests living there or back here at home. They gave absolution
to the merchants and *tangosmaos*.

I believe, Molina says, that the penitents not only do not
confess these things but even have no doubt about them in
confession, nor are they asked about them by the confessors.
And if there is any penalty imposed by the bishop or the governor on the *tangosmaos* it is only because they had not fulfilled
their Easter duty or had slept with some pagan or for some
other excess but not because they had been involved in the
slave trade. What my own opinion about all of this is, he
concludes, will be discussed in the next disputation. "At this
point we are only concerned with the facts of the case." [55]

São Tomé

In 1473 the Portuguese navigators [56] discovered the island
of São Tomé uninhabited and, according to the law of nations
as *primi occupantes*, legitimately took possession. It became
a suffragan episcopal see to the Archbishop of Lisbon. From
this island the Portuguese began their trade by ship with the
nearby areas of Africa. [57] These regions are now known as
Lower Guinea.

The first region is the kingdom of Manicongo [58] which some

---

[55] "Modo solum narramus factum," II, 34, 168A.

[56] Molina places São Tomé south of the equator (*sub linea aequinoctiali
Insulam Divi Thomae*). The equator touches the southern portion of the
island so technically the island or the greater portion of it lies north of the
equator.

[57] "It was, however, the island of São Tomé which first came to be the
centre of the slave traffic in the Gulf of Guinea. Negroes were taken to
São Tomé from Benin and from many other places on the coast between
Benin and Cape St. Catherine, while slaves from Angola, called Angolares,
were also carried to the island. Most of these unfortunate captives were
shipped either to Portugal or Pernambuco in Brazil. The trade expanded considerably during the century so that, by 1602 [two years after Molina's death]
a number of slave marts had been established by the Portuguese all around
the coast of the Gulf." Blake, "The Slave Trade (ii)," p. 277.

[58] Mani-Congo was the name given to the rulers and the area south of
the Congo River. The name itself means Lord of the Congo. The Portuguese
association with the people of this kingdom began in friendship and alliance.
One of the early rulers, Nzinga Mbemba was baptized Dom Affonso. Emissaries went back and forth between Europe and Africa and even the Vatican.
A son of Mani-Congo was appointed in Rome itself a bishop of his country.

years ago together with its king accepted the faith and is under
the spiritual jurisdiction of the Bishop of São Tomé. [59]   Since
all these people are Christians there are no slaves taken from
here nor are any subjected to slavery because of crimes committed.   The Portuguese who live in this region are called *pom-
beros*, [60] just as in Upper Guinea they are called *tangosmaos*.
These men and some Africans buy a huge supply of slaves
which they bring bound to the coast and sell to the Portuguese
merchants there.

Angola

Still further south there is the country of Ambundia, which
the Portuguese call Angola. [61]   About 80 years ago [62] one of the
chiefs, who "are called Sobas [63] there," succeeded, with the help
of the Portuguese, to subjugate a large area of land.   His name
was Angola Inene, the "Great" who ruled in the capital city
Cabaea.   It is with this king that the Portuguese were waging
war.   To this king time and time again, with himself asserting
that he wanted to be a Christian, many priests from Portugal
and the Island of São Tomé and even a monk of the order of

A summary of this history can be found in Basil Davidson's *The African Slave
Trade: Precolonial History 1450-1850* (Boston: Little, Brown and Company, 1961),
pp. 117-162.

[59] The Jesuits were the early missionaries in this region of Africa.   An
account of their first efforts can be found in Laurenz Kilger, O.S.B.   "Die
ersten Jesuiten am Kongo und in Angola (1547-1575)" *Zeitschrift für Missionswissenschaft* XI, 1921, pp. 16-33.   Kilger does not make mention of Molina's
history of the period.

[60] "Not infrequently did the Portuguese send their *pombeiros* (European
but almost invariably mulatto or black African traders or emissaries) into the
interior to stir up a local war in expectation of being able to buy the prisoners." Ronald H. Chilcote, *Portuguese Africa*, p. 56.

[61] Molina describes Angola as a huge area (*vastissima*).   Even to this day
it is considered large, fourteen times the area of Portugal.

[62] Circa 1500.

[63] "The authority of the tribal chiefs (called *sobas* or *sovas* in Angola)
was very great, and in some cases, absolute."   Boxer, "The Slave Trade (iii)"
from *Africa from Early Times to 1800*, p. 285.

"Slaves could be thus had very cheaply, whether from the Jagas, or from
the *sobas* (*sovas*) or chiefs of the other tribes."

A *soba* who has sworn allegiance to the governor of Angola was entrusted
by him to a Portuguese soldier or official.   "This soldier seeth he have no
wrong; and the lord (*soba*) acknowledgeth him to be his master; and he doth
maintain the soldier, and maketh him rich.   Also, in the wars he commandeth
his master's house to be built before his own, and whatsoever he hath taken
that day in the wars, he parteth with his master.   So that there is no Portugal soldier of any account, but he hath his Negro sova or lord." *Ibid.*, p. 285.

St. Bernard were sent. Because this ruler was interested in trade relations with the Portuguese rather than in the salvation of his soul there was no reason for the missionaries to stay. After the death of many of the priests the others returned to Portugal. Their chalices and other sacred ornaments were later found in that area.

After a passage of time when the king saw that he was missing the Portuguese trade he sent ambassadors to King John III of Portugal [64] urgently requesting priests affirming that he was willing to receive baptism along with his people and offering to the king the richest silver mines in his kingdom and the promises of the slave trade. He desired European wares from the Portuguese and for this reason, not because of religious fervor, he asked for some missionaries. Around the year 1560 then, four members of the Society of Jesus departed for this country. [65] Accompanying them was the royal delegate Paulo Diaz Novais [66] and a number of businessmen.

When they arrived they discovered that Angola Inene had died. The missionaries and the Portuguese businessmen, who were there to trade for slaves, were at first cordially received by Dambi Angola, the son and successor of Angola Inene. But then Dambi confiscated all of the businessmen's wares, saying that he would procure the proper number of slaves in return. He pretended to do as he had promised, but then took back all of the slaves, so that the Portuguese had to return home poor and robbed of their goods. In the meantime, two of the

---

[64] John III, king of Portugal (1521-1557). His reign saw the Portuguese empire at its apogee. The great Asiatic possessions were extended by further conquests. Brazil also flourished.

[65] For Jesuits in Dias de Novais' expedition. Francisco Rodrigues, S.J., *História da Companhia de Jesus na Assistência de Portugal* (4 vols.) (Porto: 1931-1950), II, 2, 509 sq.

[66] "The advocacy of the Church militant fitted in well enough with the proposals of Paulo Dias de Novais, a grandson of the discoverer of the Cape of Good Hope, who was then pressing his scheme for the conquest and colonization of Angola upon a somewhat hesitant court. The charter that was finally given him by the Crown in 1571 envisaged the colonization of at least a part of Angola by peasant families of Portugal, who were to be provided with 'all the seeds and plants which they could take from the kingdom and from the island of São Tomé.' But when Paulo Dias' expedition arrived off Luanada in February 1575, the slave-trade was already in full swing; malaria and other tropical disease proved an insuperable obstacle to white colonization for the next three centuries; and the high ideals of the royal charter were soon abandoned for the unrestrained procurement of *peças*, 'pieces,' as the Negro slaves were termed." C. R. Boxer, *Race Relations in the Portuguese Colonial Empire 1415-1825* (Oxford: Clarendon Press, 1963), p. 23.

missionaries had succumbed to the hardships of the climate.
The delegate, Paulo Diaz Novais, and the two other missionaries
were forcibly detained by the king. Only through a ruse did
the delegate and one of the fathers escape. The other father,
Francisco Govea, [67] died after several years of captivity.

Angered by the injustice which had been done to his delegate and the missionaries, King Sebastian [68] sent Paulo Diaz
Novais and a fleet from Portugal to Angola in the year 1574.
"I myself have seen the royal orders," which had been formulated "after lengthy discussions" by the personal council of
the king. The orders were first to demand reparation peace-
ably, and to commence hostilities only in the case of a refusal
(to give reparation). If these instructions were observed carefully, "certainly [a cause for] just war, would have been given."
A few Jesuits also took part in this expedition, and "from their
report I have learned a number of things." [69]

Dambi Angola had died. His successor became friends with
Paulo Diaz Novais. For four years everything was fine. The
seat of government was at Loanda. [70] Then, one day there arrived 13 or 14 ships from Europe, filled with wares. Moved
"by the greed for such a large mass of wares," the king mali-
ciously ordered the 30 or 40 Portuguese who were present to
be killed and claimed all of the goods, excusing his act by
saying that "the Portuguese intended to take over his kingdom."

----

[67] "Padre Francisco de Gouveia, S.J., who was detained for many years
at the kraal of the Ngola, or the chief from which Angola derives its name,
and who then owed a shadowy allegiance to the Congo king, explained that
these Bantu were barbarous savages who could not be converted by the
methods of peaceful persuasion that were employed with such cultural nations
as the Japanese and Chinese. Christianity in Angola, he wrote, must be imposed by force, although, once the Bantu were converted, they would make
excellent Christians. This was, and for a long time remained, the general view
among Portuguese layment and missionaries alike." Boxer, *Race Relations in
the Portuguese Colonial Empire 1415-1825, op. cit.*, pp. 22-23.

[68] Sebastian, king of Portugal (1557-1578). He was the grandson and successor of John III. His grandmother acted as regent in 1562, then his uncle
Henry (a cardinal and later king) was regent until Sebastian was declared
of age in 1568. He was killed on an expedition into Morocco in 1578.

[69] II, 34, 170A.

[70] "During the sixteenth century, thousands of slaves were obtained on
the coast of the Kingdom of Angola, and Loanda, which was founded in 1578,
and grew to be the largest sea-port of that province, and became the centre
of a very flourishing commerce." J. W. Blake, "The Slave Trade (ii)" from
Africa from Early Times to 1800 (edited by P. J. M. McEwan) (London: Oxford
University Press, 1969), p. 277.

Thus, war was inevitable. "Without a doubt this war is just. Thus the prisoners of war can be justifiably enslaved." [71]

But there are also many others who are traded off as slaves. In fact, Molina gathered the following information "in part from others, but above all from our own Jesuits who are there." [72] In each tribe there are four distinct societal levels: the nobility, called the "*mocatos*"; the "Sons of Miranda," who are free men engaged in agriculture and the trades; the "*quisico*," who are bonded slaves since ancient days and whose function it is to work in the fields; and finally, the "*mobicas*," who are the personal slaves. This fourth group has traditionally been sold on the slave-markets. The Portuguese are also involved in this trade. [73] These actual slaves originate for the most part from various wars. However, many of them find themselves in this position because they or their relatives have somehow erred, in which case the whim of the tyrannical Sobas (chief) plays a large role. [74] "Among other examples, the following one was also reported to me: A chief gave away as a present, in the presence of one of our missionaries, a noble young boy as a slave. When the Jesuit asked what the boy's crime had been he learned that the boy had looked at one of the chief's wives. As a consequence his entire clan had been enslaved as a punishment for insulting the majesty of the chief." [75]

Another example of injustice was the peacock law. The king of Angola had a monopoly on peacocks. If a person removed one feather from a royal peacock, he had all his relatives were dispossessed and either killed or sold into slavery. [76]

It is further reported, Molina continues, that on some of the rivers slaves were brought to the Portuguese ships only at night; further, that many of the blacks sell their wives and children merely to acquire a mirror; [77] that the blacks them-

---

[71] II, 34, 170D. Molina testifies that the war in Angola was just on the part of the Portuguese. There is a long and quite involved description of the lengthy war. Accounts of these same events by modern historians, who have access to many more sources, reinforce the complexity of the issue as can be readily illustrated in Ronald H. Chilcote's history, *Portuguese Africa* (Englewood Cliffs: Prentice Hall, Inc., 1967), pp. 65-68.

[72] II, 34, 170E.

[73] II, 34, 171A-D.

[74] *Ibid.*

[75] *Ibid.*

[76] II, 34, 172E.

[77] For a discussion of the bartering system employed in the slave traffic on the Guinea coast in Molina's time see Walter Rodney, "Portuguese Attempts

selves instigate slave-hunts in order to be able to trade for
European goods; and that there are other similar stories. This
trade is very suspect. [78] Thus, "year by year, whole herds of
slaves" are brought from Africa to Portugal, Brazil, and other
parts of the New World, where they are employed in the sugar
plantations, in the gold and silver mines, and in many other
occupations. [79]

Neither the bishop of São Tomé nor the secular priests
who are there, seem to scruple over this trade, the same situation which prevailed in upper Guinea. [80] Molina minces no
words in his description of these conditions. Joseph Höffner's
opinion is that Molina's description is by and large correct.
"Recent research—based on documents and reports at that
time—corroborate Molina's view." [81]

> He is above all correct in his assertion that at this time
> the Africans themselves, enticed by European goods, to a great
> extent were actively involved in procuring "black ivory." The
> Portuguese crown bought up enormous masses of tinsel and
> junk in order to have the necessary "cash" for the trade in
> human beings. Thus the Fuggers on January 20, 1548 signed
> a contract with the representative of the Portuguese king for
> the following delivery: 6,750 hundred weight of copper rings
> of the type the Africans wear on their arms and legs for trade
> with Elmina, 750 hundred weight for the trade with Guinea,
> 24,000 pots, 1,800 bowls, 4,500 shaving mugs, 10,500 copper
> cooking kettles. [82]

Sofala [83] and Monomotapa [84]

In 1501 the Portuguese established a post on the east coast
of Africa. [85] Strong (*robusta*) slaves of great height (*procerae-*

---

at Monopoly on the Upper Guinea Coast, 1580-1650," *Journal of African History*
VI (1965), pp. 307-322.

Karl Polanyi discusses the commercial devices introduced at a later date
by the Europeans to supplement the barter system. "Sortings and Ounce
Trade in the West African Slave Trade," *Journal of African History* V (1964),
pp. 381-393.

[78] "Quae sane negotiatio valde est suspecta"; II, 34, 173A.

[79] *Ibid.* « quotannis greges manciporum."

[80] II, 34, 173C.

[81] Höffner, *op. cit.*, p. 276.

[82] *Ibid.*

[83] *Manica e Sofala* is the name of a district of modern Moçambique on
the east coast of Africa.

[84] For a discussion of the region see A. da Silva Rego, "Portuguese Contributors Towards the Geographical Knowledge of Africa During the XVIth
and XVIIth Centuries," *Estudos de Ciências Políticas e Sociais*, N°. 58 (Lisboa:

que magnitudinis) called *caferes* were first shipped to India and then to Portugal. [86] In 1569 Francisco Barreto, [87] former governor of India, was sent by King Sebastian on an expedition into the Monomotapa kingdom. A Jesuit, [88] Gonçalo de Silveira, [89] had been killed by some members of the Mohammedan sect. To seek redress for that death [90] and also to search for mineral wealth, [91] Barreto had set out on the expedition with royal instructions which Molina himself saw similar to those given to Paulo Diaz de Novais. [92] The resulting conflict dragged on for some time until exhausted by the effort the troops withdrew to India.

1962), pp. 192-198. For reports of Jesuits from Monomotapa during this period see *Documenta Indica VIII, passim.*

[85] By an interesting coincidence, a Dominican from Évora is one of the chief sources of information upon the Portuguese presence on the African east coast during the last years of the sixteenth century. He was Friar João dos Santos, and his book *Ethiopia Oriental* was printed at the Dominican convent in Évora in 1609. "Santos arrived at Moçambique from Portugal in 1586. He ministered in Sofala, Sena, Tete, Moçambique, and the Querimba islands. He left south-east Africa for India in 1597 and sailed around the coast in 1600 on his return to Portugal. His book was printed in Évora in 1608 and published in 1609." E. Alexson, *The Portuguese in South-East Africa, 1600-1700,* (Witwatersrand, 1960), p. 230.

[86] II, 34, 174A.

[87] Franciso Barreto was the Portuguese governor of India 1555-1558 who died in Monomotapa in 1573 during an African expedition in that year. See Gaspar Correa, *Lendas da India* (4 vols.). (Lisboa: 1860-1922), IV, 651; *Grande Enciclopedia Portuguesa e Brasileira,* IV, 276-277. Luiz de Figueiredo Falção, *Livro en que se contém toda a fazenda e Real Patrimonio dos Reinos de Portugal, India e Ilhas adjacentes e outras particularidades copiado fielmente du manuscripto original* (Lisboa: 1859), p. 162.

[88] Molina mentions that some Jesuits accompanied Barreto. One of those was Francisco de Monclaro, S.J. who wrote several accounts of the expedition. See *Documenta Indica X,* 673-739; IX, 360-370.

[89] Gonçalo da Silveira was a Portuguese Jesuit born in 1521 who was sent to India in 1556 and died as a martyr in Monomotapa in 1561. *Documenta Indica V,* 126-129. See Antonius Franco, S.J., *Imagem da Virtude em o Noviciado da Companhia de Jesus de Coimbra em Portugal. Na qual se contem as vidas e sanctas mortes de muitos homens de grande Virtude, que naquella Sancta caza se criaram.* 2 vols. (Évora: 1719), (II-1-63). Francisco Rodrigues, S.J., *op. cit.* I/I, 316. Bertha Leite, *D. Gonçalo da Silveira.* (Lisboa: 1946). This early Jesuit mentioned by Molina is also discussed in a study by António Alvis de Cruz, S.J., *Contribução dos jesuitas portugueses para a ocupação, pacificação e nacionalização da Zambézia portuguesa, ou a terceira campanha dos jesuitas portugueses para a conquista da Zambézia a Jesus Cristo e a Portugal.* (Lisboa: 1938), pp. 6-7.

[90] "Hanc itaque praecipue ulturus injuriam"; II, 34, 174C.

[91] " Nec sine magna spe obtinendi locupletissimas auri fodinas"; *ibid.*

[92] *cf supra,* II, 34, 169E.

Molina felt the prisoners captured in this just war were legitimately held as slaves. But slaves taken from this area prior to the Barreto expedition or those taken after it or those purchased by the slave traders were subject to the norms laid down in the discussion of Upper Guinea—straight larceny. [93] So much for the African story.

India and Asia

Slaves from many different Asian nations ended up in Portugal. To summarize the moral issue involved one could say: if the slaves are from those areas where the Portuguese have been engaged in a just war, one should not hesitate to accept them as legal slaves. An area singled out for special mention was Calicut. [94] A constant state of warfare had existed between the rulers of Calicut and the Portuguese. "I hear that in 1586 a peace treaty was signed." [95] To be included among the areas where a just war had taken place is the Golden Peninsula (present Malay Peninsula,) the island of Sumatra, [96] and the region around Malacca. [97] The island of Sumatra had once been joined to the Asian continent by an isthmus, but an earthquake (maris irruptione) [98] separated it from the peninsula. The Jesuits called the Sumatrans Dachens and the other peoples Malois. The inhabitants of Java [99] are to be mentioned also. Facial

---

[93] "Latrocinia"; II, 34, 174E.

[94] Calicut is the present port city by the same name in Kerala, India on the Arabian Sea. In 1498 Vasco da Gama made it is his first Indian port of call. The term calico was first applied to Calicut cotton cloth which is still an important manufacture.

[95] II, 34, 175B.

[96] Sumatra, an island of the present Republic of Indonesia in the Indian Ocean south and west of the Malay Peninsula and northwest of Java. The first European to visit Sumatra was Marco Polo in 1292. The Portuguese came in 1509 but were, by the time of Molina's death (1600), driven out by the Dutch, who had gained control.

[97] Malacca, in present Malaysia on the southern tip of the Malay Peninsula, was a rich center of commerce in Molina's day. It is on the Straits of Malacca, one of the world's great arteries of sea-borne commerce linking the Indian Ocean with the South China Sea. In 1511 it had been seized by the Portuguese under Alfonso de Albuquerque. St. Francis Xavier preached there. It fell to the Dutch in 1641.

[98] II, 34, 175B.

[99] Java, an island of the Republic of Indonesia separated by the Sunda Strait from Sumatra. Home of early man (Pithecanthropus erectus was discovered in Java in 1891), the island was claimed by the Portuguese in the sixteenth century until the Dutch arrived in 1596. Sixteen years after Molina's death the Dutch East India Company had established its chief post at Batavia.

features and bodily build indicate that all these peoples are mid-way between the natives of Africa and India. Though some writers have claimed that Sumatra was the Golden Peninsula, others insist that the term should be applied to Ceylon. Cambay [100] and Pegu [101] are cited as sources of the slave trade where no just war had taken place.

Japan

Among the rulers of Japan there have been almost constant civil wars; it is difficult, he says, to judge the merits of each conflict. When Christian rulers were involved in these wars, their participation may be presumed just "because the Jesuits preach among them and hear their confessions and would not permit any injustice be done to others." [102] It is difficult to know, continues Molina dryly, whether the Portuguese merchants bother to discover if the persons they buy are captured in a just war and licitly enslaved. [103]

Chinese

Even greater doubt is cast upon the legitimacy of the Chinese slave trade. Since the provinces of China enjoy perpetual peace there could not be any prisoners of war. Because of their affluence there could be no great want to justify selling their children into slavery. Finally, the Chinese judges are not accustomed to subject persons to slavery in punishment of a crime. Therefore none of the legitimate titles for slave holding discussed in Disputation 33 apply to the Chinese trade. Any Chinese slaves may be presumed to be illicitly acquired by the Portuguese. Those persons holding such slaves are bound to restitution and must give the slaves their freedom. "After I had written the above, I took it to a Jesuit priest who had lived a long time in China and even penetrated into its interior; he approved everything." [104]

---

[100] Cambay is a city northwest of Bombay in India. Once a flourishing commercial center, its harbor has been rendered useless by silting.

[101] A city in present Burma on the Pegu river, a tributary of the Rangoon. From the late XV century, it was the center of one of the three chief states of Burma and in the sixteenth century, it was the capital of the Burmese kingdom.

[102] II, 34, 176A.

[103] *Ibid.*

[104] II, 34, 177A.

The Ethics of the Slave Trade

At the beginning of Disputation 35, Molina examines his conscience. After making as careful an historical investigation as possible, he is convinced that the whole issue of the slave trade is laden with moral uncertainties. In order to carry out his responsibility as a teacher and also to clear his conscience, he has reluctantly (*invitus*) decided to speak out. He would hardly presume to have the last word on these complex questions. Perhaps, he reflects, his investigations would be the source of some stimulation to resolve these issues.

The best solution would be for the King of Portugal to allow the entire matter to be investigated by wise and conscientious men who would recommend a binding course of action as Charles V had done for the New World. In that case Charles V had declared the Indians of America free Spanish subjects. In a similar manner the Portuguese government should be expected to decide clearly and specifically what was permissible in this slave trade and what was forbidden. Only then would the public perturbation about the assumed or actual injustice be calmed.

> I do not doubt at all that if King Philip II, [105] Manuel, Sebastian or Henry ever had these matters presented to them and any injustice in the issue were discovered, they would have at once ordered an investigation. One has to remember that these practices take place a long way from Portugal and were introduced little by little. A successor is not likely to overrule what was begun by a predecessor, especially if it appeared morally justifiable at that time. Only rarely do competent investigators visit these remote areas. Even more rarely do

---

[105] A fascinating recent study of Philip II might help to throw some light on the moral attitude of this unusual ruler. See Leon E. Halkin's, "The Moral Physiognomy of Philip II" in John C. Rule and John J. Tepaske (editors), *The Character of Philip II: The Problem of Moral Judgments in History* (Boston: D. C. Heath and Company, 1963). Halkin does not mention specifically the African slave trade but gives evidence that King Philip II was scrupulous in moral matters.

[106] Historians have long noted Philip II's attention to the details of his administration. Garrett Mattingly writes: "There was true asceticism in the way he toiled, eyes red-rimmed, bones aching, fingers stiff, at his self-imposed task of Chief Clerk of the Spanish empire. Increasingly as he grew older, he gave up for it not only the hunting, dancing, and feasting which were the conventional diversions of kings, but the things he really loved, flowers and pictures, country excursions and the company of his children." Rule and TePaske, *op. cit.*, p. xviii. Philip was the monarch of both Spain and Portugal when Molina wrote his evaluation. Philip died in 1598, two years before Molina.

you find those persons who are able or who dare to discuss these matters with the highest officials. It should come as no surprise, then, to learn that these matters have not come to the attention of the king who is busy with so many other matters.[106] He probably hasn't ever been consulted about them up to this very moment.[107]

Only at this point does Molina feel justified in making the following observations:

First Conclusion

In those areas where the Portuguese, as described above, are engaged in a just war, the dealers may buy up the slaves offered them without further investigation. As long as there are no unusual circumstances, it may be assumed that the slaves under consideration are prisoners of war. After all, he concludes, the trade in Moorish and Turkish slaves is carried on in a similar way.[108]

Second Conclusion

Anyone enslaved by a court of Africans because of a crime, may be bought up and led away by the Portuguese. This does not extend to the innocent children and relatives of the criminal, however, unless the father was involved in so serious a crime that, for the welfare of the state and as a deterrent to others, wise judgment demands the extension of enslavement to the children as punishment also. This is, however, in all eventuality, unlikely, so that the general rule may be construed that *per se*, a son may never be bought who has been enslaved only because of his father's crime. In those countries the following crimes might be considered punishable by enslavement: all those transgressions which are punished by sentencing to the galleys in the West, for adultery, for serious thefts, and similar crimes. Thefts of a minor order may on occasion be punished by enslavement if the common good demands it. For it has been observed that the African slaves in Europe are most thievish, but in Africa, because of the severe punishment, thievery is supposedly rare. One should not maintain lightly that the enslavement of the people in those regions on account of minor theft is just, nor should one condemn such a practice pre-

---

[107] II, 35, 178B-C.
[108] II, 35, 179B.

maturely. For it could be, the Africans are discouraged from greater personal crimes only by the unequivocal punishment of even the smallest thievery.

Third Conclusion

Portuguese dealers may, when there is danger of starvation, acquire the starving Africans and their children in return for foodstuffs, if the parents agree to the enslavement of themselves and their children without duress. [109] In case the Africans are able and willing to pay for the food, it is not permitted to claim that the food is available only in return for the enslavement. That would be sinful.

New problems appear when one inquires about the price of a slave. The Portuguese in India sometimes acquire a slave for four to six *reales* [110] and in Guinea for a mirror no better than one owned by a poor woman in Portugal, or for half a cubit of blue, green or red cloth or for trinkets made of glass and copper which have limited value here at home. Presumably, the slaves are bought dirt cheap [111] since the slave traders make enormous profits despite the high tariff paid to the crown, despite the costs of transport and despite the mass deaths enroute.

Molina was too shrewd to become trapped into a discussion of the economic worth of a man. "One must not concern himself with the question what is the worth of a man as man nor that he has been bought with the blood of Christ. [112] Re-

---

[109] "Enslavement in South-east Africa, it should be mentioned, arose from selling by the parents of their children in times of need, i.e., famine, or another emergency; from kidnapping; from capture by chiefs for crimes; and from capture in war." E. Axelson, "South-east Africa in the Early Seventeenth Century" in *Africa from Early Times to 1800*, p. 230.

[110] "Interdum pretio quatuor aut sex regalium argenti" (II, 35, 182D). The question of currency equivalents is tricky. Molina refers in Latin to silver *regales* or in Spanish *reales*. John H. Elliot in his *Imperial Spain 1469-1716* (New York: St. Martin's Press, 1964) attempts to specify: "In 1534 a new gold coin of less fineness, the *escudo*, was introduced, and gradually replaced the ducat, although this continued to be used in reckoning. Where the ducat was worth 11 reales [sic] and 1 *maravedí*, or 10 silver *reales*. It was raised to 400 *maravedís* in 1566, and to 440 in 1609," p. 114.

In another part of his study Elliot cites a tax collector in the 1620's who calculated that a poor man would spend 30 *maravedís* a day. (p. 280.) In light of the above, Molina's report of four to six *reales* for one slave in India, would be the equivalent of what a poor man in Spain, shortly after Molina's death, would spend in one week.

[111] "vilissimo pretio," II, 35, 182E.

[112] II, 35, 183B.

member that the question is the legitimate buying of a person who is in grave need. The just price (*commoditas*) is a matter of economics." [113]

In all probability, relatively few of the slaves from Africa were acquired by one of the first three methods, discussed by Molina. The vast number came as a result of predatory raids on Africans by Africans, and those captured were sold to the Portuguese.

Fourth Conclusion

This brings Molina to the fourth conclusion which, buried deep in the Disputation, seems to have been overlooked by most of his critics. Because of its importance, a large portion of it will be directly translated here:

> There are some who would like to assuage the consciences of the traders who are engaged in the slave trade in upper and lower Guinea and the Southeast coast of Africa by claiming that this trade is just and licit. In my opinion it is more likely that this business of purchasing slaves in those regions and transporting them from there is unjust and wicked and all who engage in it sin mortally and are in a state of eternal damnation, except for an individual whom invincible ignorance excuses. I would make bold to maintain that not one of them is in this condition. Further the king and all who share in the royal authority and the bishops of Cape Verde and of St. Thomas' Island and whose who hear the confessions of all these persons, each according to his rank and position, is obliged to take steps that matter be examined and that it be determined what is permitted and that acts of injustice for the future be effectively prevented unless something in the context is known to them which escapes me, or other principles of which I am ignorant enlighten them. I am of the opinion that it is a mortal sin not merely against charity but also against justice with the obligation of restitution, to purchase items about which there is or rightly ought to be a likely presumption that they have obtained under an unjust title. About such a presumption, blinding avarice pays no attention. The sin is not the sellers'. Consequently if anyone purchases items about which there ought to be a likely presumption that they have been acquired by theft, and if with a view towards permanent possession anyone makes the purchase without a previous examination by which it would be clearly established that the items were not obtained by theft,

---

[113] *Ibid.*

such a person sins mortally, and from the start he is not
an owner in good faith, but is bound later to make proper
efforts to determine whether the purchased item belongs to
another person, and if this is established, he is obliged to
restore it completely. If he is unable to arrive at certainty
in this matter, in proportion to the doubt that remains about
the ownership he is obliged to restore a greater or lesser
portion of its value in proportion to the amount of his doubt.
On the basis of what was said in the preceding disputation
and in view of the present explanation, when anyone buys
slaves of the type under discussion from infidels, with good
reason he should be convinced that generally speaking these
slaves have been reduced to slavery without a just title. Consequently by buying slaves without investigating the title under
which they were reduced to slavery and without any reason
for rejecting the presumption which is or ought to be against
it, the purchaser sins mortally, and further he is under obligation as often as an opportunity arises to seek out the truth.
If there is no such opportunity, as will normally be the case,
he is under obligation to make restitution to the slave in
violation of whose liberty the sale was made, in proportion
to the presumption that remains. This restitution is not for
the portion of the slave's value but for the portion of the
slave because his freedom was a matter of importance to
him, a far greater matter than the advantage which others
derive from his slavery and greater than the value of a slave
in comparison with other things. I have stated that the purchaser must restore the portion of the slave because his freedom was a matter of importance to him, since that is the
loss the purchaser caused the slave, and this is what must
be restored and not precisely the slave's value so that he
may be a slave to someone else. [114]

The wars among the Africans, Molina continues, are presumed to be unjust. As a result, those persons who are acquired
in this manner he considers to be *kidnapped* rather than
prisoners of war. "And I learned these things from the traders
themselves." [115]

Molina in one of his rare lapses from objectivity, employing the rhetorical device of preterition, movingly closes the
fourth conclusion:

I pass over in silence the cruelty to which the slaves are
subjected when they are being transported from the interior
to the coastline... I pass over in silence the cruelty to which

[114] II, 35, 187E-188C.
[115] II, 35, 190B.

they are subjected while on a ship, how crowded they are in order that more money can be made, how many die in route as in a prison. I pass over in silence the sexual abuses which the *Tangos-maos* commit on the women they transport. I say nothing of the sexual abuses of the slaves among themselves, men and women lying intermixed aboard the ship... All these things are the weighty responsibility of those en-engaged in the trade. It may well be a punishment for all the horrors that very few or hardly any of these slave traders, as I have heard from the buyers themselves, ever achieve lasting wealth. God grant that—as some predict—even greater misfortune does not strike due to this trade which has been carried on for so long in the dark. [116]

Fifth Conclusion

Even though the slave trade has one positive result, the conversion of African to Christianity, it would be still far better if zealous missionaries were to go to these regions and spread Christianity while slavery would be forbidden totally. "If we seek the kingdom of God and are satisfied with legitimate forms of trade, God who is the generous rewarder of good works would with ease unlock the riches in gold and silver mines in these regions and would equalize the profit which is now created by the slave trade and protect all our undertakings there." [117]

On this positive note, Molina concludes his 35th Disputation.

Molina's Critics

It is time now to consider the criticisms brought against Molina's teaching by the persons mentioned earlier in this chapter.

David B. Davis wrote:

Molina at times criticized the cruelty and violence practiced against the slave trade, but the Abbé Grégoire was quite incorrect in classifying him as an opponent of the slave trade. [118] Despite the reputation given him by Grégoire and others, Molina believed that in a just war even the innocent members of an enemy population might legitimately be enslaved as a way of punishing the entire state. Their children

---

[116] II, 35, 190E-191A.
[117] II, 35, 191E.
[118] Davis is citing Saco, *Historia de la esclavitud*, V, 44, as his source.

might also be enslaved in order to punish the parents, according to Johann Kleinhappl, *Der Staat bei Ludwig Molina* (Innsbruck, 1935), pp. 145-146. [119]

Davis' contention should be analyzed in parts. He says that Grégoire was quite incorrect in classifying Molina as an opponent of the slave trade. In light of the exposition of Disputation 34 earlier in this chapter, it seems evident that Molina opposed the slave trade and was a highly articulate critic of it. In fairness to Davis, it should be noted that he appears to be relying on others for his opinion of Molina. Had he read Disputation 34 himself, he would likely have come to a different conclusion.

Regarding the charge that Molina believes that in a just war even the innocent members of an enemy population might be enslaved, the statement is accurate. Molina so states in Disputation 33 and elsewhere. [120] The reason he gives is the following: The enemy in a just war suffers the results of losing—among which is the loss of personal liberty. Molina says this is the common experience. It appears to be the teaching in common with Grotius, who was writing some twenty-five years after Molina's death.

> But in the law of nations, which we are now discussing, slavery has a somewhat larger place, both as regards persons and as regards effects. For if we consider persons, not only those who surrender themselves, or promise to become slaves, are regarded as slaves, *but all without exception who have been captured in a formal public war become slaves from the time when they are brought within the lines,* as Pomponius says. *And no crime is requisite,* but the fate of all is the same, even of those who by their ill fortune, as we have said, are caught in the enemy's territory when the war has suddenly broken out. [121] [Emphasis added.]

While at first, Molina's and Grotius' opinions might seem to be harsh, their point of view, at least in practice, seems to be accepted even to this day. Though few students of international relations might characterize it as enslavement, certainly the occupation of Japan by the armed forces of the Allies under the command of Douglas MacArthur in 1945, did in effect, place all the citizens of Japan (and the same was true

---

[119] Davis, *op. cit.,* p. 108.
[120] II, 33, 158B; II, 120, 471A.
[121] Grotius, *De Jure Belli ac Pacis,* p. 690. (Emphasis added).

in Germany), innocent and guilty, combatants and non-combatants, under the subjugation of the armed forces of the victorious countries and the subjection lasted several years. Individuals were not sold into slavery by the victors but were, in effect, treated as subjects captured in a just war.

The third part of Davis' objection to Molina's teaching is the point that the children of those captured in a just war may be enslaved in order to punish their parents. Molina so states in the Treatise on War. [122] He also states that this practice is customary. [123] In conclusion, Molina says that Vitoria agrees with this opinion.

Regarding the issue of punishing the parents by enslaving the children, Molina and the others were speaking within the confines of the principles which they had outlined, i.e., in a *just* war, prisoners and even their children could be enslaved. This was the opinion not only of Molina but also of Grotius and of Vitoria and, as Molina noted, was customary, It is a far cry from Molina and others attempting to justify the slave trade which Davis implies by his citation.

Another criticism of Molina was that he was cited by the Spanish Council of the Indies in defense of the African slave trade. That the Spanish Council of the Indies cited Molina is correct:

> Tambien ay quien hace distincion de los mercaderes que ban á comprar, al tercero que compra despues de conducidos con buena fe u de segunda mano, dando por licita la retencion del Esclavo en este caso, como es el Padre Thomas Sanchez y el Padre Molina en la disputazion treinta y seis, numero primero, y en el numero tres y quatro. [124]

Fortunately, the references of the Spanish Council of the Indies to Molina are precise: "Disputation 36, numbers one, three and four." Disputation 36 follows immediately on those which have just been reviewed in the present chapter and is entitled: "May those in this country [Portugal and Spain] and elsewhere who are in possession of slaves discussed in the Fourth Conclusion of the preceding disputation, licitly retain them? May they be purchased?" [125]

---

[122] II, 120, 471C.

[123] "Ut testatur receptissima consuetudo," *ibid.*

[124] Georges Scelle, *La Traite Négrière aux Indes de Castille*, 2 vols. (Paris: Librairie de la Société du Recueil J. B. Sherry & Du Journal du Palais, 1906), Vol. I, p. 838.

[125] "Utrum qui in hoc regno, et aliis possident mancipia, de quibus con-

In the Fourth Conclusion of Disputation 35, Molina stated his opinion that the buying and transporting of slaves from the Guinea regions were unjust and wicked and that those who engaged in it sin mortally and were in a state of eternal damnation. What is to be done, he now asks, by those persons who had come into possession of such slaves and have just now learned that the original enslavement was likely illicit?

Throughout his reply, Molina speaks of the "possessor in good faith." [126]   The term, classical in moral theology, deserves some explanation.   The authors, cited earlier, of a twentieth century text on moral theology define a possessor in good faith in this way:

> There are three kinds of unlawful possessors:
>
> (a) the possessor *in good faith*, who is one that has been invincibly ignorant of the unlawfulness of his possession, but now learns his error, e.g., a buyer who discovers that the horse he purchased did not belong to the seller but was stolen property;
>
> (b) the possessor *in doubtful faith*, who is one that has serious reasons for fearing his possession is unlawful, e.g., the buyer of a horse learns that the seller is known to have sold some stolen property, or that the price charged for the horse was remarkably small;
>
> (c) the possessor *in bad faith*, who is one that knows his possession is unjust, e.g., a buyer who purchases a horse he knew had been stolen by the seller. [127]

It is to be noted that the possessor in good faith is an *unlawful* possessor. It is to be noted also that Molina is careful to specify that he is not speaking about the slave traders (about whose activities he has no doubt—they are morally wrong) but about the purchase of a slave from a third party who has come into the possession of these slaves. [128]   With these notations, how does Molina answer the question he posed?

---

clusione quarta praecedentis disputationis dictum est, licite illa retineant, & an licite emi possint," II, 36, 192E.

[126] *"bonae fidei possessor,"* II, 36, 194B.

[127] McHugh and Callan, *op. cit.,* II, p. 76.

[128] "Quare in hac disputatione sermo non erit de mercatoribus, qui ex illis locis ea asportant, sed de reliquis possessoribus, ad quos inde derivantur," II, 36, 192E-193A.

First Conclusion

The possessor in good faith. Whoever in good faith has acquired slaves, may licitly continue to retain these slaves. Even if he begins to doubt that the person is being held licitly, he may still retain him until he is fully certain the person was not acquired by a legitimate title, which happens rarely.[129] If he has any way of finding out the truth of the matter, he is bound to make the inquiry.

Second Conclusion

If the possessor in good faith is certain the slave in his possession is being held illicitly, he is required to emancipate him immediately, no matter what price had been paid.

Third Conclusion

When one suspects that slaves, transported from Africa and purchased from a possessor in good faith, are unjustly held, he may go ahead and purchase the slaves, but he is held to make a diligent inquiry to determine if the slaves bought were licitly reduced to bondage. If nothing can be discovered in this matter (which is the common experience) or, if nothing can be established for certain, he may continue to retain the slaves.

Fourth Conclusion

Those who buy slaves from the African traders and either did not have any reason for doubting the legitimacy of the titles or have come into possession from a possessor in good faith, may continue possession until it has been established with certainty that the slaves were originally acquired unjustly: *Melior est conditio possidentis.*

Fifth Conclusion

Whoever begins to doubt, for reasons noted in these disputations or for any other reason, that the slaves he is holding were acquired in good faith, is bound to make restitution to the slave, in greater or lesser degree, according to the degree of uncertainty.

---

[129] "Quod tamen raro continget", II, 36, 193A.

One final word about Molina and his critics. The Council
of the Indies' citation of Molina was highly selective. An ob-
jective reading would confirm that in Disputation 36 Molina
was addressing the specific problem of a possessor in good
faith and that he was not justifying the entire slave trade.
Further in the same Disputation, the Council authors con-
veniently omit all references to the Second and Fifth Conclusion
in the same disputation which would not support their point
of view.

From the above exposition and especially from the context
of the whole treatise (Disputations 32-36), it would appear
obvious that Molina's approach to the question of the morality
of the slave trade was first of all to review facts carefully as
far as he could know them, next to outline the norms according
to which slaves could legitimately be acquired and then to give
his judgment, climaxing in a blistering denunciation of the
illegal slave trade in the Fourth Conclusion of Disputation 35.

* * *

Pablo Neruda, the Chilean poet who received the 1971 Nobel
Prize, has written with moving intensity about many human
conditions. In the *Canto general* of *Alturas de Macchu Picchu*
he spoke of the slaves who built the beautifully constructed
stone city of the Andes. Molina could make his own the words
with which Neruda closes his poem:

> Tell me everything, chain by chain,
> link by link, step by step,
> sharpen the knives you kept with you,
> drive them into my breast and my hands
> like riving bolts of light,
> like a springing of jaguars under ground,
> and let me weep, hours, days, years,
> blind ages, stellar centuries.
> Give me silence, water, hope.
> Give me struggle, iron, volcanoes.
> Fasten your bodies like magnets to me.
> Come into my veins and my mouth.
> Speak through my words and my blood. [130]

---

[130] Quoted in *The New Republic*, December 25, 1971.

CHAPTER IX

THE PHILOSOPHY OF LAW

J. Frank Dobie once remarked that the average doctoral thesis is nothing but the transference of bones from one grave-yard to another.[1]   In no part of this study does Dr. Dobie's figure of speech have more relevance that in this chapter on Molina's philosophy of law.   Recent writers seem to conspire in employing funereal figures when discussing the history of the natural law.   John Courtney Murray remarks that fifty years ago it would have been highly improbable that anyone would have been invited to discuss the subject:

> If someone perchance had been assigned this subject, his discourse would doubtless have had the tone of a funeral oration, spoken without tears. At about the turn of the century it was generally believed in professional circles that the Scholastic idea of natural law, as an operative concept in the fields of ethics, political theory, and law and jurisprudence, was dead.... This was by no means the case.... The ancient idea of natural law is as inherently perennial as the *philosophia perennis* of which it is an integral part. And its reappearance after its widely attended funeral is one of the interesting intellectual phenomena of our generation.[2]

Etienne Gilson says that the natural law always buries its undertakers[3] and Judge Robert Wilkin concludes that we are witnessing the obsequies of the natural-law morticians of our day.[4]

---

[1] J. Frank Dobie, *A Texan in England* (Boston: Little, Brown and Co., 1945), p. 26.

[2] John Courtney Murray, S.J., "The Natural Law" in *Great Expressions of Human Rights* ("Religion and Civilization Series," ed. R. M. MacIver for the Institute of Religious and Social Studies of the Jewish Theological Seminary of America; New York: Harper & Bros., 1950), p. 69.

[3] Etienne Gilson, *The Unity of Philosophical Experience* (New York: C. Scribner's Sons, 1937), p. 306.

[4] Robert N. Wilkin, "Status of Natural Law in American Jurisprudence" in *University of Notre Dame Natural Law Institute Proceedings*, II (Notre Dame, Inc.: College of Law, University of Notre Dame, 1949), p. 125.

This phoenix cycle of the natural law is an interesting study in itself.   Heinrich Rommen has described the philosophy of natural law's rise in the sixteenth century from the ashes of Occamism.

> The great line of Natural Law philosophers [of the Renaissance] begins with Vittoria, who introduced the *Summa Theologica* instead of the Sentences of Peter Lombard as the basis of teaching—a practice which became general when St. Ignatius ordained that the professors of his order make the *Summa* the basis of their studies and courses and reaches to St. Robert Bellarmine.   Though originating in the Iberian Peninsula, and in its world famous universities, such as Salamanca the Great, and Coimbra the Glorious, attended by students from all nations, this second flowering of Scholasticism, spread through the whole Christian civilization, as is proven when one considers the publication places of the works of Suarez, Soto, Lessius, Bellarmine and Molina and their use as texts in the leading universities of France, Italy and Germany. [5]

The Occamism against which the scholastic writers of the sixteenth century reacted was derived from the teachings of an English Franciscan, William of Occam, who died two centuries before Molina's birth.   Occam held that God is primarily absolute and omnipotent Will and that the natures and essences of things are not recognizable by man's intellect and, consequently, that the natural order of being, which belongs to practical reason, advising us what ought to be done or omitted, is not knowable to us.   In God, so Occam says, there can be no necessity; the decree of God, the *Lex Aeterna* and the *Lex Naturalis,* do not issue necessarily from the Essence of Him who promulgated them.   All the precepts of the Eternal Law and the Natural Law are only absolutely arbitrary decrees of God's omnipotent Will.   No Law is immutable.   God could without inner contradiction ordain that the creatures hate Him and that this hatred should be meritorious.   For Occam the natural

---

[5] Rommen, "Renaissance Period," *op. cit.*, p. 91. Another work by the same author, *The Natural Law*: A Study in Legal and Social History and Philosophy (St. Louis: B. Herder Book Co., 1947), is an indispensable guide to the history and content of the natural law tradition from the Greek period to the present. In this chapter the summary of Occamism and the natural law in the sixteenth century is based in part on these two works.

For a study of the relation of St. Thomas' teaching to the early Jesuits, see V. Beltrán de Heredia, O.P., "La enseñanza de Sto. Tomás en la Compañía de Jesús durante el primer siglo de su existencia," *Ciencia Tomista*, XI (1915), 388-408; XII (1916), 34-48.

moral law is positive law, divine will. Law is pure will without any foundations in reality, without foundations in the essential nature of things. Occam held that the precepts of the
Decalogue could all be reversed, if God so willed. Molina summarizes and refutes Occam's teaching. [6] His refutation begins
with the scathing sentence: "Adversus hanc vero adeo absur-
dam sententiam sic primo argumentor." [7]

Occamism had wrought havoc in theology as well as in
metaphysics and ethics. The Reformers of the early decades
of the sixteenth century had drawn the ultimate conclusions
from Occamism with respect to theology. Contemptuous of
reason, they had arrived at a voluntarism in theology as well
as at doctrine of *natura corrupta*, nature corrupted by original
sin. Traditional natural law became speculatively impossible. [8]
Yet, as Rommen points out, it would be foolish to deny that
the Reformers explicitly rejected the natural law; they did that
as little as the Occamists. They followed the tradition, cited
the natural law, used the term, and slowly—if at all—became
aware that between the natural law and their theology there
existed an irreconcilable contradition. [9]

Such was the condition of the natural-law tradition in the
middle of the sixteenth century. The task of the scholastic
writers of the period was, as Petavius points out, to work out
further, to develop fully and completely, what the thinkers of
the earlier age of scholasticism had taught implicitly in their
outline. In their theology and psychology these scholastic
thinkers restored to honor the teaching of St. Thomas on the
divine essence as the source of the entire moral order and,
with it, the primacy of the intellect over the will. For them,
the natural law was founded in essence and reason, not in
mere absolute will. For the later scholastics law belonged more
to the reason than to the will. The natural moral law is a
judgment of reason which presents actions as commanded or

---

[6] "De hac itaque re prima opinio est Ocami in 2. dist. 19. asserentis, non
solum praecepta omnia decalogi dispensari a Deo posse, sed etiam Deum praecipere posse contraria eis omnibus praeceptis. Ut posse praecipere odium sui
ipsiusmet Dei, quo dato, inquit, laudabile esset prosequi odium Deum. Hanc
vero suam sententiam non aliter probat, quam ex illo sequenti in ore illius
ad similia principio: quod non implicat contradictionem, Deus efficere potest:
nulla vero in hoc cernitur contradictionis implicatio" (V, 57, 3146).

[7] *Ibid.*

[8] See Franz X. Arnold, *Zur Frage des Naturrechts bei Martin Luther*: Ein
Beitrag zum Problem der natürlichen Theologie auf reformatorischer Grundlage (München: Hueber, 1937).

[9] Rommen, "Renaissance Period," *op. cit.*, pp. 96-97.

forbidden by the Author of reason, because the light of reason shows them to be in agreement or disagreement with man's essential nature; and at the same time, reason judges, God wills that which accords with nature. In its essence and intellectual content the natural law is absolutely dependent upon the divine intellect; in its real existence, it is dependent upon the divine will.

In this chapter no attempt will be made to present a comprehensive view of Molina's teaching on law. As the titles indicate, all of Molina's five mammoth volumes concern themselves with law and justice. For the most part, his treatment of the philosophy of law is confined to the first few disputations of the First Tract and the twenty-seven disputations at the end of the Fifth Tract. The latter section alone extends through two hundred and forty-three columns in folio. [10] The first disputation in this section lengthens into forty columns. Even a summary of Molina's teaching on law would be an enormous task; it would be much more than a volume in itself. Therefore, in this chapter, the study will be confined to those aspects of his treatise on law which more closely pertain to his political thought, [11] i.e., (1) definition of law and its divisions, (2) natural law and the *jus gentium*, and (3) positive civil law in relation to some economic political problems: taxation, price, fixing, and monopolies.

Definition of Law

> It is a command or precept of the legislative authority in a perfect society permanently promulgated; not for one or another member, but for all, either without qualification, or for all those for whom, by reason of their status, place, time and other circumstances, its observance is intended; and accepted by them when, to have any effect, it needs their consent. [12]

---

[10] The American Library Association considers a book more than 30 cm. in height to be a folio. Molina's volumes measure about 35 cm.

See Elizabeth H. Thompson, *A. L. A. Glossary of Library Terms with a Selection of Terms in Related Fields:* Prepared under the Direction of the Committee on Library Terminology of the American Library Association (4th rinting; Chicago: American Library Association, 1956), p. 65.

[11] "Eine Frage von zentraler Bedeutung, die gelöst werden muss, bevor an die eigentliche Darstellung de Staatslehre herangegangen werden kann, ist die nach dem Verhàltnis von Staat und Recht" (Rommen, *Franz Suarez*, p. 43).

[12] "Est imperium seu praeceptio a suprema ad id potestate in republica permanenter lata ac promulgata, non uni aut alteri, sed omnibus, aut sim-

The above definition applies to human law but Molina adds that, properly understood, it would apply to all law.[13] Law is primarily an act of the intellect and Molina expressly states that he understands the terms in the same sense which St. Thomas does in his definition of law.[14] When Molina's definition is applied to the eternal law, the term *command* is taken in the wide sense by way of metaphor.[15] *Commonwealth* in the same definition, when applied to the eternal law is to be understood of the whole universe, embracing all creatures.[16] *Promulgation* when applied to the eternal law is to be understood in the sense of the production of creatures endowed by God with faculties to attain their ends.[17]

St. Thomas' definition is: "Est rationis ordinatio ad bonum commune ab eo, qui curam communitatis habet, promulgata." Both Navarrus and Soto accept this but the latter adds the term *praeceptio*, which addition Molina includes in his own definition.[18] The act of the intellect—ordination and precept— supposes a previous act of the will.[19] It was Soto who sub-

---

pliciter, aut ad quos id pro eorum conditione, loco, tempore, ac aliis circumstantiis servare spectat, et acceptata, quando, ut vim habeat, acceptatione indiget" (V, 46, 3055).

[13] "Definitio autem legis a nobis tradita, si verba in ea proprie intelligantur, solum convenit legi omni proprie sumptae, ut comprehendit omnem talem legem, sive divinam sive humanam: non vero convenit legi minus proprie sumptae et per similitudinem ad veram ac propriam legem" (V. 46, 3056-3057).

[14] "Nomine vero ordinationis intellectus, idem, quod imperium seu praeceptionem, divus Thomas in sua definitione intellexit, ut Sotus recte exposuit" (V, 46, 3056).

[15] "Quod si ad illam extendenda sit defensio [definitio?], nempe ad legem Dei aeternam comparatione creaturarum libero arbitrio non praeditarum, tunc, imperium in ea definitione sumendum est late, ut ad imperium per similitudinem ac metaphoram, quo Deus ejusmodi rebus imperare dicitur, se se extendit" (V, 46, 3057).

[16] "Nomine item reipublicae in ea definitione intelligi etiam debet hoc totum universum quoad creaturas omnes, quibus constat" (*ibid.*).

[17] "Et nomine promulgationis intelligi etiam debet productio creaturarum et collatio actualis virium illis ad suos fines a Deo datarum, et reliqua ejus definitionis admodum improprie ad eam legem ac creaturas libero arbitrio non praeditas erunt extendenda" (*ibid.*).

[18] "*Divus Th. 1. 2. q. 90. art. 4.* in fine corporis ejus articuli hanc tradit definitionem legis in genere: *Est rationis ordinatio ad bonum commune ab eo, qui curam communitatis habet, promulgata.* Eam amplectuntur *Navarrus ubi supra a. num. 8. Sotus. 1. de just. q. 1. art. 1.* et plerique alii. Sotus vero magis eam definitionem explicando, particulae, *rationis ordinatio,* addit, *et praeceptio*: in quo a Navarro dissidet, et a ratione legis consilia excludit, quae Navarrus in ea divi Thomae definitione comprehendi autumat" (V, 46, 3054).

[19] "Ordinatio autem et praeceptio intellectus, praevium actum voluntatis ad intellectu [sic] ordinandum ac praecipiendum supponit ac includit" (*ibid.*).

stituted *respublica* for *communitas* to remove any doubt that St. Thomas had meant a perfect society and not just any community. Statutes and other legislative acts of communities less than a perfect commonwealth are not to be considered laws in the strict sense. [20]

Schumpeter makes a long leap from St. Thomas to Molina but lands deftly in the center of Molina's natural-law teaching:

> Molina clearly identified natural law, on the one hand, with the dictates of reason (*recta ratio*), and with what is socially expedient or necessary (*expediens et necessarium*), on the other. These propositions, in themselves, are nothing but Thomism formulated more pointedly. But he took a further step (*tract.* 1 *disp.* 4): after repeating the Aristotelian definition he added, apparently by way of explaining its meaning: "that is to say," the naturally just is that which obligates us by virtue of the nature of the case (*cujus obligatio oritur ex natura rei*). But this is not at all what Aristotle meant. Molina does not interpret his meaning but adds a new one: He definitely married natural law to our rational diagnosis, with reference to the Common Good, of the cases—whether individual contracts or social institutions—which we observe in research and practice. Molina's view about the "nature of the natural law" is mentioned only as an example of what was the general opinion of the doctors in his and even earlier time. De Soto's concept of the Command of Reason (*rationis ordinatio*) amounts to the same thing. [21]

Following the definition of law, a consideration of its divisions is in order. Molina begins by stating that he will consider the term *jus* in a wider sense than did St. Thomas in the *Summa*. *Jus* stands not only for the object of law but

---

[20] "Loco autem ejus partis definitionis divi Thomae: *ab eo, qui curam communitatis habet* apponit Sotus, ab eo, qui curam reipublicae gerit, quasi nomine communitatis intelligit divus Thomas non quamcumque communitatem, sed rempublicam integram. Ea statuta enim et constitutiones lata a curam gerentibus earum communitatum, quae respublicae integrae non sunt, sed partes duntaxat integrae reipublicae, non dicuntur leges, nisi admodum late ac inusitate sumpto vocabulo, sed constitutiones ac statuta vocantur, ut supra explanatum fuit" (*ibid.*).

For Soto's philosophy of law, see Venancio Carro, O.P., *Domingo de Soto y su doctrina jurídica* and *Domingo de Soto y el derecho de gentes*.

See also, by Vincente Beltrán de Heredia, O.P.: "El maestro Domingo (Francisco) de Soto en la Universidad de Alcalá," *Ciencia Tomista*, XLIII (1931), 357-373; XLIV (1931), 28-52; and "El maestro Domingo de Soto, catedrático de vísperas en la Universidad de Salamanca (1532-1549)," *ibid.*, LVII (1938), 38-67 and 281-302.

[21] Schumpeter, *op. cit.*, pp. 109-110.

for law itself.   After explaining the various divisions of *jus*, Molina sets down that division which he prefers. [22]

First of all, law is divided into natural and positive. Positive law is subdivided into divine and human; human law is of three kinds: law of nations, civil law, and canon law. [23] Natural law is defined as that which everywhere has the same force, whose obligation arises from the nature of that which is commanded, which obligation is known by the light of reason. [24] The obligation of positive law arises from the command and will of the legislator. [25]   The acts prohibited by the natural law are prohibited because they are evil; they are not evil because they are prohibited; acts of positive law are not prohibited because they are *in se* evil. [26]   The rule of thumb which Molina furnishes to determine whether something pertains to natural or positive law is this: if the obligation arises from the nature of the thing commanded, then it belongs to the natural law; if the obligation does not arise from the nature of the thing but from the precept and will of the legislator, it pertains to positive law. [27]

[22] "Licet D. Tho. 2. 2. q. 57. art. 2. et 3. solum videatur locutus de divisione juris, quod objectum est justitiae particularis, quae virtus est cardinalis, dividendum tamen nobis est jus latius sumptum, ut objectum est cujuscunque legis, aut moris, qui vim legis habeat: cujusmodi sunt, rerum divisio, immunitas legatorum, et pleraque alia, quae consuetudine perscripta sunt de jure gentium, aut civili: eaedem quippe divisiones sunt juris utroque modo sumpti. Imo cum disputatione praecedente ostensum sit, jus non solum dici de objecto legis, sed etiam de lege ipsa: et quam late lex patet, tam late pateat ipsius objectum; sane eodem modo dividi potest jus sumptum pro lege, et sumptum pro legis objecto" (I, 3, 9).

[23] "Secundo, dividendo jus in naturale, et positivum.   Deinde positivum in divinum, et humanum.   Rursus humanum, in jus gentium, civile et canonicum" (*ibid*.).

[24] "Jus naturale definitur ab Aristotele esse illud quod ubique eandem vim habet ... cujus obligatio oritur ex natura rei de qua est praeceptum, et non ex arbitrio praecipientis: et quia res eandem naturam retinet apud omnes" (I, 4, 10).

[25] "E contario vero obligatio juris positivi oritur a praecepto et voluntate praecipientis, indeque derivatur in objectum" (*ibid*.).

[26] "Quo loco accipe egregium hoc discrimen inter jus naturale, et positivum.   Quod obligatio juris naturalis oritur a natura objecti, indeque se diffundit in praeceptum.   Ea vero de causa dici consuevit, ea, quae sunt juris naturalis, prohibita esse, quia mala, et non ideo mala esse qui prohibita. ... Atque idcirco de iis, quae juris sunt positivi, dici consuevit, ea esse mala, quia prohibita, et non ideo prohibita, quia in se mala" (*ibid*.).

[27] "Regula ergo generalis ad dignoscendum, num aliquid ad jus naturale, an ad positivum pertineat, haec est.   Si obligatio oritur a natura rei, quae praecipitur aut prohibetur, quia videlicet in se est necessaria ut fiat, ut est subvenire extreme indigenti, vel quia in se est illicita et mala, ut furari, adulterari, mentiri, tunc praeceptio aut prohibitio pertinet ad jus naturale: si vero obligatio non oritur a natura rei quae praecipitur aut prohibetur, sed a prae-

Certain acts are so clearly contrary to nature that they are seen to be in themselves evil and illicit—e.g., stealing, adultery, lying. But, Molina warns, in other matters nature is not such a clear teacher. It is possible in these areas to make mistakes in deducing conclusions from the natural law.

Besides the acts commanded or prohibited by the natural law, there is the whole institutional framework of society. Marriage, the family, and political society flow from the natural law. [28] Positive law comprises all the precepts derived from using the legislative power given by God. [29] The law of nations is positive human law which all or almost all nations use. A consent of all men or almost all nations is necessary for the law of nations to be valid. [30]

Civil law is to be taken as the law which is proper to each state or commonwealth, in which sense it does not include either the natural law or the law of nations. [31] Canon law is that law which, approved by the sovereign pontiffs, pertains to the government of the universal Church. [32]

---

cepto et voluntate prohibentis, esto ex parte rei sit congruitas, et exigentia quaedam ut praecipiatur aut prohibeatur, pertinet ad jus positivum" (I, 4, 10-11).

[28] See *supra*, chap. II.

[29] "Jus vero humanum sunt reliqua praecepta, quae homines tulerunt accepta a Deo potestate pro ministerio et dignitate cujusque ad leges condendas" (I, 5, 14).

[30] "Jus gentium est jus humanum, quo omnes aut fere omnes gentes utuntur" (*ibid.*).

Cf. Saint Isidore, *Etymologiarum*, Bk. V, chap. vi, PL, LXXXII, col. 199-200: "Jus gentium est sedium occupatio, aedificatio, munitio, bella, captivitates, servitutes, postliminia, foedera, paces, induciae, legatorum non violandorum religio, connubia inter alienigenas prohibita, et inde jus gentium, quod eo jure omnes fere gentes utuntur."

[31] "Altero modo potest jus civile usurpari pro eo, quod est proprium cuique civitati aut regno. Sumptum vero hoc modo, distinguitur a jure naturali et a jure gentium, estque membrum dividens nostrae divisionis" (I, 3, 10).

In the Fifth Tract Molina offers another definition of civil law: "Civilis una, supremorum principum rerumpublicarum, rerumve ipsarum publicarum quoad eos, quibus condendi leges juxta varia regimina earundum rerumpublicarum ab ipsismet rebus publicis concessa est" (V, 46, 3046).

[32] "Quamvis si stricte, et proprie de jure canonico loquamur, sit illud solum, quod ad regimen universalis ecclesiae a summis pontificibus traditum approbatumve est: constitutiones vero particulares ministrorum ecclesiasticorum non, nisi ut illas a jure seculari secernamus, sint cum canonico jure annumerandae" (I, 3, 10).

"Altera vero pars legis humanae est jus canonicum, a summis Pontificibus Christi autoritate reipublicae ecclesiae ad finem spiritualem ac supernaturalem latum. Licet autem multa conciliorum provincialium et sanctorum Patrum continent; non tamen illa rationem legum simpliciter comparatione totius corporis ecclesiae habent, nisi quatenus autoritate summorum Pontificum corpori ecclesiae ut leges servandae sunt propositae" (V, 46, 3047).

Natural Law and "Jus Gentium"

As a rule, the scholastics of the sixteenth century employed the terms *lex naturalis* and *jus naturale* as synonyms. [33] Molina favors the latter form, although he seems to use the terms interchangeably. For him, the natural law is related to God's essence, to His reason whence emanates the eternal law of which every law is a participation. Molina distinguishes two aspects of the eternal law. The first aspect is the eternal law as it exists in God by which he judges what is in conformity with his nature and what is not. [34] The second aspect of the eternal law is that by which God provides for and governs all things, directing them to their ends. [35]

Molina clearly states that the natural law is derived from the eternal law and that the natural law obliges by reason of a precept of the eternal law. [36] The natural law and its precepts

---

[33] Rommen, *The Natural Law*, p. 67.

Molina does not seem to make the distinction which Rommen notes of Suárez and Bellarmine: "But Suarez and Bellarmine, for instance, made a distinction when they expressly declared that violations of the *lex naturalis* on the part of the Indians by no means constitutes grounds for a just war: hence Christian princes are not justified in subjugating these *gentes* by alleging their transgressions of the *lex naturalis*. Only an offense against the *jus naturale* warrants such action" (*ibid.*).

[34] "Primo autem loco distinguitur Lex Dei aeterna et incommutabilis in ipsomet Deo existens, qua imprimis judicat, quid ex ipsamet rei natura rectum sit, quidque turpe et a recta ratione dissonum, si fiat tum a creaturis mente praeditis sua omnipotentia possibilibus, tum etiam si ab ipsomet Deo fieret" (V, 46, 3039).

[35] "Deinde eadem lege aeterna Deus cunctis rebus providet et cuncta gubernat, ratioque dirigendi res omnes in suos fines, eisque ad eosdem fines providendi in Deo existens, ad legem Dei aeternam pertinet: quae determinata per suam voluntatem ad res, quas creare ac gubernare statuit illas ad suos fines dirigendo, rationem integram providentiae circa easdem res sortitur, cujus actus Dei externus est creatio ac gubernatio ipsa rerum exequutione [sic] mandata" (V, 46, 3040).

"In the essential nature is likewise founded essential oughtness, the eternal law, which is God's wisdom so far as it directs and governs the world as first cause of all rational creatures and of all movements of irrational beings. The eternal law, ... is the governance of the world through God's will in accordance with His wisdom. This law is thus the order of the world" (Rommen, *The Natural Law*, p. 45).

[36] "Item, ut in hac etiam disputatione explanamus, lex naturalis non solum a lege Dei aeterna derivatur, sed etiam praeceptum, ratione cujus illa obligat, est praeceptum legis Dei aeternae, quod nobis per legem naturalem, tanquam per actum externum legi Dei aeternae, et tanquam per legem in cordibus nostris a Deo scriptam ... quare lex naturalis lex est Dei" (V, 46, 3036-3037).

are so dependent on the existence of the eternal law that in
the impossible hypothesis of God's non-existence, the dictates
of reason would not have the formal notion of law and acts
contrary to nature and reason would not be culpable. [37]   The
same problem hypothesis was considered by Grotius fifty years
later, but the great Dutch jurist came to the opposite conclusion: "What we have been saying would have a degree of validity
even if we should concede that which cannot be conceded without the utmost wickedness, that there is no God, or that the
affairs of men are of no concern to him." [38]

Rommen points out that one of the efforts of the scholastics
of the Renaissance was to abolish the distinction between a
primary natural law as it existed before the Fall of Man and
a secondary natural law valid after that event. [39]   Molina distinguishes between the various conditions (*status*) of man, [40] mak-

---

[37] Molina pauses to refute an opinion of Gerson, who held that natural
law should not be considered as emanating from God: "Illud quidem darem
Gersoni, si per impossibile non esset Deus, solumque a nobis ipsis haberemus
lumen naturale intellectus, quo intelligimus, quae bona sint facienda, et quae
mala fugienda, ut in officio nos contineremus, virtutesque conservaremus, et
in vitia et mala non incideremus, dictamina illa intellectus non haberent tunc
rationem legis proprie, quoniam non essent alicujus superioris, nec proinde
essent culpae et peccata adversus Deum" (V, 46, 3037).

For a further discussion of this point, see José M.ª Díez-Alegría, S.J., *El
desarrollo de la doctrina de la ley natural en Luis de Molina y en los maestros
de la Universidad de Evora de 1565 a 1591*: estudio histórico y textos inéditos
(Barcelona: Consejo superior de investigaciones científicas, 1951), pp. 94-118.
The author points out that "la posición de Molina quien de este modo viene
a situarse en una postura radicalmente diversa de la que vendrá a adoptar
De Groot cinco lustros más tarde" (p. 112).

"Para Molina, como aparece claramente en este texto, considerado en su
contexto propio, la negación mental de Dios implica formalmente la negación del derecho natural en cuanto absolutamente vinculatorio. La obliga-
toriedad moral perfecta es esencialmente teológica. ... El pensamiento de
Molina coincide exactamente en este punto con el de su predecesor Domingo
Soto" (*ibid.*, p. 114).

[38] Grotius, *De Jure Belli*, p. 13.

According to Anton-Hermann Chroust ("Hugo Grotius and the Scholastic
Natural Law Tradition," *The New Scholasticism*, XVII [1943], 126): "This
famous passage from Grotius is but a rebuke of William of Occam's and Hobbes's voluntarism or 'positivism'—by that we mean something valid because
of its being posited or willed by someone—and an indirect proof of Grotius's
belief, quite in accordance with the Thomistic tradition, in the *perseitas boni
et justi.*"

[39] Rommen, "Renaissance Period," *op. cit.*, p. 103.

[40] "Secundo autem loco distinguitur lex naturalis, ad finem naturalem humanae felicitatis moralis ac speculativae ordinata" (V, 46, 3045).

"Tertio vero loco distinguitur lex status innocentiae, quae naturalem legem
comprehendebat, quatenus finis naturalis felicitatis moralis subordinatus est

ing it clear that the natural law as such is unchanged whether one considers a condition of natural felicity (which never existed historically) or one of innocence (which did exist historically), or the condition of fallen and redeemed nature (which does exist historically).

A Spanish Jesuit, Jose Mª. Díez-Alegría, has done careful research in the manuscripts of Molina to trace the development of the doctrine of natural law at the University of Evora. [41] His study clearly shows that the professors at Evora were in great part concerned with the problem of the mutability or immutability of the natural law. The problem, old as the natural law itself, is a heritage of Greco-Roman and Christian thought. It goes back to Cicero, the Stoics, and the great moralists of antiquity and to its great poets, particularly Sophocles. [42] Antigone, who was aware that in transgressing the human law and being crushed by it she was obeying *the unwritten and unchangeable laws*, is the heroine of the natural law: for, as she puts it, they were not born out of today's or yesterday's sweet will, but live always and forever, and no man knows from where they have arisen. [43]

---

fini supernaturali sempiternae felicitatis, ad quam homines fuerunt conditi, mediaque ad eum naturalem finem necessaria quoque in adultis sunt ad finem supernaturalem" (*ibid.*).

"Quarto loco distinguitur lex status naturae post peccatum: quae ob eandem rationem legem etiam naturalem comprehendebat" (*ibid.*).

"Et quidem in statu innocentiae non alias leges scimus primis parentibus a Deo ad finem supernaturalem supra naturae legem fuisse additas" (V, 46, 3033).

"Dissoluta vero natura per peccatum, promissoque primis parentibus ipsis, et ipsorum posteris, redemptore, in eo statu legis naturae, qui tunc incepit, eadem lex naturae jam antea ipsis promulgata permansit" (*ibid.*).

[41] Díez-Alegría, *op. cit.*

See also by the same author, *Etica, derecho e historia* (Madrid: Sapientia, S.A. de Ediciones, 1953), pp. 91-133.

[42] Rommen, *The Natural Law*, pp. 11-12.

Jacques Maritain, *Man and the State* (7th ed.; Chicago: Phoenix Books, The University of Chicago Press, 1958), p. 85.

[43] "Antigone: I hear it not from Heaven, nor
                  came it forth
            From Justice, where she reigns with
                  God below.
            They too have published to mankind a
                  law.
            Nor thought I commandment of such
                  might
            That one who is mortal thus could
                  overbear
            The infallible, unwritten laws of
                  Heaven.

In the Christian era interest in the problem of the mutability of natural law was heightened in connection with the exegesis of certain passages in the Old Testament. The thesis of the immutability of the natural law presupposes the intrinsic immorality and unlawfulness of certain actions, and excludes any dispensation from the norms of the natural law. [44] Such a position seemed to conflict with some Old Testament accounts, such as Yahweh's command to Abraham to offer up his son Isaac in sacrifice, [45] the polygamy of the patriarchs, God's instruction to the prophet Osee: "Go, take thee a wife of fornications"; [46] the injunction laid on the Jews or the permission accorded them at the time of the Exodus to take away with them vessels of silver and gold lent them by the Egyptians; [47] divorce openly allowed to husbands in the Mosaic legislation.

> Not now or of yesterday they have
>   their being,
> But everlastingly, and none can tell
> The hour that saw their birth. And
>   I would not
> For any terror of man's resolve
> Incur the God-inflicted penalty of
>   doing them wrong."

(Lewis Campbell, *Sophocles*: The Seven Plays in English Verse [Oxford: Oxford University Press, 1936], p. 16).

[44] Rommen, *The Natural Law*, pp. 42-43.

[45] Gen. 22:2.

[46] Osee 1:2.

[47] Exodus 3:21, 11:2, and 12:35.

Biblical exegesis is far richer in its research methods than it was in Molina's day. In very recent years significant works on the Old Testament have been added to the wealth of knowledged already accumulated. See John L. McKenzie, S.J., *The Two-Edged Sword*: An Interpretation of the Old Testament (Milwaukee: The Bruce Publishing Co., 1956); also Bruce Vawter, C.M., *A Path Through Genesis* (New York: Sheed & Ward, 1956); and A. Robert and A. Tricot (eds.), *Initiation Biblique*: Introduction à l'études des Saintes Ecritures (Paris: Desclée & Cie, 1954).

J. H. Crehan, S.J. ("The Inspiration and Inerrancy of Holy Scripture" in *A Catholic Commentary on Holy Scripture*, ed. Dom Bernard Orchard *et al.* [London: Thomas Nelson and Sons, 1953], p. 52) treats some of these classic cases: "Inerrancy implies in Scripture absence of immoral teaching, and it is therefore necessary to give some lines of explanation by which difficulties against the moral teaching of the Bible (the OT mainly) can be met. ... Sometimes commands may be given such as the command to despoil the Egyptians, ... which at first sight seem to be immoral, but (as here) can be explained on moral grounds. The Israelites were entitled to some compensation for their labours in Egypt and God, as lord of all creation, could certainly tell them to take it where he willed."

St. Thomas was the first to offer an adequate solution of the problem. [48]

In St. Thomas' *Commentary on the Sentences* he treats for the first time the problem of the institution of marriage among the Jews and in connection with it the problem of the immutability of the natural law. He distinguishes two classes of precepts of the natural law: primary precepts and secondary precepts. The former are immutable; the latter admit of dispensation by God. [49] Commentators acknowledge a certain fluctuation in the terminology (if not the thought) of St. Thomas on this question. [50] Maritain says it is unfortunate that his ideas on this point were expressed in an insufficiently clarified vocabulary. [51] One can note in Molina a certain development of his own thought on this question. [52]

Molina first began to discuss the matter of the natural law in his lectures at Evora in 1570, commenting on the *Summa*: "In 1-2, qq. 98-108: *De Lege Veteri*." [53] He adopts Soto's dis-

---

[48] See Michael Wittmann, *Die Ethik des Hl. Thomas von Aquin in ihrem systematischen Aufbau dargestellt und in ihren Geschichtlichen, besonders in den antiken Quellen erforscht* (München: M. Hueber, 1933); and Odon Lottin, *Le droit naturel chez Saint Thomas d'Aquin et ses prédécesseurs* (2d ed.; Bruges: C. Beyaert, 1931).

[49] Lottin (*op. cit.*, pp. 76 and 102) maintains that this distinction between the primary and secondary precepts was a creation of St. Thomas and was not found in his predecessors.

After his work was published there appeared an article by G. Meersse- mann, "Le droit naturel chez S. Thomas d'Aquin et ses prédécesseurs," *Angelicum*, IX (1932), 63-76. This article contained a previously unedited commentary of St. Albert the Great on Nicomachean Ethics of Aristotle in which, it is maintained, Albert had distinguished between the primary and secondary precepts of the natural law.

[50] "En cuanto a las fórmulas de expresión de la doctrina acerca de la inmutabilidad o de la dispensabilidad del Derecho natural (en general, de la ley natural), se nota en la obra de Santo Tomás una cierta fluctuación, sin que la diversidad de explicaciones pueda ser referida con fijeza a la sucesión cronológica de los trabajos" (Díez-Alegría, *Etica, derecho e historia*, p. 119).

[51] Maritain, *op. cit.*, p. 85: "Especially because the vocabulary of the *Commentary on the Sentences*, as concerns the 'primary' and 'secondary' precepts of the Natural Law, is at variance with the vocabulary of the *Summa theologica* (i-ii. 94)."

[52] "El enfoque y solución del problema de la indefectibilidad vinculatoria de los preceptos de la ley natural, por lo que toca a Molina y los maestros de Evora, nos ofrece un ejemplo muy interesante de evolución doctrinal progresiva, que es sugestivo analizar" (Díez-Alegría, *El desarrollo*, p. 165).

[53] The manuscript of these lectures is preserved at Lisbon in the Biblioteca Nacional and is printed in full as Appendix C of Díez-Alegría's *El desarrollo*, pp. 203-224.

tinction: [54] "La posición de Molina en la lecturas de 1570 parece, pues, coincidir plenamente con la de Soto, y queda como la de este último bastante imprecisa." [55]   The precepts of the Decalog do not admit dispensation.   Other conclusions from the natural law may be dispensed.   The classic example is that concerning the secondary precept: *reddere depositum domino*. This could be dispensed from or would not oblige, for example, if what was to be returned was a sword and the owners was in a rage.   It would be contrary to the natural law to endanger his life and those of others by returning what belonged to him. [56]

---

[54] "Igitur quando praecepta per se intrinsece continent ... ordinem ipsum justitiae ... nunquam contingere potest ut facere contra illa non adversetur intentioni legislatoris.   Exempla rem ipsam patefaciunt, si jussio legis reipublicae esset haec: ... Nullus injuste agat.   Profecto rationi intrinsecae et nativae talium legum repugnaret dispensatio: implicatio enim est contradictionis, licere cuipiam injuste agere.

"Hoc quod est adulterium facere, quod est in Decalogo, et mentiri aut fornicari, quae implicite illic latitant ... tam intrinsece mala sunt (ut de odio Dei proxime arguebamus) quam est homini esse rationalem: ergo naturae suae justitia repugnat ac probitas: Deus autem dispensare nequit nisi ubi aliqua est ratio aequi et boni: ergo in his dispensare non potest: aut (quo temperantius loquamur) disponibilia non sunt" (Soto, *De justitia et jure*, l. II, quaest. 3).

Before Soto, Vitoria had developed the same distinction.   See Francisco de Vitoria, O.P., *Comentarios a la Secunda Secundae de Santo Tomás*, ed. V. Beltrán de Heredia, O.P. (5 vols.; Salamanca: Biblioteca de teólogos españoles, 1932-1935), V, 210: "In secundo argumento petit: si Deus praeciperet aliquid contra jus naturale, an esset parendum illi, ita quod qui illi pareret, non peccaret, sicut si praeciperet quod perjurem.   Videtur quod sic, quia Abrahae praecepit occidere filium suum.   Item, Judaeis praecepit quod furarentur vasa Aegyptiorum; et Oseae quod acciperet mulierem adulteram quod tamen est contra castitatem.   Ergo.

"Respondetur quod Deus in omnibus istis non fecit contra jus naturale nec contra justitiam, nec dispensavit in aliquo praecepto.   Dato quod Deus non esset legislator, sed creator, et alius v. gr. Deus esset legislator qui diceret, non occidas etc., nihilominus Deus ipse creator, licet praeciperet alicui occidere aliquem, non faceret contra praeceptum, nec dispensat cum illo cui praecipit occidere alium, quia vita illius quem praecipit occidere, est bonum suum, quia Deus est dominus et auctor vitae et mortis.   Ita cum filiis Israel, quibus praecepit accipere res et vasa Aegyptiorum, non dispensavit, quia vasa illa erant bona sua.   Et quia Deus est dominus omnium, ideo potuit dare illa cui voluisset, et sic dedit Judaeis.

"Similiter nec praeceptum datum Oseae, ut mulierem adulteram acciperet, fuit contra castitatem, quia Deus ipse est ordinator generationis humanae, et ideo ille est legitimus et debitus modus utendi mulieribus quem Deus instituit."

[55] Díez-Alegría, *El desarollo*, p. 168.

[56] "Ad primum ergo, dicendum est quod, sicut in naturalibus quaedam sunt invariabilia omnino et quaedam quae regulariter loquendo sublatis impedimentis semper eodem modo se habent, raro tamen superveniente aliquo impedimento deficiunt, ita in moralibus quaedam sunt de jure naturali quae omnino sunt invariabilia et quaedam quae secundum se nulla superveniente

The second stage of the development of Molina's thought on this question may be found in Tract 1, published during his life time. Relying on a metaphor from the physical world, Molina says there are certain things in the physical world which could never be changed—fire is necessarily hot, and man must have the capacity for intellectual activity. Certain other things can change: The right hand is usually stronger than the left, but some people are left-handed. [57] In the moral world there are likewise two types of laws: certain things are so closely connected with the natural law that they cannot be changed. Such are the precepts of the Decalog. Not even divine omnipotence can change them. Other laws are connected with the natural law but admit of change. Normally one is obliged to return to the owner whatever has been left as a deposit. However, should the owner return in a rage and demand his sword, then the obligation ceases. [58]

There is a difference between variations in the natural law and positive law. Changes in the natural law do not come about because of a mutation in the law itself, but because of circumstances which remove an object from the comprehension of the law. Positive law may bring it about that something which had been contrary to the natural law, in certain circumstances no longer is. [59] The example Molina uses is the law

---

circumstantia non variantur, superveniente vero aliqua circumstantia non inconvenit raro variari. Prioris generis sunt praecepta Decalogi, in quibus nulla cadit dispensatio, posterioris vero generis sunt ea de quibus loquitur ibi Aristoteles, in quibus non inconvenit cadere aliquando dispensationem. In casu tamen proposito absque ulla dispensatione proprie dicta licet non reddere depositum, per interpretationem juris, quod non intelligitur quando is cui reddi debebat incidit in furiam et depositum erat gladius" (ibid., p. 222).

[57] "Dubium tamen est circa rem praesentem, an ea, quae juris sunt naturalis. ... Ut enim inter res naturales quaedam sunt necessariae omnino, quae variationem non patiuntur, ut ignis ita est calidus, ut esse nequeat frigidus, et homo suapte natura ita vim habet ad intelligendum, ut nequeat ea privari; et quaedam sunt ita suapte natura tales, ut possint aliquando aliter se habere, sicut, licet dextera manus naturaliter fortior sit, quam sinistra, interdum tamen sinistra evadit fortior, quam dextera" (I, 4, 11).

[58] "Ita in rebus moralib. quaedam sunt de jure naturali ejus conditionis, ut nequeant non esse, cujusmodi sunt quae in Decalogo praecipiuntur, eo modo quo praecipiuntur; in quae, sic spectata, ne divina quidem potentia cadit dispensatio. ... Alia vero ita sunt de jure naturali, ut possint aliquando deficere, et non esse de jure naturali. Hoc modo licet reddere depositum sit de jure naturali, si tamen rei depositae dominus in furiam incidat, periculumque sit ne se, vel alium ea interficiat, de jure naturali est contrarium, nempe dum periculum illud imminet, rem depositam ei non reddere" (ibid.).

[59] "Est tamen notandum latissimum discrimen inter variationem eorum quae sunt de jure naturali, et eorum quae sunt de jure positivo. Variatio

of prescription by which one who in good faith possesses something belonging to another for a set period of time; at the expiration of that time he becomes its owner. Likewise, by a kind of eminent domain, a ruler may take what belongs to his subjects and transfer it to another when the common good demands it. [60]

Secondly, custom may introduce changes. For example, the goods of the earth are, according to the natural law, possessed in common. By the law of nations, a division of property was introduced. [61] This came about as a result of original sin. It was seen by men that it was better to divide property among themselves, both for better administration and also to promote peace. Therefore by positive law, according to the tacit or expressed consent of all men, private property, once contrary to the natural law, now no longer is. [62]

---

namque eorum, quae sunt de jure naturali, non evenit propter variationem, aut mutationem, quae in lege naturali fiat, sed propter adventum circumstantiae, quae extrahit objectum a numero eorum, quae lex ea comprehendebat, quare fit sine ulla dispensatione, aut mutatione legis, lumine intellectus dictante et interpretante, quod persistente lege in se ut antea erat, non intelligatur in eo eventu, talique superveniente circumstantia" (*ibid.*).

[60] "Primum est, jus positivum humanum efficere posse, ut aliquid liceat, quod secluso tali jure, esset contra jus naturale: non quasi jus humanum praejudicare possit juri naturali, ipsum in aliquo derogando; sed quod possit apponere circumstantiam ex parte objecti, qua id esse desinat de jure naturali, quod foret seclusa ea circumstantia. Exemplum accomodatum habemus in lege praescriptionis, qua ei, qui bona fide possedit aliquid alienum toto tempore dato ad praescribendum, fas est, transacto eo tempore, retinere illud, esto resciat fuisse alienum" (I, 4, 12).

"Sed princeps potestatem habens jure naturali spoliandi subditos dominio rerum suarum, illudque in alios transferendi, quando id bono Reipublicae, viderit expedire, eo ipso, quod ad rescindendas lites, et quasi in poenam negligentiae propriorum dominorum, ne id in posterum publicam tranquillitatem turbaret, legem justam praescriptionis condidit, qua statuit, ut qui bona fide rem aliquam certo quodam tempore possideret, compararet dominium illius, priorque dominus illud amitteret, apposuit circumstantiam ex parte objecti, qua id, quod seclusa ea lege esset alienum, ac proinde cujus retentio esset contra jus naturale, stante ea lege, neque alienum sit, neque illius retentio sit contra jus naturale" (*ibid.*).

[61] "Secundum est, in quo sensu verum sit, quod communiter dici consuevit, nempe de jure naturali fuisse omnia communia, jure vero gentium introductam, factamque fuisse rerum divisionem" (*ibid.*).

[62] "Sane homines post lapsum in peccatum, postulante id recta ratione, dividere eas inter se potuerunt, reque ipsa diviserunt: tum ut melius administrarentur: tum etiam ut pax inter homines servaretur, quae sane, si omnia omnibus universim essent communia, servari nulla ratione posset. Jus ergo positivum, ex communi hominum tacito vel expresso beneplacito ... efficere potuit, ut quod ante rerum divisionem esset contra jus naturale, ea facta,

Thirdly, by the law of nations there may be introduced a situation of life that is contrary to man's natural condition. If, for example, a certain people is captured in a just war in which it was permitted to kill them, it is licit according to the law of nations to enslave them, commuting their death sentence into perpetual servitude. At this point slavery is introduced by the law of nations. [63]

Civil law, Molina continues, may add to or take from natural law. Sometimes it adds but a further determination of the natural law and sometimes completely new statutes. For an example Molina cites the natural law which requires worship of God; that God be worshipped by this or that particular sacrifice is not required by the natural law but is determined by the will of men. The Sacrifice of the Mass in the New Law pertains to positive divine law. Punishment of a criminal is of the natural law but the manner of punishment—hanging, whipping, or assignment to the galley—is a determination of human civil law. [64]

The third stage of the evolution of Molina's thought on the question of the immutability of natural law is to be found in Tract Five, edited and published by his fellow Jesuits at Madrid after his death. In the posthumous work Molina distinguishes three grades of those things which pertain to the natural law. [65]

---

advenienteque circumstantia ex parte objecti appropriationis rerum, juri naturae non repugnaret" (I, 4, 13).

[63] "Sensus autem horum omnium est, spectata praecise prima rerum constitutione homines ita jure naturali nascituros fuisse liberos, ut servitus esset contra naturam, jusque ipsum naturale, atque adeo injusta. Commissa autem culpa per aliquos populos, ortoque bello justo, quo fas fuit eos interficere, non solum jure gentium servitutem esse licitam, minimeque contra jus naturale, eo ipso quod ex parte objecti ea circumstantia licitae eorum interfectionis resultavit, sed etiam authoritate propria cujusque populi aut principis, qui jus simile ad interficiendum quancunque ex causa haberet, potuisse licite introduci, commutando mortem iis, qui illa digni erant, in perpetuam eorum servitutem" (ibid.).

[64] "Quibus verbis affirmat, jus civile aliquando addere juri naturali et gentium, aliquando vero aliquid ab eis detrahere. Addit quidem nonnumquam solam determinationem ad quaedam particularia, nonnumquam vero nova omnino statua. V. g. de jure naturali est, Deum coli debere: quod vero hoc vel illo sacrificio in particulari colatur, non est de jure naturali, sed ex arbitrio hominum pendet, ... Eodemque modo determinatio sacrificiorum in lege veteri et sacrificii missae nova lege, ad jus divinum positivum spectat. Item de jure naturali est, malefactorem puniri debere: quod vero hac vel illa poena in particulari, ut quod latro suspendatur, vel flagelletur, aut triremibus adigatur, non est de jure naturali, sed ad jus humanum civile spectat id constituere" (I, 4, 13-14).

[65] "Accipe ergo tres gradus eorum, quae de jure sunt naturali. Primus

The first grade contains those things which are so intrinsically evil that no circumstance whatever will justify them: perjury, lying, hatred of God. [66] The second grade contains those items which under certain aspects are so intrinsically evil they can never be justified. Under certain other aspects, however, because of special circumstances they may be removed from the strict obligation of natural law. For instance, the taking of what belongs to another who is reasonably unwilling that it be taken is so intrinsically evil that it does not admit of dispensation, even by God. There are, however, circumstances where on the command or permission of God, who is universal lord of all things, property belonging to another may be taken even if the owner is reasonably unwilling. [67] The third grade contains those items which belong to the natural law, but can cease to bind because of certain circumstances. To this group belongs the famous example of returning a deposited sword to an owner who is in a rage. Regarding the Decalog, Molina states categorically that none of them admit of dispensation even by God, with the possible exception of the third commandment in its ceremonial aspects. [68]

---

est eorum, quae ita intrinseca sunt mala, ut nulla superveniente circumstantia cohonestari possint" (V, 49, 3072).

[66] "Nulla tamen circumstantia efficere potest, ut illicitum et contra jus naturale esse desinat, falsum testimonium dicere, mentiri, odio prosequi Deum, aut malum morale ac culpae non fugere" (*ibid.*).

[67] "Secundus est eorum, quae sunt quidem de jure naturali, quaequae accepta sub certa ratione formali adeo sunt intrinsece mala, ut remanente eadem ratione formali, nulla ratione possint licita reddi, attamen adveniente aliqua circumstantia, quemadmodum extrahi per illam possunt ab ea ratione formali intrinsece mala, sic licita quoque reddi possunt ac extrahi ab objecto juris naturalis. Ejusmodi est contrectatio rei alienae invito domino, quae jure naturali est prohibita, rationemque furti sortitur, atque, quoad rationem furti, ita est intrinsece mala, ut nulla ratione possit esse licita, aut non prohibita jure naturali: et quia septimum praeceptum decalogi furtum, quoad rationem furti, prohibet, sane quod illo praecepto prohibetur, sub ea ratione, qua prohibetur, est intrinsece malum, neque in eo cadere potest dispensatio, etiam divina potentia" (*ibid.*).

"Nihilominus si permissu Dei, qui dominus universalis est omnium, quod alienum erat, contrectetur, eo, cujus erat, invito, quemadmodum id jam ex ea circumstantia furti rationem non retinet, quia accipitur condonatum a Deo, sic nec eadem acceptio manet, intra limites prohibitae [sic] jure naturali, sed potius manet extra limites talis objecti" (*ibid.*).

[68] "Tertius vero est eorum, quae licet per se, seclusa alia circumstantia, sint de jure naturali, ex circumstantia tamen desinunt esse de jure naturali, imo reddi possunt contra jus naturale, ratioque ipsorum formalis ad utrumque se extendit, nec perit adveniente, juxta communem cursum naturae, ea circumstantia. Ejusmodi est, reddere depositum domino illud petenti. Id enim de se, seclusa omni alia circumstantia, quae id impediat, aut quae licitum efficiat

Jus Gentium

The concept of the *jus gentium* can be as elusive as a drop of quicksilver. Maritain says it is difficult to define exactly because it is intermediary between natural and positive law. [69] Rommen calls it that somewhat vague medium between the *Jus Naturale* and the *Jus Civile*. [70]

> The great accomplishment of the Late Scholastics lay in the domain of the *jus gentium*. They cleared up, before Grotius, the ambiguous distinctions of Roman law that had crept in during the course of centuries. *Jus gentium* in the proper sense is not *jus naturale*, although the precepts of the latter are evidently valid for the ordering of the community of peoples. Thus differentiated, *jus gentium* is the quasi-positive law of the international community: it is founded upon custom as well as upon treaty agreements. [71]

Molina defines *jus gentium* as human law which all or nearly all nations observe. [72] Universal acceptance is not necessary for something to belong to the *jus gentium*. The Christian practice of not enslaving other Christians captured in war does not prevent the practice of non-Christian nations taking slaves

---

illud non reddere, est de jure naturali: ex circumstantiis tamen, secundum naturae cursum supervenientibus desinere potest esse de jure naturali" (V, 49, 3073).

"Est ergo nobis amplectenda sententia ... omnia videlicet praecepta decalogi nec divina potentia dispensari posse, praeter tertium, ea ex parte qua caeremoniale ac de jure positivo est" (V, 57, 3153).

[69] Maritain, *op. cit.*, p. 98.

[70] Rommen, "Renaissance Period," *op. cit.*, p. 119.

[71] Rommen, *The Natural Law*, pp. 68-69.

See Clementinus Vlissingen, O.F.M. Cap., *De evolutione definitionis juris gentium*: Studium historico-juridicum de doctrina juris gentium apud Auctores Classicos Saec. XVII-XVIII (Romae: Apud Aedes Universitatis Gregorianae, 1940); also A. H. Dantas de Brito, *La philosophie du droit des gens*: Une étude de critériologie juridique (Washington: The Catholic University of America Press, 1944). Both books contain extensive bibliographies.

Also Ernest Nys, "Les juresconsultes espagnols et la science de droit des gens," *Revue de droit international et de législation comparée*, 2d série, XIV (1912), 360-387, 494-524, and 614-642.

[72] "Jus gentium est jus humanum, quo omnes, aut fere omnes gentes utuntur. ... Neque enim, ut aliquid sit de jure gentium, necessarium est, ut omnes universim gentes illud exerceant. Etenim licet inter Christianos sit in more positivum, ut qui ab aliis Christianis in bello justo capiuntur, mancipia non fiant, id non tollit, quominus de jure gentium sit, ut capti in bello justo servitutem contrahant" (I, 5, 14).

as prizes of war from being considered as part of the *jus gentium*. The division of the goods of the earth into private property is an example of the *jus gentium*. The consent of all men was necessary before that which was owned in common should be divided. It is also according to the *jus gentium* that what belongs to no owner becomes the property of the first who occupies it. The privileges of legates and the sanctity of contract belong to the *jus gentium*. [73]

In Molina's division of laws he leaves no doubt that the *jus gentium* belongs under the heading of positive human law. His relatively brief treatment of the question does not indicate that he considers *jus gentium* to be of minor importance. He devotes a full disputation [74] to an explanation of the ways the lawyers, in contrast to the theologians, [75] try to group *jus gentium*. His attempt leaves the reader bewildered, bringing to mind the student conversing with Mephistopheles in Faust:

> As if a wheel turned in my head,
> I feel confused by what you have said.

Molina's own classification is clear. His definite grouping of *jus gentium* under positive human law removes, for him at least, any ambiguity about its status. He would associate *jus gentium* with the natural law as a sort of compass, indispensable to the navigation of human living, but requiring a great deal of skill in its use to allow for variations and deviations in human conduct.

Civil Law

The third type of positive human law Molina calls a civil law. He defines it as an act of political prudence, derived from the eternal and immutable law of God, consonant with right

---

[73] "In primis ergo rerum divisio est de jure gentium. Communis quippe est omnibus rationibus, ad illamque necessarius fuit consensus hominum, ut ea, quae alioquin omnibus in commune a Deo donata fuerant, dividerentur. De jure etiam gentium est, ut facta rerum divisione, res, quae domino carent, sint primo occupantis: item legatorum non violandorum religio, et fere omnes contractus, quos homines communiter exercent, et pleraque alia" (*ibid.*).

Goyau, *op. cit.*, pp. 125-129.

[74] "De Divisione juris tradita a jurisconsultis, et qua ratione cum divisione hactenus explicata concilianda sit" (I, 6, 15-16).

[75] M. J. Laversin, O.P., "Droit naturel et droit positif d'après S. Thomas," *Revue Thomiste*, XXVIII (1933), 1-50 and 177-217; F. Heydte, "Francisco de Victoria und sein Völkerrecht," *Zeitschrift für öffentliches Recht*, XVI (1936), 487-495.

reason and accommodated to the common good. [76] But there
is much of the human element in positive law, depending in
great part on the will an disposition of the legislator. [77] Civil
law, though derived from natural and the eternal law of God,
should conform with the customs of the area. [78] For example,
Molina continues, it often happens that in parts of Spain there
is a great abundance of grain and in other parts a great lack
of the same. A result of this is that the normal price varies
in different localities. A law which would attempt to set up
one constant price of grain for all Spain would be unjust. [79]

Tax Laws

The area of taxation provides an opportunity of demonstrat-
ing how carefully Molina considered the problems of his day. [80]

---

[76] "Ejus modi quoque leges omnes humanae, tam ecclesiasticae quam civiles, si non iniquae, (tunc enim rationem legis nec mererentur nec haberent)
sed rationabiles sint, quin et praecepta omnia, non iniqua et irrationabilia,
a legitimis superioribus quibuscunque suis inferioribus lata, a lege Dei incom-
municabili et aeterna descendunt ac derivantur" (V, 46, 3047-3048).

"Dicendum est tertio, legem omnem humanam positivam ... esse debere
rectae rationi consentaneam, ab illave minime dissonam, bonoque communi
reipublicae accomodatam" (V, 68, 3213).

[77] "Dicendum est deinde, multas humanas leges derivari a naturalibus per
arbitramentum ac dispositionem humanam, consentaneam quidem juri illi naturali, a quo ita derivantur, non tamen necessariam, quasi sine tali dispositione
naturale id jus non posset salvum consistere: qua de causa tales dispositiones
ac leges non sunt de jure naturali, sed de jure humano positivo" (V. 68,
3212-3213).

"Lex vero positiva ab arbitrio ac dispositione legislatoris eam ferre volen-
tis pendet, ideoque positiva lex nuncupatur" (V, 47, 3059).

[78] "Addit vero non expedire ut feratur lex contra consuetudinem patriae,
quae nec mala sit nec bona, nec utilis nec inutilis, ne forte talem legem contra similem consuetudinem ferendo, perturbatio et malum aliquod oriatur in
republica. ... Evenire facile posse, ut quae lex uni loco est conveniens ac
justa, alteri loco conveniens non sit, sed injusta, et ut quae lex uno tempore
est conveniens et justa, alteri tempore conveniens non sit, sed injusta" (V,
69, 3217).

[79] "Ut, verbi gratia, (quod quam saepissime in Hispaniis evenit) si in eodem
anno in una parte Hispaniarum, ut in Betica, in Legione ac Castella veteri,
in regno Toleti, aut in minoribus partibus harum praecipuarum partium, quae
eisdem legibus Regis Hispaniarum gubernantur, eveniat, magnam esse copiam
frumenti, et in aliis magnam penuriam, ita ut pretium naturale justum frumenti merito in eisdem variis locis sit valde inaequale, non video legem posse
esse justam, quae aequale pretium in omnibus eis locis taxet, esto permittatur
accipi insuper pretium transportationis ex uno loco in alium" (ibid.).

[80] This summary on Molina's position on taxation is based in part on
the study by Laures, The Political Economy of Juan de Mariana, pp. 171-227.

Molina declares at the beginning of his treatise on taxation, "Now we shall speak ... of taxes, which are due to the lay authorities because of their jurisdictional dominion and for the common good of the state." [81] The common good Molina identifies as salaries for public officers, repair of bridges, public buildings, and town walls, common utilities, and the needs of defense. [82]

Molina carefully distinguishes between taxes and other revenues of the king. He also sees clearly the difference between taxes by assessment and taxes on transportation and exchange of commodities. The first he calls *tributum* and the other two *vectigal* and *quasi-vectigal*. He begins with a discussion of the use of these terms in the Roman Empire; then he enumerates the various types of taxes in Spain and Portugal by analogy with those of Rome; next he finds that there existed in Rome a tax on land and on immovables in general which was determined by assessment. This assessment was valled *census*, the same name being applied to the tax itself. A similar tax existed in Castile during Molina's day. He also speaks of a per capita tax and a number of other payments to the king.

Moreover, he lists a per capita tax in Castile and Leon which was assessed according to the number of persons in the family. It was a sign of subjection to the king and was called *moneda forera*. The *Martinega*, another form of tribute, was levied every year upon each independent individual and was collected regularly on St. Martin's Day, the eleventh of November. [83]

Quite different in nature were the taxes on the transportation and sale of goods. They were called *vectigalia* and *quasi-vectigalia* and were mainly charges on imports and exports (*portoria*, Spanish *aduana*), on transportation (*pedagia*, Spanish *guidagia*), and on sales and all other kinds of business transactions (Spanish *alcavala*). [84] This latter tax played an important role in Spain and was characteristic of Spanish finance. Mariana

---

[81] "Nunc autem disserendum consequenter nobis est de tributis, quae laicis potestatibus, ratione dominii jurisdictionis, quaeque in commune reipublicae bonum debentur" (II, 661, 201-203).

[82] "Unde si, quae illi [principi] a populis tributa sunt, non sufficiunt ad stipendia competentia ministrorum publicorum, ad reparationes pontium, domorum publicarum, moenium, et ad similes, aut majores utilitates ac necessitates publicas, aut ad resistendum hostibus, tunc princeps imponere potest nova tributa, aut antiqua augere, quantum et quandiu similes causae postulaverint" (II, 667, 220).

[83] II, 661, 203-206.

[84] II, 662, 207-209.

and De Lugo speak almost exclusively of this tax. It was the chief source of public revenue. [85]

According to Molina, the *alcavala* originally amounted to one-thirtieth of the value of the goods involved in the transaction but was later raised to one-twentieth. After the state bankruptcy under Philip II, it was raised again and amounted to one-tenth. Formerly it had been exacted with leniency; now it was collected most rigorously and fraudulent returns were punished severely. [86] Practically the whole of De Lugo's treatise [87] and the greater part of Molina's are devoted to this general sales tax.

Only a few commodities enjoyed freedom from the *alcavala*. Of the necessities of life, bread was exempt but grain was taxed. When the baker bought grain, he could pay by furnishing a certain number of loaves tax-free; but if he offered bread for sale to a farmer in exchange for grain the tax had to be paid. Another concession was made in favor of the poor peasant. Should he sell a grown and broken-in horse with saddle and harness, he was free of the *alcavala*. But if he sold a young animal, or one grown up that had not been broken-in or was not harnessed at the moment of the sale, he was compelled to pay the tax. [88]

Books, even when imported from abroad, bore no tax. Dowries were considered presents made to the bridegroom and thus passed tax free. An inheritance was exempt from the *alcavala* when it was divided among the heirs without involving money, mutual exchange, or sale. When a heritage was made over to a pious cause, it was considered *ipso facto* property of the Church and as such free from taxation. [89]

For persons who think that the principles and burdens of twentieth-century taxation are modern problems, the disputations of Molina would be a surprise. Molina and the other Jesuit writers were very much aware of the differences between taxes borne by the taxpayer and those shifted to other persons. The tariffs and the *alcavala* were of the latter type: indirect taxes. One finds Molina with a detailed knowledge of the difference between direct and indirect taxes, taxes on property

---

[85] Laures, *op. cit.*, p. 179.

[86] II, 663, 10-213.

[87] Juan de Lugo, S.J., *Tractatus de Justitia et Jure* (Parisiis: Apud Ludovicum Vives, 1863), V, 443-778.

[88] Laures, *op. cit.*, p. 179.

[89] II, 670, 223-225.

and persons, and on commodities. The former are taxes in
the strictest sense of the word while tariffs and sales taxes are,
as he believed, always shifted to the consumer. [90]

Philosophical Basis of Taxation

Molina, along with the other scholastic writers of his day,
based the principle of taxation on the natural law. Molina's
interpretation is that taxes are due according to the nature
of the matter and the obligation of the subjects to the state
and to the sovereign—i.e., for the good of the state, for its
conservation, administration, and defense. [91] Taxes are a necessary consequence of the nature of the state.

It is natural enough that their discussion of political power
and taxation be bound up with actual conditions in Spain and
Portugal. Because Spain was a monarchy, the person of the
sovereign and the state are used almost synonymously. Consequently, it is not surprising that the maintenance of the king
and government expenditures are often indiscriminately associated. Molina, however, does distinguish between them, point-
ing out that the maintenance of the king is but one item in
the disbursments to be covered by taxation.

> It is, as it were, a proper stipend to the prince from his sub-
> jects and is to be numbered among the needs of the state.
> With regard to this stipend and the reverence and obedience
> which the subjects owe and exhibit to their sovereign, he in
> turn is bound, as it were, by a contract to rule and defend
> them, to administer justice and to care for the common
> good. [92]

Molina considers the relationship between the king and his
subjects to be a relationship of quasi-contract, not indeed in

---

[90] Laures, *op. cit.*, p. 181.

[91] "Sed deberi [tributa] ut res solvi praecepta juxta id, quod postulat natura rei, ac debitum subditorum suae reipublicae, ac principi vi institutionis
ipsius reipublicae, in reipublicae bonum ac conservationem atque pro administratione ac defensione reipublicae, esseque proinde res eo ipso ex justitia
debitas" (II, 674, 228-229).

[92] "Quippe est quasi proprium stipendium a subditis principi debitum,
computaturque inter reipublicae necessaria. ... Ratione vero hujus stipendii,
reverentiae, atque obedientiae, quae subditi principi suo debent, ac praestant,
ipse vicissim, tanquam ex contractu, tenetur eos gubernare, ac defendere, admi-
nistrare illis justitiam, et curare bonum commune ipsorum" (II, 667, 220).

the sense of Hobbes, Locke, or Rousseau, but in the sense that an onerous transfer of power has been conferred on the king by the people, the king being bound to use this power for the good of the commonwealth and being granted the right to demand the necessary means; the people in turn oblige themselves to obey their sovereign and to supply the means needed to promote the common interests.

Taxes are considered the natural obligation incumbent upon members of a body politic to contribute their share toward defraying expenses incurred for the common good: "The members of the commonwealth are each obliged to aid on behalf of the common good and the public needs according to his ability."[93] Far from considering the measures of taxes by the private wants of the sovereign, Molina states clearly:

> The people are not for the prince, but the prince is for the people, since he has been set upon his throne for the good and benefit of the people. For this reason, taxes are not to be measured by the will and benefit of the prince but by the public good and the needs of the community, as whose administrator, defender, watchman and ruler he was constituted. He must, therefore, be satisfied with a proper a proper maintenance and the means for his own expenditures as the prosperity and the dignity of the commonwealth warrant. He must also content himself with what is sufficient for the common needs; nor are his subjects obliged to contribute more.[94]

If taxes are destined to defray the expenses incurred in the common good, it follows that they can be imposed only by those who have charge of the common good; usually this is the sovereign.[95] But the question arises whether he is the

---

[93] "Partes enim reipublicae juxta vires cujusque subvenire tenentur communi bono necessitatibusque publicis" (II, 668, 221).

[94] "Neque enim populus est propter principem, sed a contrario princeps est propter populum, qui est praepositus, in bonum ac commoditatem illius: eaque de causa tributa non ad voluntatem, et utilitatem principis sunt admetienda, sed ad utilitatem ac necessitatem publicam ejus communitatis, cui tamquam administer, defensor, custos, ac rector est constitutus: contentusque esse debet princeps iis quae ad competentem sustentationem et sumptus ipsius, pro qualitate status et reipublicae, et ad publicas necessitates sufficiunt, neque plus respublica subditorum tenetur ei tribuere" (II, 667, 220).

[95] "Dicendum est consequenter, quae conditiones necessariae sint, ut tributa sint justa, ac debeantur in conscientiae foro. Atque prima conditio ad id necessaria est, ut imponatur ab habente ad id autoritatem.... ejusmodi sunt legitimi Imperatores, Reges, et consilia universalia. Nomine Regum intelliguntur, qui non recognoscunt superiorem ut fere omnes Reges hodie eum non recognoscunt in temporalibus. Aut saltem, qui quoad administrationem

only one who has the right to impose taxes. With the exception of Mariana, all the Jesuit writers hold that, directly, only the sovereign may impose taxes. Where the laws of the country require the consent of the legislature, the king is bound to submit to their decision. But, unless the people have reserved the right, the sovereign is free to tax without consulting any persons or group of persons. [96]

Although the king has the right to increase taxes, Molina nevertheless maintains that he should exercise this right only when all other means have failed and then only for as long as the need exists. Molina requires that a tax be imposed "for a just reason, that no more be demanded than the cause requires, and that with the disappearance of the cause, the tax must likewise cease." He then gives his reasons:

> For the subjects who are members of the commonwealth are obliged to come to its aid by exhibiting and exposing not only their property but their lives as well, when the common good and the public need require it. Thus they may be compelled, whenever the common good demands it and no other means is available, to contribute as much as and as long as the public good and the common welfare demand it. [97]

Molina admits that the general sales tax appears to be contrary to the principle of equality because the poor are burdened more heavily by it than the rich. [98] Yet he would not venture to condemn the sales tax as unjust. [99] Actually, people in general do not find the *alcavala* unbearable. In point of

---

sui regni, tributorumque impositionem, eum non recognosceret. Intelliguntur praeterea respublicae liberae, quae superiorem in temporalib. similiter non habent" (II, 666, 219).

[96] Laures, *op. cit.*, p. 193.

[97] "Secunda conditio necessaria, ut tributum sit justum, et debeatur conscientia est: Ut imponatur ex justa causa, neque plus exigatur, quam causa postulat: et ut cessante causa ... cesset etiam ipsum tributum.... Etenim subditi reipublicae, cujus sunt partes, subvenire tenentur, non solum sua, sed et se ipsos exhibendo, ac exponendo, quando bonum ac necessitas publica id ita efflagitat; eaque de causa, exigente id communi, publicoque bono, cui non possit aliter commode subveniri, cogi possunt contribuere, quantum postulat, et quandiu id postulat, publica necessitas ac bonum" (II, 667, 220).

[98] "Sane in contributione illa ad tributum solvendum, non servatur geometrica aequalitas, ut pro quantitate facultatum cujusque, plus aut minus, contribuant, sed saepe evenit, ut quis sic minores habuerit facultates, plus contribuat, quam qui habuerit majores" (II, 668, 222).

[99] "Ego vero licet videam eum modum colligendi id tributum, expositum esse illi inaequalitati, non tamen auderem illum condemnare: praesertim cum usu sit receptus plurimis in locis" (*ibid.*).

fact, should a tax on property be substituted for it, the opposition of the people would prove serious and its reintroduction would be demanded. [100] Molina believes that a direct tax by assessment would bring in its wake numerous brushes between the people and the royal assessors, and that enforcement of it would require a host of such officers. This, in turn, would be followed by additional taxes in order to supply the salaries of the numerous taxing staff. [101] An assessment of each citizen would occasion great violence, injustice, and hatred, and cause much uneasiness in conscience. [102]

Other Economic-Political Problems

The foregoing excursion into Molina's treatises on taxation provides but a sampling of the wealth of material contained in the disputations of his five huge volumes. Only someone who has worked the mine could realize the vast, still unexplored caverns it contains. For example, this present volume has made reference to about fifty disputations out of the seven hundred and fifty-eight disputations of the Second Tract. Rich veins of ore have been uncovered yet many remain unworked. Bernard Dempsey did pioneer work on Molina and the question of usury. Of that work Schumpeter wrote that it "combines to a degree that is quite exceptional, thorough familiarity with scholastic and with economic thought, so that the interested reader may be referred to it with confidence." [103]

Another work which Schumpeter does not mention deserves to be included here. It is Joseph Höffner's monograph on economic theory in the sixteenth and seventeenth centuries. [104] He singles out Molina among the scholastic writers of the period.

---

[100] "Si attentaretur mutari, ut singuli non illo modo, sed simul contribuerent pecuniam pro cujusque divitiis, omnes reclamarent, ut potius priori hoc alio modo colligeretur" (ibid.).

[101] Ibid.

[102] "Ducor, quoniam populus minus gravatur, minoremque molestiam sentit, ita per partes adeo minutas solvendo tributum illud dum res emunt, quam si illud solveret simul. Praesertim cum, ad solvendum illud simul, necessarii essent exactores, qui impignorationibus, et stipendio ea de causa ipsis debito, occasio essent longe majorum sumptuum, molestiarum, ac inquietudinum" (ibid.).

[103] Schumpeter, op. cit., p. 95, n. 19.

[104] Höffner, Wirtschaftsethik und Monopole.

15

Both Höffner [105] and Schumpeter [106] call attention to the remarkable way Molina analyzes economic activity. He does not simply speculate but does all the fact-finding possible for him in an age without statistical services. His generalizations invariably grow out of discussions of factual patterns and are copiously illustrated by practical examples. Molina sallies forth to interview businessmen about their methods. [107] Rommen points out that, when Molina studies the problem of slavery, he makes inquiries about the Negro slave trade with ship owners and with traders, with port authorities, and with central authorities, citing pertinent documents in nine columns of his work. Höffner [108] and Schumpeter [109] cite Molina's study of the Spanish wool trade as a model monograph.

Molina showed special interest in the free exchange market. Among the unethical practices which interfered with the free market was monopoly. [110] He says that private monopolies are in general (*regulariter*) unjust and harmful to the public good. [111] State monopolies are accepted on the condition that they serve the common good, because they may be considered as a source of public revenue; they must never serve private interest in the form of privileges. His doctrine here is a logical conclusion from his position on the natural market price. He distinguishes between natural and regulated price. The former price is natural "because it is deduced without human law or decree from things themselves, although dependent on many circumstances which can change it." [112] The just natural price possesses a certain degree of flexibility dependent on circumstances. [113] Not so the officially fixed price. Molina makes it

---

[105] *Ibid.*, pp. 67 ff.

[106] Schumpeter, *op. cit.*, p. 99.

[107] *Vide supra*, Chap. 1.

[108] Höffner, *op. cit.*, p. 68.

[109] Schumpeter, *op. cit.*, p. 99.

[110] Höffner, *op. cit.*, pp. 135ff.

[111] "Dixi monopolia regulariter esse iniqua, et Reipublicae injuriosa" (II, 345, 385).

[112] "Sed naturale dicitur, quoniam ex ipsismet rebus, seclusa quacunque humana lege ac decreto consurgit, dependenter tamen a multis circumstantiis, quibus variatur, atque ab hominum affectu, ac aestimatione, comparatione diversorum usuum, interdum pro solo hominum beneplacito et arbitrio" (II, 347, 390).

[113] "Quia ergo ejusmodi pretium non mere ex naturis rerum consurgit, sed a circumstantiis, quibus variatur pendet, et, quod plus est, ab hominum affectu, et aestimatione rerum pro suo beneplacito, inde proficiscitur, ut non consistat in indivisibili, sed habeat certam latitudinem justi ac commensurati merci" (*ibid.*).

unmistakably clear that he is opposed to price regulation. [114]
Fixed prices are only just when they remain within the scale
of the just natural price. The peculiar nature of the fixed price
lies precisely in that it prescribes an exactly determined price
within the area of natural prices to safeguard the good of the
state and prevent abuses. [115] Fixed prices which fall outside
the scale of natural prices do not obliged in conscience. The
objection that the common good requires price regulation in
the interest of the poor at the time of a shortage of grain is
not valid. The poor may be helped by welfare agencies and
not by forced unjust prices. [116]

The complex question of value was explored by Molina and
his contemporaries and the Aristotelian distinction between
value in use and value in exchange was deepened and developed
into a fragmentary but genuine utility theory of exchange.
Molina makes it quite clear that cost, though a factor in the
determination of exchange value or price, is not its logical
source or cause. He especially points out that utility is a principal source or cause of value. He is careful to note that this
utility is not an endowment of goods themselves or identical
with any of their inherent qualities but is the reflex of the uses
the individuals under observation propose to make of these
goods and of the importance they attach to their use. [117]

Rommen's observation is apt:

> Molina's views thus show, in accordance with the general ten-
> dency, a highly positive evaluation of liberty in the economic
> exchanges in a free market, as a natural condition for the

---

[114] Höffner, op. cit., pp. 113-114.

[115] II, 347, 390.

[116] II, 364, 465-466.

[117] "Illud in primis observandum est, justum pretium non ex naturis
rerum secundum se, quo ad earum nobilitatem ac perfectionem esse judican-
dum, sed quatenus ad humanus usus inserviunt: eatenus enim ab hominibus
aestimantur, atque in commerciis commutationibus hominum inter se pretium
habent" (II, 348, 391).

"Observandum est deinde, pretium justum rerum non etiam attendi solum
penes res ipsas quatenus veniunt in usus hominum, quasi ex natura, et necessitate usus cui res inserviunt, absolute sumatur quantitas pretii, si caetera
paria sint; sed pretii quantitatem pendere plurimum ex aestimatione, qua homines plus, vel minus, aestimare volunt rem aliquam ad ejus usum" (ibid.).

"Justum itaque pretium rerum multum pendet a communi hominum aestimatione in unaquaque regione: quare quando absque fraude, monopoliis ...
communiter res aliqua vendi consuevit pretio aliquo in aliqua regione, aut loco,
id habendum est pro mensura, et regula judicandi pretium justum rei illius
in ea regione, aut loco, interim dum circumstantiae non variantur, quibus merito pretium accrescat, vel decrescat" (II, 348, 392).

realization of the just price. This positive attitude toward ordered liberty in economic life is further accentuated by his strong criticism of unfair monopolistic practices and by his diffidence toward Government controlled markets and prices. [118]

The emphasis laid on the subjective factors which determine the price of goods was extended also to the value of money. The exchange value of money, Molina held, depends largely on the estimation in which money is held; and the estimation of money, like that of goods, fluctuates with variations in supply and demanded, utility, the safety of money in question, etc. Monetary theory is thus rendered a flexible instrument which can be applied successfully to most varied circumstances. [119]

There are two ways, Molina relates, in which a given money may be more valuable in one place than another. First, by virtue of public law or accepted custom, the value of money in terms of other moneys may vary from place to place.

> In Portugal the ducat is worth 400 *reais* and in Castile 375 *maravedís;* the silver *real* is worth 34 *maravedís* in Castile and 40 in Portugal, while in the kingdom of Valencia it is worth less, and in Catalonia more, of the small bronze coins known as *dinars;* and its value is different in other places. Though 11 silver *reales* are worth 375 *maravedís* in Castile, they are equivalent to 475 *reais* in Portugal, omitting other places for the present. The gold *escudo,* which at one time was worth 10 silver *reales* and 10 *maravedís* in Castile or 350 *maravedís,* was worth 11 *julios* and one *dimidio* in Rome, although the *julio* corresponds to the silver *real.* The *escudo* was priced differently in France and elsewhere, and it is struck today at a value of 400 *maravedís* in Castile. [120]

Also, money may be worth more in one place than another because of its scarcity. All other things being equal, wherever money is most abundant, there it will be least valuable for exchange purposes. Just as an abundance of goods causes prices to fall, so does an abundance of money cause them to rise. In Spain, Molina continues, the purchasing power of money is far lower, on account of its abundance, than it was eighty years before his time.

---

[118] Rommen, "Renaissance Period," *op. cit.,* p. 123.

[119] For an excellent study of the scholastic monetary theory in Spain in Molina's day, see Marjorie Grice-Hutchinson, *The School of Salamanca*: Readings in Spanish Monetary Theory, 1544-1605 (Oxford: At the Clarendon Press, 1952).

[120] *Ibid.,* pp. 112-113, citing Molina.

A thing that could be bought for two ducats at that time is nowadays five, six or even more. Wages have risen in the same proportion, and so have doweries, the price of estates, the income from benefices, and other things.[121]

Money is likewise far less valuable, Molina explains, in the New World (especially in Peru, where it is most plentiful), than it is in Spain. But in places where it is more scarce than in Spain, there it will be more valuable. Nor will the value of money be the same in all other places but will fluctuate because of the variations in its quantity.

> Value in this sense is not indivisible, *but enjoys a certain freedom,* just as goods whose price is not legally controlled are priced according to the judgment of prudent merchants.[122]

It is clear, as Grice-Hutchison traces the development, that the monetary theory of the School of Salamanca spread through many countries during the early decades of the seventeenth century. It spread in great part through the works of Jesuits in the field of moral theology. They produced a vast number of manuals for the use of confessors, in which were often discussed knotty problems of commercial ethics along the lines laid down by the School of Salamanca.

> It may be assumed that their doctrines filtered down through to the laity. I do not suggest that these tedious works constituted the favourite reading of the average *honnête homme,* but we have only to turn to Pascal's *Provincial Letters* to realize how great an influence the Jesuit theologians exerted on the ordinary life and thought in France at this period. Pascal employs all his accustomed verve and irony in attacking many of the writers whose works we have been considering (he devotes the English Letter to impugning their doctrine of usury), and it is evident that, writing in 1656, he looked upon our Spanish writers and all their works as a force both living and dangerous.[123]

---

[121] *Ibid.,* p. 113, citing Molina.

[122] Grice-Hutchinson, *op. cit.,* p. 114. Italics added.

[123] "A typical and popular example was the *Theologia Moralis* of Antonio de Escobar. This manual, which was published in 1652, was a compendium of twenty-four earlier works on moral theology, mostly by Spanish authors such as Molina, Suarez, and Lugo. Escobar says that the natural price of an article depends on the estimation of men, taking into account the scarcity or plenty of goods, buyers, sellers, and money, the manner of sale, the utility of the article in question, and the labour and expenses of merchants. Escobar was attacked with particular virulence by Pascal, and his name now figures in

* * *

Luis de Molina's *De Justitia et Jure* belongs to those master-pieces of intellectual fabric in which

> One treadle sets a thousand threads in motion,
> The shuttles shoot to and fro,
> Unperceived the threads flow. [124]

The fundamental intellectual principles of Molina's work can be grasped only as each pattern takes shape on the huge tape-stry. To trace one color or thread risks missing the effect of the whole work. Yet the effect in light and shadow is appre-ciated only when it is discovered that chromatic variety is but the close-knit strands of unbroken threads.

One treadle sets a thousand threads in motion. For Molina it is the concept of the dignity, liberty, and freedom of the human person. St. Ignatius had given instructions to his sons not to lose sight of the importance of human liberty. [125] Molina's doctrine in the *Concordia*, explaining how divine grace can coexist with human liberty, was but carrying out the in-structions that came with the loom. His theological concept lends a strongly emphasized justification to the social and political autonomy of man in his role as a citizen.

One of the characteristics of Molina's social metaphysics, as was mentioned above, was its basic *realism*. Man is always considered in the concrete in all his activities, with contingent historical reality and the autonomous and independent values of social and political life accorded full recognition. In the present study it as often been pointed out that Molina is slow to generalize before he has collected the available data, whether

---

French dictionaries as the very symbol of prevarication" (*ibid.*, p. 74, n. 2).

Schumpeter (*op. cit.*, p. 97) makes the same observation: "It is within their [Molina, Lessius, and de Lugo] systems of moral theology and law that eco-nomics gained definite if not separate existence, and it is they who come nearer than does any group to having been the 'founders' or scientific eco-nomics."

For a comparatively recent reply to Pascal see James Brodrick, S.J., *The Economic Morals of the Jesuits*: An Answer to Dr. H. M. Robertson (London: Oxford University Press, 1934).

[124] "Wo ein Tritt tausend Faden regt
   Die Schifflein herüber hinüber schiessen
   Die Faden ungesehen fliessen."
(Goethe, *Faust*, Part I, ll. 1924-1926).

[125] *Vide supra*, Chapter I.

on conditions in the remote jungle areas of Africa or on the rate of monetary exchange in Spain.

Molina's social teaching is also distinctly *personal*. The concrete living person stands in the center of all studies concerning the essence and purpose of the state, society, and economy. The people are not for the prince for the prince is for the people, he repeats again and again. State and society exist through men and for men. All ordering of state and society, all economic activity derive their sense and purpose from the one fact they serve the human person who is both their origin and their end.

There is a *democratic* orientation to Molina's social metaphysics which determines the role that authority will play in political and social life, yet preserves the autonomy of men. This democratic orientation will oppose usurpation of authority by a dictatorship based on massed totalitarianism.

Molinism, in these broader aspects, bloomed during the St. Martin's summer of scholasticism in the sixteenth century. Withstanding all efforts to uproot it, Molinism became the distinctive flower of Jesuit thought. In the *Concordia* Molina concludes a long proof of his celebrated doctrine on *scientia media* with an exhortation which rings with the moving oratory of the pulpit rather than the cold and impersonal tone of a philosophical discourse. Liberty is ours, so indisputably ours, that, with the help of God's gifts, it lies in our power to avoid all mortal sin and to attain eternal life. Freedom belongs to the sons of God. [126]

---

[126] Pegis, *op. cit.*, p. 90.

INDEX

Abbott, Walter M., S.J., 162.

Acton, Lord, 63, 64.

Adams, John, 64.

Adrian, Pope, authority to declare war, 104, 121; probabilism, 143.

Africa, 158, 164, 170, 174, 176, 177, 178, 180, 184, 187, 189, 190, 191, 192, 197, 231.

Albertus Pighius, papal authority, 80.

Albuquerque, Alfonso de, 186.

Alcala, 79; Jesuit college, 5; Molina's legal education, 4.

Alcavala, 220, 221, 224.

Aldama, J.A., S.J., Molina and the just war theory, 96.

Aldrin, Buzz, 163.

Alexander, Edgar, 12, 13.

Alexson, E., 185, 190.

Allen, J.W., *A History of Political Thought in the Sixteenth Century*, 60, 61, 69.

Alto Alentejo, 8.

Amado, G., 102.

Amboyna, 120.

America, 132, 158, 166.

American Libray Asociation, 202.

American Revolution, 64.

Amorrhites, 114.

Andersonville Prison, 137.

Andrade, Alonso de, 4.

Angola, 158, 175, 180, 182, 183.

Angola, Dambi, 181, 182.

Angola, Inene, 180, 181.

Anselmo, B. S.J., 96

Antoninus, St., papal authortiy, 73.

Antwerp, 18.

Aquaviva, Claudio S.J., 16; Molina's wrtiing, 9, 17; just war, 98, 99; Molina's background, 3, 9, 15; Molina and the just war theory, 97; Molina's philosophy of law, 21; right of liberty, 158.

Aquinas, St. Thomas, authority to declare war, 104; civil society, 28, 218; *Commentary on the Sentences*, 211; definition of law, 203; governmental power, 33. 43; indirect power of the pope, 87; just war theory, 97, 98, 112; just causes of war, 113, 116, 117, 132; influence on Molina, 16, 20, 24; natural law, 41, 42, 169, 200, 201, 204, 210; neutrality, 133; origin of the family unit, 25; papal authority, 81; political sociology, 24, 27, 34; right of resistance, 67; *Secunda Secundae*, 16; slavery, 170, 171; *Summa Theologica*, 8, 211.

Aragon, 110.

Araoz, Antonio de S.J., Jesuit provincial, 4, 5.

Aristotle, 20, 25, 34, 47, 86, 107, 110; democratic government, 43; origin and nature of the family, 24; justice, 17; philosophy of law, 205; political society, 24, 27; slavery, 165. 169, 171; usury, 227.

Armstrong, Neil, 163.

Arnold, Franz X., Bellarmine's theory of political authority, 40; natural law, 201.

Asia, 186.

Astrain, Antonio, S.J., *Historia de la Compañia de Jesús en la Asistencia de España*, 9.

Athens, 59.

Augustine, St., authority to declare war, 104; influence on Molina, 10, 20; just causes of war, 113; *Jus in Bello*, 144; just war theory, 99, 101, 117, 135; original justice and sin, 28; political law, 29; sovereignty and war, 107.

Augustinus, Triumphus de Ancona O.S.A., papal authority, 73.

Australia, 129.

BIBLIOTHECA INSTITUTI HISTORICI SOCIETATIS IESU

1. Félix Zubillaga S.I. *La Florida. La misión jesuítica (1566-1572) y la colonización española.* 1941, xiv-475 p.

2. Alessandro Valignano S.I. *Historia pel principio y progreso de la Compañia de Jesús en las Indias Orientales (1542-1564),* Herausgegeben und erläutert von Josef Wicki S.I. 1944, 108*-510 p.

3. 7. Ignacio Iparraguirre S.I. *Historia de los Ejercicios espirituales de san Ignacio de Loyola.*
   I. *En vida de su autor (1522-1556).* 1946, 54*-320 p. 3 cartes.
   II. *Desde la muerte de san Ignacio hasta la promulgación del Directorio oficial (1556-1599).* 1955, 48*-588 p.
   III. V. n. 36.

4. Joseph de Guibert S.I. *La spiritualité de la Compagnie de Jésus.* Esquisse historique. 1953, xl-659 p.

5. Guillermo Kratz S.I. *El tratado hispano-portugués de límites de 1570 y sus consecuencias.* 1954, xvi 313 p.

6. Pietro Pirri S.I. *Giovanni Tristano e i primordi dell'architettura gesuitica.* 1955, xv-299 p., 40 ill.

7. V. 3, II.

8. Alfred Desautels S.I. *Les « Mémoires de Trévoux » et le mouvement des idées au XVIIIᵉ siècle (1701-1734).* 1956, xxvii-256 p.

9, 13, 16, 17. Francisco Javier Alegre S.I. *Historia de la Compañía de Jesús en Nueva España (1566-1766).* Nueva edición por Ernest J. Burrus S.I. y Félix Zubillaga S.I. — 1956, xxxii-640 p.; 1958, xxxii-13*-747 p.; 1959, xxxvi-14*-502 p.; 1960, xxx-15*-663 p.

10, 11. Pedro de Leturia S.I. *Estudios ignacianos.*
   I. *Estudios biográficos.* 1957, xxxii-475 p.
   II. *Estudios espirituales.* 1957, viii-544 p.

12. Pierre Moisy. *Les églises des jésuites de l'ancienne Assistance de France.* I. Texte. II. Illustrations. 1958, xx-580 p. et c ill.

13. V. 9.

14. Pietro Pirri S.I. *L'interdetto di Venezia del 1606 e i gesuiti.* Silloge di documenti con introduzione. 1959, xv-409 p.

15. Jean Vallery-Radot. *Le recueil des plans d'édifices de la Compagnie de Jésus conservé à la Bibliothèque National de Paris.* 1960, xxvi-100*-560 p., 39 ill.

16, 17. V. 9.

18. Joseph Sebes S.I. *The Jesuits and the Sino-Russian Treaty of Nerchinsk (1689). The Diary of T. Pereira S.J.* 1961, xxxvi-344 p.

19. Estanislao Olivares S.I. *Los votos de los escolares de la Compañia de Jesús. Su evolución jurídica.* 1961, xx-250 p.

20-23. Georg Schurhammer S.I. *Gesammelte Studien.*
   I. *Die zeitgenössischen Quellen zur Geschichte Portugiesisch-Asiens und seiner Nachbarländer zur Zeit des Hl. Franz Xaver.* 2. Auflage. 1962, 6*-xlv-652 p., 30 ill.
   II. *Orientalia.* 1963, lxiii-815 p.
   III. *Xaveriana,* 1964, xx-703 p.
   IV. *Varia* (2 Teile mit Generalindex und 77 Tafeln). 1965, xxiv-1055 p.

24. Nicholas P. Cushner S.I. *Philippine Jesuits in Exile. The Journals of F. Puig S.I.* 1964, xvi-200 p.

SUBSIDIA AD HISTORIAM SOCIETATIS IESU